VOLUME 457   SEPTEMBER 1981

THE ANNALS

of The American Academy *of* Political
and Social Science

ISSN 0002-7162
RICHARD D. LAMBERT, *Editor*
ALAN W. HESTON, *Associate Editor*

NATICNAL SECURITY POLICY
FOR THE 1980s

Special Editor of this Volume
ROBERT L. PFALTZGRAFF, Jr.
Professor of International Politics,
Fletcher School of Law and Diplomacy
President,
Institute for Foreign Policy Analysis, Inc.
Massachusetts

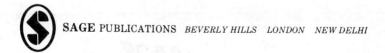

SAGE PUBLICATIONS *BEVERLY HILLS   LONDON   NEW DELHI*

THE ANNALS

© 1981 *by* The American Academy *of* Political *and* Social Science

For information about membership* (individuals only) and subscriptions (institutions), address:

SAGE PUBLICATIONS, INC.
275 South Beverly Drive
Beverly Hills, Calif. 90212 USA

From India and South Asia, write to:

SAGE INDIA
P.O. Box 3605
New Delhi 110 024
INDIA

From the UK, Europe, the Middle East and Africa, write to:

SAGE PUBLICATIONS LTD
28 Banner Street
London EC1Y 8QE
ENGLAND

**Please note that members of The Academy receive THE ANNALS with their membership.*

Library of Congress Catalog Card Number 81-52757
International Standard Serial Number ISSN 0002-7162
International Standard Book Number ISBN 0-8039-1704-X (Vol. 457, 1981, paper)
International Standard Book Number ISBN 0-8039-1705-8 (Vol. 457, 1981, cloth)

Manufactured in the United States of America. First printing, September 1981.

The articles appearing in THE ANNALS are indexed in *Book Review Index; Public Affairs Information Service Bulletin; Social Sciences Index; Monthly Periodical Index; Current Contents: Behavioral, Social, Management Sciences;* and *Combined Retrospective Index Sets.* They are also abstracted and indexed in *ABC Pol Sci, Historical Abstracts, Human Resources Abstracts, Social Sciences Citation Index, United States Political Science Documents, Social Work Research & Abstracts, Peace Research Reviews, Sage Urban Studies Abstracts, International Political Science Abstracts,* and/or *America: History and Life.*

CONTENTS

BOOK DEPARTMENT

INTERNATIONAL RELATIONS AND POLITICS

AFRICA, ASIA, AND LATIN AMERICA

EUROPE

UNITED STATES

SOCIOLOGY

ECONOMICS

PREFACE

The international security environment of the late twentieth century poses numerous dangers and problems for the United States. In designing a strategy in support of its national interests, the United States faces the need to mold into a coherent framework numerous instruments of statecraft, of which military power remains an indispensable element. Each of the contributors to this issue of *The Annals* addresses one or more dimensions of American defense policy. The development of an effective national security policy within government, and an evaluation of such policy outside government, depends necessarily upon an understanding of numerous aspects of defense, strategy, and weapons systems. These include contrasting Soviet and American approaches to deterrence and nuclear weapons; the measurement of strategic force levels and the comparison of defense budgets; the relationship between offensive and defensive strategic capabilities, and between nuclear and general purpose forces; strategic force vulnerability issues; the hypothesized role of military power in diplomacy of crisis management; the formidable task of strengthening, or maintaining, extended security guarantees by the United States to its allies, as well as equitable sharing of defense burdens; the concepts of a rapid deployment force and power projection capabilities; the Soviet-American maritime balance, including American naval force modernization needs; the defense mobilization base of the United States, both in personnel and technological-industrial infrastructure; and the future of arms control in American national security policy.

The purpose of this special issue is not to provide specific policy guidance, but rather to examine in broad context the national security issues that will shape the ongoing debate in the United States about the necessary levels, scope, prospective emphases, and priorities in programs in support of the common defense of the United States and other nations in the years ahead.

ROBERT L. PFALTZGRAFF, Jr.

ANNALS, *AAPSS*, **457**, September 1981

Soviet Strategic Doctrine and the Soviet-American Global Contest

By URI RA'ANAN

ABSTRACT: Soviet Military Doctrine, despite the exigencies of the thermonuclear age, continues to follow Clausewitz in viewing war as a continuation of politics by other means. Accordingly, war is regarded both as feasible and winnable, provided the USSR continues to maintain the initiative, to pursue the offensive, and to utilize surprise and deception. These factors mean that an initial blow against an adversary may prove ultimately decisive, but without ensuring that conflict necessarily would be short. Preparations have to be adequate for protracted warfare, with particular emphasis on reserves, military and economic. Pacifist rejection of wars as such is condemned in the USSR for failing to distinguish between just and unjust conflicts, that are judged by their class content—not by the question of who started the fighting. There is little evidence for the view that the Soviet Military Doctrine is the product of military rather than civilian (Party) leaders. In accordance with the dialectic, the USSR believes that balance, or stalemate, is unfeasible as a long-term concept since, ultimately, there are only victors and the defeated.

Uri Ra'anan is professor of international politics and chairman of the International Security Studies Program, The Fletcher School of Law and Diplomacy, as well as Fellow of Harvard University's Russian Research Center.

ASYMMETRY is a key to any realistic evaluation of the international balance between the superpowers. It is essential to treat this factor as a point of departure, not merely because of the obvious contrast between the United States and the USSR with regard to geographic location and the resulting force structures, but, perhaps even more significantly, in view of mutual incompatibilities as far as their respective approaches toward doctrine are concerned.

The unity of theory and action is a commonplace of the ideology that provides both the analytical concepts and the jargon which assist Soviet leaders in appraising the international situation and in articulating the operational conclusions that are to be drawn. In this context,

Military Doctrine provides the broad parameters within which the Kremlin elaborates the specifics of "military science" and its derivative, "military art."

Soviet leaders do not differentiate sharply between "military" and "civilian" aspects of doctrine—a concept, it seems, related somewhat more closely to classical "grand strategy" (reflected particularly in German politico-military literature) than to circumscribed Western definitions of military doctrine. The fact is that, in Soviet thought, "war" and "peace" are not mutually exclusive antitheses, as they might be perceived by Western minds. In some aspects, the Leninist world view is beholden to social Darwinism as much as were ideologies at the other extreme of the political spectrum. Like Engels, Lenin viewed conflict as the norm of social and political organisms no less than of nature itself. In that context, war and peace constitute no more than hash marks between which the course of permanent conflict meanders.

STALIN AND AFTER

Despite the oversimplifications of some historians, the eventual inevitability of global confrontation, in its most violent form, as the appropriate way of resolving the inherent tension between two social systems was posited more starkly before Stalin and since his demise than it was during some periods in the reign of that grim personality. Paradoxically, the dictator's eight last "dark years" were precisely the time he chose to advance the theory that war was more probable among the "imperialists" themselves than it was between them and the Soviet state. The specious reason he provided was that one imperialist state could defeat the other without destroying the contemporary, final stage of capitalism, whereas that system could not survive defeat at the hands of the USSR.

However, the actual cause for the publication of this thesis seems to have been Stalin's gnawing doubt—foreshadowed by his "Letter to Comrade R." in 1946—whether the advent of the new weapons systems had not transformed the nature of war itself. (Stalin stated that Clausewitz might be outdated, since the "manufacturing" stage of warfare was being superseded by a new age in which the "machine" would dominate the battlefield.) This doubt appears to have been shared by his immediate successor, Malenkov. The irony of history is that a far more light-headed, less cautious and responsible ("adventuristic") attitude on this vital issue came to be characteristic of the subsequent "good days," the age dominated by Khrushchev and his successors.

It was not the tensions and fears of the Cold War, therefore, but the more buoyant atmosphere of "peaceful coexistence" and "détente" that witnessed the predominance of a Soviet Doctrine favoring "war-waging" and "war-winning" scenarios, rather than "deterrence" and "war-avoidance." The explanation is that weakness and fear in the face of American nuclear preponderance motivated Stalin, while subsequent generations of Soviet leaders have become somewhat "dizzy with success" in the thermonuclear field.

"IDEOLOGICAL STRUGGLE"

To be sure, when dealing with conflict in the current international arena, Soviet literature places emphasis on "ideological struggle." However, Russian publications leave little doubt that this term is not intended to confine confrontation to the ethereal realm of the contest of ideas. Rather, it emerges that such struggle encompasses a veritable gamut of means—conventional and unconventional, overt and covert—through which one system is to attain irreversible hegemony over its adversary, if not eliminating the latter entirely.

Thus, Soviet statements emphasize that the USSR will not allow its opponents to implement even primarily defensive countermeasures—subsumed conveniently under the heading of "export of counterrevolution"; judging from the examples provided, this category covers Western efforts to ward off the overthrow or defeat of friendly governments. (This posture is somewhat reminiscent of the apocryphal claim of a pretender to supreme power in some small principality, alleging that he felt compelled to stage a coup, since the current ruler was "plotting to retain the throne.") Consequently, the status quo is accepted as viable only with regard to the possessions of one of the parties, but remains entirely fluid where the territories and spheres of its adversary are concerned.

To date, the ideological struggle against export of counterrevolution has embraced (1) Soviet organization, training, arming, and logistical infrastructure for surrogate forces operating in remote regions including Cubans, East Germans, and others; (2) similar support for the expanding terrorist international, leaving in abeyance whether or not this implies Soviet control; (3) not to speak of the increasingly direct intervention of Soviet armed forces (for example, Afghanistan). In few, if any, of these instances has the role of the USSR been "reactive"—that is, it has not been compelled to respond to any military initiatives

by the adversary, jeopardizing the territorial integrity of the Soviet Union itself. Rather, these have been cases either of Soviet offensives resulting from opportunism, particularly in the Third World, or of Soviet attempts to resolve primarily political problems that have "threatened" (that is, questioned) the entrenched power monopoly of a communist party and/or of a pro-Soviet regime, with regard to prestige or legitimacy much more than in military terms.

INITIATIVE AND DECEPTION

The USSR's rejection of the role of a mere "reactor" reflects an essential ingredient of Soviet doctrine: namely, that it is imperative to seize and to maintain the initiative in military and political arenas alike. This element is linked integrally to two other components of the doctrine—specifically, the penchants for "the offensive," and for "surprise and deception." These are characteristics with profound implications not only for Soviet strategy but also for tactics. It is hardly necessary to define the role these factors can assume in a thermonuclear age. Strategically, "the offensive" wedded to "surprise and deception," may be translated into "first strike" without undue effort of the imagination.

It should not be deduced from these propositions, however, that the Soviet leadership necessarily is committed to short war scenarios. To be sure, Soviet literature stresses that the side enjoying the initiative and resorting to the offensive, with maximal exploitation of surprise and deception, may be able to achieve major, probably decisive, advantages at the initial stages of a global conflagration. This does not mean, however, that under all circumstances conflict termination will be achieved rapidly. On the contrary, the Soviet leadership remains convinced of the (typically "continental") view that final victory requires seizure and occupation of enemy soil.

MOBILIZATION AND RESERVES

Consequently, such factors as surge mobilization—economic, technological, and in terms of manpower—continue to be essential components of Soviet Military Doctrine (which anticipates the possibility of a prolonged interval between the initial surprise, however traumatic may be the blow inflicted on the other side, and war termination, including not only the eviction of the opponent from the territories of his friends and allies and their occupation by the Red Army but the collapse of his system and his total surrender). These aspects, reminiscent of more conventional warfare scenarios, assume protracted conflict to be probable and call for the necessary preparations, irrespective of the unprecedented and esoteric dimensions of such a conflagration—spilling over into outer space as a zone of combat.

In this context, a decisive role is assigned to the "reserves," hardly an invention of Leninism but nevertheless a factor to which the creed ascribes particular importance. This applies especially to the strategic nuclear forces, the leaders of which, imbued still with the traditions of the Russian artillery, think and plan in terms of repeated "salvos," with victory rewarding the side that retains sufficient reserves for a potential last salvo, when the opponent has exhausted his supply of warheads. The other branches of the Soviet armed services tend to share these views. Their spokesmen and writers reminisce incessantly about the halcyon stage of the Great Patriotic War, when the injection of fresh Soviet reserves first broke the backbone of the seemingly relentless German advance and then gained the initiative during the huge armored battles that finally ground down the sophisticated German military machine.

Indeed, the Soviet force posture—on Warsaw Pact territory, along the frontiers of the USSR, and in the Soviet Military Districts—is based on the rapid mobilization of reserves to flesh out the permanent skeletal infrastructure of additional military units, established in accordance with the Soviet traditional three echelons of preparedness (that range from the combat-ready to the easily mobilizable entities).

It should not be assumed, however, that a single Soviet doctrine has persisted unchanged throughout the whole period since the creation of the Red Army, despite the revolutions in technology that have occurred.

THE HERITAGE OF CLAUSEWITZ

Certain general principles, in fact, continue to dominate Soviet military concepts, these changes notwithstanding. Lenin's copy of Clausewitz, heavily annotated in the Soviet leader's own hand, has been published. It reveals not only his penchant for Clausewitzian terminology, that was to permeate so much of his work, but his fundamental agreement with the proposition that warfare essentially is an extension of politics. The concept that war qualitatively is not to be viewed as on a plane higher than related forms of political, diplomatic, civil, economic, or social conflict has been expressed in Soviet literature from Lenin's time onward.

In this respect, the thermonuclear age (with some brief exceptions mentioned earlier) has failed to bring about a basic revision. Nor has there been a tendency to review the tenet that conflict is endemic, that it will continue from time to time to take the form of international warfare, and that there are no compromises—only the victors and the defeated. In other words, the USSR subscribes to a dynamic, not a static, view of history. For that matter, the literature continues to posit that "ideological" struggle is bound to end in the annihilation of one system by the other, as a result not merely of verbal but of extremely physical conflicts.

Quite a few of the more specific components of Soviet Military Doctrine, however, as opposed to these broader concepts, have undergone modification and revision. Stalin's famous five "Permanent Operating Principles" of warfare were not superseded formally until the Twentieth Congress of the CPSU; although, as has been mentioned, Stalin himself appears to have begun to doubt this essentially conventional—indeed, classical—approach to the subject, at least from 1946 onward. This is not to say that these principles have been overtaken entirely by subsequent developments. Such ingredients as morale, the quality of command personnel, the stability of the rear, and the level of armaments continue to play their role. Moreover, in traditional Russian fashion current Soviet leaders, like Stalin, still are enamored of sheer size and numbers quite apart from quality, believing that "more is better."

KHRUSHCHEV AND AFTER

The Twentieth CPSU Congress initiated a reexamination of certain aspects in light of the technological innovations of the postwar period. By 1960, Khrushchev enunciated a new doctrine, based on the assumption that strategic blows would *precede* an offensive by theater forces, unlike earlier periods of history. In other words, in response to the exigencies of the thermonuclear age a reorientation took place, paying primary attention to surprise attack by means of nuclear missiles that would cause the adversary's interior to suffer prior to the front lines. In this context, heavier initial emphasis was to be placed on firepower than on mobilized manpower. Significantly, Khrushchev continued to adhere to the views he had espoused in his famous 1953-54 "debate" with Malenkov, to the effect that nuclear war (whether inevitable or avoidable) would not mean the end of civilization, but that the USSR would survive despite serious losses, while the West would be destroyed—at least as a viable political and socioeconomic system.

Following Khrushchev's ouster, one major modification was made toward the end of the 1960s, rehabilitating the role of theater forces (downgraded by Khrushchev, in part because of demographic exigencies, as opposed to the newly established Strategic Rocket Forces). Such upgrading of the significance of ground, air, and naval forces has continued unabated, accompanied, during the 1970s, by increased emphasis on the projection of Soviet military power into remote corners of the globe (a role stressed particularly, but not exclusively, by the leaders of the Soviet Navy).

SHORT AND LONG WARS

It is because of the modifications of the late 1960s and the 1970s, that short war scenarios, which seemed fashionable for a brief period previously, have been revised. While Soviet leaders continue to believe that an initial nuclear strike may be decisive in breaking the adversary's back, it need not necessarily be conclusive—that is, it might have to be followed by protracted operations to finalize victory.

Indeed, it would be more correct to speak not so much of an initial strike as of a series of such blows (salvos), with the decision going in favor of the side that retained residual missiles when the opponent had exhausted his supply—a factor at least as significant as the ability to inflict greater damage in the initial exchange. (Incidentally, the publications of Soviet military theoreticians and planners stress the need for paralyzing the adversary's C³ system in the opening stage, obviously not sharing the preoccupation of Western analysts with the thought that functioning C³ systems would be required to enable both sides to negotiate a halt in an escalatory process.)

In the context of war survival and recovery, to which Soviet mobilization scenarios pay appropriate attention, a particularly important role is assigned to active and passive defense, represented by PVO (antiair), PRO (antimissile), and the Civil Defense Command. This posture makes much more sense on the assumption that active and passive defense will need to deal only with U.S. residual strategic forces following a Soviet first strike, and that the USSR will abrogate the ABM Agreement (in accordance with its provisions).

THE SHADOW OF POWER

Soviet Military Doctrine, as one might expect, does not neglect the possibility that the penumbra of military power may prove sufficiently potent for the purpose of achieving political hegemony, precisely because Soviet war-fighting scenarios seem increasingly credible; consequently, actual resort to military might—at least as far as its most devastating strategic manifestation is concerned—may not prove necessary. It is in this sense that one should perhaps interpret the remaining echoes of Khrushchev's contribution to the issue of the "inevitability of war" (which he questioned). If the *threat* of force will suffice, then, indeed, use of force may not be essential. Nevertheless, the literature of recent years is replete with war-fighting assumptions (with very few caveats), apparently as the most realistic point of departure for the work of Soviet planners and decision makers; Western war-avoidance theories, on the other hand, are mentioned usually with contempt.

"JUST" AND "UNJUST" WARS

The Soviet leadership obviously does not feel it is feasible to eschew war altogether as an instrument of policy. A major doctrinal reason is that Moscow continues to posit a sharp distinction between "just wars" and "unjust wars" and, in this context, goes on to denounce sharply Western pacifists who oppose all wars, irrespective of their class content. Soviet Doctrine maintains flatly that wars waged by "socialist countries" against "imperialists," by their very nature are just with regard to the former and unjust as far as the latter are concerned, irrespective of how the conflict originated and who was the initiator. The same concept applies to "wars of national liberation" and to civil wars between the proletariat and the bourgeoisie. Since at least the latter two cases are regarded as endemic, because of the dynamic assumptions of historical and dialectical materialism, and because, in these instances, the export of counterrevolution by the imperialists is taken for granted, high probability of a U.S.-Soviet military confrontation is implicit.

Moreover, Soviet Doctrine assumes that military conflict between the superpowers, regardless of how and where it started, most probably will escalate to the nuclear level, so that the respective strategic nuclear forces may be expected to come into play. There are, to be sure, exceptions to this proposition, but they refer only to wars between bourgeois states and to such local wars as may be viewed by the superpowers as being of marginal importance, so that they can be contained.

However, even the latter case is not free of Soviet caveats, since the concept of wars of national liberation applies not merely to guerrilla actions against established governments but even to military operations between sovereign states whenever the USSR sees fit to promote one of them to honorary membership in the National Liberation Movement. Readers will note the failure of Soviet literature to address one other obvious contingency—wars *between* socialist states. Obviously, this possibility flies in the face of the class conflict assumptions that continue to underlie not only the domestic but also the international facets of the Soviet ideology. Hence the desire both of Moscow and of Beijing to excommunicate one another.

"CIVILIAN" AND "MILITARY" VIEWS

This intensely political approach to the question of war explains, at least in part, why distinctions between the "military" and the "civilian" aspects of Soviet Doctrine are arbitrary and misleading, since one is dealing with a highly integrated theory encompassing both elements. It is equally artificial to reduce the analysis of the Soviet decision-making process to some imaginary tug-of-war between civilian doves and military hawks, with the latter "lobbying" for increased "appropriations." This paradigm reflects "mirror imaging" at its most simplistic level.

Although military figures in the USSR frequently write about individual aspects of current military doctrine, there are few, if any, examples demonstrating their ability to shape or modify that doctrine. On the contrary, as in other cases linking doctrinal and operational issues, it is the leadership of the CPSU that enjoys an unchallenged monopoly over decision-making. This is emphasized constantly in Soviet literature and is substantiated by many known examples from the history of the USSR. From the beginning, the Kremlin has shown a marked aversion to any and all potential rivals to the leadership of the Party; such professional military figures as Marshal Zhukov, who came close to attaining an independent political role, were promptly ousted and banished. The "man on the white horse" continues to be a specter haunting CPSU leaders, and appropriate measures are in force to exorcise this phenomenon.

Although instances of internal debates in the Kremlin are not lacking with regard to the issues analyzed here, there are few, if any, documented cases pitting civilian against military personalities. Consequently, it is less than scientific, and potentially counterproductive, to ascribe doctrinal innovations or modifications to elements other than the Party leadership.

SOVIET DEFENSE LITERATURE

It is equally misleading to view the international affairs and defense literature of the USSR as "purely propagandistic," or "for internal consumption only (!)"—or, for that matter, as mere deception. To be sure, there are specifics to which the open literature alludes, but which are discussed more overtly and concretely in the restricted or classified organs, which Western analysts have been able to obtain in some instances. However, few serious observers of the Soviet scene will challenge the view that the Kremlin leadership spends an inordinate amount of time and energy discussing, drafting, and vetting doctrinal statements, even in the open publications, because they serve to guide Soviet "cadres" (even of the middle and lower-middle level) who are meant to draw operational conclusions.

The objection that Moscow must be concerned lest valuable information be given away to the West in this manner lacks validity: Over the decades, the Soviet leadership has learned that relatively few Western analysts attempt to "decipher" such literature. Their conclusions, moreover, do not appear to have much impact on Western decision makers and policies, while, in any case, Western institutional memo-

ries are notoriously short. Thus, there is no convincing reason why the Kremlin should deprive itself of an effective and simple overt channel of communications with its own cadres and with clients abroad.

SOVIET AND WESTERN APPROACHES

To return to the asymmetry mentioned at the outset, perhaps it would be more accurate to refer to two asymmetries. One refers to the lack of relationship between Soviet reality and the way it is perceived by many Westerners who prefer to make assumptions based on their own world view rather than on careful examination of documentation published in the Soviet Union (and analyzed in the context of Soviet operations and other "hard data"). The other asymmetry relates to the West's own doctrines—to the extent that a somewhat amorphous set of views can be subsumed appropriately under this elevated title.

Western doctrines seem to reflect (1) our own Weltanschauung, (2) our misreading of the Soviet Gestalt, and (3) our capabilities (available or in an advanced stage of development). While it may be argued that the first two of these factors apply to the USSR as well (although in rather different fashion), in the third instance a contrast becomes apparent: The USSR develops capabilities to reflect the requirements of doctrine, rather than the other way around.

This is not as difficult to demonstrate as some might think. Analysts of Soviet military affairs have noted cases in which doctrinal revisions anticipated by a number of years the existence of new capabilities that became visible at a subsequent stage. (In this connection the crucial factor of lead time cannot be ignored, since the military R&D stage may precede deployment of new systems by quite a few years.) In other words, one may assume that Soviet Doctrine, from time to time, calls for the enhancement of capabilities in certain areas and is articulated in modified form as soon as Soviet science and technology indicate the feasibility of developing the appropriate software and hardware. (Final Soviet decisions on such matters seem to be made at an earlier stage in the R&D process than in most Western instances.)

This is not the only problem in assessing Soviet realities. "Mirror-imaging" appears to be a professional hazard of Western analysis of unfamiliar environments. It is amazing with what ease Western thinkers assign to the Soviet scene the concepts (accurate or otherwise) they apply to their study of bureaucratic and legislative processes in Western capitals. Consequently, terms like "military-industrial complex," "lobbying for appropriations," "interservice rivalries," and so on abound in Western publications concerning the USSR. There appears to be such eagerness for "systemic convergence" that many appear reluctant to ask the appropriate questions—Do their descriptions bear much resemblance to the manner in which the Soviet decision-making system actually functions?

More surprising is the rather light-hearted vein in which certain artifacts of Western military thought (embraced affectionately, at one time or another, by systems analysts) are ascribed also to Soviet theoreticians—irrespective of whether Soviet literature, the Soviet posture, or Soviet capabilities and operations bear out these assumptions to any meaningful extent.

"Mutual assured destruction," "mutual war-deterrence," "defense is destabilizing in the strategic nuclear arena," and similar gems readily come to mind. The creators and supporters of these concepts in many instances undoubtedly were motivated by sincere hopes and expectations. Regrettably, "Wishing Will Make It So" is not necessarily applicable in this case.

Perhaps the most remarkable aspect of this syndrome is the fact that Soviet defense literature not only implicitly but, on many occasions, explicitly has rejected these Western constructs and the accompanying terminology as "bourgeois," "reactionary," and "unrealistic." At least as far as the last of these adjectives is concerned, one finds it difficult to disagree. Not only is it unreasonable, therefore, to conclude that the USSR accepts what it so clearly rejects, but the very approach inherent in Western concepts is incompatible with the ideological foundations upon which Soviet Doctrine rests.

STATIC AND DYNAMIC CONCEPTS

The Western terms mentioned assume a static world, governed by genuine "equilibrium," long-term compromise, and "stability." The dialectic, on the other hand—the repository of the ideological remnants that continue still to guide both Soviet analysis and action—reflects a highly dynamic view of warfare, as of politics, socioeconomic relationships, and of nature itself. It does not allow for prolonged, global deadlock, or lasting compromise, but envisages ongoing conflict, resulting in victors and in the vanquished (who are consigned to the "rubbish bin" of history), with the victors, in turn, presumably having to confront another set of antagonists (although this is a contingency discreetly ignored in Soviet literature, whenever it predicts the ultimate triumph of the Socialist bloc).

The Soviet term "correlation of forces" does not refer to balance but to power *trends*, with one side overtaking or falling behind its adversary. Even during the brief moments of overall parity, relative to one another, the more dynamic of the protagonists will attempt to produce a favorable "correlation" at least locally, concentrating his forces to dominate a key area.

While Soviet publications allow that technological innovation leads to different *forms* of warfare, they reject the belief that a qualitative change has occurred with respect to the role of conflict itself, including its most extreme manifestation—war. To be "winnable," however (indeed, credible), Soviet war-waging requires an effective network of active and passive defense, to the extent that losses in life and infrastructure should not be exponentially in excess of the casualties and damage caused by the Nazi invasion. Consequently, Soviet analysts and the Russian leadership view PVO, PRO, and Civil Defense in an altogether positive light, whereas quite a few Western publicists have insisted for years that defensive measures are "destabilizing."

It should not be assumed from the foregoing, however, that war is the only or perhaps even the essential ingredient for achieving Soviet policy aims. Negotiations, political pressure, and psychological ploys are other extensions of diplomacy no less than war itself. If they can provide the desired results, from the Soviet point of view, the CPSU no doubt would be happy to do without the damage and the possible internal stresses (given an apathetic and cynical Soviet population) that a major conflagration may be expected to produce. This cannot be done, on the other hand—as the Soviet leaders see it—unless the USSR's posture and capabilities, as well as its military doctrine, provide credible orchestration of the options at Moscow's disposal: the attainment of goals either by political or by "other" means.

U.S. and Soviet Strategic Force Levels: Problems of Assessment and Measurement

By THOMAS A. BROWN

ABSTRACT: The problem of measuring the strategic balance has been viewed by some as a meaningless exercise, by others as a matter of comparing simple static indicators, and by still others as a complex process of assessing likely war outcomes. As the strategic power of the Soviet Union has grown, there has been a trend toward the latter view. To assess likely war outcomes, one must go substantially beyond the standard static indicators, such as warhead count, equivalent megatons, and hard target kill capability, into problems of command and control, long-term endurance, and the dynamics of escalation. To assess the likely outcomes of extended nuclear exchanges which stop short of all-out attacks on cities, it is necessary to employ fairly detailed war games. The use of such games to measure the strategic balance raises problems of how to report the results and how to use the games in posture design.

Thomas A. Brown is a partner in Booz, Allen & Hamilton, Inc. He served as Deputy Assistant Secretary of Defense (Strategic Programs) from December 1977 through February 1981. He is coauthor of the book Swords from Plowshares: The Military Potential of Civilian Nuclear Energy *(University of Chicago, 1979) and has written numerous articles on operations research, strategic forces, and national defense policy.*

BEFORE discussing the problem of measuring strategic forces, it is necessary to clarify what we want to use our measures for. There are at least four separate applications for measures of strategic force, and each application drives one toward different sets of measures. First, there are "figures of merit" used by systems analysts as an aid in making force posture decisions. Second, there are measures of the extent to which military forces burden a nation's economy. A third application of measures of strategic forces is as an element in arms control agreements.

The subject of this article, the fourth application of measures of strategic forces, is the assessment of the strategic balance. What do we mean by "the strategic balance?"

There are three distinct points of view on this question. The first point of view holds that, once you have passed a certain level, the strategic balance becomes meaningless; the second holds that the strategic balance is primarily a matter of perceptions; the third maintains that the strategic balance is essentially a question of probable outcomes of strategic conflict. These differing viewpoints reflect, to a certain extent, the opposing perspectives in Western strategic thought between deterrence achieved through "assured destruction" and deterrence achieved through "war-fighting capability." The first school holds that, once we reach certain levels, we could simply ignore the size of the Soviet strategic arsenal. This view was popular in the late 1960s, as expressed in the following passage:

In terms of numbers of separately targetable, survivable, accurate, reliable warheads, U.S. strategic forces have remained consistently superior to those of the Soviet Union. However, the relationship of this "superiority" to U.S. military and political objectives is unclear. In a conventional war, a numerical advantage in men and firepower can often defeat or force the retreat of enemy forces. Superior conventional forces can end a conventional war and are a source of political power in peacetime. However, once each side has enough nuclear forces virtually to eliminate the other's urban society in a second strike, the utility of extra nuclear forces is dubious at best. In this context, notions of nuclear "superiority" are devoid of significant meaning.

Strategic nuclear forces cannot seize territory, even when they are superior in numbers; they can only destroy it. As a result there is now no feasible way of ending a strategic nuclear war short of the total destruction of both sides, except through mutual control and restraint. Thus, such "nuclear superiority" as the United States maintains is of little significance, since we do not know how to use it to achieve our national security objectives. In other words, since the Soviet Union has an assured-destruction capability against the United States, "superior" U.S. nuclear forces are extremely difficult to convert into real political power. The blunt, unavoidable fact is that the Soviet Union could effectively destroy the United States even after absorbing the full weight of a U.S. first strike, and vice versa. Nor do we see that this is likely to change in the future.[1]

A second group views the strategic competition as primarily a competition for prestige, similar in many ways to the space race of the 1960s. It is suggested that actual nuclear conflict between the superpowers would be so destructive for all sides that actual use of nuclear weapons is absolutely out of the question. Proponents of this approach recognize, however, that a widespread perception that one side or the other is ahead in all the "standard indicators of strategic power" would have adverse political effects both nationally and internationally. Former Secretary of Defense Harold Brown expressed this point of view in testimony before the House Armed Services Committee that followed the decision of the Carter administration in 1977 to cancel the B-1:

Our analyses show that, over a range of wartime events, our current forces could ride out such a massive Soviet first-strike and retaliate with devastating effect. . . . In terms of wartime capability, this situation is acceptable for the national security. However, there are other issues that we must consider: the need to hedge against the unexpected, and the impact of comparative capabilities with the Soviet Union on interna-

1. Alan Enthoven and K. Wayne Smith, *How Much is Enough?* (New York: Harper & Row, 1971), pp. 183-84.

tional perceptions (Soviet, third party, and our own). . . . There is no generally accepted way to make this comparison. However, the two methods used most often are (1) comparing static indices and (2) comparing capabilities after a first strike by one side or the other.[2]

Secretary Brown then compared the Soviet and U.S. forces in warheads, megatons, throw-weight, and hard-target kill potential, referring to these as "the primary static measures of the strategic balance." He went on to distinguish clearly between the balance of indicators and hypothesized war outcomes:

The advantage to the Soviets of a possible lead in the primary measures of comparative capability is ill-defined in terms of useful wartime capability. But it might have some political value during peacetime or in a crisis. The perception of the U.S.-Soviet strategic balance has been and will be shifting away from that of U.S. advantage and becoming more favorable to the Soviets. Such perceptions can have an important effect. We must be sure that perceptions are such that no doubt as to our capability or our will exists in the minds of the Soviet leaders, or in the minds of our allies, or even in our own minds should we be faced with a moment of deep crisis.[3]

The third group assumes that, while actual nuclear conflict may be unlikely, the possibility of nuclear war casts a long political shadow. In this view, the important perceptions are those of professional military analysts, those who advise world leaders in times of crisis. This group views nuclear war as a complex phenomenon that could take a variety of forms, such as an extended series of exchanges in which each side would attempt to destroy the military for-

ces of the others but neither would launch direct attacks against the other's cities. Even if such a struggle were likely to escalate to city attacks early in a nuclear engagement, the expected outcome would still have a strong influence on the behavior of nations in crises far below the level of nuclear conflict. This approach is distinguished from the previous school of thought by its deep concern over the possible outcomes of actual nuclear conflict. Its proponents use static indicators as a tool to gain insights into this problem, rather than as an end in themselves.

In the course of his tenure as secretary of defense, Harold Brown seemed to move somewhat away from the "pure perceptionist" position he articulated so clearly in 1977 toward a recognition of the importance of hypothesized war outcomes for deterrence and for political influence. In 1980, at the Naval War College, Secretary Brown gave cogent expression to the "potential war outcome" point of view:

. . . deterrence must restrain a far wider range of threats than just massive attacks on U.S. cities. We seek to deter any adversary from any course of action that could lead to general nuclear war. Out strategic forces also must deter nuclear attacks on smaller sets of targets in the U.S. or on U.S. military forces, and be a wall against nuclear coercion of, or attack on, our friends and allies. Strategic forces, in conjunction with theater nuclear forces, must contribute to deterrence of conventional aggression as well.

In our analysis and planning, we are necessarily giving greater attention to how a nuclear war would actually be fought by both sides if deterrence fails. There is no contradiction between this focus on how a war would be fought and what its results would be, and our purpose of ensuring continued peace through mutual deterrence. Indeed, this

2. Statement of Secretary of Defense Harold Brown before the House Armed Services Committee, 2 August 1977.
   3. Ibid.

focus helps us achieve deterrence and peace, by ensuring that our ability to retaliate is fully credible.[4]

Readers may find paradoxical the trend toward a more serious interpretation of the significance of the strategic balance as the United States' position relative to the Soviet Union has declined. This is really a natural consequence of our attitude toward military force. While we have not desired to exploit the advantages of strategic superiority when we have had it, we are also unwilling to concede strategic superiority to another nation that might not be so forbearing.

The analysis of the strategic balance from the standpoint of assessing war outcomes is far more difficult than a strict perceptionist approach through "accepted" static indicators. This more difficult approach includes the use of some static indicators, as well as dynamic indicators, assignment of forces against specific target sets, and war games. I will consider each element in this approach to the measurement of strategic capabilities.

STATIC INDICATORS

Secretary Brown identified warheads, megatons, throw-weight, and hard-target kill capability as the "standard" static indicators. Others might add equivalent megatons, linear kill potential, strategic nuclear delivery vehicles, equivalent weapons, and lethality to the list. The advantages and disadvantages of these individual indices have been much discussed.[5] I will limit my dis-

4. Harold Brown, remarks prepared for delivery at the Convocation Ceremonies for the 97th Naval War College Class, 20 August 1980.

5. For example, see Thomas A. Brown, "Number Mysticism, Rationality, and the Strategic Balance," *Orbis* (Fall 1977): 479-97.

cussion to the general principles behind static indicators. All of the static indicators named are numerical quantities that may be evaluated for an individual weapon and then simply added up to obtain an indicator for the entire force. Almost all of the static indicators relate to the theoretical effectiveness of the weapon against a particular type of target.

On the surface, the standard static indicators seem to be objective and independent of scenario; each appears to provide a yardstick for comparing Soviet and American strategic forces. Serious issues arise, however, when attempting to apply these measures. First of all, what portion of the force should be included when summing up the static indicators? Should all the forces in the inventory be included? Should the bomb capacity of the old B-52s in storage, essentially unflyable, with no crews assigned to them, be included? Should missiles in storage without launchers be included? Should submarines in overhaul be included?

Some would go even further and sum up the static indicators only over ICBMs, bombers on alert, and submarines at sea. The argument for this approach is that all other forces would easily be destroyed in a surprise attack and thus should not enter into a calculation of the strategic balance. But, if we count only U.S. forces on peacetime alert, what should we assume for the Soviet Union, which maintains a smaller fraction of its bombers and submarines on continuous alert? Yet, one would suppose that if the Soviet Union decided on a surprise attack, it would be able to increase the usable fraction of its force without alerting us. One way to finesse this problem is to argue that "surely" a nuclear exchange would be preceded by a crisis so severe that both sides would have all their forces on full alert.

Unfortunately, the history of this century gives numerous examples of major wars that began with a surprise attack by the aggressor that caught the victim totally by surprise, even after a long period of tension. So we see that the supposed scenario-independence of the standard static indicators is really an illusion if one attempts to apply them seriously in estimating probable outcomes of nuclear conflict.

DYNAMIC INDICATORS

Were one willing to postulate a particular scenario for war outbreak, one might be able to calculate alert rates, survival probabilities, penetration probabilities, and reliability factors that, when multiplied by the appropriate static indicators, give some insight into the likely outcome of the war. These scenario-dependent indicators are termed "dynamic indicators."

Some analysts consider scenario-dependence a great blemish in any measure of the strategic balance because the results of analysis can be controlled by varying the scenario assumptions. A responsible analyst, however, would not simply pluck a scenario out of the air. One must assume that each side pursues a strategy which makes the best use of its available forces and that the best estimates are used in assessing the technical characteristics of those forces (these estimates are required even for calculating the static indicators). Nevertheless, legitimate disagreements can arise about the likelihood or importance of alternative scenarios. For example, to what extent could the Soviet Union

increase its forces on alert without detection by the United States? Is generated alert or day-to-day alert the more likely condition at the start of a nuclear exchange? Would the Soviet Union be willing to accept the risk of detection inherent in a sneak bomber attack, a wave of sabotage, or some other "unusual" way of striking the first blow? Should we consider the outcome if the United States strikes first in evaluating the strategic balance, or should we limit our attention to cases in which the Soviet Union strikes the first blow? These are important questions, closely related to our strategic policy as a whole, and there is no mathematical trick that will make them disappear. A technique for measuring the strategic balance that suppresses these questions is itself somehow flawed and incomplete—at least to those who accept the idea that the strategic balance is primarily a matter of what would be the likely outcome if war were to break out. In other words, scenario-independent measures, not scenario-dependent measures, are the ones that are blemished.

Even within the context of a single scenario, and even if the difficulties in calculating such factors as prelaunch survivability and penetration probability are ignored, the indicators discussed so far represent quantities attached to individual weapon systems that are simply summed up in order to produce an indicator for the entire force. Therefore they must miss out on any synergy or interference that may exist within the force. They also fail to take account of any special advantages or disadvantages flowing from the relationship of the arsenal to the potential target set.

INDICATORS LINKING ARSENALS TO TARGET SETS

It should be obvious that the power of a weapons arsenal cannot be evaluated without considering the nature of the target set it is intended to attack. The equivalent weapons concept attempts to do this by taking the harmonic mean of a single weapon's effectiveness against point targets, area targets, and hard targets in proportion to the percentage of the total target set represented by each type of target. Summing up the "equivalent weapons" in an entire arsenal, however, can give a misleading impression of the arsenal's strength if it contains a wide spectrum of different types of warheads.[6] The equivalent weapons concept totally fails to consider that individual weapons would be assigned primarily against those targets against which they were most capable. Thus the efficiency and effectiveness of a diverse arsenal will be substantially understated.

This failure to take into account the power of diversity in an arsenal affects every one of the static indicators related to effectiveness against targets of a given type. The following example is artificial, but it makes the point well.

Let us suppose that we wish to compare two arsenals. Arsenal A consists of one 1.2-megaton warhead and one 45-kiloton warhead. Arsenal B consists of three 500-kiloton warheads. Assume each weapon to be perfectly accurate. A little calculation shows that Arsenal B is bigger than Arsenal A in terms of every relevant indicator discussed above: Warheads, equivalent megatons, megatons, linear kill potential, hard-target kill capability, linear kill potential, and equivalent

6. Ibid., pp. 489-90.

weapons all favor Arsenal B. But now consider what these arsenals could do to a target set consisting of exactly four point targets, each of 8.5-psi hardness. Assume three of the targets to be at the vertices of an equilateral triangle 20,000 feet on a side, and the fourth target to be more than 20,000 feet away from any of the others. The radius of effectiveness of 500-kiloton warheads against targets of this type is 9000 feet. Hence Arsenal B can destroy only three out of the four targets. The radius of effectiveness of a 1.2-megaton warhead against these targets is somewhat less than 12,000 feet. If such a warhead were to be detonated at the center of the triangle of targets, it would destroy all of them. Thus Arsenal A can destroy all four targets. In other words, Arsenal A is 33 percent more effective against this target set, even though it is inferior to Arsenal B in every static indicator.

There appears to be no way to calculate the effectiveness of a given arsenal against a given target set, except to work out a specific assignment of weapons against targets using the appropriate optimization tools. This approach requires the use of computers if the target set and arsenal are reasonably large. The concept of "relative force size" (the term used in the 1981 Defense Report[7]) or "U.S. retaliatory potential" (the term used for essentially the same indicator in the 1982 Defense Report[8]) is an implementa-

7. Report of Secretary of Defense Harold Brown to the Congress on the FY1981 Budget, FY1983 Authorization Request, and FY 1982-1986 Defense Programs, 14 January 1981.

8. Report of Secretary of Defense Harold Brown to the Congress on the FY1982 Budget, FY1983 Authorization Request, and FY1982-1986 Defense Programs, 14 January 1981.

tion of this concept. This approach to calculating the effectiveness of given arsenals versus given targets was developed in late 1976 by Paul Groover, Ed Kownacki, and Joseph Prukop at Science Application Incorporated. The technique involves several steps in completing the calculation.

In the first step of the technique, a target set and desired damage level are specified. In the case of the calculations presented in the latest Defense Report, the target set selected was a comprehensive group of military, leadership, war-supporting industry, and economic recovery targets in the Soviet Union and Warsaw Pact. The desired damage level was not given in the published Defense Report. The next step is to calculate, by means of a specific assignment of weapons to targets, the size of the arsenal (consisting of weapons in precisely the same proportions as the arsenal being measured) required to achieve the specified damage level. The ratio of the size of the arsenal being measured to the arsenal just adequate to achieve the specified damage level is defined to be the "relative force size" or "U.S. retaliatory capability." This index takes into account the value of diversity in the force and the advantage gained by using weapons against targets that give them the greatest relative effectiveness. It is a complex measure, however, and has often been misunderstood. It is incorrect to interpret it as a measure of adequacy. The damage level specified is arbitrary, and numerous important factors are not taken into account in this measure.

Other criticisms related to the above technique include the target base used as a standard. In the Defense Reports for fiscal years 1979 and 1980, the relative force size

concept was used to measure both U.S. and Soviet forces. In order to compare the two forces on a common scale, they were both measured against a Soviet target base. Evaluating Soviet forces on the basis of targets in the Soviet Union was derided by some critics, who urged that such forces should be measured by their capability against targets in the United States. It is difficult, however, to make up two lists of targets and two specified damage levels for two different countries and to certify that they are, in some sense, equivalent. If target sets and damage levels could be identified that accurately reflect each country's nuclear targeting objectives, then the comparison would be meaningful, but we have little detailed knowledge of Soviet targeting objectives. This difficulty and the need for justifying the equivalence of the two target lists in an open forum led to the decision to apply this measure only to U.S. forces in the Defense Report for fiscal years 1981 and 1982.

Strategic Air Command analysts and the Studies, Analysis, and Gaming Agency at the Joint Chiefs of Staff now assess arsenals by allocating them to specific target sets, using methods similar to those employed in the Defense Report but with some difference in detail. These approaches all offer a way to include the advantages of a diverse force, with each weapon used against a target appropriate to it—an important consideration. These complex measures are superior to the standard static and dynamic indicators in that regard; however, numerous factors are not taken into account. Normally, these measures assume rather ideal conditions. For example, communications work perfectly, and commanders reassign surviving weapons so that each will go where it will do the most good. Also, the target bases used consist entirely of fixed, preplanned targets so that the problem of hunting down mobile targets, or restriking targets that may have survived the initial attack, is totally absent. The problem of endurance, of keeping forces alive through an extended period of conflict, is not modeled by this technique. No light is shed on the possible reuse of bombers. The interactions between strategic nuclear forces and conventional forces are not represented. Viewing the nuclear balance in terms of the likely outcome of a nuclear war, considerations such as these are just as important as the raw nuclear firepower available to the two sides.

WAR-GAMING

There is no substitute for some sort of war game to determine the likely outcome of an actual nuclear conflict, especially in consideration of the complex interplay of forces and information structures that changes dramatically over the course of the conflict. Such a war game must be complex enough to capture realistically the problems of command and control, endurance, and interactions between conventional and nuclear forces, yet simple enough to be played in a few days by individuals with a minimum of instruction. Perhaps the game that comes closest to these criteria is the Global Wargame at the Naval War College in Newport, Rhode Island; however, that game takes about two weeks to play and emphasizes sea combat rather than realistic land combat. There have also been recent efforts at the Rand Corporation to design a game for assessing the nuclear balance. Considerable progress has been made in developing this war game.

The rapid progress evident in computers and displays has made such war games more realistic and playable than ever before. As problems of game design are overcome, two more methodological problems will be recognized as of increasing importance. First, how does one communicate the results of these games to people who have not actually played them? Most people who participate in such games find the experience very instructive and come away with a better understanding of the strategic balance. But how does one package this increased insight for transmission to political leaders and to the public at large? Reading synopses of games played by others is dull; it does not give the player the same insight as playing himself and having to make moment-to-moment decisions. One approach to this problem of communications would be to create a vocabulary or mathematical structure for representing scenarios so that the results of many games could be reported in a single display. Rather than trying to develop this vocabulary in a vacuum, it would be better to work with a collection of synopses of actual games to evolve an optimum means of presentation. This would communicate the richness of the game experience to a nonparticipant and would make it easier to save and accumulate the results of individual games into a substantial body of "artificial history." Another way of stating this problem is: What information do you save about a game? With modern recording equipment it is, of course, possible to save everything: every discussion of every team, every move, every random number that is drawn. This has been tried. A single game, played over two or three days, can generate 100 hours of videotape and many pounds of computer printout. Saving everything creates an impenetrable unstructured mass that is virtually useless. The solution to the problem of how to edit and report the information generated in the play of a game is therefore critically important to any attempt to use war games as a systematic measure of the strategic balance.

Second, there is the problem of using results of war-gaming analysis in force posture design. I have already noted that measures of the strategic balance and figures of merit for force posture decisions are not synonymous, but one of the characteristics of the traditional static indicators of the balance is that they suggest fairly directly corresponding figures of merit for force posture decisions. If the increased insight we hope to gain from war-gaming is to be of any practical use in improving the strategic balance, we must somehow translate the results of war-gaming into desiderata for individual systems. War games measure the entire force, with all its internal interactions at once (indeed, this is one of their most important advantages). The impact of a single force posture decision on a total war outcome is likely to be relatively small and difficult to detect in the midst of the random noise generated by interaction of large forces. This means that the obvious approach, of simply running the game once for each of a number of alternative posture decisions and seeing which works out best, is likely to be unproductive. To get rid of statistical uncertainty, a series of runs would be required for each possible alternative. This could soon become prohibitively expensive and time-consuming. War-gaming on the scale appropriate for measuring the strategic balance may be appropriate only for evaluation of major force posture decisions, such

as the relative weight to put on nuclear and conventional forces, rather than for the more detailed individual weapons system choices.

CONCLUSIONS

The standard static indicators and their derivatives were perhaps adequate measures of the strategic balance when the United States had an overwhelming preponderance across the board. Now that we have entered a period of, at best, rough equivalence, we must turn to more complex and delicate measures. We must pay close attention to factors such as command and control, endurance, and relations to conventional forces that defy straightforward quantification. Careful attention to the many different ways a nuclear war might be fought, and evaluation of our total posture in such a context, is essential for deterrence. As former Secretary of Defense Brown noted in his Naval War College speech,

By definition, successful deterrence means, among other things, shaping *Soviet* views of what a war would mean—of what risks and losses aggression would entail. We must have forces, contingency plans, and command and control capabilities that will convince the Soviet leadership that no war and no course of aggression by them that led to the use of nuclear weapons—on any scale of attack and at any stage of conflict— could lead to victory, however they may define victory.[9]

This view of deterrence requires that we evaluate our forces against those of the Soviet Union under many different scenarios rather than a few stereotypes. There seems to be no way to evaluate strategic

9. Harold Brown, Naval War College speech, 20 August 1980.

postures against one another in adequately diverse contexts except by means of a series of war games. This approach should be pursued with resolution, but it does raise the problems, in addition to designing a game complex enough to be realistic but simple enough to play, of communicating the results to nonplayers and applying the games to the problems of force posture design that arise daily.

Strategic Offense and Defense: Enhancing the Effectiveness of U.S. Strategic Forces

By DANIEL GOURÉ

ABSTRACT: The United States is faced with a series of imminent strategic force posture decisions, the most critical of which focuses on measures to reduce the vulnerability of the land-based ICBM. Other decisions involve improvement to the survivability and effectiveness of the bomber and submarine legs of the Triad, U.S. space-based assets, and command and control capabilities. Complicating resolution of force planning issues are growing concerns about the adequacy of current U.S. strategic doctrine and persistent disagreements over alternative strategic policies. The most promising solution to the ICBM vulnerability problem appears to be a combination of rebasing and active defense. Active defense against ballistic missiles is a technically plausible strategic option in the 1980s. The increased viability of strategic defenses and their improving cost-effectiveness calls into question existing strategic doctrine with its emphasis on offensive systems and deterrence via threat of retaliation. A potential answer to the problem of an uncertain strategic vision may be movement toward a more balanced offense-defense posture or even to a "defense-heavy" strategic posture and corresponding strategy based on assured survival.

Daniel Gouré is a senior associate with the firm of Jeffrey Cooper Associates, Inc. He is also a member of the Soviet studies department of the Johns Hopkins University School of Advanced International Studies, where he is completing his doctoral dissertation on Soviet views of U.S. military power, 1945-1980.

IN the 1980s the United States is faced with the prospect of attempting to ensure its national security with a strategic force pos-

ture that is increasingly vulnerable, seriously obsolescent, relatively unresponsive to policy direction, and, in the view of a growing number of defense analysts, of diminishing deterrent value.[1] Over the past decade and a half, the Soviet Union has undertaken a general arms buildup which, where it has not already permitted Moscow to surpass the United States according to virtually all static indicators, has significantly closed previous gaps.[2] The change in the U.S.-Soviet balance since the mid-1960s has been most pronounced in the area of strategic forces, both offensive and defensive. In a period when the United States undertook expensive but militarily marginal improvements of its strategic forces, the Soviet Union deployed an array of offensive and defensive systems that pose direct threats not only to U.S. strategic systems but also to long-cherished notions of strategic stability. U.S. ennui and an excessive dependence on arms control formulae inhibited and delayed necessary response to the Soviet buildup, to the point where some question the capacity of the United States in the current decade to do more than reduce the rate of strategic decline.[3]

Lest the future be held captive to the myths of the past, it is important to state from the outset that the current strategic imbalance is not simply the product of the evolution of strategic technology, nor of the decisions by past administrations to limit the size of U.S. strategic forces and accept the reality of Soviet acquisition of a secure retaliatory capability.[4] Any force improvement, whether offensive or defensive, raises uncertainties regarding their impact on the survivability and operation of opposing forces. However, the situation confronting the United States today is fundamentally the result of a deliberate and long-term Soviet effort to acquire a preemptive counterforce capability coupled with an equally serious investment in systems designed to limit damage to the Soviet Union and, not incidentally, deny the United States an assured destruction deterrent.[5]

This situation is no more stable considering that the United States, with its existing force posture, even in the absence of Soviet strategic defenses, is incapable of posing a similar disarming threat to Soviet ICBMs.[6] The result is that the Uni-

1. Colin S. Gray, "Soviet Strategic Systems: Implications for the U.S. Deterrent Posture," in *The Emerging Strategic Environment: Implications for Ballistic Missile Defense* (Special Report) (Cambridge, MA: Institute for Foreign Policy Analysis, 1979), p. 45.

2. While arguments on specific balance measurements are to be expected, the general trend—and trends in strategic forces in particular—is indisputable. See John M. Collins, *U.S.-Soviet Military Balance: Concepts and Capabilities, 1960-1980* (New York: McGraw-Hill, 1980).

3. "In sum, the trends in relative military strength are such that, unless we move promptly to reverse them, the United States is moving toward a posture of minimum deterrence in which we would be conceding to the Soviet Union the potential for a military and political victory if deterrence failed." Paul Nitze, "Assuring Strategic Stability in an Era of Detente," *Foreign Affairs* 54(2): 227 (January 1976).

4. This claim was made most recently by a former advisor in the Kennedy and Johnson administrations: McGeorge Bundy, "The Future of Strategic Deterrence," *Survival* 21(6): 268-72 (November-December 1979).

5. Former Secretary of Defense Harold Brown, "Brown Says Soviets Long Sought Way to Knock Out U.S. Missiles," *New York Times*, 31 May 1979, p. A4. Also Leon Gouré et al., *The Role of Nuclear Forces in Soviet Strategy* (Coral Gables, FL: Center for Advanced International Studies, University of Miami, 1974).

6. Keith B. Payne, "Deterrence and Essential Equivalence," *International Security Review* No. 4, p. 349 (Winter 1979-80). Also Thomas A. Brown, "Missile Accuracy and Strategic Lethality," *Survival* 18(2): 52-59 (March-April 1976); and House Armed Services Committee, *Study on the Vulnerability of U.S. ICBM Forces* (Washington, DC: Government Printing Office, 1977).

ted States is increasingly at a disadvantage in any plausible exchange scenario, so much so that the outcome would appear to favor the Soviet Union regardless of the character of the conflict.[7] Clearly, such a balance contradicts the minimum desiderata for stability. Moreover, the ability to extend the deterrent shield to protect U.S. allies is becoming increasingly questionable. The absence of credible limited options on the forces to execute them and a growing Soviet invulnerable retaliatory capability serve to undermine confidence in U.S. commitments.[8]

The United States is entering perhaps the most critical decade since the end of World War II. Imminent decisions on new strategic systems, based on the ongoing strategic debate begun in the last administration, promise to be the most critical for U.S. national security since that of the early 1960s, which produced Minuteman, the B-52, and Polaris. Difficulties abound if only for the number of new and alternative capabilities. Under consideration often for competitive roles are a new intercontinental ballistic missile (the MX); upgrades to existing Minuteman forces; a mobile basing mode for either MX or Minuteman; a shallow underwater missile system (SUMS); a new, manned penetrating bomber; a longer-range, higher-accuracy ballistic missile for the Trident/Polaris fleet; an entirely new ballistic missile submarine; renewed air defenses; some

7. Paul Nitze, "Deterring Our Deterrent," *Foreign Policy*, 25: 195-210 (Winter 1976-77); and T.K. Jones and W. Scott Thompson, "Central War and Civil Defense," *Orbis* 22(3) (Fall 1978).

8. Edward Luttwak, "The Problems of Extended Deterrence," in *The Future of Strategic Deterrence*, Adelphi Papers 160 (London: International Institute for Strategic Studies, 1980), pp. 35-37.

form of ballistic missile defense (either for silo- or mobile-based ICBMs or for area coverage); and possible development of exotic technologies (lasers, particle beams). The protracted time frame for any major weapons system development and acquisition virtually guarantees that the U.S. force posture will not change in the near future. The United States faces, at the very minimum, several years of high ICBM vulnerability. Delays in implementing measures to improve force survivability could perpetuate the threat into the 1990s.

Analysts, while generally agreeing on the need to upgrade the U.S. strategic posture, differ sharply on the urgency of strategic force posture changes and the preferred options for implementation. Complicating the difficulty of correcting even glaring deficiencies in the U.S. strategic posture are SALT constraints and the insistence by some arms control advocates that SALT be preserved even at the price of perpetuating dangerous defense asymmetries.

What most distinctly divides the various factions in the debate on U.S. strategic force improvements is not the specific, short-term, and all-too technical issues which have dominated the discussions to date, but rather basic assumptions about deterrence, the objectives of U.S. strategic planning, and the utility of nuclear weapons. In the absence of consensus on nuclear strategy it is little wonder that there exist no clear choices among competing systems or even between action and inaction. How can the United States determine the role and effectiveness of various prospective force posture changes unless it is in the context of a well-developed strategy? Debates on the relative merits of arms control solutions versus unilateral measures to improve strategies for effectiveness thus take place in a vacuum. Charles Burton Marshall noted with reference to these circumstances:

> Reversing adverse strategic trends is an essential component—necessary but not of itself sufficient—in the task of restoring the United States to a proper position in world affairs. Much else must be done to correct a general tackiness that has come to characterize the conduct of external affairs.[9]

To this prescription must be added the need to correct the tackiness of strategic thought that has dominated U.S. strategic planning for almost two decades.

OFFENSE AND DEFENSE: SURVIVABILITY AND ENHANCED EFFECTIVENESS

Colin S. Gray correctly noted that the United States cannot be expected to postpone resolution of urgent force posture problems while first addressing tendentious doctrinal issues.[10] That luxury was affordable only so long as the United States enjoyed unquestionable strategic superiority. The Reagan administration, unlike its predecessor, recognizes the immediacy of the need to bolster a deteriorating military balance and has responded with a general upgrading of the status of, and budgetary allocation to, national defense.[11] However, as of this writing, the key strategic program decisions have yet to be made. It is to these imminent and crucial choices that we must first turn.

The current debate on measures to redress the strategic imbalance has focused most of its energies on the doubtful survivability and limited utility of the existing force of land-based intercontinental ballistic missiles. There is now general agreement regarding the imminent vulnerability of silo-based forces.[12] Less well recognized is the problem posed by the demands of current U.S. strategy for a reliable and highly flexible ICBM force capable of executing limited attacks or functioning under conditions of protracted crisis/conflict.[13] A further complication is persistent uncertainties regarding the status and capabilities of the other two legs of the Triad, both of which are undergoing extensive modernization to guard against system failure in the face of improving Soviet strategic defenses.[14] An open issue is the

9. Charles Burton Marshall, "Strategy: The Emerging Dangers," in *From Weakness to Strength: National Security in the 1980's* (San Francisco: Institute for Contemporary Studies, 1980), p. 439.

10. Colin S. Gray, "The Strategic Forces Triad: End of the Road?" *Foreign Affairs* 56(4): 772 (July 1978).

11. Clarence A. Robinson, Jr., "Reagan Details Defense Boost," *Aviation Week and Space Technology* 10 November 1980, pp. 14-16.

12. Former Secretary of Defense Harold Brown, *Annual Report, FY 1981* (Washington, DC: Government Printing Office, 1980), pp. 5-6. Also Colin S. Gray, *The Future of the Land-Based Missile Force*, Adelphi Papers 140 (London: International Institute for Strategic Studies, 1977), p. 4; Richard Burt, "Search for an Invulnerable Missile," *New York Times Magazine*, 27 May 1979, pp. 34-38. Considerable uncertainties exist regarding the Soviets' ability to translate a theoretical capability into a usable targeting strategy. See *Counterforce Issues for the U.S. Strategic Nuclear Forces* (Washington, DC: Congressional Budget Office, January 1978), pp. 9-21; and John D. Steinbruner and Thomas M. Garwin, "The Balance Between Prudence and Paranoia," *International Security*, 1(1) (Summer 1976).

13. Such a requirement appears inherent in a "countervailing" strategy. Harold Brown, *Annual Report, FY 1980*, pp. 77-79 and *Annual Report, FY 1981*, pp. 65-67. Also Desmond J. Ball, "PD-59: A Strategic Critique," *FAS Public Interest Report* October 1980, pp. 5-6.

14. Daniel Gouré and Gordon H. McCormick, "Soviet Strategic Defense: The Neg-

urgency of the ICBM problem. Decisions made today on survivability improvements will take a number of years to implement. Reliance on the other legs of the Triad is problematic at best in light of the delays in the cruise missile, B-1, and Trident submarine programs.

Complicating the decision on ICBM modernization is the possible desirability of a new missile. Arguments in favor of a new missile have less to do with the issue of survivability than with concern about the declining ability of U.S. strategic forces to strike an increasingly hardened and proliferated Soviet target set and the disparity between proposed strategic options and existing capabilities.[15] Added to this is the growing recognition that a strategic posture capable only of an assured destruction response may be incredible to those the United States seeks to deter.[16] Opponents of ICBM upgrades tend to argue not the essentials of U.S. strategic requirements, but the impact of U.S. actions on the Soviet Union and on strategic stability. At the same time, they tend to ignore the problem of the declining political and military utility of U.S. ICBMs. Either the MX or an improved version of the existing Minuteman III would offer

the prospects of hard-target capability, flexibility, and timeliness necessary in an ICBM force intended to perform military missions other than simple deterrence via countervalue retaliation.[17]

It is unclear whether the strategic bomber force is more or less vulnerable than the ICBM forces. The B-52 has questionable survivability against a ballistic missile attack (including the use of depressed-trajectory SLBMs) designed to eliminate bombers on the ground and to interdict fly-out corridors.[18] However, launching such a strike would be a difficult problem for the Soviet Union.[19] Furthermore, the Soviet air defense network, the largest and most complete system ever created, calls into question the ability of surviving U.S. bombers to perform their mission.[20] Although the

17. William R. Graham and Paul Nitze, "Viable U.S. Strategic Missile Forces for the Early 1980's," in William R. Van Cleave and W. Scott Thompson, eds., *Strategic Options for the Early 1980's: What Can Be Done?* (New York: National Strategy Information Center, 1979), pp. 137-40; Jacquelyn K. Davis, Patrick J. Friel, and Robert L. Pfaltzgraff, Jr., *SALT II and U.S.-Soviet Strategic Forces* (Cambridge, MA: Institute for Foreign Policy Analysis, 1979), pp. 17-21; Clarence A. Robinson, Jr., "MX Deployment Urged for Parity," *Aviation Week and Space Technology* 5 December 1977, pp. 12-15.

18. Francis P. Hoeber, *Slow to Take Offense: Bombers, Cruise Missiles, and Prudent Deterrence* (Washington, DC: Center for Strategic and International Studies, Georgetown University, 1977), pp. 77-100; and Goure and McCormick, "Soviet Strategic Defense."

19. There is no hard evidence to suggest that the USSR has practiced depression-trajectory launch of SLBMs. In addition, the deployment of numbers of Soviet SSBNs in attack position would provide warning permitting the dispersal or launch of U.S. bombers. However, such warning may not apply in a protracted crisis with continuous stationing of SSBNs off U.S. coasts.

20. Alexander H. Flax, "Strategic Defensive Systems," *National Defense* 63(349): 41-42 (September-October 1979). Also Michael

lected Dimension of the U.S.-Soviet Balance," *Orbis* 24(1): 117-23 (Spring 1980). Also *Counterforce Issues*, pp. 22-30; and Gray, "Soviet Strategic Systems," pp. 6-66.

15. Colin S. Gray, *Strategy and the MX ICBM*, Hudson Paper (HI-3075-P) (Croton-on-Hudson, NY: Hudson Institute, 1979), pp. 46-80; idem, "Strategic Forces and SALT: A Question of Strategy," *Comparative Strategy* 2(2): 122-26 (1980); and Payne, "Deterrence and Essential Equivalence."

16. Colin S. Gray and Keith B. Payne, "Victory is Possible," *Foreign Policy* 39: 16-18 (Summer 1980). On Soviet views of assured destruction see Michael J. Deane, *Strategic Defense in Soviet Strategy* (Washington, DC: Advanced International Studies Institute, 1980), pp. 1-14.

bomber penetration problem was apparently addressed in the decision to deploy cruise missiles on the B-52 and to begin to develop a cruise missile carrier, it is by no means certain that further upgrading of Soviet air defenses will not be able to counter current U.S. bomber improvements.[21] In view of U.S. dependence on the bomber to maintain essential equivalence and to perform critical non-time-urgent hard-target strikes, the lack of assured penetrability should be the object of concern.

The third leg of the Triad, the fleet of ballistic missile submarines (SSBNs), remains relatively invulnerable at sea; SSBN survivability is essentially a function of the area in which the submarine can hide. Improvements in existing capabilities are being made in the form of the Trident submarine and the C-4 long-range SLBM also being fitted to most of the Poseidon fleet.[22] SSBNs constitute the only truly assured destruction capability available to the United States. Unfortunately, the existing SLBN capability is sufficiently inaccurate to be of little use against hardened

targets.[23] Furthermore, at least 40 percent of the fleet is in port at any time and thus subject to preemptive attack. Critical command and control problems limit the effectiveness and flexibility of the at-sea force.[24] Nor is the survivability of the SSBNs assured for longer than they can remain at sea—for perhaps six months in the event of war. Finally, the ability of the United States to meet even limited destruction criteria in the face of Soviet active-passive defense is increasingly in doubt.[25]

Compounding these force posture problems are similar vulnerabilities in support functions. The U.S. command, control, communications, and intelligence (C³I) infrastructure is particularly vulnerable to preemptive attack. Ground-based stations and satellite downlinks are few in number and not hardened. Space-based systems are equally vulnerable. The present Soviet ASAT program may be capable of destroying low-altitude intelligence-collecting satellites; subsequent generations may be able to strike at early warning satellites in syn-

J. Deane, "Soviet Military Doctrine and Defensive Deployment Concepts: Implications for Soviet Ballistic Missile Defense," in *The Soviet Union and Ballistic Missile Defense* (Cambridge, MA: Institute for Foreign Policy Analysis, 1980), pp. 50-54; and idem, *Strategic Defense in Soviet Strategy*, pp. 95-102.

21. The new Soviet strategic air defenses include look-down/shoot-down interceptors, airborne warning aircraft, and high-velocity missile defenses. See Clarence A. Robinson, Jr., "U.S. Upgrades its Strategic Arsenal," *Aviation Week and Space Technology* 9 March 1981, pp. 31-33; idem, "Soviets Press Production, New Fighter Development," *Aviation Week and Space Technology* 16 March 1981, p. 56; and R. Evans and R. Novack, "Does Russia's SA-10 Eclipse the Cruise Missile?" *Washington Post* 17 February 1978, p. A30.

22. *Annual Statement, FY 1981*, pp. 131-32.

23. The combination of low-yield warheads and targeting inaccuracies inhibits the hard-target potential of the SSBN force. Jacquelyn K. Davis, "End of the Strategic Triad," *Strategic Review* 6(1): 39-40 (Winter 1978).

24. U.S. SSBNs are dependent on external sources for precision navigation and targeting. Also, the present mode of communication with submerged SSBNs requires that they approach the surface and trail an antenna, both of which increase the chances of detection. See Donald G. Brennan, "Command and Control," in Francis P. Hoeber and William Schneider, Jr., eds., *Arms, Men and Military Budgets* (New York: Crane, Russak and Company, 1977), pp. 334-42; and Albert Langer, "Accurate Submarine Launched Ballistic Missiles and Nuclear Strategy," *Journal of Peace Research* 14(1): 45-51 (1977).

25. Gouré and McCormick, "Soviet Strategic Defense."

chronous orbit.[26] The interdiction of C³I may, in itself, be sufficient to paralyze a U.S. response; the next war may be won in space without any nuclear strikes against ground targets.[27] In the absence of adequate survivability measures, existing U.S. C³I assets could be degraded in the initial moments of conflict. The residual capabilities would then be inadequate to meet the requirements in current U.S. strategy, much less those for sustaining a protracted conflict.

The prospect of changes in U.S. strategic policies, an evolving Soviet threat, and uncertainties regarding the direction or even the future of SALT militate against the positions of those who would advocate that the United States essentially do nothing about ICBM vulnerability but rely either solely on a policy of launch-on-warning or move to a dyad of bombers and submarine-launched ballistic missiles.[28] All these nonsolutions are predicated on the belief that strategic forces perform no useful mission aside from deterring nuclear strikes on the forces themselves or

on the U.S. homeland. Were this true, a vulnerable ICBM force—particularly one tied to a launch-on-warning trigger—may be more destabilizing in a crisis than a less vulnerable force which can successfully withstand a Soviet strike. Development of a dyad founders on uncertainties regarding the current modernization programs for the bomber and SSBN forces and potential improvements to Soviet strategic defenses. Providing equivalent capability in a dyad to that which exists in the current Triad is likely to be at least as expensive as improving ICBM survivability. Furthermore, acceptance of ICBM vulnerability or elimination of the capabilities represented in the land-based ICBM force risks serious negative impact on both U.S. and Soviet perceptions of the strategic balance. The Soviet Union clearly places great store in the political and military utility of the land-based ICBM. In view of official expressions of doubt concerning the adequacy of the U.S. deterrent, weakening the Triad by failing to deploy a survivable land-based ICBM appears an unwarranted risk.

As a consequence, the United States is left with two alternatives to preserve the capabilities represented by the land-based ICBMs: (1) force proliferation, including changes to the "front ends" of the Minuteman force, or an increase in the number of launchers/warheads but at the expense of any arms control limitations; and (2) defense of ICBMs, either active, passive, or a combination of the two. Should U.S. policy dictate a need for a nuclear war-waging capability, this would require an expansion of the ICBM force as well as enhanced survivability, which, in turn, would clearly involve a combination of both (1) and

26. "Gains by Soviet Reported in Test to Kill Satellites," *New York Times* 19 March 1981, p. A1; Richard Burt, "U.S. Says Russians Develop Satellite-Killing Laser," *New York Times* 22 May 1980, p. A9.

27. Colin S. Gray, "Strategic Stability Reconsidered," *Daedalus* (Fall 1980) 144-45; Donald Hafner, "Averting a Brobdignagian Skeet Shoot," *International Security* 5(3): 42-43 (Winter 1980-81).

28. The best summary of the alternatives to retention of the land-based ICBM is provided in Gray, "The Strategic Forces Triad," pp. 778-83; idem, *The Future of the Land-Based Missile Force* pp. 9-18. For a discussion of the concept of launch-on-warning/launch-under-attack, see Richard L. Garwin, "Launch under Attack to Redress Minuteman Vulnerability?" *International Security* 4(3) (Winter 1979-80); Francis Hoeber, "How Little is Enough?" *International Security* 3(3) (Winter 1978-79).

(2), as in the MX missile deployed in a mobile basing arrangement.

Improvements to the ICBM force have tended to focus on deployment of the MX missile in one among a number of alternative deceptive basing modes.[29] The intent is to force the attacker to expend a sufficiently large fraction of his available warheads (RVs) in attacking a target set consisting primarily of empty structures so as to make a counterforce effort costly, if not impossible. The multiple protective shelter (MPS) system currently in fashion envisions some 200 MX missiles dispersed among 23 horizontal shelters of minimum hardness (600 psi per missile) in a series of closed roadways, or "racetracks."[30] A widely discussed alternative envisions fields of vertical shelters or silos with ICBMs in movable cannisters. In order to ensure destruction of the missiles, the Soviet Union must use at least one, and perhaps two, RVs per shelter. This has the effect of creating some 2300 additional hard targets and requires the expenditure of up to 4600 RVs, thereby stressing plausible Soviet hard-target kill capabilities.[31] In theory,

any system would have sufficient latitude to permit the deployment of additional shelters or to increase the number of ICBMs either to meet a demand for a U.S. war-waging capability or to thwart Soviet efforts to saturate the MPS system.

MX/MPS in either horizontal or vertical deployments suffers from two serious flaws: It permits the Soviet Union excessive leeway in responding to such deployments, because MPS is essentially a passive defense and it maintains the classical offense-dominant strategic posture. Under SALT limitations it appears that the Soviet Union would have little incentive to target an MPS system. However, the present system is extremely sensitive to a failure to deceive, thereby allowing an attacker preferentially to target the occupied shelter.[32] Furthermore, the certainty of exhausting Soviet hard-target capabilities assumes little or no cheating.[33] Finally, in the absence of SALT, the Soviet Union, albeit at great cost, may proliferate its hard-target capabilities to a point at which MPS ceases to be effective.[34] MX/MPS is a

29. On the various basing modes suggested for a new land-based ICBM, see William Schneider, Jr., "Survivable ICBMs," *Strategic Review* 6(4) (Fall 1978); Gray, *The Future of the Land-Based Missile Force* pp. 18-24; K. M. Tsipis, "The MX Missile: A Look Beyond the Obvious," *Technology Review* 81(6): 59-64 (March 1979).

30. "Work on MX System Speeds on Though its Base isn't Picked Yet," *New York Times* 19 March 1981, p. A1; and Colin S. Gray, *MX and the Future of the Land-Based Component of the Triad*, Hudson Paper (HI-3267-P) (Croton-on-Hudson, NY: Hudson Institute, December 1980), p. 5.

31. Under present SALT limitations, the Soviet Union could deploy between 7,000 and 10,000 ballistic missile RVs, the majority of which would have hard-target capability. Davis, Friel, and Pfaltzgraff, *SALT II and U.S.-Soviet Strategic Forces*, pp. 18-19; Paul

Nitze, "SALT II and American Strategic Considerations," *Comparative Strategy* 2(1): 14-15 (1980); and William T. Lee, "Soviet Targeting Strategy and SALT," *Air Force Magazine* September 1978, pp. 126-29.

32. This is a particularly thorny issue because of the verification requirements associated with mobile basing. See Stephen M. Meyer, "Verification and the ICBM Shell-Game," *International Security* 4(2) (Fall 1979).

33. Two obvious ways the Soviets might cheat is through deploying additional RVs on existing launchers and stockpiling launchers for silo reload. Edgar Ulsamer, "Alarming Soviet Deployments," *Air Force Magazine* November 1980, pp. 22-23; and Richard Burt, "Likelihood of SALT's Demise Changes the Strategic Options," *New York Times* 23 March 1980, p. E4.

34. "Soviets' Nuclear Arsenal Continues to Proliferate," *Aviation Week and Space*

reactive deployment, not merely in the immediate sense of responding to Soviet hard-target capabilities but also in a broader strategic sense.

An alternative to a passive defense system and to the overreliance on offensive forces for U.S. security would be increased reliance on active defenses, particularly ballistic missile defense (BMD). An active defense complicates the attacker's targeting, since he must engage in a more difficult strategic interaction than that presented by a simple passive defense. The defender can manipulate an active defense in such a manner as to increase further the attacker's uncertainty. To the extent that uncertainty weighs on predictions of the attack outcomes, the incentive to strike can be reduced. Moreover, strategic defenses can affect requirements for offensive systems, insofar as deterrence is assured by the ability to defeat an attack, rather than by the certainty of retribution. A combination of passive and active defenses may negate any plausible counterforce scenarios, thereby countering the tendency in both U.S. and Soviet ICBM forces toward high fractionation of missile payloads, in favor of smaller numbers of higher-yield countervalue weapons.

The Reagan administration is looking at the deployment of a low-altitude defense system (LoAD) consisting of a small radar and a high velocity nuclear armed missile intended to intercept Soviet RVs at low altitudes and designed to be compatible with the MX/MPS system.[35] The LoAD system would also

be deceptively based and would preferentially defend the occupied shelter/silo.[36] Active defense of deceptively based ICBMs would enforce an additional burden on an attacker by requiring the use of several RVs on each shelter/silo.[37] The presence of an active defense may serve to complicate an attacker's strategy: While a south-to-north attack pattern against silo-based ICBMs might be desirable in order to allow for retargeting and limit the effects of fratricide, active defense may be best met by a north-to-south pattern, which could interfere with BMD radars.[38] While the exact point of tradeoff between additional shelters and LoADs is difficult to determine, clearly the addition of active defense complicates the problem for an attacker.

LoADs may be only the first stage in the development of U.S. active defenses. The system envisioned by the ballistic missile defense community would involve an "overlay" system composed on an exoatmospheric interceptor using advanced optical sensors and a nonnuclear

Technology 16 June 1980. Some estimates suggest that the USSR may be able to deploy from 12,000 to 21,000 RVs.

35. George C. Wilson, "Army Now Sees ABM as Blockbuster's Guard," Washington Post 15 November 1979, p. A6; William A.

Davis, Jr., "Ballistic Missile Defense into the Eighties," National Defense 63(349): 60-61 (September-October 1979); and G.E. Barasch et al., Ballistic Missile Defense: A Potential Arms-Control Initiative (Los Alamos, NM: Los Alamos National Laboratory, 1981), pp. 8-10.

36. W. Davis, "Ballistic Missile Defense into the Eighties," p. 60.

37. William A. Davis, Jr., "Current Technical Status of U.S. BMD Programs," U.S. Arms Control Objectives and the Implications for Ballistic Missile Defense, symposium proceedings (Cambridge, MA: Harvard University, 1979), pp. 46-48.

38. Other countermeasures, such as a precursor attack to "flush" the defense, increase the difficulty of executing the preemptive counterforce strike and in themselves constitute attrition of Soviet RVs. See Colin S. Gray, "A New Debate on Ballistic Missile Defense," Survival 23(2): 6 (March-April 1981).

infrared and multiple kill vehicle to intercept Soviet RVs in space.[39] To the extent that impact-point prediction is possible, the exoatmospheric overlay may be able to defend preferentially against attacks on the LoAD system or the hidden ICBM.[40] The layered defense concept is intended to enforce extremely high attrition rates on a Soviet attack; in addition, the layered concept reduces the stress on any single component, since none are required to be 100 percent effective. This "layered" defense system is also less sensitive to Soviet countermeasures than simple MPS or LoAD defenses. A recent evaluation of the layered defense concept stated:

Combination of exoatmospheric, infrared, non-nuclear intercept technology and endoatmospheric, small radar, nuclear-intercept technology into a layered defense system offers a number of synergistic advantages over either system operating alone.[41]

Active defenses also have significant potentials for lessening the vulnerability of other components of the strategic force posture. The overlay component of a layered defense could significantly reduce the deliverable megatonnage in a Soviet attack; a combination of overlay and some form of underlay system could be used to protect at least time-critical targets such as SAC bases, SSBN ports, and C³I.[42] Active defense would also increase the effectiveness of passive measures designed to protect strategic forces such as rebasing of bombers and hardening of C³I.

The test of strategic defenses is not, as past critics of ABM held, the certainty of protection, but rather the uncertainty which they enforce on an opponent.[43] By maximizing Soviet uncertainty, the incentive to strike is reduced. Active defense compounds the problem created by passive systems, insofar as different countermeasures are required at each layer. At the very least, the requirement for countermeasures or retargeting is a cost to an attacker. A sophisticated BMD system can be defeated by a combination of decoys, maneuvering RVs, precursor attacks, and direct

39. Barasch et al., *Ballistic Missile Defense*, pp. 6-8. The exact character of the nonnuclear kill mechanism is yet to be determined. A variety of nonnuclear devices are being studied, including cannisters of metal pellets and a "flying umbrella." See Philip J. Klass, "Ballistic Missile Defense Tests Set," *Aviation Week and Space Technology* 16 June 1980, pp. 213-18. Also George C. Wilson, "U.S. Developing Umbrella Against Rain of Warheads," *Washington Post* 11 April 1980, p. A4.

40. Also known as "adaptive preferential defense," such a system makes use of the additional time and distance provided by exoatmospheric intercept. W. Davis, "Ballistic Missile Defense into the Eighties," p. 58.

41. Among the advantages of a layered system are:

- Multiplication of leakage factors resulting in a system with an overall low leakage rate

- Different sensor technologies limit the effectiveness of decoys

- Lower cost per intercept than with single layer system

- Greater simplicity at each layer due to synergistic operation

- Exoatmospheric defense enhances threat assessment for endoatmospheric defenses.

Barasch et al., *Ballistic Missile Defense*, p. 10.

42. "Defense Department to Examine Ballistic Missile Program," *Aviation Week and Space Technology* 30 March 1981, pp. 18-19. Other uses for a layered BMD were suggested by Wayne R. Winton, "Applications of BMD Other Than ICBM Defense," in *U.S. Arms Control Objectives*, pp. 92-95.

43. On the issue of strategic uncertainty and its uses see Stanley Sienkiewicz, "Observations on the Impacts of Uncertainty in Strategic Analysis," *World Politics* (October 1979).

attacks on defensive sites.[44] Such steps are not cost-free. They exert what is termed "virtual attrition," the diversion of valuable payload capacity to countermeasures.[45] The result is that an attacker's already difficult problem of calculating expected gain is rendered even more problematic.

Measures to ameliorate the vulnerability and declining utility of other elements of the strategic posture are not as well developed or conceived. The U.S. response to the threat to space-based assets is the development of ASAT.[46] This fails to consider the asymmetry in U.S.-Soviet dependence on space-based assets, and the potential gain to the attacker from a preemptive strike against C³I dedicated to U.S. retaliatory forces.[47] The time-sensitive character of many strategic space-based assets reduces the effectiveness of a response in kind, and hence the deterrent value of a U.S. ASAT threat. While a U.S. ASAT may have relevance in other scenarios (such as against Soviet Roarsat and Eorsat oceans reconnaissance capabilities), it is of uncertain utility given the retaliatory character of U.S. nuclear strategy.

In the near term (the 1980s), passive measures hold the greatest

prospect for protecting U.S. space-based assets. Among the possible responses to a Soviet ASAT are increasing the number of platforms, use of manuevering satellites, silent spares, and a quick replacement.[48] Successful development of more exotic technologies—laser weapons in particular—may provide both an effective time-urgent ASAT and a means of protecting critical satellite assets from Soviet attack.[49]

Few measures appear to have a significant impact on the survivability against a preemptive attack of the other legs of the Triad. The bombers, essentially soft targets, are highly sensitive to preemption; increasing alert rates—already a practice in crises—and an expanded basing structure appear to offer the prospects for at least marginal survivability improvements.[50]

Soviet active and passive defenses threaten the postlaunch survivability and targeting capabilities of the bomber force. While deployment of the cruise missile offered some prospect for defeating existing Soviet air defenses by a combination of saturation and maneuver, development of a Soviet AWACS, look-down/shoot-down interceptor and terminal defenses threaten to negate this approach.[51] Near-term responses to

44. Such options are more difficult to deploy under conditions of limitations on offensive systems.

45. Gray, "A New Debate," p. 67.

46. Craig Covault, "Antisatellite Weapon Design Advances," *Aviation Week and Space Technology* 16 June 1980, pp. 243-47. The U.S. program involves the use of a Miniature Homing Vehicle (MHV), launched by an F-15 into a direct ascent to the orbit of the Soviet satellite, which would be destroyed either by being hit by the MHV or through the use of a nonnuclear warhead.

47. Ibid., especially p. 247. Also see Thomas Blau and Daniel Gouré, *Military and Diplomatic Issues in Active Space Defense*, report prepared for the Defense Advanced Research Projects Agency, September 1980.

48. "Space Surveillance Deemed Inadequate," *Aviation Week and Space Technology* 16 June 1980, pp. 249-52. One objective of the U.S. Space Defense Program is improving the survivability of U.S. space-based assets.

49. Richard Burt, "Experts Believe Laser Weapons Could Transform Warfare in the 80's," *New York Times* 10 February 1980, p. A1.

50. High alert rates (80 percent of available bombers) cannot be maintained for protracted periods except at great expense and wear to the aircraft and crews. Rebasing also has some difficult cost considerations.

51. For the argument in favor of the cruise missile solution to the air defense problem, see Alton H. Quanbeck and Archie L. Wood, *Modernizing the Strategic Bomber*

the growing threat involve both pro-liferation of penetrators (essentially cruise missiles deployed in large numbers aboard dedicated carriers) and development of a new penetrat-ing bomber incorporating an ability to defeat Soviet AWACS and inter-ceptors.[52] Longer-range solutions might include counterair defense measures, including precursor attacks by ballistic missiles or even space-based (laser) systems intended to blind or otherwise degrade Soviet air defense.

The SSBN problem is certainly the least critical but also possibly the least soluble save by a restructuring of the force. Ensuring the surviva-bility of the SSBN force has less to do with defense against Soviet ASW than provision for refit and reconsti-tution. Current basing arrange-ments and vulnerable C^3 limit the flexibility and responsiveness of the SSBNs. Construction of the "Sea-farer" Extremely Low Frequency (ELF) communications systems would address the C^3 problem in peacetime.[53] A wartime C^3 system would likely involve multiple, har-dened, and redundant C^3 sites possi-bly protected by site BMD defense.

In summation, the ICBM force is in the most immediate need of improvements to its survivability and also the component of the Triad with the greatest potential. The deployment of BMD defenses, both the LoAD underlay and exoatmos-pheric overlay, to protect ICBMs promises potentially significant col-lateral benefits for the other legs of the Triad and for survivable C^3.[54] More important, perhaps, than the exact configuration of the proposed force posture is the impact such changes may have on perceptions of the rate—if not the static measurements—of U.S. strategic decline. The United States has depended for the last 15 years on a favorable qualitative technological balance to maintain essential equi-valence against a growing Soviet quantitative superiority, a fact not unrecognized by Moscow.[55] In recent years the Soviet Union has caught up with, and often sur-passed, the United States in many qualitative and quantitative indices of strategic power. For the United States to maintain credible essential equivalence, which many still see as the foundation of the U.S. deter-rence posture, it is necessary to effect the perception, particularly in Soviet eyes, that U.S. strategic power cannot be neutralized. This, rather than the specifics of improved exchange-ratios, force loadings, or kill rates, should consti-tute the rationale for U.S. action.

The critical dimension of strategic policy is not technological but political, and the necessarily vague technical fac-tors may in the end count for much more than detailed estimates of weapons per-formance.[56]

Force: Why and How (Washington, DC: The Brookings Institution, 1976). An excellent critique of the Quanbeck and Wood study is provided in Hoeber, Slow to Take Offense.

52. For a detailed discussion of possible improvements to the bomber force, see B. T. Plymale, "Strategic Alternatives: Airbreath-ing Systems," in Van Cleave and Thomp-son, Strategic Options for the Early 1980's, pp. 33-58.

53. The failure of several administrations to build a secure communications system for the SSBN force has continued to hamper its security and responsiveness. Gray, "The Stra-tegic Force Triad," pp. 782-83; and Brennan, "Command and Control," p. 340.

54. Gray, "A New Debate," p. 67.

55. Leon Gouré, "Developments in Soviet Ballistic Missile Systems: Offensive and Def-ensive Capabilities," in The Emerging Stra-tegic Environment, pp. 26-27.

56. Edward Luttwak, Strategic Power: Military Capabilities and Political Utility.

Solving the ICBM vulnerability problem is certain to be complex and costly. Moreover, weapons systems acquisition problems and the likelihood of Soviet countervailing actions suggest that no solution will be swift, nor will any single "fix" meet all U.S. force posture requirements. While the most critical requirements are clearly to preserve and improve the ICBM leg of the Triad, the bomber force and, to a lesser extent the ballistic missile fleet also pose both offensive and defensive problems. Related to these issues is that of secure C^3I and particularly the protection of critical and highly vulnerable space-based assets. Clearly, to solve only the ICBM or bomber problems is to fail to treat the "systemic" disease which affects U.S. strategic policy. This requires, inter alia, recognition of the need for balance between offensive and defensive measures. The United States must look toward a comprehensive program of "fixes" if it is to reduce strategic force posture vulnerability and provide the necessary offensive capabilities to achieve its strategic objectives.

STRATEGY AND THE OFFENSE-DEFENSE INTERACTION

In an era when no defense against nuclear weapons appeared credible and when the United States enjoyed unquestionable strategic superiority, reliance on offensive forces and on deterrence via the threat of punitive retaliation appeared the simplest, if not the only, viable strategy.[57] Soviet attainment of a strategic nuclear capability gave the appearance of precluding efforts at offensive demage limitation. This, in turn, engendered a U.S. search for stable deterrence predicated on the mutual vulnerability of the homelands of both superpowers and the invulnerability of their respective retaliatory forces.[58] Only by ensuring that a nuclear exchange would be a global holocaust was it possible, in the view of proponents of mutual assured destruction, to maintain deterrence and to avoid the escalation of local conflicts to general war.[59] While it was always recognized that deterrence could fail, measures to mitigate the resulting destruction in the event of war were viewed as destabilizing and ineffective against improving offensive technologies.[60]

57. Bernard Brodie, *Strategy in the Missile Age* (Princeton, NJ: Princeton University Press, 1959), chs. 6 and 7; idem, "The Development of Nuclear Strategy, *International Strategy* 2(4) (Spring 1978); Jan Lodal, "Nuclear Strategy and Deterrence," *Daedalus* (Fall 1980).

58. Richard Rosecrance, *Strategic Deterrence Reconsidered*, Adelphi Papers 116 (London: International Institute for Strategic Studies, 1975), pp. 5-27; McGeorge Bundy, "Maintaining Stable Deterrence," *International Security* 3(3) (Winter 1978-79); Gray, *Strategy and the MX ICBM*, pp. 25-34.

59. The best-known argument of this sort is presented in K. H. Panofsky Wolfgang, "The Mutual-Hostage Relationship Between America and Russia," *Foreign Affairs* 53(1) (October 1973).

60. This view was inchoate until the ABM debates of the late 1960s brought it into public prominence. Jeremy J. Stone, *The Case Against Missile Defenses*, Adelphi Papers 47 (London: International Institute for Strategic Studies, 1968); Abram Chayes and Jerome Weisner, eds., *ABM: An Evaluation of the Decision to Deploy an Antiballistic Missile System* (New York: Harper & Row, 1969); Michael D. Solomon, "New Concepts for Strategic Parity," *Survival* 19(6) (November-December 1977) for a reprise of earlier works.

Washington Papers 38 (Beverly Hills, CA: Sage Publications, 1976). On the political and strategic implications of perceptions of strategic power see Benjamin S. Lambeth, "The Political Potential of Soviet Equivalence," *International Security* 4(2) (Fall 1979); and Richard Pipes, "Soviet Global Strategy," *Commentary* 4: 35-36 (April 1980).

The focus of U.S. nuclear strategy has changed over the past few years. Deterrence by punitive retaliation appears increasingly incredible given the disparities in U.S. and Soviet strategic force postures, both offensive and defensive. Additionally, the prospect of a U.S. force posture able to perform only a single suicidal mission is readily perceived to be of little military or political utility. In light of growing official U.S. concern over dissimilarities in U.S. and Soviet strategic doctrines, it seems reasonable to question the deterrence-via-destruction strategy that has dominated U.S. defense planning for some 20 years.[61]

Faced by the increasing uncertainty regarding what constitutes a reliable deterrent, the United States has sought ways to bolster confidence in the credibility of the existing force posture while avoiding recourse to actual use of the assured destruction threat.[62] To date, such efforts have been limited essentially to changes in targeting strategies for which little force posture alterations were required.[63] War aims, such as they were defined, focused on such nebulous concepts as "escalation control" and "conflict termination." The effort to devise credible limited nuclear options (LNOs) is confounded by force posture inadequacies and the United States' inability to limit domestic destruction.[64] More important, no effort has been made to take advantage of emerging technologies which offer improved prospects for national survival and damage limitation thereby permitting greater flexibility in the use of strategic offensive forces.

Recent developments in BMD technologies offer the prospect for increasing the impetus toward change in U.S. strategic doctrine. Even erstwhile opponents of BMD are admitting that defense is preferable to proliferation of offensive systems.[65] Moreover, it is no longer evident that improvements in offensive technologies can successfully overwhelm the defense, or even that exchange calculations will favor the former. U.S. and Soviet force posture changes have reaffirmed the dynamic balance between offensive and defensive technologies. A U.S. strategy for the 1980s should look first at grasping that dynamic relationship.

61. U.S. uncertainties were clearly limned in both the FY 1980 and 1981 *Annual Reports*. For a scholarly view see Fritz W. Ermarth, "Contrasts in American and Soviet Strategic Thought, *International Security* 3(2) (Fall 1978).

62. Desmond Ball, *Deja Vu: The Return to Counterforce in the Nixon Administration*, California Arms Control and Foreign Policy Seminar, Foreign Scholar Theories, December 1974; Colin S. Gray, "Rethinking Nuclear Strategy," *Orbis* 17(4) (Winter 1974); Gray, *Strategy and the MX ICBM*, pp. 25-45.

63. Current U.S. nuclear strategy seeks to pose a more credible deterrent by engaging in "countervailing" strikes against high-value Soviet military and command and control target sets. Yet no consideration has apparently been given to the proliferated and hardened character of Soviet military/C³ assets. Desmond Ball, "Counterforce Targeting: How New? How Viable?" *Arms Control Today* 2(2) (February 1981). On alternative targeting strategies see Colin S. Gray, *Targeting Problems for Central War*, Hudson Paper (HI-3068-P) (Croton-on-Hudson, NY: Hudson Institute, October 1979); and William R. Van Cleave and Roger W. Barnett, "Strategic Adaptability," *Orbis* 18(3) (Fall 1974).

64. Benjamin S. Lambeth, *Selective Nuclear Options in American and Soviet Strategy Policy*, Rand Note No. R-2034-DDRE (Santa Monica, CA: Rand Corporation, December 1976).

65. Bernard T. Feld and K. M. Tsipis, "Land-Based Intercontinental Ballistic Missiles," *Scientific American* 241(5): 56 (November 1979); and Herbert Scoville, Jr., "The Arms Control Implications of New Ballistic Missile Defense Technologies," in *U.S. Arms Control Objectives*, p. 105.

Strategic defenses offer the prospect for improved national security and survivability should deterrence fail and avoidance of the limitations of deterrence via assured destruction. Opponents of strategic defenses acknowledge that deterrence is maintained by the limited tolerance of all states for even relatively low levels of societal devastation.[66] No defensive posture can promise to preclude serious national destruction in the event of a major attack. Yet, deterrence is always a precarious thing. While the likelihood of a U.S.-Soviet nuclear war is not high, the results would be such as to warrant attention by the United States to measures designed to enhance the prospects for survival and recovery. In the unlikely event of a general war, the United States must have one aim uppermost: assured survival. No retaliatory action or strategy for defeating Soviet forces is credible in the absence of national defense.

The deployment of BMD for the protection of strategic forces constitutes only the first step in the movement toward an assured survival capability.[67] Logical follow-ons to BMD include civil defenses, protection of the national command authority, and industrial survival. While civil defenses have been criticized by some as being of limited utility in the absence of active defenses, the deployment of the latter will stimulate the requirement

for the former. The current asymmetry in strategic defenses, while rarely factored into the strategic balance, has had a profound effect on perceptions of relative strategic capability and on U.S. war planning and SALT proposals.[68] Current Soviet civil defense measures are believed to be able to reduce casualties from a U.S. retaliatory attack to from 8 to 10 million, approximately one-tenth of those possibly lost by the United States in the event of a major Soviet attack. The Soviet Union is also better prepared to deal with the physical consequences of a nuclear war and the requirements for postattack recovery. Such a situation is intolerable for the United States.

Critics have attacked BMD and efforts at assured survival as entailing an offensive-defensive arms race and increasing the likelihood of war. The evidence of the past 20 years does not sustain either contention. Indeed, it is equally plausible to suggest that the deployment of defensive systems will prove stabilizing. Certainly, if both sides seek to maximize societal survival—a defensive arms race—this cannot prove more threatening than the current race in offensive systems.[69] Nor have previous efforts at strategic defenses proven to stimulate crises or reduce the inherent deterrent value of

66. George Rathjens and Jack Ruins, "Nuclear Doctrine and Rationality," *Daedalus* (Winter 1981).
67. Richard B. Foster, "From Assured Destruction to Assured Survival," *Comparative Strategy* 2(1). On the broader implications of such a move see Donald G. Brennan, *Alternatives to MADness*, California Arms Control and Foreign Policy Seminar, Conference on Arms Competition and Strategic Doctrine, June 1974.

68. Leon Gouré, *War Survival in Soviet Strategy* (Coral Gables, FL: Center for Advanced International Studies, University of Miami, 1974); T. K. Jones, "The U.S.-Soviet Strategic Balance: Options and Non-Options," *Journal of International Relations* 2(3): 255-67 (Fall 1977).
69. Donald G. Brennan, *BMD Policy Issues for the 1980s*, Hudson Paper (HI-3134-P) (Croton-on-Hudson, NY: Hudson Institute, 1980), pp. 19-22; Gray, "A New Debate," pp. 68-70; Donald G. Brennan, "The Case for Missile Defense," *Foreign Affairs* 47(3) (April 1969).

nuclear weapons. Furthermore, deterrence may be improved to the extent that the United States is no longer faced with the option—for example, in response to regional Soviet aggression—of a general conflict if it should threaten the use of nuclear weapons.[70] The Soviets have long insisted that the threat of nuclear retaliation at the risk of the attacker's own destruction is not credible. Strategic defense may serve to increase the credibility of the U.S. deterrent in Soviet eyes.

A more symmetrical offensive-defensive balance is likely to be less stable in the sense used by arms controllers. The United States will be required to shift its frame of reference from stability as a static indicator to that of a dynamic and fluid state. This need not be less secure than the current strategic balance. Stability can be maintained by ensuring that Soviet force posture changes are met with corresponding or countervailing U.S. efforts. So long as the uncertainty of success remains high, the prospect of maintaining crisis stability is greatly enhanced.

As yet unmentioned are the prospects for more exotic defense technologies. Space-based lasers (SBL) based on advanced optical and infrared sensor and either chemical or nuclear power plants imply targeting capabilities and kill rates that are awesome. A ring of SBL satellites could intercept a Soviet ballistic missile strike in the boost-phase, before decoys and jamming capabilities can be deployed.[71] Preferential targeting could permit the SBL to attack Soviet hard-target capable heavy ICBMs, thereby denying the Soviet Union a preemptive counterforce capability. SBL also has as yet unexplored potential in other uses, notably in the continental United States (CONUS) air defense, and air threat suppression roles, and as an ASAT weapon.[72] As the first stage in a multilayered defense deployment including nonnuclear exoatmospheric intercepts and point defense of critical targets, SBL could successfully defend against even large-scale ballistic missile attacks on urban-industrial targets.[73] Countermeasures to negate the SBL would exact a stiff penalty in the form of reduced missile throw-weight and payloads. The most plausible long-term countermeasure, shifting from a few high-payload missiles to many low-payload missiles, would place less stress on other layers of the defense. Coupled with civil defense and industrial protection measures, layered defense involving SBL could permit the United States to develop a strategy of damage limitation, if not damage denial.

Clearly, we will not soon see a full strategic defensive deployment that includes SBL and conventional BMD, civil defense, industrial protection, and the rest. However, the trend appears clear. The United States faces the prospect of moving toward what may become essentially a defense-"Heavy" if not a defense-dominated environment. This has implications not only for the character of U.S. defensive for-

70. Gray, "A New Debate," p. 68.

71. Clarence A. Robinson, Jr., "Advance Made in High-Energy Laser," *Aviation Week and Space Technology* 23 February 1981, pp. 25-27.

72. Clarence A. Robinson, Jr., "Laser Technology Demonstration," *Aviation Week and Space Technology* 16 February 1981, pp. 16-19.

73. At present, the immaturity of the technologies involved in both SBL and exoatmosphere interception does not permit greater specificity as to the characteristics of such a layered defense.

ces but for the composition and use of offensive capabilities as well. The current U.S. focus on maintaining deterrence through an escalatory ladder of increasingly painful punitive blows may prove less relevant in a defense-dominated environment. Indeed, deterrence via positive threat of nuclear retaliation may be increasingly ineffectual. Adequate deterrence of strategic conflicts then would rest with the ability of the defender to deny the attacker a successful outcome. Since no defense is leak-proof, there is likely still to be an adequate deterrent for most crises. Strategic analysts have long agreed that the failure of deterrence need not be synonymous with absolute societal destruction.[74] Some have suggested the likelihood of self-restraint when decision makers are faced with the prospect of initiating irrational retaliatory strikes.[75] Strategic defenses may increase the incentive toward bargaining and conflict termination and lessen the bias in current U.S. strategy toward specified levels of urban-industrial damage.

Strategic defenses could permit or require considerable alteration in strategic offensive forces. The high certainty of survivability reduces the requirement for proliferated or redundant systems. Similarly, the current emphasis on time-urgent hard-target capabilities could be relaxed if both U.S. and Soviet strategic forces were survivable. Indeed, enhanced survivability can lessen the incentives for immediate use of available weapons, thereby permitting the withholding of strategic forces either for protracted conflict or for intrawar bargaining. Rather than the spasmodic, all-out massive strikes envisioned by U.S. strategy, general conflict under conditions of upgraded strategic defenses would resemble a dual between two master swordsmen, each attempting to pierce the other's defenses and strike at a vulnerable spot. To implement such a concept, the United States will require improved reconnaissance and C^3, enhanced strategic force flexibility, and a withhold/withdrawal capability, all of which are absent in current U.S. forces. Supplementing dedicated war-fighting assets will likely be a retaliatory reserve composed of large-yield weapons targeted on urban-industrial centers and intended to effect a minimum damage level consonant with practical deterrence needs.

It has been claimed that strategic defenses would effectively mean the end of strategic arms limitations. This need not be true. Indeed, a case can be made that strategic defenses provide a rationale for maintaining existing limitations on offensive systems. The planning for strategic defense requirements is rendered easier if the character of the offensive threat is specified and its numbers limited. It may prove easier to justify present SALT ceilings on offensive forces, and even asymmetries in such categories as heavy missiles and SLBMs, if current limitations provide a ceiling against which to plan strategic defense deployments.[76] Clearly, a negotiated move toward increased defense deployments is preferable to one based on pure competition.

74. Hedley Bull, "Future Conditions for Strategic Deterrence," in *The Future of Strategic Deterrence*, pp. 16-19.

75. Herman Kahn, *On Thermonuclear War* (Princeton, NJ: Princeton University Press, 1960), pp. 19-39; idem, "Issues of Thermonuclear War Termination," *The Annals* (November 1970).

76. Brennan, *BMD Policy Issues for the 1980s*, pp. 22-24.

Having gone far down the road of speculative inference, it is important to return at the end to some basic postulates. The first is that U.S. strategic force survivability is a sine qua non of deterrence. The past dependence on offensive forces and deterrence via punitive retaliation may be difficult to maintain in the future. Second, strategic defenses appear to offer the promise of significant improvements to strategic force survivability in the near term and national survival in the mid-term. Third, once started on the path toward defensive deployments, both sides are likely to pursue this avenue with great intensity. The result may well be a return to a more balanced offensive-defensive force posture, one which is more dynamic according to current indicators of strategic stability. This in turn requires that we adjust our notions of stability, deterrence, and warfighting to accord with the new reality.

ANNALS, *AAPSS*, 457, September 1981

The Shift in Soviet National Priorities to Military Forces, 1958-85

By W. T. LEE

ABSTRACT: This article traces the shift in Soviet national economic priorities from civilian uses, primarily consumption, to support of the Soviet military establishment since the late 1950s. It treats certain methodological issues involved in international comparisons, outlines the methodology used to estimate Soviet defense expenditures from published Soviet economic data, and compares the results with the CIA's estimates before and after the CIA was forced to double its estimates by new information which confirmed my estimates. A brief list of some of the major weapons systems whose development, procurement, and operations have driven the shift in Soviet national priorities from civilian to military uses is provided and the article concludes on the prospects for further increases in the military burden on the Soviet economy in the 1980s.

William T. Lee received his B.A. degree from the University of Washington and attended Columbia University for graduate work in Russian and Chinese area studies. Lee was an employee of the Central Intelligence Agency from 1951 to 1964, of the Stanford Research Institute from 1964 to 1972, and has been a consultant on Soviet military and economic matters from 1972 to the present. His book, The Estimation of Soviet Defense Expenditures, 1955-75 *was published by Praeger in 1977. Lee also has published numerous articles and studies on Soviet military matters and is co-author of a forthcoming book on Soviet military policy since World War II.*

HOW much is the Soviet Union spending for defense? How fast have Soviet defense expenditures grown over the past two decades? How heavy is the defense burden on the Soviet economy? How do Soviet defense expenditures compare with U.S. outlays? These have been contentious issues for some 25 years. Before 1976 the CIA consistently estimated Soviet defense expenditures to be essentially the same as the official Soviet "Defense" budget, plus about two-thirds of reported Soviet outlays for "Science" to account for military R&D and the Soviet space program. Many academics accepted the same figures. With very few exceptions, those who rejected the official Soviet defense budget did not offer an alternative to take its place.

Since 1970 official defense has declined by nearly one billion rubles. Yet it is generally recognized that Soviet military capabilities continued to grow rapidly in the 1970s. In fact, the import of Soviet military policy formulated under Khrushchev in the late 1950s and maintained with few changes by Brezhnev was not generally perceived by most Western observers until the 1970s. In 1975 the CIA discovered that the Soviet Union had spent some 50 billion rubles for defense in 1970 compared with the CIA estimate of 24 billion rubles (including some 8 billion rubles for military R&D and the space program). In 1976 the CIA doubled its estimates. Currently, the CIA estimates Soviet spending to be roughly 65 billion "constant 1970 rubles," or more than double official defense plus two-thirds of science. As will be discussed later, this estimate once again understates Soviet outlays by a factor of two, or nearly so.

Meanwhile, the CIA has admitted that its so-called constant 1970 rubles are not Soviet rubles at all. CIA defense "rubles" are simply CIA constructs. Consequently, despite all the prattle about Soviet defense expenditures in testimony by senior intelligence officials to Congress and in official documents such as the annual reports by secretaries of defense, the U.S. government does not have an accurate estimate of Soviet defense expenditures. Nor does the U.S. government have an estimate of the burden of defense on the Soviet economy.

The question of how much the two superpowers are spending for defense can become an arcane subject very quickly. Let us begin with why the question arises in the first place and then consider some of the methodological problems involved.

WHY COMPARE U.S. AND SOVIET DEFENSE EXPENDITURES?

Expenditures for military establishments represent one basic dimension of any comparison of superpower defenses. How a nation spends its money tells us something about its policy objectives. When accurately measured, changes in defense expenditures provide good indicators of a nation's objectives. Moreover, trends in expenditures tell us something about a nation's priorities. In the United States, debate over priorities centers on how the budget is divided among such categories as defense, social and welfare programs, improving the environment, and public transportation. Similarly, we allocate our gross national product among the three basic end uses of consumption, investment, and defense. Trends in our national budget and in apportioning Gross National Product (GNP) tell us a great deal about our national priorities.

The same is true of the Soviet budget and national income. The latter differs from GNP by the exclusion of most personnel services, but Soviet GNP can be roughly approximated from published Soviet data. In analyzing trends in Soviet national priorities among consumption, investment, and defense, it does not matter much whether one uses Soviet national income or estimates of Soviet GNP as long as the data are reasonably reliable and consistent. However, it is much easier to reconstitute Soviet national accounts to fit GNP definitions than it is to decipher how defense outlays are treated in Soviet national income ("net material product") accounts.

It is often argued that defense expenditures constitute a heavy burden on the U.S. economy, even when their share of GNP is down to five or six percent compared with about ten percent a decade ago. But what is the burden of defense on the Soviet economy? As we shall see, it now is more than three times the U.S. burden in terms of its share of GNP. But this is a crude measure. The real measure in both superpowers is the "opportunity cost"—that is, what the United States and the Soviet Union give up in investment or consumption, or in some combination of the two, in order to support a given level of defense expenditures. Unfortunately, we do not have good estimates of the opportunity cost of defense expenditures in the Soviet Union.

Trends in national priorities and even crude measures of the burden provide insights into the political utility a nation ascribes to military power. If defense priority is low and the burden light, the political utility ascribed to defense is likely to be low, unless some exceedingly fortuitous political and economic conditions make military power unusually cheap. But under the best of conditions, powerful defense establishments are never free. If a country's defense establishment is consuming a rising share of GNP (or national income), it seems reasonable that the national decision makers must ascribe considerable political utility to military power. Comparable measures are required for international comparisons. Let us first examine a few of the salient methodological problems.

Some methodological issues

It is not uncommon to hear that the Soviet Union is "spending" this or that many billions of dollars for defense. Whether U.S. expenditures are discussed in the same way in Moscow is unknown. Keep in mind, however, that in both Washington and Moscow domestic expenditures are made only in domestic currencies. Rubles can be converted to dollars, and vice versa, but the data are fraught with uncertainties and the results should be used cautiously, if at all. For policy analysis, we should confine the discussion to expenditures in the domestic currencies of both countries.

Ideally, comparisons of U.S. and Soviet defense expenditures, and their major components, would be measured in rubles and dollars in four ways:

—Soviet defense spending in rubles;

—U.S. defense spending in dollars;

—Soviet defense outlays converted to dollars; or

—U.S. defense spending converted to rubles.

In practice, we have only the first two measures, although rough approximations of the third measure are available for some years. Data required to price U.S. procurement and RDT&E in rubles are lacking. The CIA estimates what it would cost to buy the Soviet defense establishment in the United States but is careful not to call these dollar costs Soviet defense spending in dollars. Others, however, carelessly refer to the CIA's dollar cost estimates as Soviet "defense expenditures" in dollars. The CIA has attempted to compare "defense" expenditures of both superpowers in rubles, but no details of data or methods used have been released. According to CIA testimony before the House Select Committee on Intelligence, the Soviet defense establishment costs more than the

U.S. defense establishment when both are costed in dollars and in rubles.[1]

When we convert goods and services produced by one superpower into the monetary values of the other, we seek the cost of replicating one country's basket of goods in the other country. For example, we replicate the cost of a Soviet missile when produced by the particular combination of capital, labor, and management engaged in producing missiles in the United States. Thus we attempt to translate Soviet outputs into comparable U.S. outputs in dollars. Conceptually, we may do this either by pricing out the Soviet missile directly in dollars or by applying an appropriate ruble/dollar conversion ratio if we know the ruble price.

When we seek the comparable value of Soviet output in U.S. prices, we are adjusting for the differences in the level of productivity in the two countries. The Soviet basket of goods valued at U.S. prices reflects American productivity. However, using U.S. prices introduces a basic ambiguity. Those prices represent the cost of producing U.S. goods. If the United States actually produced Soviet (or some other) goods instead, U.S. prices would be different from the goods the United States actually produced.

Since estimates of what it would cost the United States in dollars to replicate the Soviet defense establishment exceed what we are spending on defense, the conventional wisdom is that costing the U.S. establishment in rubles would yield

1. *CIA Estimates of Soviet Defense Spending*, Hearings before the Subcommittee on Oversight of the Permanent Select Committee on Intelligence, House of Representatives, Ninety-Sixth Congress, Second Session, September 3, 1980 (Washington, DC: Government Printing Office, 1980), p. 9.

a larger ruble number than the Soviet Union is spending on defense. This is the so-called index number effect. The relative costs depend on whose prices one uses.

But the military establishments of the United States and the Soviet Union represent a special case that confounds the conventional wisdom in one sense and confirms it in another. To understand this better, let us take some simplified examples. Assume that countries X and Y purchase five defense goods and services. These are identical—technologically—on both sides, but each side purchases different quantities. Three of the five are purchased in larger quantities by country X and the other two by country Y. Because prices correlate negatively with quantities, the conventional wisdom holds. Which country is the bigger defense spender depends on whether one is in Moscow or Washington (Table 1).

The actual situation is quite different. The Soviet Union is buying more of all five goods. Under these circumstances it makes no difference where one is. The Soviet Union is the bigger spender regardless of whether both defense establishments are priced in dollars or in rubles. As shown in Table 2, country X, which buys the most of all five defense goods, is the larger spender no matter how prices correlate to quantities.

Now for the paradox. The Soviet Union buys more of almost everything. But "everything" here really means *only* those things that are within the state-of-the-art in both countries. The United States still buys a few high-technology weapons that the Soviet Union does not buy because such advanced weapons are still in the R&D stage in the Soviet Union. To illustrate, what

TABLE 1
ILLUSTRATIVE EXAMPLE OF THE "INDEX NUMBER PROBLEM,"
THE USUAL CASE

WEAPON SYSTEMS	QUANTITIES PURCHASED IN COUNTRIES		PRICES IN COUNTRIES		VALUES			
	X	Y	X	Y	QXPX	QYPY	QXPY	QYPX
A	50	5	1	5	50	25	250	5
B	10	100	10	2	100	200	20	1000
C	20	10	5	4	100	40	80	50
D	10	70	10	5	100	350	50	700
E	100	50	10	20	1000	1000	2000	500
Totals	190	235			1350	1615	2400	2255

QXPX	QYPX	
1350	2255	Y > X

QXPY	QYPY	
2400	1615	X > Y

TABLE 2
ILLUSTRATIVE EXAMPLE OF THE "INDEX NUMBER PROBLEM,"
THE CONTEMPORARY U.S.-USSR CASE

WEAPONS SYSTEMS	QUANTITIES PURCHASED IN COUNTRIES		PRICES IN COUNTRIES		VALUES			
	X	Y	X	Y	QXPX	QYPY	QXPY	QYPX
A	100	5	7	10	700	50	1000	35
B	100	10	5	10	500	100	1000	50
C	300	5	20	100	6000	500	30000	100
D	60	50	120	120	6000	6000	7200	6000
E	200	100	40	60	8000	6000	12000	4000
Totals	760	280			21200	12650	51200	10185

QXPX	QYPX	
21200	10185	X > Y

QXPY	QYPY	
51200	12650	X > Y

	X	Y	X	Y	QXPX	QYPY	QXPY	QYPX
A	100	5	20	10	2000	50	1000	100
B	100	10	10	5	1000	50	500	100
C	300	5	50	100	15000	500	30000	250
D	60	50	20	10	1200	500	600	1000
E	200	100	30	10	6000	1000	2000	3000
Totals	760	280			25200	2100	34100	4450

QXPX	QYPX	
25200	4450	X > Y

QXPY	QYPY	
34100	2100	X > Y

would it have cost the United States to have produced a Minuteman III missile in 1960, in 1965, and in 1970? In 1960, one Minuteman III missile could not have been produced for all the GNP of the planet Earth. By 1965, the GNP of the United States *might* have purchased one overweight Minuteman III. Yet by 1970 the United States was able to start volume production of Minuteman III missiles at several million dollars per copy. Volume production of Soviet MIRVs did not begin until about 1974.

Now consider assigning ruble prices to U.S. weaponry that is not within the Soviet state-of-the-art. Assign all the rubles there are and still there will not be enough. But in a few years the Soviet Union will probably be turning out much larger quantities than the United States. The Soviet Union currently is producing one major weapon system that the United States cannot build—the Alpha-class submarine. Unless and until the United States spends a large amount of R&D time and money learning how to fabricate large titanium hulls, we cannot buy such a submarine at any price—unless, of course, the Soviet Union would be willing to make a barter deal for American grain.

Finally, we know that the Soviet Union has about twice as many military personnel as the United States, although manpower costs present their own difficulties. Among them is the disparity between the pittance paid to Soviet conscripts and U.S. pay for the volunteer army; whether to value manpower at Soviet or U.S. pay scales, in dollars or in rubles; uncertainty as to which establishment uses more civilian employees; differences in tax structures and consumption patterns; and opportunity cost. Perhaps the least bad

solution here would be to show defense costs in the two countries with military manpower valued both at going pay scales and at opportunity cost, as best the latter may be approximated. The consequences for total defense expenditures (in dollars or in rubles) would be explicit, and U.S. critics would have to find something else to complain about.

Another alternative would be to drop—or at least deemphasize—the question of how much it would cost the United States to purchase the Soviet defense establishment in dollars, and vice versa. If analysts would concentrate on how much each superpower is spending in its own currency, then we could legitimately talk about expenditures instead of simulated costs, to say nothing of the problems peculiar to converting one currency to another. Plenty of realistic and meaningful problems would remain, such as:

—How much does the Soviet Union spend in any given year?

—What is the trend in Soviet expenditures over time?

—What share of its budget, national income, and GNP does, and will, the Soviet Union devote to defense?

—How does the Soviet Union apportion its defense expenditures among personnel costs, operations and maintenance, procurement, and RDT&E?

—How do Soviet trends in national priorities and expenditures compare with U.S. trends and proportions?

To answer these questions, we need to know how much the Soviet Union is spending in rubles. The subsequent discussion concentrates on the latter question.

Limits of the evidence

The Soviet Union publishes virtually no information directly relating to weapons procurement beyond pictures of parades, unit training, and an occasional film. It is necessary, therefore, to keep in mind some of the limits of the evidence and the methods used to estimate Soviet outlays for procurement and defense. First, numbers and characteristics of individual Soviet weapons systems are provided almost entirely by the "national means of verification" available to the United States. There are many gaps in the data provided by these collection systems. Second, the CIA estimates the distribution of Soviet defense expenditures, according to its direct costing methodology, by major mission and by branch of service. In 1975-76, the CIA was forced by new evidence to double its estimates of Soviet defense expenditures in 1970. Current CIA estimates are subject to similar margins of error for the same reasons as before. CIA estimates of expenditures by major mission and by branch of service probably are even less reliable than are its estimates for total outlays. Third, total Soviet defense expenditures, in rubles, can be derived from published Soviet economic data within a tolerable degree of uncertainty. The trend (growth rate) of these expenditures over time is more reliable than the magnitude for any given year. Fourth, Soviet outlays by major mission and by branch of military service cannot be derived from published Soviet economic data. The latter provide the basis for distributing total expenditures by only three components: procurement; pay, maintenance, operations, and military construction; and research, development, test, and evaluation. Nevertheless,

reasonable judgments can be made concerning major shifts in funding by major mission and, to a lesser extent, by branch of service.

The estimates of Soviet expenditures presented in this statement are derived entirely from published Soviet economic data that have proven to be, when properly understood, the only reliable source of such estimates. When the CIA had to double its estimates in 1976, the Soviet economic data estimates used herein did not need to be changed. Outlays for weapons procurement are the most reliable component of Soviet defense expenditures derived from Soviet economic data. Data on specific Soviet procurement programs are taken from various unclassified publications. Directly or indirectly, most such information is derived from the "national means of verification."

METHODOLOGY FOR MEASURING USSR DEFENSE EXPENDITURES BASED ON SOVIET DATA

The estimates of Soviet defense expenditures from published Soviet economic data in this article are the sum of three components:

—personnel pay and maintenance, operations and maintenance of the Soviet military establishment, and military construction (POMC);

—military research, development, test, evaluation (RDT&E), and space; and

—procurement.

The methodology for estimating military procurement is outlined in Table 3.[2]

2. William T. Lee, *The Estimation of Soviet Defense Expenditures, 1955-75* (New York: Praeger Publishers, 1977), pp. 36-37.

TABLE 3
OUTLINE OF METHODOLOGY FOR
ESTIMATING SOVIET MILITARY PROCUREMENT

Soviet production and allocation of durables to the MOD is derived as a residual of the GVO of the M&MW sector of Soviet industry, the essential steps in the procedure are as follows:

(1) establishment (or commodity) M&MW GVO as reported by Soviet TSU/GOSPLAN
(2) less GVO of metal working (MW) and repair
(3) equals GVO of machine building (MB)
(4) less all intermediate products (inter- and intra-industry)
(5) equals final demand (FD) of MB
(6) less exports
(7) equals domestic FD of MB
(8) less producer and consumer durables net of imports
(9) equals national security hardware as residual

For illustrative purposes, this list may be restated in three steps:

(1) M&MW GVO – MW + repair = MB GVO
(2) MB GVO – Intermediate Products = MB FD
(3) MB FD – Exports + Imports – Producer & Consumer Durables = NS Durables

SOURCE: William T. Lee, *The Estimation of Soviet Defense Expenditures, 1955-75* (New York: Praeger, 1977), pp. 36-37.

Until 1970, the official defense budget served as a reasonable surrogate for POMC outlays, although there is no guarantee that official defense covered all such outlays in 1970 and prior years. Since 1970, however, official defense has declined slightly, from 17.9 to 17.2 billion rubles, while POMC outlays obviously have been rising. Because there is no independent method for estimating POMC, except for personnel costs, the estimates for 1970-80 are an extrapolation from the 1970 base of 17.9 billion rubles.

Estimating Soviet military RDT&E is another thorny problem. The conventional wisdom on this subject has been: (1) reported "Science" expenditures include all Soviet RDT&E, military and civilian; and (2) military RDT&E constitutes the lion's share of science, usually estimated at about two-thirds. No empirical evidence to support either of these assumptions appears to exist, except some data from the late 1950s that were interpreted, (wrongly, as it turned out) to mean that science consisted of mostly military R&D. Since the early 1960s a great deal of evidence has accumulated indicating that (1) science outlays fall far short of total Soviet spending for R&D, and (2) not much of science is military.[3]

The estimates of total Soviet outlays for R&D in this analysis represent the sum of identifiable inputs: wages, materials, construction of R&D plants, and certain overhead costs of the R&D performing institutions. Some of the input data appear to be fairly reliable; the reliability of other components is difficult to assess. Moreover, these input data do not cover R&D performed by Soviet higher educational institutions (VUZy), series production factories, R&D activities performed by

3. Ibid., pp. 14-20, for a summary of the evidence on coverage of military R&D outlays in reported Soviet expenditures for "Science."

uniformed military personnel, and possibly some other R&D activities. To try to allow for all of these uncertainties, the sum of identifiable inputs is taken to be the minimum measure of total Soviet R&D outlays. This sum is then increased by 30 percent in order to arrive at a range—sum of inputs to said sum plus 30 percent—which might bound Soviet R&D outlays. From this range derived from input data, a rough approximation of what appears to be the civilian R&D component of science outlays is subtracted in order to arrive at an estimate of military R&D outlays.

This method leaves much to be desired, but it appears to be the best available until the Soviet Union releases better data or until someone succeeds in gaining unique insights into Soviet financial accounts. For all its defects, this method is preferable to the CIA's use of science expenditures to derive military R&D outlays because that approach is demonstrably wrong on the basis of the available evidence.

TRENDS IN SOVIET DEFENSE EXPENDITURES

In the aftermath of World War II the Soviet Union reduced its armed forces to 2.8 million men and made corresponding cuts in procurement. Except for copies of U.S. B-29 bombers, jet fighters, and radars, there was little new procurement in the 1945-50 period. However, R&D on new technology was pushed hard and fast, particularly on nuclear weapons and missiles. The high-level organization created to run the Soviet missile program included two civilians who are still prominent: D. F. Ustinov and L. I. Brezhnev.

During the Korean War the Soviet Union doubled the size of its military establishment to nearly six million men and procured much new weaponry. Production of civilian machinery and equipment was frozen at 1950 levels through 1953; during these years almost all of the increase in machinery output went to the military in the form of weapons. In order to mask their rearmament programs, it removed procurement from the official "defense" budget. Total Soviet defense expenditures rose from around 9 billion rubles in 1950 to about 14 billion in 1955.

From the end of the Korean War to the beginning of the SALT era in 1970, the most rapid growth in Soviet military expenditures occurred in the years 1959-63 and 1966-70. In the former period Soviet military expenditures increased from about 13 to about 23 billion rubles (in 1955 prices), or nearly 75 percent; in the latter period Soviet outlays nearly doubled, from about 25 to about 50 billion rubles (in 1970 prices). The years 1963-65 represented a lull that is difficult to interpret; it may have been due simply to "normal" transitional factors as the Soviet Union moved from one set of deployment programs to another; or it may have been the consequence of a shift in Khrushchev's priorities from armaments to basic economic investment after the Cuban missile crisis.[4]

Trends in the allocation of Soviet GNP in the 1955-70 period are shown in Table 4.[5] Note the decline in consumption's share and the modest increase in investment's share in the 1955-70 period. Despite the rapid growth of military outlays

4. Ibid., pp. 65-66.
5. William T. Lee, "USSR Gross National Product in Established Prices, 1955-1975" in *Jahrbuch der Wirtschaft Osteuropas* (Gunter Olzog Verlag Minchen-Wien, 1979), pp. 412, 415.

TABLE 4
TRENDS IN STRUCTURE OF USSR GNP, 1955-70
(1955-59 and 1969-70 estimates and current prices)

	CONSUMPTION		INVESTMENT		MILITARY		CIVIL R&D & BUDGET AD-MINISTRATION		GNP	
	Billions of Rubles	% of GNP	Rubles	%	Rubles	%	Rubles	%	Rubles	%
1955	69.8	60.3	29.9	25.8	14.0	12.1	2.1	1.8	115.8	100
1958	95.5	62.1	41.6	27.1	14.0	9.1	2.6	1.7	153.7	
1960	107.6	61.6	47.6	27.2	16.5	9.4	3.0	1.7	174.7	
1965	151.0	60.8	65.8	26.5	26.5	10.7	4.9	2.0	248.2	
1968	186.2	56.0	99.0	29.8	41.0	12.3	6.3	1.9	332.5	
1970	215.1	55.6	116.0	29.8	49.0	12.6	7.7	2.0	357.8	

SOURCE: William T. Lee, "USSR Gross National Product in Established Prices, 1855-75," in *Jahrbuch der Wirtschaft Osteuropas* (Gunter Olzog Verlag Minchen-Wien), pp. 412, 415.

after 1959, the military share of GNP in 1970 was not much above the 1955 level, due in large part to the relatively high growth rates for GNP in the period as a whole.

Trends in Soviet defense expenditures in the 1970s

To put it mildly, SALT has had no discernible effect on Soviet defense expenditures. True, the growth rate in the 1970s in total expenditures has been less than the frantic pace of 1959-63 or of 1966-70. But the pace of general economic expansion has slowed much more. Consequently, the burden of military forces on the economy has risen faster in the 1970s than in the 1960s. The diversion of resources from investment to the military in the Tenth Five Year Plan (1976-80) is comparable to that of the Korean War period.[6]

The magnitude and growth of Soviet defense expenditures from 1966 to 1980 is shown in Table 5 in constant 1970 prices (as the Soviet Union reckons constant prices), and the trend in the share of GNP in Table 6.[7] Note that the growth rate since 1970 has averaged more than 8 percent per annum; Soviet defense expenditures (in constant prices) in 1980 were more than double the 1970 level. Note also the rapid rise in defense outlays as a share of Soviet GNP from 12 to 13 percent in 1970 to about 18 percent in 1980. The latter trend is due in part to the declining growth rates of Soviet GNP, which in turn is largely due to the rising burden of defense. Several other factors are at work—notably, declining growth in the labor force, increasing costs of basic materials, and the perennial problems of Soviet agriculture —but the growth in defense expenditures is one of the most important reasons the rate of Soviet GNP has

6. For an extended discussion of the Soviet military expenditures in the SALT era, see William T. Lee, *Soviet Defense Expenditures in the Era of SALT*, (Washington, DC: United States Strategic Institute, 1979).

7. R&D estimates are mostly in current prices because a satisfactory method of converting R&D outlays to constant prices is lacking. William T. Lee, *Trends in Soviet Defense Expenditures* (Analytical Assessments Co., AAC-TR-10001/79), pp. 17, 19.

TABLE 5
ESTIMATE OF USSR DEFENSE EXPENDITURES IN 1970 PRICES
(billions of rubles)

	PROCUREMENT OF WEAPONRY	PAY, MAINTENANCE, OPERATIONS, AND CONSTRUCTION	RDT&E AND SPACE	DEFENSE EXPENDITURES
1966	7.6-8.6	14.7	4.8-7.9	27.1-31.2
1967	10.1-11.2	15.3	5.3-8.8	30.7-35.3
1968	12.6-13.8	17.1	6.2-10.1	35.9-41.0
1969	15.2-16.6	17.9	6.3-10.4	39.4-44.9
1970	17.8-19.5	17.9	7.5-12.4	43-50
1971	21.2-23.0	19.2	8.0-13.3	48-56
1972	24.3-26.4	19.9	8.4-14.2	53-60
1973	28.5-31.0	21.3	9.4-15.8	59-68
1974	32.2-35.1	22.1	10.2-17.1	64-74
1975	37.2-41.5	22.9	11.3-18.6	71-83
1976	41.3-46.1	24	11.8-19.4	77-90
1977	45.1-51.0	25	12.4-20.3	82-96
1978	51.4-57.6	26-27	12.9-21.3	90-106
1979	58.5-65.1	27-28	13.5-22.2	99-115
1980	66-74	28-29	14.1-23.2	108-126

declined so much in the last decade.

The Politburo obviously took into account its expectations concerning the content and timing of the SALT II Treaty when, in 1975, it set priorities for the Tenth Five Year Plan (FYP). The basic economic priorities set by the Politburo in 1975 for the 1976-80 period were as follows:

—Consumption was to increase at about the same rate as national income (and GNP)—about 25 to 30 percent for the five-year period.

—Investment was to grow by only 16 to 17 percent (with a somewhat larger increase in producer durables); hence it would decline as a share of national income and, correspondingly, of GNP.

—Total defense outlays were to increase by about 50 percent; hence the share of defense in both national income and GNP was to increase sharply.

For the Soviet Union this was a relatively unique set of economic priorities. With the possible exception of 1940-41, this is the first time the Soviet Union has planned to cut investment as a share of national income (or GNP) since Stalin decreed forced industrialization in 1929. The decision not to reduce consumption's share of national income (and of GNP) also was a unique feature, particularly in light of the priority given to defense outlays.

During the first two years (1976 and 1977) of the Tenth Five Year Plan and in the annual plan for 1978, the Soviet Union followed its game plan rather precisely. The actual performance for 1978-80, however, allocated more resources to investment than was originally planned, evidently as a result of rising imports of machinery and equipment —financed by Western credits and skyrocketing prices for oil and gas— and by once again failing to provide promised increases in consumption. Rather than increasing only about

TABLE 6
ESTIMATE OF USSR GNP BY END USE IN ESTABLISHED PRICES
(billions of rubles)

	INVESTMENT	CONSUMPTION	DEFENSE*	CIVIL R&D AND ADMINISTRATION	GNP
1966	85.7	161.4	31.2	5.5	284
1967	94.4	172.2	35.3	5.9	308
1968	99.0	186.2	41.0	6.3	332
1969	98.5	200.1	44.9	7.3	351
1970	116.0	215.1	50.0	7.7	389
1971	119.7	227.6	56.0	8.5	412
1972	128.8	240.6	60.0	9.3	439
1973	140.8	251.6	68.0	10.0	470
1974	149.2	265.5	74.0	10.7	499
1975	158.5	282.9	83.0	11.4	536
1980 forecast			= 126		650

*Defense represents the high side of the range in Table 2 because the evidence indicates it is more likely.

16 percent, as was planned, investment in 1980 exceeded the 1975 level by about 18 percent.[8] Figure 1 sets forth the trends in the structure of Soviet GNP since 1960 as it was projected in the Tenth Five Year Plan for 1976-80.[9]

Things are turning out somewhat different from the Tenth FYP projections shown in Figure 1. Soviet GNP in 1980 was about 20 percent above the 1975 level instead of 25 to 30 percent as implied by the Plan. Investment in 1980 was about 18 percent above the 1975 level instead of about 16 percent, thanks to larger imports of machinery and equipment than expected. Hence the share of investment remained at 30-32 percent of Soviet GNP. Defense spending, however, probably met the original Tenth FYP goals, which means that consumption declined instead of remaining a more or less constant share of Soviet GNP as envisaged by the planners five years ago.

8. *Ekonomicheskie Gazeta*, No. 5, 1981.
9. Lee, *USSR Gross National Product*, p. 419.

One of the best indicators of the impact of rising defense expenditures on the Soviet economy is the rapid growth in the share of weapons procurement in domestic production of machinery and equipment. Between 1966 and 1980 procurement rose from about 20 percent to well over half of Soviet domestic production of machinery and equipment, as shown in Figure 2.[10] Allocations of machinery output to civilian uses—producer durables for capital investment and consumer durables for use in households and by individuals—declined correspondingly from about 80 percent of domestic output in 1966 to a little over 40 percent in 1980.

The impact of this shift in priorities from civilian machinery and equipment to production of weaponry has been eased considerably by rapidly rising imports of machinery and equipment, particularly in the last few years. This trend can be illustrated by data for 1978. Net costs of intermediate products,

10. Lee, *Soviet Defense Expenditures*, USSI Report 79-1, p. 17.

Figure 1: Structure of USSR GNP, 1960-80

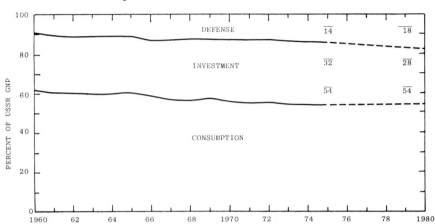

SOURCE: William T. Lee, "USSR Gross National Product in Established Prices, 1955-1975," in *Jahrbuch der Wirtschaft Osteuropas* (Gunter Olzog Verlag Minchen-Wien, 1979), p. 419.

Figure 2: Military Procurement as a Share of Total Machinery Output

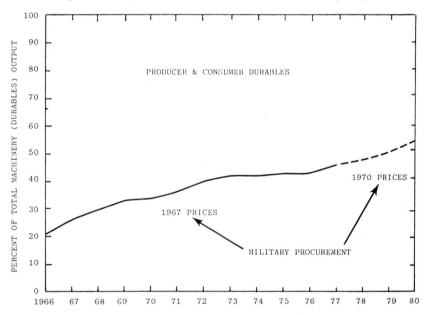

SOURCE: William T. Lee, Soviet Defense Expenditures, United States Strategic Institute Report 79-1, p.17.

imports of machinery and equipment in foreign trade prices, increased by about 2.6 billion rubles in 1978.[11] In domestic prices, these

11. *Narodnoe Khoziaystvo SSSR v 1978 G* (M. 1979), pp. 547, 551.

imports probably were valued at between 2.8 and 4 billion rubles. Meanwhile, allocations of producer durables to capital investment rose by about 3.6 billion rubles in 1978, while production of consumer durables increased by about 0.8 billion rubles. In other words, increased imports of machinery and equipment in 1978 probably accounted for the increase in allocations to producer durables in that year. Consequently, most of the growth in domestic output of machinery and equipment in 1978 was in the form of weaponry for the Soviet armed forces. The rapid growth in Soviet machinery imports in the 1970s ceased in 1979.[12] This, however, probably was only a temporary interruption in the trend. Soviet foreign trade jumped sharply in 1980, and the growth of machinery imports was probably resumed.[13]

Much of the recent growth in Soviet machinery imports is from the United States and its NATO allies. Such machinery generally incorporates higher technology than the Soviet Union can produce itself or can import from Eastern Europe. Increased imports from the West have been financed largely by Western loans and credits, by higher prices for Soviet petroleum products and natural gas thanks to OPEC, and by higher gold prices resulting from U.S. inflation and the decline of the dollar. It is difficult to see how the Soviet Union could have maintained its military buildup since the early 1970s without the assistance of these external factors. It is equally difficult to see how they can continue the buildup in the 1980s, as they evidently plan to do, without the benefits of growing trade with the West.

Devoting such a large share of Soviet machinery output to weapons procurement has resulted in a dramatic increase in the procurement share of Soviet defense expendi-

tures. Note that in Table 5 procurement accounted for about 28 percent of the Soviet defense budget in 1966 and about 40 percent in 1970. Currently procurement's share has risen to over 60 percent. Meanwhile, operating costs, while rising absolutely, have declined to about 25 percent of the Soviet budget. Personnel costs (excluding pensions) represent only about one-eighth of the Soviet defense budget, compared with nearly three-fifths of the U.S. budget.

COMPARISON WITH CIA ESTIMATES

Figure 3 compares the estimates of Soviet defense expenditures from Tables 4 and 5 with the prior and revised CIA estimates. Figure 4 makes the same comparison for procurement. For both total expenditures and procurement, the revised CIA estimates show about the same rate of growth as before. This was predicted before the CIA published its revised estimates. Consequently, one can replicate the revised CIA estimates easily at very low cost. Simply plot the prior CIA estimates from the 1974 testimony of William Colby, former director of the CIA, to Senator Proxmire's Subcommittee.[14] Double the 1970 estimate and through that point draw a line parallel to the prior estimates. A parallel line so drawn does not differ significantly from the revised CIA estimates, as was predicted before the revision. The revised CIA estimates for total defense expenditures

12. *Narodnoe Khoziaystov SSSR v 1979 G* (M. 1980), pp. 567, 569.

13. *Ekonomicheskie Gazeta*, No. 7, 1981.

14. *Allocation of Resources in the Soviet Union and China.* Hearing before the Subcommittee on Priorities and Economy in Government of the Joint Economic Committee, Congress of the United States, Ninety-Third Congress, Second Session, 12 April 1974 (Washington, DC: Government Printing Office, 1974), p. 68.

Figure 3: Comparative Estimates of Soviet Defense Expenditures

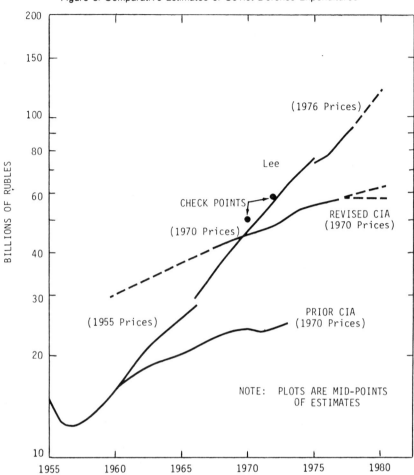

do not grow at the rate of 4 to 5 percent per annum, as the CIA claims. For the midpoint, the revised CIA estimates grow at the rate of about 3.8 percent per annum since 1967 and about 3.5 percent since 1975. The revised CIA estimates have not come anywhere near a growth rate of 5 percent per annum for any extended period.

Compared with the estimates derived from Soviet economic data in Table 2, the revised CIA estimates overstate Soviet outlays for defense and procurement prior to 1970 by the same degree that the prior CIA estimates understated them. The further back before 1970 the revised estimates are extended, the more the overstatement becomes, and the conflict with other Soviet data—budget, machinery output, labor and capital inputs— becomes increasingly gross. The revised CIA estimates overstate Soviet defense expenditures by nearly 50 percent in 1965 and by nearly a factor of two in 1960. After 1970, the discrepancies between estimates derived from Soviet economic data and the revised CIA estimates are essentially the same as

Figure 4: Alternative Estimates of Soviet Procurement Outlays in 1970 Prices

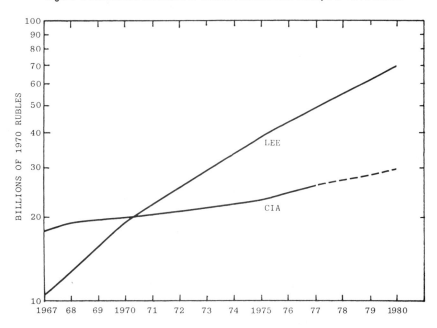

between the prior CIA estimates and those derived from Soviet economic data.

The two checkpoints acquired independently from Soviet sources shown in Figure 2 fall on the high side of the estimates derived from Soviet economic data according to the methodology summarized at the beginning of this article. The checkpoint of 50 billion rubles for 1970, acquired in 1975, forced the CIA to double its estimates. The checkpoint of 58 billion rubles for 1972 was acquired earlier but was distorted by the CIA to say that its prior estimates were off by about 20 percent instead of by more than a factor of two. The revised CIA (doubled) estimates (midpoint) are about 10 billion rubles short of the second checkpoint already by 1972.

Aside from admitting that its direct costing method does not work, which the CIA is evidently not willing to do, the only explanation the CIA seems to have for the discrepancy between its estimates and those plotted in Figures 3 and 4 is overpricing of new products. The inadequacy of this explanation has been discussed at length elsewhere and is too long and involved to be repeated here.[15] Actually, the comparisons between the estimates used in this article, which were corroborated by the checkpoints from Soviet sources, and the CIA estimates have little meaning since the CIA has admitted that its so-called constant 1970 rubles are not Soviet ruble prices. The CIA's constant 1970 rubles for procurement and some operating costs are constructed quite differently than Soviet constant 1970 rubles for the same goods. In effect, the CIA's constant rubles are simply constructs generated by the CIA's direct costing

15. See footnotes 1 and 2 and the testimony of Prof. Steven Rosefields in the reference cited in footnote 1.

model. The Soviet Union does not spend CIA rubles any more than it spends dollars. Nor does the Soviet Union keep its accounts or make decisions in CIA rubles. The Soviets use their own rubles for such purposes.

In the summer of 1977, a senior CIA analyst in this area, Derk Swain, agreed with me that CIA "constant rubles" are not Soviet constant rubles. Swain then said that the CIA would so state publicly in 1978. In the latter year in a second conversation he again agreed that CIA constant rubles were not Soviet rubles and admitted that the CIA had not so stated as he had promised a year before. "Maybe next year," Swain said in 1978. In testimony before Senator Harry Byrd's Subcommittee on General Procurement on 8 November 1979 Donald Burton of the CIA admitted, in response to Senator Byrd's question, that CIA and Soviet constant prices are constructed by different methodologies.[16]

Estimates of Soviet defense expenditures in Soviet rubles tell us a great deal about Soviet objectives, policies, and national priorities. Soviet rubles may be used to calculate the burden of defense on the economy and provide essential insight into the willingness of Soviet leaders to build up their military power at the expense of economic growth and domestic consumption. But estimates of Soviet defense expenditures in CIA constructs, mislabled "rubles" by the admission

of senior CIA analysts, may not be used to analyze Soviet policies, objectives, and national priorities, or to calculate the burden on the Soviet economy. When CIA rubles are used for these purposes, the results are not only erroneous and misleading but quite irrelevant.

Inasmuch as the CIA is the official and only source of Soviet defense expenditures in the U.S. government, it has neither an estimate of Soviet defense expenditures nor an estimate of the burden on the Soviet economy, all official testimony to Congress and Department of Defense posture statements notwithstanding.

WHERE HAS THE MONEY GONE?

From the information available in the public domain, it is possible to construct a representative list of major Soviet procurement programs in the 1960s and 1970s. The list is not complete, of course, because much information is not available in the public domain. The intelligence community can count major additions to the visible inventory, but such numbers cannot be equated to reliable estimates of Soviet weapons production. It is one thing to count the number of missile launchers deployed but quite another thing to determine how many missiles have been produced. Much procurement, such as ammunition production, simply cannot be counted by national means of verification. But the following list of visible acquisitions should help the reader to understand the high rates of growth shown in Figures 3 and 4, remembering that unit costs for each successive generation of weapons systems have been rising due to increasing complexity and the cost of technological innovation.

16. *Soviet Defense Expenditures & Related Programs.* Hearings before the Subcommittee on General Procurement of the Committee on Armed Services, United States Senate, Ninety-Sixth Congress, First & Second Sessions, 1, 8 November 1979; 4 February 1980. (Washington, DC: Government Printing Office, 1980), p. 130.

Thus in the period 1958-70 the Soviet military establishment procured the following:

—some 700 IR/MRBM launchers and associated support equipment, several times that many missiles and nuclear warheads;

—nearly 1400 ICBM launchers—support equipment, additional missiles, and warheads;

—the majority of their 10,000 SAM launchers, 6,000 radars, who knows how many missiles, and large quantities of equipment for command, control, and communications (C³);

—at least 1,500 and probably about 2,000 interceptors, thousands or air-to-air missiles (AA-1 through AA-5), and large quantities of C³ and support equipment;

—41 first-generation nuclear-powered missile submarines—32 E-Class cruise missile SSNs and 9 H-Class ballistic missile submarines;

—39 diesel-powered missile-launching submarines—23 G-Class ballistic missile and 16 J-Class cruise missile boats;

—about 16 Y-Class ballistic missile submarines and a total (all classes) of about 350 SLBM launchers;

—some 100 heavy and at least 1,000 medium bomber aircraft for the Long Range Aviation (LRA) armies and a large number of air-to-surface missiles—AS-1 through AS-6—for these bombers*;

—about 15 first-generation nuclear-powered attack submarines (N-class and V-class)

*Allows for bombers procured prior to 1958.

primarily for strategic antisubmarine warfare (ASW);

—some 40 large surface ships (3,800 to 18,000 tons loaded) for open ocean operations, since 1960 primarily for strategic ASW operations;

—probably about 2,000 tactical fighters and fighter bombers for Frontal Aviation (FA), some 1000 transports for Military Transport Aviation (VTA) and several thousand helicopters for FA and VTA;

—several hundred launchers and many more missiles for air defense of Soviet Ground Forces in the field—SA-2, SA-4, and SA-6;

—at least 20,000 and possibly 40,000 or more tanks, several tens of thousands of other armored vehicles (mostly wheeled), and several thousand (probably more than 10,000) artillery pieces and large mortars; and

—on the order of 300 tactical missile launchers (SCUDs) for nuclear and chemical fire support of Soviet-Warsaw Pact Fronts and armies and around 500 tactical rocket (FROG) launchers for nuclear and chemical fire support of Soviet-Pact divisions. This in turn requires procurement of several thousand (no one in the West knows how many) missiles and rockets.

The list of major weapons procurement since SALT began (and through 1980) is also impressive:

—several hundred later model SS-11s with multiple warheads, 700 to some 800 third-generation large, liquid-fueled ICBMs (SS-17, 18, and 19) with MIRV warheads, some 250-300 mobile

SS-20 MIRVed IRBM launchers (probably about 1000 missiles), on the order of 8000 to 10,000 nuclear warheads;

—about 20 Y-Class and 30 D-Class SSBNs with a total of some 700 missile tubes, probably the first ship of the "Typhoon" class SSBN, and 1000-2000 nuclear warheads;

—at least 150 Backfire bombers, several hundred ASMs for this and older model bombers, and a corresponding number of nuclear bombs and warheads;

—more than 60 major surface ships, mostly for strategic ASW operations, and other lesser combatant and support ships for a net increase of over 1 million metric tons (after retirements) in the surface ship Navy, many hundreds to several thousand rockets, cruise missiles and (naval) SAMs; some 20 to 25 nuclear powered attack submarines—equipped with antiship cruise missiles;

—more than 11,000 SAM (SA-3 and SA-5) launchers, perhaps 10,000 or more missiles; more than 1,000 high performance interceptors, some with an initial "look-down/shoot-down" capability, several thousand air-to-air missiles; these deployments in turn must have required a large investment in new radars, equipment for the ground control environment, and probably a large number of nuclear warheads; at least two over-the-horizon radars;

—about 1 million men added to active duty military personnel and about 20 divisions (about equal to the entire U.S. Army) to the Ground Forces; about 30,000 tanks, more than 30,000

armored personnel carriers and other armored vehicles, more than 20,000 artillery pieces and heavy mortars;

—some 2100 interceptors, fighter bombers, and high-performance reconnaissance aircraft for Frontal Aviation; about 600 helicopter gunships; who knows how many thousands air-to-surface and antitank missiles;

—at least 1750 to 2000 SAM launchers (SA-4, SA-6, and SA-8) for Ground Force air defense, and thousands of missiles; more than 2,500 SA-9 (Redeye type) launchers and corresponding numbers of missiles; on the order of 2500 ZSU-23/4 anti-aircraft guns; and

—about 250 large (AN-22 and IL-76) transport aircraft and more than 1000 cargo/troop transport helicopters.

Once again we must remember that such litanies are merely (1) what can be detected by the "national means of verification," and (2) that portion thereof which is available in the public domain. Much is missing from the list.

As a result of all the new weaponry being acquired, procurement has risen rapidly as a share of Soviet defense outlays, as shown in Figure 5.[17] RDT&E and space have remained constant, accounting for about 25 percent of Soviet defense expenditures. Although outlays for pay, operations, maintenance, and military construction (POMC) have risen absolutely, the rate of growth has been slow compared with procurement and RDT&E. Hence the share of pay, operating costs, and military construction has declined

17. Based on the estimates in Table 4.

Figure 5: Structure of USSR Defense Expenditures

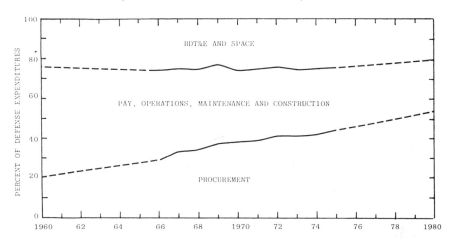

markedly as a share of total defense expenditures, as shown in Figure 2.

Two factors appear to be contributing to the declining share of POMC: the low (direct) cost of conscripts and Soviet training and maintenance practices. Soviet conscripts are well fed (by Soviet standards) and well clothed but are paid less than the price of a bottle of vodka per month. Officers are very well paid, but their compensation probably grows at about the same rate as that of civilian workers. Consequently, manpower costs grow steadily but slowly.

Soviet training practices emphasize use of training vehicles and weapons rather than unit equipment whenever possible. Soviet military aircraft fly fewer hours, and Soviet ships steam fewer miles each year than their U.S. counterparts. These practices keep operating costs down and make it possible to maintain a high percentage of unit equipment in reliable operating condition. It is generally thought, however, that such practices result in lower unit proficiency. But it is one way of keeping operating costs down and unit equipment reliability up.

The decline in direct manpower costs (excluding pensions) has been dramatic, from about 25 percent of defense expenditures in 1960 to about 15 percent in 1970 and about 10 percent currently. Adding pensions would increase the share but would not alter the trend significantly. In terms of the opportunity cost—that is, what the conscripts would have produced if employed in the Soviet economy—of course, the economic cost of Soviet military manpower is quite high. But to military budgeteers, manpower costs increase slowly and take a smaller share of total outlays each year.

PROSPECTS FOR THE 1980s

The Eleventh Five Year Plan adopted at the 26th Party Congress in March 1981 continues the shift in Soviet national economic priorities toward defense. The economy as a whole is to grow by about 3.5 percent per annum, consumption by 3 percent, and investment by 2 percent per annum, or less.[18] Evidently, defense expenditures are planned to

18. *Pravda*, 28 February 1981.

increase by 6 to 7 percent per annum, while procurement probably is scheduled to grow at 10 percent per annum (or more) through 1985. Consequently, defense will rise as a share of Soviet GNP from the current level of about 18 percent to well over 20 percent.

Analysis of the driving forces behind this continuous shift in Soviet national priorities to defense since the late 1950s would require another (and longer) analysis. Suffice to say here that we are observing the high cost of Soviet attempts to acquire the military capabilities required to fight and "win" a nuclear war. The 1980s will be the decade of Soviet strategic defense—air, missile, space, antisubmarine warfare (ASW), anticarrier/navy and civil defense. Other forces will be modernized and perhaps expanded somewhat, but the emphasis will be on strategic defenses because these are the areas where Soviet capabilities lag well behind requirements. Many of the air defense, ASW, and other strategic defensive programs are already evident. Others, such as the all but inevitable Soviet breakout from the ABM Treaty, may not be visible for a few more years. Nevertheless, the resources have been committed to building up Soviet strategic defenses despite the high price in terms of very low economic growth rates. And all the other indicators appear to be present. Without nationwide ballistic missile defenses, the vast Soviet investment in all other damage-limiting measures—counterforce capabilities, air defense, ASW, and the rest—will be for naught.

ANNALS, *AAPSS*, 457, September 1981

Strategic Forces, General Purpose Forces, and Crisis Management

By COLIN S. GRAY

ABSTRACT: The 1980s could prove to be an unusually dangerous decade because of the simultaneous maturing of Soviet multilevel military superiority and of very severe Soviet domestic problems. It is not clear that the Western "window of military vulnerability" will be defined by the Soviets as a "window of opportunity," but the West has been very imprudent in permitting such a question ever to have potential policy salience. Unlike the situation in the 1960s and 1970s, fairly plausible scenarios for war between the United States and Soviet Union can be drafted for the 1980s. Western understanding of how acute crises should be managed almost certainly is outdated as a consequence, in good part, of the cumulatively dramatic change in the East-West military balance. U.S. defense planning should recognize the essential unity of military and crisis bargaining problems and appreciate that one cannot prudently choose to emphasize, for example, the modernization of the general purpose forces at the expense of the "less usable" strategic forces. Indeed, if anything, the United States can least afford relative weakness at the higher potential end of the escalation spectrum.

Colin S. Gray is director of National Security Studies at Hudson Institute, Croton-on-Hudson, New York. Prior to joining Hudson Institute in 1976, Dr. Gray was Assistant Director at the International Institute of Strategic Studies in London. He studied at Manchester and Oxford Universities. Dr. Gray's most recent books are The MX ICBM and National Security *(Praeger, 1981), and* Strategic Studies: A Critical Assessment *(Greenwood, 1981).*

This article represents the views of its author. Although it originally appeared as Hudson Institute Paper HI-3317-P, it has not been widely circulated among Institute staff and has not been formally reviewed. No opinions, statements of fact, or conclusions contained in this document can properly be attributed to the Institute, its staff, its members, or its contracting agencies.

T HERE is broad consensus in the United States today on the belief that the adverse trend in relative military power that persisted throughout the 1970s must be reversed. Furthermore, it is widely believed that the trend has progressed to the point where the West faces a "window of military vulnerability." Some commentators take this argument one stage further and claim that the Soviet Union will enjoy the benefits of a "window of military opportunity" that should endure through most of the 1980s.

Consensus breaks down on the subject of just how dangerous the 1980s will prove to be. Some people, while acknowledging the need for an increased level of Western defense preparation, choose to take comfort from what they see as offsetting Soviet weaknesses. Frequently the point is made that the development of military power is the only Soviet success story. On the negative side of the contemporary Soviet condition may be listed such factors as a cumulatively dramatic drop in the rate of economic growth (since the 1960s); growing manpower (and particularly skilled manpower) shortages; political instability in the empire in Eastern Europe; a noticeably declining standard of living; and—very generally—a continuing resistance at the highest levels to adaptive change. The Brezhnev leadership has provided stability and steadiness of course, but at the cost of foreclosing on timely reforms.

Underpinning this article is not the conviction that the Soviet Union has been granted, and should be expected to exploit, a five- to ten-year window of military opportunity; rather, is it the belief that a malign combination of relative military strength and perceived domestic weakness could make the Soviet Union a particularly dangerous player in the international politics of the 1980s. Soviet domestic weaknesses, far from offsetting the near-term military strength of the country, could well provide the needed incentive to external adventure.[1] It is not, on the basis of the historical record thus far, "the Soviet way" consciously to court very high risks in the hope of registering positive gains. However, the Soviet Union has never before been as militarily strong, relative to defined external enemies, as it will be over the next five to seven years, and a bitter and probably protracted political succession struggle has never before been waged against the backdrop of such military strength.[2]

I am not at all convinced that the Soviet Union sees the evolving military (im)balance in "window of vulnerability/opportunity" terms. Moreover, it would be unduly alarmist to claim that some candidate Soviet leader or leaders will seek to achieve unambiguous foreign policy success by way of reinforcing a claim to Brezhnev's throne. Nonetheless, one could be wrong. What, surely, is beyond reasonable dispute is that the United States and its friends and allies have behaved most imprudently in permitting the multilevel military balance to deteriorate to the point where American—and presumably

1. See Colin S. Gray, "The Most Dangerous Decade: Historic Mission, Legitimacy, and Dynamics of the Soviet Empire," *Orbis* 25(1): 13-28 (Spring 1981).

2. On the Soviet political succession in the 1980s see Seweryn Bialer, *Stalin's Successors: Leadership, Stability, and Change in Soviet Union* (Cambridge [U.K.]: Cambridge University Press, 1980); and Jerry F. Hough, *Soviet Leadership in Transition* (Washington, DC: The Brookings Institution, 1980).

Soviet—defense planners can design not wholly implausible theories for the military solution of actual, and possible, Soviet political problems.

The West is in serious trouble when NATO's Supreme Allied Commander, testifying before Congress, feels moved to say:

> NATO has now been surpassed—or soon will be—in all categories of forces necessary to implement its strategy: strategic nuclear, theater nuclear and conventional.[3]

No one can predict what crises will erupt in the 1980s. The point is that the Western governments have chosen to live far more dangerously than they had any right (given their responsibilities) or need to. Military power is not the only factor influencing crisis outbreak, dynamics, and outcome. Scarcely less important may be degree of perceived commitment (relative to the adversary) and skill in diplomacy and communication. However, freedom of action in foreign policy is related to the quantity and quality of military options available to a president. In the last resort one may have to fight. Clever strategy is always desirable (as a force multiplier, or even substitute), but it has its limits. For example, General David Jones, Chairman of the Joint Chiefs of Staff, in language mildly reminiscent of John Foster Dulles, recently invoked the idea of "compound escalation."[4] That is, a United States at a military disad-

vantage in an acute crisis in one specific geographical area (such as Iran and the Gulf) might seek political-military action in some other region where it had the geopolitical advantage (vis-à-vis Cuba).

This idea of the imaginative "knight's move" in strategy offers more the illusion than the reality of intelligent defense planning. After all, compound escalation is a game which more than one can play. As a generic scenario for a complex crisis which overloads the decision-making capacity of governments, and hence would offer major incentives for the military simplification of the situation, this idea has few close competitors. Although, up to a point, superior strategy and tactics can substitute for ready military muscle (historically, many materially inferior armies have won), Americans should disabuse themselves of the notion that they are somehow "smarter" than Russians. Some of the current defense problems of the United States and NATO can be traced to the hubristic belief that American strategic thinkers were on the frontier of understanding, while backward Soviet general staff analysts were trailing five or more years behind. The Soviet general staff has studied Western strategic concepts very carefully indeed, and—by and large—has rejected them.[5] Soviet military science matches almost ideally the precepts offered by Russian strategic culture, and the product is a philosophy of defense preparation that Americans typically have great difficulty comprehending.

The issue here is not which strategic culture—the American or the

3. Testimony of General Bernard W. Rogers, SACEur, before the House Armed Services Committee, reprinted in *Soviet Aerospace* 30(8): 59 (2 March 1981).

4. See General David C. Jones, *United States Military Posture for FY 1982* (Washington, DC: Government Printing Office, 1981), p. VI. Also see Herman Kahn, *On Escalation* (New York: Praeger, 1965), p. 6.

5. See Robert Bathurst, "Two Languages of War," in Derek Leebaert, ed., *Soviet Military Thinking* (London: Allen and Unwin, 1981).

Soviet—is right (and wrong); rather, it is what that Soviet culture prescribes, and provides, for possible conflict in the 1980s. Soviet crisis-time decisions in the 1980s are going to be made on the basis of *Soviet* beliefs and perceptions (however foolish to some Westerners).

The proper way to justify President Reagan's rearmament program is not exclusively with reference to evidence of growing Soviet military strength, linked to somewhat forced (and seemingly simple-minded) predictions of Soviet crisis propagation; rather, it should be with reference to the genuine indeterminacy of political events over the next decade. Western democracies typically find their preferred defense programs to be vulnerable to the skeptical cry of "give me a plausible scenario." Neither 1914 nor 1939 (nor 1870—for the Franco-Prussian War) were "plausible scenarios," with reference to a time period appropriate to the preparation of military programs that might have served to provide the deterrent clout needed to avert the crisis slide to war: plausible, that is, in the eyes of the relevant foreign policy makers, given their contemporary mindsets.

The truly severe crisis possibilities for the 1980s lie in the basic structure of the Soviet empire and the political instability, actual or potential, in some of the littoral states of Eurasia. The geopolitics of the maritime alliance led by the United States require that the Soviet Union not be granted a hegemonic position on one shore of the Persian Gulf. In addition, President Reagan has decided, very sensibly, that the forward encroachments of Soviet power through client, candidate-client, and occasional-client states is a process that must be arrested. Military power in support of foreign policy requires local (or, at minimum, not too distant) access. Denial of (safe) access to what Zbigniew Brzezinski called the "arc of crisis" around the North-Central littoral of the Indian Ocean does not require control of all potential American entry points to the region; simply a position where such entry points are relatively few and militarily exposed should suffice.

MILITARY PLANNING AND THE NEED FOR STRATEGY

The potential requirements of crisis management vis-à-vis a first-class superpower adversary must embrace defense planning for all levels of possible military engagement. The beginning of planning wisdom is recognition of the following considerations.

—The United States cannot always choose which political and military events it will define as a crisis challenge. "Vital interests" tend to be defined as interests that are worth fighting for[6]—but such interests, not infrequently, are more or less vital according to shifting political circumstance.

—Some crises can be deterred (crises can be planned and engineered as deliberate acts of policy). However, other crises can erupt and unfold according to nobody's game plan. In short even very high-quality defense planning, and a matching posture, offer no guarantee that crises can be prevented or managed either nonviolently or

6. See the discussion in Bernard Brodie, *War and Politics* (New York: Macmillan, 1973), ch. 8.

with only a low level of violence leading to a satisfactory political outcome.

—In defense planning, everything —potentially—is connected to everything else. This dictum is unusually pertinent to conflict involving a superpower that does not share the American understanding of what is strategic and tactical—and indeed has an additional category, of "operational."[7]

Force remains the ultimate sanction of states, albeit a sanction threatened and exercised with historically extraordinary caution for reason of the destructive potential or nuclear-equipped military arsenals. If the Soviet imperium is to be contained within its existing boundaries, let alone eroded at the margins, the United States has no alternative but to back its foreign policy with the appropriate quality and quantity of military power. What is or is not appropriate is, in substantial part, dictated by military postural decisions taken by the Soviet Union. American defense planners today, unlike some theorists in the early 1970s, cannot prudently assume that East-West relations are set on a course of increasing political stabilization so that matters of military balance and imbalance will become less and less important. The defense planner lacks access to a crystal ball, but he does have access to the trends and details of recent history. He is not required to predict whether and where U.S. forces might be committed to combat, but

7. See Harriet F. Scott and William F. Scott, *The Armed Forces of the U.S.S.R.* (Boulder, CO: Westview Press, 1979), p. 70. Also relevant is Edward N. Luttwak, "The Operational Level of War," *International Security* 5(3): 61-79 (Winter 1980/81).

he is required to assume that it could be any time, anywhere from the North Cape of Norway around the periphery of Eurasia-Africa to South Korea and Japan. He should not assume the worst case (which would include a reversal of de facto alliance ties on the part of Beijing, and Soviet achievement of strategic and tactical surprise), but he should assume a bad case. Perhaps above all else, the American defense planner logically is compelled to consider small-scale conflict in the context of conflict on a much larger scale.

Proponents of a program for the across-the-board rebuilding of Western defenses are not—or, at least should not be—arguing for the purchase of everything, on each service's "wish list," in lieu of strategic thought on the determination of priorities (that is, "bottom-up planning"—the tendency to decide first on forces and later on strategy). Instead, the case for across-the-board rearmament rests on an appreciation of the extent to which relative military coercive potential has shifted to the Soviet Union since 1970,[8] and on recognition of the essential unity of military action.

The United States is not at liberty to choose to rebuild a particular kind of combat capability (general purpose, naval and amphibious, theater-nuclear, strategic-nuclear) at the expense of others. Until the late 1960s, the United States enjoyed the benefits of a theater- and strategic-nuclear superiority which could hold the ring around a local conflict. Even if the United States was not often moved to consider

8. For a useful overview see John M. Collins, *U.S.-Soviet Military Balance: Concepts and Capabilities, 1960-1980* (New York: McGraw-Hill, 1980).

theater-nuclear escalation, there was virtual certainty that the Soviet Union would see no advantage in involving itself directly in local crises in a strategic context where it had no plausible theory of victory.

Conditions are different in the 1980s. Soviet asserted interests in the world, far beyond its traditional sphere, are much more extensive today than in the past. More specifically, the Persian Gulf area, a region of vital importance to noncommunist industrialized countries, and of considerable strategic significance to the Soviet Union, is in the process of a protracted crisis of political and social modernization; while, overall, the West has major deficiencies in all categories of military power. Without denying the great reluctance of Soviet leaders to court the dangers of nuclear war, the structure of any acute East-West crisis in the 1980s cannot help but be determined in part by each side's perception of its own and the other's military choices.

In keeping with its novel nuclear-age theory of limited warfare,[9] the (new, post-1945, that is) American "way of war" and defense planning has been to seek to minimize costs and risks (of unwanted escalation) by taking military quarter- and half-measures on behalf of limited political objectives. This fact, however intelligent in theory, had a major negative impact upon the quality of American combat performance in Korea and Vietnam, and has promoted some highly dangerous ideas to the level of national policy with respect to nuclear weapon employment policy (NUWEP).

It is essential that the United States have a limited or small-war philosophy—and that it not be locked into a military system, as occurred with the French in March 1936 (over the occasion of Hitler's military reoccupation of the Rhineland), where the policy choice is narrowed to full mobilization (and all-out war) or inaction. However, American forces should not be committed to battle on so modest a scale, or with so restricted a permitted freedom of action, that political objectives cannot be obtained. A United States prepared to commit forces in what is intended—and hoped—to be only a limited operation should be a United States with a good theory of higher-level military cover for that operation. Because the American defense community continues to decline to confront honestly and squarely issues of nuclear warfighting, *strategic* reasoning typically stops at a relatively low level of potential violence. For example, there is virtual unanimity over the idea (though not over the organizational or deployment details) of a Rapid Development Force (RDF) for use particularly in the Persian Gulf area, but interested citizens will search in vain for plausible official explanations of the higher-level "cover" behind that force. Should that force be defeated or stalemated, then how would the war be conducted? Or, U.S. NUWEP at the very low end of the employment spectrum has, since 4 April 1974,[10] retailed the idea of limited nuclear options (LNOs); but, again, what should be done if U.S. LNOs are either met in kind or responded to by means of a very large leap up the escalation ladder—how should the

9. An excellent critical essay is Robert E. Osgood, *Limited War Revisited* (Boulder, CO: Westview Press, 1979).

10. The date when President Nixon signed the NUWEP directive on "Policy Guidance for the Employment of Nuclear Weapons," which expressed the sense of NSDM 242 of 17 January 1976.

war be waged? and in pursuit of what political goals?[11]

Each part of the U.S. defense posture should be related in terms of complementarity of capability, credibility for threat or execution of escalation, and overall integrity, to every other part. U.S. so-called strategic forces (really nuclear-capable central systems) should not be regulated for essential equivalence with their Soviet counterparts, because the United States and the Soviet Union place different foreign policy supportive burdens on those forces. Soviet strategic forces are (or should be judged) adequate—for a very un-Soviet concept—provided they can function as a robust counterdeterrent to U.S. strategic forces. The reverse is not true. American strategic forces are not required solely to neutralize the threat posed by, or deter the employment of, Soviet strategic forces. Instead, their task, in extremis, is to provide compensation for deficiencies in locally deployed forces.

Defense planning, as Richard Burt has argued persuasively, should be governed by putative operational needs, not by political slogans that point to essentially static "input" or political-perceptual characteristics of a military relationship.[12] "Parity," "sufficiency," and "essential equivalence" are the loose concepts of the political speech maker, and point to the region of easiest negotiability in an interstate arms control process; they have little or nothing to offer the defense planner who is obliged professionally to provide military threat and employment options in potential support of unique American foreign policy requirements.

There is no elementary mechanical relationship between general purpose and strategic forces. There is some truth to the claim that the weaker the one, the stronger should be the other. However, the horrors of central nuclear war are so well (and possibly overly) appreciated that the threshold for central nuclear employment is likely to be very high almost regardless of the (im)balance in theater forces. NATO traditionally has sought to bridge the credibility gap between theater-conventional defeat and strategic (central-system) use by means of theater-nuclear forces. In general, if the United States and its allies must choose to be deficient at one level, it is probably better for that level to be in the theater rather than with respect to central nuclear forces. The Organization of the Joint Chiefs of Staff offered this opinion:

U.S. capability to avoid coercion and exert leverage in a crisis is eroding in direct relation to continuing Soviet force improvements and the aging of U.S. strategic nuclear systems. *This erosion contributes more than any other to the danger confronting U.S. interests in the 1980's* [emphasis added].[13]

Since the mid-1960s, American and NATO defense planning has had, at its core, a theory of a seamless web of deterrence which, if it ever broke down, could easily have translated into a seamless web of disaster. The pre- and intrawar deterrence (as opposed to defense) focus of allied "defense" planning, however attractive for peacetime interallied political accord and for an elegantly comprehensive theory

11. See Colin S. Gray, "Targeting Problems for Central War," *Naval War College Review* 33(1): 3-21 (January-February 1980).
12. Richard Burt, "Reassessing the Strategic Balances," *International Security* 5(1): 50 (Summer 1980); "The Relevance of Arms Control in the 1980's." *Daedalus* 110(1): 170-71 (Winter 1981).
13. Jones, *United States Military Posture for FY 1982*, p. 23.

of war prevention, has the all-too-obvious problems that "the buck rests" nowhere in particular. No particular element in the NATO-allied arsenal is designed to arrest and defeat Soviet military aggression. There is no "theory of victory" underlying U.S./NATO strategy,[14] while even the extant theory of victory-denial is distinctly fragile. NATO's theater-conventional forces are intended not to defend against conventional attack, but rather to guarantee a "major war," to deny a coup de main.[15] NATO's theater-nuclear force posture is not designed to provide an effective local war-fighting offset to conventional weakness, but rather a speedy transmission belt to central nuclear war. U.S. strategic forces, in their turn, are not designed so as to defeat Soviet strategic forces and, ipso facto, defend the United States—instead, they are designed (if that is the appropriate term) to promise the infliction, in extremis, of catastrophic damage upon the Soviet Union.[16]

The above thumbnail characterization is admittedly a simplification of official American and NATO reasoning, but not by very much. In principle, there are several major

thresholds to which (Western-style) rational statesmen should be attentive: nuclear use, nuclear use abroad, (central) nuclear use against the homeland of the other superpower; central nuclear use against urban-industrial targets. But American and NATO officials seem not to have thought through the logic of their (in)security condition. What if it is the U.S./NATO that is driven to consider fracturing escalation thresholds? That is, what if the burden of escalation is placed upon the West rather than the Soviet Union?

Defense planning should have integrity from the top down rather than the bottom up (somehow, "bottom-up" planning never takes the top levels very seriously, if it reaches them at all). For reasons both of general prudence (for example, war could occur regardless of the quality of defense posture and doctrine) and optimum deterrent effect, the United States should identify, as the core of its defense planning, the need to limit damage to the United States to an acceptable level given the political circumstances of a total challenge to American values. A United States paralyzed by fear (of retaliation) from stepping on the topmost rungs of the escalation ladder should be a United States self-deterred from stepping onto that ladder at all. At the present time U.S. defense planning appears to take no account whatsoever of the critical issue of which side would be the deterrer and which the deterree. The strategist should consider the likely net effect of the actions he recommends.

14. See Colin S. Gray, "Nuclear Strategy: The Case for a Theory of Victory," *International Security* 4(1): 54-87 (Summer 1979).

15. Kenneth Hunt, *The Alliance and Europe: Part II Defence With Fewer Men*, Adelphi Paper No. 98 (London: International Institute for Strategic Studies, Summer 1973), p. 20.

16. PD 59 of 25 July 1980, and its implementing NUWEP, did not change this situation. See Desmond Ball, "Counterforce Targeting: How New? How Viable?" *Arms Control Today* 2(2): 1-2, 6-9 (February 1981); and Colin S. Gray, "Presidential Directive 59: Flawed But Useful," *Parameters* 11(1): 29-37 (March 1981).

CRISIS MANAGEMENT

Much, if not most, of the research on crises conducted by Western academics over the past two decades has produced little fruit worthy of harvesting.[17] A general theory of desirable crisis behavior, if attainable, would be so general as to offer no policy advice sufficiently specific to be useful. Moreover, the gathering of a cumulative wisdom from historical crises in different periods appears to be impossible because of the historical distinctiveness of each crisis—and the indeterminacy of much of the crucial data. This is not to say that the study of history is not valuable—far from it. But that the familiar concept of "crisis management" convenys an aura of authority and comprehension that is quite inappropriate to the reality.

There is some value to be found in the scholarly literature of crises and crisis management, but what may effect the demise of the West in the 1980s are some novel, or apparently novel, features in the structure of acute East-West crises. The more rigorous of the academic crisis management studies tend to be less than empathetic to local political and strategic culture. Critical to the course of an acute East-West crisis in the 1980s (or beyond) will be Soviet assessments of the state of "the correlation of forces"[18]—this is a Soviet concept that tends not to be widely appreciated among Western scholars of international relations. How the Soviets assay this correla-

tion will have a major impact on how they choose to behave. Soviet leaders, save for Nikita Khrushchev, have not been adventurers—they move no further than they believe the correlation of forces permits, but also no less.

The differences between Soviet and American approaches to the risks of war and crisis management (to the extent to which these are different subjects) are quite startling, if ill-understood. In the authoritative Soviet view, war is a political experience to be prevented or decided upon for reasons of political calculation. It is not the duty of Soviet defense planners to design a force posture so that technical crisis instability potential is minimized.[19] The Soviets do not believe that war can be triggered, for example, by the mechanistic instabilities of "the reciprocal fear of surprise attack"[20]—that is a wholly Western notion. Furthermore, the Soviets do not appear to hold that the risks of large wars may be minimized by the application of only a very limited force in pursuit of very limited political objectives. Instead, the Soviet Union appears to have concluded that military power, when applied (rarely) to solve a political problem, should be applied massively in pursuit of very rapid results.

It is disturbing to note that the Soviet strategic literature does not entertain even rough facsimiles of such American ideas as escalation, escalation control, crisis management, and crisis bargaining. These obvious lacunae may mean much or little, but one cannot deny the strong

17. However, some useful studies are identifiable amidst the flow of scholastic pedantry. For example, see Phil Williams, *Crisis Management: Confrontation and Diplomacy in the Nuclear Age* (New York: John Wiley, 1976); and Richard N. Lebow, *Between Peace and War: The Nature of International Crisis* (Baltimore, MD: Johns Hopkins University Press, 1981).
18. See Col. S. Tuyushkevich, "The Methodology for the Correlation of Forces in War," *Voyennaya mysl'* No. 6 (1969), FPD translated 30 January 1970 (0008/70), pp. 26-37.

19. See David Holloway, "Military Power and Political Purpose in Soviet Policy," *Daedalus* 109(4): 19-20 (Fall 1980).
20. Thomas C. Schelling, *The Strategy of Conflict* (Cambridge, MA: Harvard University Press, 1960), ch. 9.

possibility that, in the Soviet perspective, military force—once applied—is to be applied effectively for the end of securing whatever political goals are in contention. If this were to prove true in practice, it could mean that the Soviet armed forces would be bent upon victory, for clearly defined reasons, while the United States or NATO were approaching the military crisis from the perspective of political bargaining.

A culturally alien Soviet approach to crisis bargaining may have been of relatively little interest in the 1950s and the early 1960s, when the United States was clearly superior in nuclear "trumps." But in the 1980s, when nuclear trumps are at best fairly evenly divided, the putative cultural differences between the superpowers could easily prove to be of critical significance.[21]

It is worth noting that although the Western scholar of crises and crisis management confronts academic problems of a severe character, the Western policy maker faces choices which, should he choose incorrectly, may prove deadly. In the 1980s, Western policy makers must conduct business with a Soviet Union that is peaking in its relative military power, yet which is subject to increasing domestic-imperial challenges. A greatly improved capability for the forward projection of military power and internal fragility may cancel each other out, or may reinforce each other—the American defense planner does not, and cannot, know which will be the more true. However, that defense planner does know that his country

is the principal guardian of international order and that, ipso facto, he cannot afford to take substantial risks.

CONFLICT IN THE 1980s

Historians tend to differ as to whether the possibility of war is endemic in a particular international system, or as to whether the details of particular crises are the controlling elements. With respect to 1914, for example, it is relatively easy to argue that the countervailing alliance structures constituted a catastrophe "in the wings" simply awaiting the right cue for disastrous "on-stage" action. Many events, in retrospect, appear to have been inevitable. However, I am sufficiently impressed with the role of the singular in history that I decline to assign any probability estimates to the prospect of Soviet-American war in the 1980s. The possible occasions for war are all too easy to identify: They include:

—Soviet imperial policing in Eastern Europe which spills over into NATO/Europe;

—a wide variety of superpower intervention scenarios in the Persian Gulf area;

—another Arab-Israeli war;

—an American military intervention in Central America which comes to include Cuba;

—a Sino-Soviet war.

None of the above have to produce World War III, but any of them could do so, and any of them can be scripted plausibly for the 1980s. It is scarcely an exaggeration to assert that the American armed forces today are functioning on the equivalent of a "Ten-Year Rule" (that there will be no major conflict

21. See Fritz Ermarth, "Contrasts in American and Soviet Strategic Thought," *International Security* 3(2): 138-55 (Fall 1978).

for ten years).[22] The United States recently chose to adopt tough anti-Soviet diplomatic positions at the very moment when it was entering a seven- to eight-year period of multi-level military vulnerability. If the Soviet leadership is deterred from inimical action by the undifferentiated threat of nuclear catastrophe, the U.S. military forces today are indeed adequate. Unfortunately, there is scant authoritative Soviet evidence to support the view that the promise of "nuclear catastrophe" per se is likely to be very relevant to Soviet crisis-time decision-making should it perceive the very survival of its political system to be at stake. Crises in the 1980s may not have so severe a character, but what if they do?

Success in crisis management does not depend only upon relative military muscle, but that valid point offers only the slimmest of a basis for optimism. Looking at what might occur in the 1980s, it is not at all obvious that the United States

22. In August 1919 Great Britain adopted the "Ten Year Rule.": This held as a planning assumption until 1932 (following the Japanese invasion of Manchuria in 1931).

can, or should, assume that it can find political commitment or tactical/strategic-operational compensation for more than 10 years of military underinvestment. The occasions for world war tend to appear somewhat irregularly, as best we can tell. Nonetheless, statesmen should have little difficulty understanding that the 1980s are unusually dangerous. This decade combines a multilevel military preponderance on the part of the superpower that has no investment worthy of note in the extant international security order with an increasingly severe set of Soviet domestic economic, social, and imperial ordering problems.

Soviet leaders may prove to be culturally so unfriendly to policy initiatives that could plausibly be branded by domestic rivals as adventurous that they would not even consider jumping through the Western window of military vulnerability. But, how could it be that supposedly prudent Western leaders have permitted a period to unfold wherein the risk of Soviet military adventurism has to be a cause of acute Western concern?

ANNALS, *AAPSS*, **457**, September 1981

Theater-Nuclear Force Modernization and NATO's Flexible Response Strategy

By JACQUELYN K. DAVIS

ABSTRACT: In October 1979 the North Atlantic Treaty Organization adopted a resolution that recommended modernization of NATO's long-range theater-nuclear forces. Based upon the deployment in Western Europe of 108 Pershing II missile and 464 ground-launched cruise missile launchers, the NATO decision was widely regraded as an essential step in redressing the deteriorating military balance in Europe. The perceived erosion of the European balance is rooted in the momentum of programs undertaken by the Soviet Union both in nuclear and nonnuclear forces. From a European perspective, however, the most worrisome aspect of Soviet modernization programs relates to improvements in theater-nuclear systems which, when juxtaposed with the development of a potential counterforce capability (against U.S. ICBMs), have reinforced doubts about the ability of the Alliance to ensure deterrence by means of the agreed strategy of Flexible Response, with its attendant concepts of defensive planning and graduated response providing for conventional and nuclear options. To enhance the deterrence posture of NATO and to provide for a contingency in which the actual use of NATO's nuclear-capable systems might become neces-theater-nuclear forces and, at the same time, revitalize its tactical planning options.

Jacquelyn K. Davis is special assistant to the president and senior staff member of the Institute for Foreign Policy Analysis. She received her Ph.D. on international relations from the University of Pennsylvania in 1980. She is the author and coauthor of several monographs on the U.S.-Soviet strategic relationship and the impact of SALT II on U.S.-Alliance relations.

AT its twenty-fifth annual session held in Ottawa in October 1979, the North Atlantic Assembly adopted a resolution that recommended a program for the modernization of NATO's theater-nuclear forces (TNF).[1] Subsequently, on 12 December 1979, at a NATO ministerial meeting, this proposal was given substance with the announcement that the Alliance would pursue the development and initiate production of a new generation of long-range theater-nuclear forces (LRTNF). While subject to ratification by the governing bodies of each of its member nations, the decision of the North Atlantic Treaty Organization to deploy 108 Pershing II missile (PII) and 464 ground-launched cruise missile (GLCM) launchers in Western Europe was widely regarded as a necessary step in redressing what was perceived in Western Europe and the United States as a deteriorating balance between the military forces of NATO and the Warsaw Pact.

The erosion of the military balance in Europe is rooted in the sustained momentum of programs undertaken by the Soviet Union

designed to effect major qualitative and quantitative improvements in Soviet offensive and defensive systems alike. Across the spectrum the Soviet Union has endeavored to strengthen its military force deployments, although from the European perspective the most worrisome aspect of Soviet modernization programs relates to improvements in theater-nuclear systems which, when juxtaposed to the development by the USSR of an intercontinental first-strike capability (against U.S. land-based strategic systems), have contributed to doubts about the ability of the Alliance to respond to an enemy attack against Western Europe by relying on the escalatory options provided for in NATO's Doctrine of Flexible Response.

Adopted by the Alliance in 1967, the NATO Doctrine of Flexible Response is predicated on the assumption that Western Europe could deter and, if need be, mount a defense against an enemy attack based upon superior conventional forces by means of the threat to employ theater-nuclear and ultimately strategic-nuclear weapons. The deterrence credibility of NATO's escalatory options was inextricably linked both to the perceived ability of the Alliance to employ its theater-nuclear systems and to the willingness of the United States to invoke its own strategic-nuclear forces in defense of Western Europe should it become necessary. With the codification of superpower strategic parity in the SALT I Accords[2] and, later, the develop-

1. According to the Resolution, Alliance governments were to agree on a program for theater-nuclear modernization and to provide for a deployment of such forces in several alliance countries in order to

shape the modernization program exclusively towards strengthening deterrence and escalation control, thereby improving the Alliance strategy of "flexible response" and assuring the stabilization of the overall strategic nuclear balance without attempting to create a separate nuclear balance in Europe.

See "Texts Originating in the Military and Political Committees, A Recommendation on Theater Nuclear Forces," in *Twenty-Fifth Meeting of the North Atlantic Assembly* (held at Ottawa, Canada) October 22-27, 1979. Report of the U.S. Delegation (Washington, DC: Government Printing Office, February 1980), pp. 810-11.

2. It will be recalled that in 1972 the first round of negotiations between the United States and the Soviet Union to restrict their respective intercontinental nuclear weapons deployments resulted in the ABM Treaty, which restricted U.S. and Soviet deployments of strategic defensive systems, and the Interim agreement on Offensive Missile

ment by the Soviet Union of a first-strike counterforce option that is considered to pose a threat to U.S. land-based strategic forces, the uppermost rung of the NATO escalatory ladder was perceived in Europe to have been broken. As a result, the importance of NATO's theater-nuclear and conventional capabilities for deterrence was increased.[3] However, the ability of the Alliance to rely on its theater-nuclear assets as a means of sustaining the credibility of NATO's escalatory option and hence its deterrent posture was itself questionable because of the augmentation of Soviet/Warsaw Pact theater forces, especially capabilities designed to destroy NATO nuclear weapons.

THE EVOLVING
EUROSTRATEGIC BALANCE

Over the last decade the Soviet Union has modernized its theater-nuclear forces, including tactical air forces and highly accurate nuclear-capable battlefield support and long-range missile systems. As demonstrated in the SU-19 Fencer aircraft, Soviet Frontal Aviation forces have

been augmented to deploy nuclear munitions for low-altitude penetration and attack against airfields and other targets deep within Western Europe, including NATO nuclear weapons sites and storage facilities. Soviet shorter-range nuclear systems have likewise been upgraded with the development of the SS-21, a follow-up to the FROG, and the SS-22 and SS-23 battlefield support systems. Each of these three new generation missiles is reported to possess improved reaction times and greater reliability, accuracy, handling characteristics, and ranges over their predecessor systems.[4] Such systems provide increased firepower support for Soviet/Warsaw Pact armored units, which are capable of operating in contaminated (nuclear/chemical-biological) environments.

However, of the new-generation Soviet theater-nuclear systems, none has generated greater concern in Western Europe than the SS-20 Intermediate Range Ballistic Missile (IRBM). The SS-20 is a highly accurate, two-stage ballistic missile that incorporates a warhead with three independently targeted reentry vehicles, each capable of employing a payload of 100 to 150 kilotons.[5]

Launchers, which provided for unequal ceilings for the United States and the Soviet Union with respect to deployment of ICBM and SLBM launchers. It was assumed that the U.S. advantage in warhead numbers at that time would offset the numerical superiority in launchers granted to the Soviet Union —1618 to 1054 in ICBM launchers and 950 to 710 in SLBM launchers, with the Soviet Union allowed a total of 62 strategic submarines, SSBNs, to 44 for the United States.

3. Helmut Schmidt, Chancellor of the Federal Republic of Germany, publicly underscored this point in a speech before the members of the International Institute for Strategic Studies in London in 1977. Chancellor Schmidt's address was reprinted in its entirety in *Survival* (the journal of the International Institute for Strategic Studies), July/August 1977, p. 178.

4. The SS-22 is the successor system to the SCUD B, while the SS-23 is a follow-on system to the Scaleboard. In addition, the Soviet Union has also developed two dual-capable artillery pieces (203 mm and 240 mm) which are currently deployed only in the USSR but which could be rapidly transferred to East European positions as necessary. See Robert Kennedy, "Soviet Theater Nuclear Forces," *Air Force Magazine* (Soviet Aerospace Almanac 1981), March 1981, pp. 78-83.

5. See Major General Edward Fursdon, "Soviet SS-20 Sites are Doubled/SS-20 Missile has Triple Warhead," *Daily Telegraph* (London) 7 February 1981. A version of the SS-20 has been tested with four warheads. Reportedly, this variant also incorporates a longer-range capability.

As a result of the deployment of as many as 180 SS-20 launchers, the Soviet Union has arrayed against Western Europe at least 600 warheads capable of striking hardened NATO targets, including nuclear weapons sites.[6] According to one assessment, the SS-20 has provided the Soviet Union with an in-theater "selective" targeting capability that it previously had lacked.[7] Together with the new generation, long-range strategic bomber (Backfire), the SS-20 has the capacity for destroying "virtually every NATO base, weapons storage site" and, in the case of the SS-20, "with negligible warning."[8] For Europeans, the capability of the SS-20 in particular contributes to the perception of a Eurostrategic balance that favors the Soviet Union. Whereas few in Europe believe that the Soviet Union would actually employ its SS-20s against Western Europe, it is widely conceded that in a crisis, Moscow—by virtue of the perceived imbalance of Eurostrategic forces—could extract from the Europeans political concessions, in effect resulting in the neutralization of NATO Europe.

Whatever the validity of hypotheses of the political leverage conferred by superior military power, it remains the case that the Soviet deployment of the SS-20 has been largely responsible for the debate in the Alliance over the deficiencies of NATO's deterrent posture. In particular, it has been widely noted that in contrast to the emphasis of the Soviet Union on a theater attack strategy and tactical employment options that provide for the use of nuclear weapons, NATO planning has consistently adhered to its Flexible Response doctrine with its attendant concepts of defensive planning, graduated response, and a nuclear firebreak or a pause before implementing its nuclear options—assuming, of course, that such remain an Alliance prerogative. In theory, the Flexible Response strategy would allow an adversary time in which to reflect upon the consequences of a decision to use nuclear weapons, in the hope that he would conclude that the risks attendant with such use would far outweigh any anticipated benefits. In practice, however, the Soviet Union, by its own admission, expects that should war occur in Europe, it is likely to involve the use of nuclear weapons, and in that context nuclear weapons employment enhances the ability of combat forces to attain surprise on the battlefield. Because of their concentration of firepower and time-urgent capability, nuclear weapons provide the basis for rapidly securing offensive operations and by their first use can predetermine the outcome of battle. In other words, the use of nuclear weapons is regarded by the Soviet Union as an opportunity to alter the balance of forces on a battlefield by destroying the strongest areas of an opponent's defense; in the case of Europe, this means NATO's theater-nuclear weapons.

6. In January 1981, U.S. Chairman of the Joint Chiefs of Staff General David Jones reported to Congress that the Soviet Union had in place some 180 SS-20 launchers, deployed in the Western Soviet Union, with over 100 Backfires assigned to Soviet European aviation forces. It is estimated that the Soviet Union will increase its inventory of Backfires with the addition of up to 30 aircraft per year. See *United States Military Posture, for Fiscal Year 1982*, an Overview by General David C. Jones, USAF, with Supplement Prepared by the Organization of the Joint Chiefs of Staff, Presented to Congress January 1981, pp. 24 and 102.

7. Quoted from paragraph 35 of "General Report on the Security of the Alliance: The Role of Nuclear Weapons," presented by Mr. Klaas G. de Vries (Netherlands), General Rapporteur, in *Twenty-Fifth Meeting of the North Atlantic Assembly*, p. 33.

8. Quoted in Kennedy, *Air Force Magazine*, pp. 78-83.

SURVIVABILITY OF
ALLIANCE NUCLEAR FORCES

In general, current generation NATO theater-nuclear systems are extremely vulnerable to preemption by Soviet/Warsaw Pact forces. For example, its 108 Pershing 1A land-based medium range ballistic missile launchers are deployed at sites that are relatively well-known throughout Europe, as are NATO's nuclear-capable aircraft. For that reason and because they possess low reaction rates, their vulnerability to preemption by enemy forces is perceived to be high; whereas, in contrast, new-generation Soviet theater-nuclear forces, especially the SS-20 (which is deployed in a mobile mode), are considered to be more survivable than their predecessor systems. Others of the Alliance's nuclear-capable systems are similarly vulnerable to enemy preemption and, in the case of NATO's Quick Reaction Alert Aircraft, are likely to be interdicted in flight by enemy air defenses, assuming they can escape destruction on the ground. Even at the battlefield level, NATO's nuclear-capable artillery and howitzers have become less survivable with the modernization of the FROG, SCUD, and SCALEBOARD surface-to-surface missile systems.

The most survivable of NATO's nuclear systems are its long-range ballistic missile forces, deployed at sea aboard Poseidon strategic submarines. However, European members of the Alliance have expressed doubts about the willingness of an American president to invoke the use of such weapons in a European contingency because of the variety of retaliatory options that would be available to the Soviet Union directed against the U.S. homeland. For that reason, the prospective contribution of long-range ballistic missiles to the deterrent posture of the Alliance is less than convincing, despite their perceived survivability. Taken together, the deficiencies of the Alliance's nuclear deterrent posture and the corresponding growth of Soviet theater-nuclear forces generated momentum within NATO in support of nuclear force modernization. The considered decision of the High Level Group to focus its initial efforts on the modernization of NATO's long-range theater-nuclear forces was based on the urgent need to "offset" Soviet deployments of the SS-20, at once the most visible and potentially the most dangerous threat, from a military-political perspective, to European security.

RATIONALE FOR A
LONG-RANGE CAPABILITY

If the need for enhanced survivability with regard to NATO TNF deployments is considered by Alliance members to be crucial to preserving the deterrent posture of NATO, the development of credible retaliatory options was assessed as essential to the viability of the tactical planning concepts of the Flexible Response strategy. With the potential of the SS-20 for attaining high accuracy of delivery and because of its capacity for reload—leading to speculation that the system has been designed for use in a "sustained military campaign"—the corresponding deficiency in NATO's ability to strike hardened targets in the Soviet Union was perceived by Alliance members as a shortcoming that had to be corrected if deterrence was to be putatively maintained. While NATO planners did not consider necessary the development of a capability precisely symmetrical to the SS-20, they did emphasize the deployment of an "offsetting" capability for assured response should deterrence fail. Essentially this meant the development and deployment of capabilities that possessed ranges and payload/accuracy combinations to strike targets in the Soviet Union itself.

In conceding the possibility that a conflict in Europe conceivably could involve the use of nuclear weapons and that the Soviet Union itself might be subjected to nuclear strikes, the latter has engaged in programs of active and passive defense designed to limit the damage to the USSR in a nuclear war. In addition to upgrading its active systems of defense, including ABM/BMD and surface-to-air radars, launchers, and interceptors, the Soviet Union has undertaken a massive program of passive defense that includes the hardening and dispersal of major command centers as well as high-priority—the so-called Class A—industries and military facilities. The effect of such programs has been to raise the targeting requirements of NATO (and U.S.) nuclear-capable systems, resulting in the need for weapons with increased accuracy potentials in combination with larger payload and throw-weight capabilities; hence the emphasis by the Alliance on systems like the Pershing II and the cruise missile having terminal guidance and a longer-range capability. In this sense, the choice by NATO of the Extended Range Pershing II and the ground-launched cruise missile as the basis of Alliance efforts to restore the credibility of its deterrent posture is also regarded by Alliance members as providing Western Europe with an important military option should deterrence fail. In other words, the NATO decision to modernize its long-range theater-nuclear forces is viewed by some strategists as the basis from which credible warfighting options could be developed.

TNF AND THE DEFENSE OF WESTERN EUROPE

In the event of a Soviet/Warsaw Pact attack against Western Europe, it is the view of some in NATO that the conventional forces of the Alliance would be unable, without the firepower afforded by battlefield nuclear weapons—including perhaps the fission-fusion Enhanced Radiation Warhead (ERW)[9]—to hold their defensive positions until reinforcements arrived from across the Atlantic. Because Soviet/Warsaw Pact forces are highly mobile, configured for a rapid advance across Western Europe, and incorporate significant firepower for breakthroughs in NATO's defense lines, it has been suggested[10] that unless Allied armies can bring to bear large concentrations of firepower against enemy forces and therein break the momentum of their attack, a NATO defense of Western Europe is unlikely to be sustained.

According to the military literature of the Soviet Union, and based on observations of Warsaw Pact maneuvers, the tactics for exploiting breeches in NATO lines are based on the echeloning of capabilities and the ability to field quantitatively superior forces in a rapid

9. The Enhanced Radiation Weapon, popularly referred to as "the neutron bomb," is in reality a low blast weapon whose release of neutrons could penetrate enemy armor and incapacitate its crew without destroying large land areas and structures. Its deployment in Europe has become a contentious issue largely because of an inadequate public understanding of its potential and technical capability.

10. See Jacquelyn K. Davis and Robert L. Pfaltzgraff, "The Shifting Euro-Atlantic Military Balance—Some Avenues of Redress," *Atlantic Community in Crisis* (Elmsford, NY: Pergamon Press, 1979), pp. 91-148.

manner. One aspect of the defense tactics of NATO forces must be to deny the Soviet/Warsaw Pact armies the means of concentrating their capabilities to exploit a breakthrough in Western Europe. Inasmuch as Soviet/Warsaw Pact second echelon forces comprise the essence of their capability for exploiting breakthroughs in allied defensive positions, Alliance planning for a European contingency needs to incorporate means of destroying Soviet/Warsaw Pact second echelon forces. One way in which this can be done is through the threat to employ theater-nuclear forces. The potential use of TNF against enemy formations would carry profound implications for the Soviet attack strategy, which relies on the massing of forces to overcome NATO defenses. The use, or threat of use, of NATO's theater-nuclear weapons would force Soviet/Warsaw Pact formations to disperse, adversely affecting the momentum of the offensive.

Operationally, the second echelon targeting concept is dependent upon the use of long-range, time-urgent, accurate capabilities such as are embodied in the Pershing II and which may eventually be incorporated into the cruise missile. From a military perspective, therefore, the modernization of NATO's theater-nuclear forces is considered necessary to support the development of a retaliatory option that would become necessary if NATO conventional forces failed to sustain a defense of Western Europe. In such a contingency, ground-launched cruise missiles would be directed against important fixed targets behind enemy lines, including perhaps staging areas and weapons storage sites in the Soviet Union and Eastern Europe. Reliance on the cruise missile to perform deep-interdiction missions against fixed targets would free existing NATO nuclear assets, including its Quick Reaction Alert aircraft, for use in more efficient manners—notably in a ground-attack support role contributing potentially to the favorable outcome of the land battle for NATO. In other words, the deployment of a mix of LRTNF offers a flexibility of strike options that is not attainable with current-generation systems. Each system is considered by NATO planners to possess distinctive characteristics that complement those of the other system, with the Pershing II having a high potential for penetrating enemy defenses and the cruise missile having lower life-cycle costs and a projected longer-range capability.

The decided preference for deployment of land-based systems was rooted in numerous considerations, not the least important of which relates to the issue of public opinion and perceptions of the Eurostrategic balance. Deployment on the territory of the European members of NATO reinforces the perception of greater commitment by the United States to the defense/deterrence of Western Europe. The deployment on land of NATO's LRTNF provides tangible evidence of the commitment of the Alliance to maintain a Eurostrategic balance and therein a credible deterrent posture in relation to the East.

Militarily, a land-based TNF deployment provides for greater accuracy in targeting and thus allows for the development of a hard-target employment policy that is consistent with the changing nature of the European security environment. Because of the variety of payload/accuracy combinations that are made possible by deployment of a land-based system, the flexibility offered by ground-based systems is unmatched by their sea-based or air mobile counterparts.

Nevertheless, there are those who argue that, deployed at sea, new-generation NATO theater-nuclear forces would be more survivable than land-based systems and for that reason NATO should review its decision of December 1979, opting instead for the deployment of sea-launched cruise and/or ballistic missiles. It cannot be emphasized too strongly that the political-psychological implications of such a decision would profoundly affect the cohesion of the Atlantic alliance, especially with regard to the perception of European allies as to the United States' seriousness of intent to engage its resources in defense of Western Europe. More fundamentally, in the view of the Europeans, the deterrence credibility of the Flexible Response strategy would be seriously eroded if the means of implementing NATO's escalatory option were removed from the theater of operations. From this perspective the threshold of deterrence would necessarily be raised at a time when there exist serious doubts about the ability of NATO's conventional forces to hold their assigned positions and repel attacks by Soviet/Warsaw Pact forces designed to break through defensive lines.

As the modernization of NATO's TNF enhances the credibility of the defense options provided for in the Flexible Response Strategy, it also accords with the adoption by the United States of a Countervailing Strategy. As the basis for strengthening the U.S. deterrent posture in relation to the Soviet Union, the Countervailing Strategy provides for the development of an array of employment options—including

counterforce as well as countervalue strikes—appropriate to a range of contingencies, from an all-out massive strategic exchange to a limited strike against Europe. Articulated in Presidential Decision Memorandum 59 (PD 59), the Countervailing Strategy is not a new strategic doctrine or a radical departure from U.S. strategic policy of the last decade. It is, according to Former Secretary of Defense Harold Brown,

more precisely, a refinement, a recodification of previous statements of our strategic policy. PD 59 takes the same essential strategic doctrine and restates it more clearly, more cogently, in the light of current and prospective conditions and capabilities—Soviet and United States—which have changed during the past ten years.[11]

Conceptually, the Countervailing Strategy and NATO's Flexible Response Doctrine are inextricably linked because the perceived credibility and strength of U.S. strategic-nuclear forces provide the basis of the American extended deterrent and hence the U.S. nuclear force deployments in Western Europe. For this reason, prescribed development under a Countervailing Strategy of employment options for a range of possible contingencies embodies planning for European scenarios in which theater- and strategic-nuclear forces might be used. In this context the planned modernization of NATO's long-range theater-nuclear forces assumes increased significance, in that it contributes to the overall

11. Statement of the Honorable Harold Brown, U.S. Secretary of Defense in *Nuclear War Strategy* Hearing on Presidential Directive 59, Committee on Foreign Relations, U.S., Senate, 96th Cong., 2nd sess. (Top Secret Hearing held on 16 September 1980, and sanitized on 18 February 1981), (Washington, DC: Government Printing Office, 1981), p. 8.

deterrent posture of the United States and the West in general.

THE POLITICAL DEBATE OVER TNF MODERNIZATION

Notwithstanding the perceived importance of TNF to maintaining the defense/deterrence posture of NATO, increasingly there are within Western Europe those who are opposed to the modernization of NATO's long-range theater-nuclear systems. In this European view, the decision to modernize these forces would be acceptable only if accompanied by negotiations with the Soviet Union designed to limit deployment of those systems. In fact, the resolution that was adopted by the North Atlantic Assembly provided for implementation of the modernization decision

in such a way that concrete results of arms control negotiations with the Soviet Union can be taken into account at any time during the period between the decision on the program (December 12, 1979) and the earliest possible deployment of new systems in 1983, including the possibility of renouncing the new medium-range nuclear weapons, if and to the degree that the Soviet Union is prepared to reduce its own long-range theater nuclear forces (LRTNF).[12]

Some NATO members suggest that the decision on modernization should be delayed until negotiations are actually underway. An amendment to that effect was introduced by Klaas G. de Vries of the Netherlands during the Twenty-fifth and Twenty-sixth Meetings of the North Atlantic Assembly.[13] While the de

12. "Texts Originating in the Military and Political Committees," p. 811.
13. The de Vries amendment recommended that the North Atlantic Council "pursue efforts in SALT III to negotiate satisfactory restrictions on theater nuclear forces

Vries proposal was rejected on the floor of the Assembly on both occasions, its substance has attracted considerable support in Europe since the adoption by the ministerial group of the TNF modernization proposal. Particularly among the youth of Western Europe, and among a broad segment of European publics as well, there exists an anathema to nuclear-related issues. Especially in the military areas and in the context of the NATO TNF decision, opposition to the modernization of Alliance forces is based on the fear of adverse reaction by the Soviet Union. Opposition arises also from the apprehension that TNF modernization would commit Western Europe to what is considered a senseless arms race that is bound to result in miscalculation and nuclear war.

This apparent alienation from defense—but particularly nuclear weapons—is thus the product of a conception of the Soviet Union as having only inherently defensive motivations and the view that the status quo that has brought unparalleled peace, stability, and prosperity to Western Europe can be sustained without major improvements in NATO forces to offset those of the Soviet Union.[14] From this perspec-

before making any decision on new deployments." Reported in *Twenty-Fifth Meeting of the North Atlantic Assembly*, p. 810.
14. For example, in recent weeks a youth organization associated with the Free Democratic Party of the Federal German Republic, the ruling coalition party with the Social Democratic Party (SPD) and the party of Foreign Minister Hans Dietrich Genscher, "has urged West Germany to abandon NATO's decision to station new medium-range nuclear missiles in Europe on the ground that the program represents only the interests of the United States." Moreover, at a party convention held in Leverkusen in March 1981, the young Democrats attacked the German Foreign Minister personally for his rejection of a proposal by the Soviet Union for a mora-

tive even the deployment of the SS-20 IRBM has been explained as a defensive requirement, rather than as part of Soviet offensive strategy. That such arguments have been advanced, notably by Herbert Wehner and others in the left wing of the Social Democratic Party in the Federal Republic of Germany, bespeaks a persistent uncertainty in Western Europe about the NATO decision that has led some analysts to question whether modern theater-nuclear systems will be deployed.

The Soviet Union, for its part, has sought to exploit intra-Alliance divisions on the TNF issue by supporting a two-pronged strategy which, on one hand, calls for a moratorium on the deployment of Eurostrategic weapons in Europe; while Moscow, on the other hand, brandishes its military power and suggests that implementation of the NATO decision would carry adverse consequences for relations with the Soviet Union. All the while, the Soviet Union continues to deploy its own

torium on deploying long-range nuclear systems in Europe. See John Vinocur, "Youth Group Tied to Bonn Assails NATO Missile Plan," *New York Times*, 9 March 1981.

long-range theater-nuclear systems at the rate of one new SS-20 launcher every five days.

Conversely, the continued Soviet military buildup in Europe could galvanize NATO members to strengthen the deterrent posture of the Alliance. At the very least, the continued erosion of the Eurostrategic balance will force NATO into an in-depth examination of the Alliance's deterrent posture and its reliance on a strategy of Flexible Response. If modernization of NATO's LRTNF is rejected by Alliance members, then the basis for the escalatory threat upon which NATO has long relied will have been destroyed. Having agreed to modernize theater-nuclear systems and thus to redress asymmetries currently favoring the Soviet Union in Europe, the Alliance confronts the need to move as rapidly as possible toward actual deployment. The failure to do so, taken in context of the need for the Alliance to redress present imbalances in forces across a broad spectrum, would cast doubt not only upon the strategy of Flexible Response, but also upon the basic premise of the Alliance: the need to deter a potential adversary at various levels, from the battlefield to the nuclear level.

The United States and Extended Security Commitments: East Asia

By HAROLD C. HINTON

ABSTRACT: In East Asia and the Western Pacific the United States faces an impressive recent Soviet military (especially naval) buildup, continuing and serious tension in Korea, a Japan that to date has not done much to put itself in a viable defensive posture, and potential for further unrest in Southeast Asia. In the last year or two of the Carter administration, accordingly, a trend begun a decade earlier toward American military disengagement from the region was reversed. The Reagan administration is almost certain to maintain this reversal and to cultivate closer relations with South Korea and Taiwan than did its predecessor, while trying at the same time to establish a strategic relationship of some sort with the People's Republic of China. The purpose of the latter move is, or would be, to help cope with rising Soviet assertiveness in the region. Moscow itself claims—prematurely, to say the least—that the United States, Japan, and China are forming an alliance against it and is especially anxious that the United States and everyone else refrain from transferring modern arms to China.

Harold C. Hinton is Professor of Political Science and International Affairs at The George Washington University. He has written and traveled widely on and in Asia since his first visit, as an Army historian in 1945. He specializes in Chinese politics and foreign policy and Sino-Soviet relations.

Note: The writer is grateful to the Earhart Foundation for support of part of the research on which this study is based.

E AST Asia abounds in superlatives. Its ocean, its populations, and its economic growth rates are the greatest in the world. In places its land masses dominate vital sealanes, especially those linking the Indian Ocean, the China Sea, and the Western Pacific. Its resources, although not overwhelming, are impressive in many categories. More people have been killed in or died from armed combat in East Asia since World War II than anywhere else.

East Asia and the approaches to it across the Pacific have held a correspondingly great interest for the United States since it expanded to the Pacific in the mid-nineteenth century. The fall of Japan in 1945, almost entirely to American military power, left the victor dominant in the Pacific and along its western littoral for a time, but not for long. The dramatic emergence of the (Communist) People's Republic of China (PRC), its alliance for a decade (approximately 1950-60) with the Soviet Union, revulsion in the United States over casualties suffered and costs incurred in Korea and still more in Vietnam, the economic and political maturation of the Asian regional states, and most recently the growth of Soviet military (especially naval) power in East Asia and the Western Pacific have all rendered an active—to say nothing of a dominant—American role in the region controversial at home and difficult to play in the field.

THE SOVIET UNION AND
EAST ASIA[1]

The Soviet Union is ruled by the only important elite in the world

1. For background see Walter Kolarz, *The Peoples of the Soviet Far East* (New York: Praeger, 1954); John J. Stephan, *Sakhalin: A History* (Oxford: Clarendon Press, 1971); John J. Stephan, *The Kuril Islands: Russo-Japanese Frontier in the Pacific* (Oxford: Clarendon Press, 1974); David J. Dallin, *Soviet Russia and the Far East* (New Haven, CT: Yale University Press, 1948); Max Beloff, *Soviet Policy in the Far East, 1944-1951* (London: Oxford University Press, 1953); Harold C. Hinton, "East Asia," in Kurt London ed., *The Soviet Union in World Politics* (Boulder, CO: Westview Press, 1980), pp. 145-71; Rodger Swearingen, *The Soviet Union and Postwar Japan: Escalating Challenge and Response* (Stanford: Hoover Institution, 1978); Donald S. Zagoria, "Soviet Policy and Prospects in East Asia," *International Security* 5(2): 66-78 (Fall 1980); Harold C. Hinton,

that drastically overestimates the political utility of large, strong military forces and an aggressive military posture; to date there is only one Finland. Moscow has never enjoyed much strictly political influence in East Asia, except for the case of China in the early 1950s. Since then shrill Soviet hostility to Peking has aroused resentment on the part of a region to which China, whatever its shortcomings, unquestionably belongs by geographic and cultural right. The Soviet Union is feared by many Asians who live around its Asian periphery and distrusted by many more throughout the region; even the Communist Parties in Asia tend to pay more attention to Peking than to Moscow. The latter's economic influence in the region is not much greater, although the lure of its Siberian resources, as yet largely untapped, exert a potent attraction on Japan and although its economic aid to Vietnam and Laos has yielded substantial dividends of various kinds—mainly military—in Indochina. The Soviet invasion of Afghanistan has greatly intensified the suspicion with which Moscow is regarded throughout Asia.

Moscow's main assets not only for protecting its Asian borders but for projecting its influence beyond them are clearly military. According to recent intelligence, they consist, in the Western Pacific and

"The Soviet Campaign for Collective Security in Asia," *Pacific Community* 7(2): 147-61 (January 1976); "Shadow of the Kremlin," *Far Eastern Economic Review* 24 August 1978, pp. 20-24, 26-28, 33-36; "A Sino-Soviet Detente?" *Far Eastern Economic Review* 31 August 1979, pp. 25-32; "Moscow's Rouble Strategy," *Far Eastern Economic Review* 7 September 1979, pp. 43-44, 49-54; Strobe Talbott, "The Soviets Stir up the Pacific," *Time* 23 March 1981, pp. 53-55; Thomas R. Robinson, "The Soviet Union and Asia in 1980," *Asian Survey* 21(1): 14-30 (January 1981).

therefore in an area directly relevant to American interests, of major established naval and/or air base complexes at Vladivostok and Petropavlovsk (on Kamchatka)—both of which, however, have ice problems in winter—and of much newer ones at Camranh Bay and Danang in Vietnam. The Soviet Pacific Fleet controls one carrier (the *Minsk*, on which both ASW helicopters and fixed-wing aircraft are based), approximately 150 Badger bombers, 11 cruisers, 25 destroyers, 48 frigates (many of the latter three types of vessels being armed with guided missiles), 80 attack submarines, and 30 strategic (nuclear missile) submarines. There is no doubt that these are by far the strongest naval forces normally on station in the Western Pacific (as distinct from the entire Pacific), or that two major semienclosed bodies of water off the Northeast Asian coast—the Sea of Japan and the Sea of Okhotsk—are virtual Soviet lakes. It is also probable (although for obvious reasons not certain) that in the event of general war—a mere regional war between the superpowers appears an unreal scenario—Soviet naval forces in the Western Pacific could in theory deny access to an opponent and interrupt, to one degree or another, Japan's vital sealanes. In reality, however, the situation is not so one-sided; American, Japanese, and South Korean units would try, probably with considerable success, to block the three key straits (La Perouse, or Soya, between Sakhalin and Hokkaido; Tsugaru, between Hokkaido and Honshu; and Tsushima, between Japan and Korea) and thereby bottle up a large part of the Soviet Pacific Fleet. The cloud enveloping this silver lining is the fact that the latest Soviet SLBNs have the capability to

strike the United States from firing positions in the Sea of Japan; in turn, this piece of bad news is alleviated by the excellence of American ASW techniques, which are more advanced than those of the Soviet adversary. The new Soviet facilities on the Vietnamese coast, acquired as a direct result of Moscow's support—limited though it was—of Vietnam during the brief Sino-Vietnamese war of 1979 and smaller than their American counterparts in the Philippines across the South China Sea, give the Soviet Pacific Fleet a position threatening the Straits of Malacca and other important areas on and around the South China Sea; however, in case of general war this position would be highly vulnerable to attack.[2] As for influence, the Soviet Pacific Fleet of course shows the flag in the Western Pacific and the Indian Ocean, with some but by no means overwhelming effect; the ASEAN states (Thailand, Malaysia, Singapore, Indonesia, and the Philippines) have refused it the right to make port calls. Singapore and the Philippines are especially conscious, for obvious geographical reasons, of a potential Soviet naval threat.

THE SINO-SOVIET CONFRONTATION[3]

It is on China that Moscow's military weight in Asia mainly bears.

2. See John M. Collins, *U.S.-Soviet Military Balance: Concepts and Capabilities, 1960-1980* (New York: McGraw-Hill, 1980), pp. 355-59.

3. For background see Howard L. Boorman et al., *Moscow-Peking Axis: Strengths and Strains* (New York: Harper & Row, 1957); Donald S. Zagoria, *The Sino-Soviet Conflict, 1956-1961* (Princeton: Princeton University Press, 1962); William E. Griffith, *The Sino-Soviet Rift* (Cambridge: MIT Press, 1964); William E. Griffith, *Sino-Soviet Relations, 1964-1965* (Cambridge: MIT Press, 1967); Richard Wich, *Sino-Soviet Crisis*

Since shortly after 1969, when the border dispute between the two giants of Eurasia, piled on a bitter political quarrel, erupted in a massive and persisting military confrontation, the Soviet Union has maintained about one-quarter of its rapidly growing military might in its Siberian and Far Eastern territories. Just as its naval and air forces in those regions are targeted mainly on Japan and on American forces in the Western Pacific, so its ground forces east and south of, say, Novosibirsk are a direct threat to China. These consist of approximately 45

divisions (heavily armed but mostly understrength and not combat ready) backed by 850 fighter aircraft, elaborate air defenses, and both tactical and strategic nuclear weapons.[4]

Against this formidable array China disposes, in its four military regions bordering on the Soviet Union and its Mongolian satellite (Shenyang or Mukden, Peking or Beijing, Lanzhou, and Xinjiang or Sinkiang), approximately 100 Main Force (first line) divisions, much weaker in arms and transport than their Soviet counterparts and stationed a considerable distance from the border for both tactical and logistical reasons, backed by almost negligible (again by contrast with the opposition) air, logistical, and other support and by several dozen not very sophisticated surface-to-surface nuclear missiles capable of hitting Soviet territory.[5] Peking understands very well its vulnerability, the danger in which it finds itself, and the need to compensate for its military vulnerability by keeping its diplomatic fences—especially those linking it with the United States—in good repair.[6]

The Sino-Soviet relationship has three basic possible futures: accommodation, war, or continued confrontation. There is at present no convincing evidence or reasonable likelihood that an accommodation is

Politics: A Study of Political Change and Communication (Cambridge: Harvard University Press, 1980); Morris Rothenberg, *Whither China: The View from the Kremlin* (Miami: Center for Advanced International Studies, University of Miami, 1977); Victor Louis, *The Coming Decline of the Chinese Empire* (New York: Times Books, 1979); Dennis J. Doolin, *Territorial Claims in the Sino-Soviet Conflict* (Stanford: Hoover Institution, 1965); George Ginsburgs and Carl F. Pinkele, *The Sino-Soviet Territorial Dispute, 1949-1964* (New York: Praeger, 1978); Thomas W. Robinson, "The Sino-Soviet Border Dispute: Background, Development, and the March 1969 Clashes," *The American Political Science Review* 66(4): 1175-1202 (December 1972); Raymond L. Garthoff, ed., *Sino-Soviet Military Relations* (New York: Praeger, 1966); Morton H. Halperin, ed., *Sino-Soviet Relations and Arms Control* (Cambridge: MIT Press, 1967); Harold C. Hinton, *The Sino-Soviet Confrontation: Implications for the Future* (New York: Crane, Russak, 1976); "The Border Issue: China and the Soviet Union," *Studies in Comparative Communism* 2(3-4): 121-382 (July/October 1969); Harrison Salisbury, *War Between Russia and China* (New York: W. W. Norton and Bantam Books, 1969); Harold C. Hinton, *The Bear at the Gate: Chinese Policymaking under Soviet Pressure* (Washington: American Enterprise Institute and Stanford: Hoover Institution, 1971); Drew Middleton, *The Duel of the Giants* (New York: Scribner, 1978); Harry Gelman, "Outlook for Sino-Soviet Relations," *Problems of Communism* 28(5-6): 50-66 (September/December 1979); Jonathan D. Pollak, "Chinese Global Strategy and Soviet Power," *Problems of Communism* 21(1): 54-69 (January-February 1981).

4. Collins, *U.S.-Soviet Military Balance*, p. 355; *Asian Security 1980* (Tokyo: Research Institute for Peace and Security, 1980), pp. 30-31; "Ivan's Arms Around Manchuria," *Far Eastern Economic Review*, 28 January 1977, p. 60.

5. *The Military Balance, 1979-1980* (London: International Institute for Strategic Studies, 1979), p. 60; *Asian Security 1980*, pp. 89-91.

6. See Henry Kissinger, *White House Years* (Boston: Little, Brown, 1979), pp. 166-67, 707.

feasible within the "foreseeable" future. War, meaning, in real terms, a Soviet attack on China, is certainly not unthinkable—Soviet capabilities for such an attack will improve markedly after the completion of the Baikal Amur Main Line Railway (BAM), 600 miles to the north of the Trans-Siberian, to the Pacific in the mid-1980s—but the risks to and disincentives for both sides, and not merely for the Chinese, are enormous and incalculable and will remain so: casualties (civilian as well as military), costs and damage, internal political stresses, diplomatic complications, and possible open-ended escalation. On balance, the most likely scenario is an indefinite prolongation—with variations, of course—of the present bizarre no-war-no-peace confrontation.

CHINA AS AN ASIAN POWER[7]

China's record since 1949 indicates that its leaders' undoubted aspirations to influence, in Asia above all, are tempered by a shrewd appreciation of the costs and risks involved. As Henry Kissinger foresaw,[8] the general Chinese tendency

7. For background see A. Doak Barnett, *China and the Major Powers in East Asia* (Washington: Brookings Institution, 1977); Harry G. Gelber, *Technology, Defense, and External Relations in China, 1975-1978* (Boulder, CO: Westview Press, 1979); Jay Taylor, *China and Southeast Asia: Peking's Relations with Revolutionary Movements* (New York: Praeger, 1974); Allen S. Whiting, *The Chinese Calculus of Deterrence: India and Indochina* (Ann Arbor: University of Michigan Press, 1975); *Asian Security 1980*, pp. 79-81, 84-86; Robert G. Sutter, *Chinese Foreign Policy After the Cultural Revolution* (Boulder, CO: Westview Press, 1978); Shinkichi Eto, "Recent Developments in Sino-Japanese Relations," *Asian Survey* 20(7): 726-43 (July 1980).
8. Kissinger, *The White House Years*, p. 177.

toward external caution has been intensified by the confrontation with the Soviet Union, both because Moscow has deflected and absorbed much of Peking's energy and because China needs the goodwill of the United States and the Asian countries as counterweights to its Soviet adversary. There is the additional important consideration that, as China's leaders have often said in recent years, Peking requires a stable international environment for the success of its modernization program, even though the program's level of dependence on foreign credits and technology has been considerably reduced by recent postponements and cancellations of overambitious contracts.

In Northeast Asia, an area of powerful neighbors and high military risks, Peking has adopted a low strategic posture. It values good relations with Japan, its most important trading partner. It encourages Tokyo to cultivate its security links with the United States and keep its distance from the Soviet "polar bear"; in August 1978 Peking and Tokyo signed a treaty of peace and friendship containing an anti-"hegemony" clause included at Chinese insistence and obviously aimed at Moscow. Since the Sino-American Shanghai Communiqué of February 1972 and the Sino-American announcement of 15 December 1978 on the establishment of diplomatic relations each also contains an antihegemony clause, there has been much speculation, especially in Moscow, that a trilateral anti-Soviet alliance is in the making in the Far East. If so, it is largely the result of heavy-handed Soviet behavior. Peking cultivates good relations with North Korea mainly in order to discourage it from tilting toward Moscow, but in reality the Chinese privately favor the retention of a strong United States-Republic of Korea security tie and the continued presence of American forces in South Korea.

The main direction in which China's assertive tendencies have made themselves felt in recent years has been that of its soft underbelly. Peking played an active although essentially secondary role—mainly logistical in nature—in Hanoi's protracted and successful drive for control over South Vietnam. But Peking claims the China Sea continental shelf and most of the islands on it, and in January 1974—mainly, it appears, in order to preempt Hanoi—it seized the Paracel Islands, about 200 miles southeast of Hainan, which are also claimed by Vietnam.[9] Hanoi's surging pro-Soviet tilt, its invasion of Cambodia (then under a pro-Chinese regime) at the end of 1978, and its expulsion of one million refugees mostly of Chinese descent infuriated Peking to the point where it launched a brief (mid-February to mid-March 1979) attack on Vietnam with the announced objective of teaching it a lesson. Considered strictly as a military operation this attack was far from impressive, and its main strategic result was probably Vietnam's prompt acquiescence in the establishment of the Soviet bases already mentioned. The Sino-Vietnamese confrontation continues, although at a somewhat less dramatic level; one of the main current issues is friction between Vietnam and Thailand, which is the friendliest of the ASEAN states to China, over Cambodia.

On 18 and 21 May 1980, China conducted two ICBM tests over the Southwest Pacific; the fact that they were highly inaccurate is probably less significant than the fact that they were monitored by a flotilla of 18 Chinese naval vessels. On this, the first occasion when China's navy had operated beyond the continental shelf, the ships performed some very complex maneuvers in a highly creditable manner.[10]

The prospect of increased Chinese military activity in and near the South China Sea is bound to exacerbate a feeling, already rather widespread in the ASEAN countries (especially Malaysia and above all Indonesia), that Peking is a serious—in fact, the most serious—external threat to the region. This apprehension, although largely unwarranted under present conditions, has been fed for many years by two undoubted facts: There are many (probably about 15 million) persons of predominantly Chinese descent and cultural orientation ("overseas Chinese") living in Southeast Asia, and Peking has long maintained, to the point of explicitly and repeatedly refusing to give up, political ties with the Communist Parties of the region. In reality, very few of the Southeast Asian Chinese would actively support a Chinese attempt to overthrow the governments of the region—an effort that in any event is not in prospect except in the case of Vietnam and its Laotian and Cambodian puppets—and the Communist Parties of the non-Communist Southeast Asian non-Communist states are in no instance a significant threat, or likely to become one, in the foreseeable future.

9. Harold C. Hinton, *The China Sea: The American Stake in Its Future* (New York: National Strategy Information Center, 1980), pp. 16-17.

10. Ibid., p. 23.

The Taiwan issue remains as a major piece of unfinished business on Peking's external—or, from its own point of view, domestic—agenda. With no observable effect on the entrenched Nationalist elite on the tight little island, Peking has promised it "autonomy," defined with increasing liberality, following unification; the older, more militant, term "liberation" is no longer used. Military tension between the two Chinas is at an all-time low, even though on the Taiwan side of the strait there is great nervousness on account of the loss of the United States as an ally at the beginning of 1980. On the other hand, Peking has stated that it will use force against Taiwan if—but, by implication, only if—the Nationalists refuse over a prolonged period to negotiate with the mainland or if the Soviet Union "interferes" in Taiwan.[11]

THE SECURITY OF JAPAN[12]

The contemporary security policy of Japan is heavily influenced by its

11. *Sino-American Relations: A New Turn* (Washington, DC: Government Printing Office for Senate Foreign Relations Committee, 1979), pp. 3-4.

12. For background see *Japan's Contribution to Military Stability in Northeast Asia* (Washington, DC: Government Printing Office for Senate Foreign Relations Committee, 1980); *Asian Security 1980*, pp. 182-95; Stuart E. Johnson with Joseph A. Yager, *The Military Equation in Northeast Asia* (Washington: Brookings Institution, 1979); John E. Endicott, *Japan's Nuclear Option: Political, Technical, and Strategic Factors* (New York: Praeger, 1975); Derek Davies, "Return of the Rising Sun," *Far Eastern Economic Review* 14 March 1980, pp. 18-22, and other articles in the same issue; Tomohisa Sakanaka, "Military Threats and Japan's Defense Capability," *Asian Survey* 20(7): 763-75 (July 1980); Yasuhisa Nakada, "Japan's Security Perceptions and Military Needs," in Onkar Marwah and Jonathan D. Pollack, eds., *Military Power and Policy in Asian States, China, India, Japan* (Boulder, CO: Westview Press, 1980), pp. 147-80.

catastrophic defeat in World War II, the acute "nuclear allergy" generated by the detonation (by the United States on Japanese soil, of course) of the only two nuclear weapons yet fired in anger, and the ensuing uniquely effective Allied (actually American) occupation. The famous Article IX of the 1946 constitution, drafted by Americans, renounces not only war but even the maintenance of armed forces. After the eruption of the Cold War in 1947-48, the Communist victory in China the following year, and the signing of the Sino-Soviet Treaty and the outbreak of the Korean war in 1950, to be sure, Japan began under American prodding to create a modest military establishment that is known to this day as the Self Defense Forces. Today the SDF, although modern and efficient in many respects, are far from adequate to defend Japan against an attack by the only likely adversary, the Soviet Union.

Japan's security therefore rests largely in the hands of the American forces in the region and the American guarantee, which, together with a generally favorable international environment, have enabled Japan to enjoy a virtual "free ride" in the matter of its security—until recently, at any rate. At the time Japan regained its independence through the peace treaty of 1951-52, it also signed, without having any real choice in the matter, a security treaty with the United States that, with some later modifications, is still in force. It obliges the Japanese side to do little more than tolerate the presence of American bases and forces and the use of the latter if necessary for the defense of Japan itself. The American side assumes the responsibility to do just that and to seek the concurrence of the Japanese government, which is tacitly assumed to be almost automatic in most cases, in the event of the tactical deployment of American forces from Japanese bases to areas outside Japan. Because of the nuclear allergy, nuclear weapons have not been stored—overtly, at least—at American bases in Japan, and this restriction was extended to Okinawa when that island reverted to Japanese jurisdiction in 1972.

Bases in Japan and Okinawa were vital to the American conduct of the Korean and Vietnam wars, and the Japanese economy contributed a mighty logistical component known in bureaucratic language as "offshore procurement." In 1969, President Nixon extracted from Premier Eisaku Sato a pledge to continue allowing the United States to use its bases in Japan for the defense of South Korea and Taiwan; the first half of this commitment is still in effect as far as can be determined, but the second clearly is not, because of the "normalization" of relations between Japan and the PRC in 1972, Tokyo's derecognition of the Republic of China at that time, and the Sino-Japanese treaty of peace and friendship of August 1978.

Current Japanese foreign policy, the matrix within which security policy is made and carried out, centers on (1) the maintenance of optimal economic relations with as many countries as possible, especially the industrial ones and the producers of important raw materials; (2) seeking the latter (oil, of course, above all) and also investment and export outlets more or less everywhere and in the case of Asia with minimum discrimination among China, Soviet Asia, and Southeast Asia; (3) a posture of nominal "equidistance" between the parties

to the Sino-Soviet confrontation while inevitably tilting in practice toward China as by far the less threatening and the culturally more compatible of the two; and (4), as already indicated, the cultivation of a close security and a profitable economic relationship with the American ally while doing the minimum necessary to redress the serious economic grievances felt in the United States—notably, the huge payments imbalance in favor of Japan and the related and well-known difficulties put in the way of American firms trying to sell or invest in Japan.

At the present time, after a decade of steady but unspectacular expansion and modernization, the SDF are organized approximately as follows. The Ground Self Defense Forces (army) dispose of 13 divisions, most of them stationed, for obvious reasons, on the northern island of Hokkaido, and appropriate equipment such as heavy tanks and heavy artillery, which are of excellent quality. The Maritime Self Defense Forces (navy) include no offensive units such as carriers but emphasize antiaircraft and antisubmarine capabilities—notably, 16 submarines designed for defensive missions. The Air Self Defense Forces (air force) control about 200 modern fighter and interceptor aircraft but no bombers. Air defenses are porous at present but improving rapidly, and the same appears to be true of ASW capabilities.

Primarily for domestic economic and political reasons, the Japanese defense budget has remained for many years at a little under one percent of GNP, the absolute figure approximating US$10 billion per year. Any proposal to increase the defense budget by even as little as one-tenth of one percent (of GNP) is controversial, but in recent years the perceived Soviet threat, as well as pure nationalism—counterbalanced, however, by a realization that rapid rearmament would be most disturbing to all of Japan's neighbors—has caused political support for a larger defense budget and stronger SDF to grow at a fairly rapid rate. The present government under Premier Zenko Suzuki has made an apparently firm, although not yet fully explicit, decision in that direction.[13] Some leading political figures seem to want a defense budget on the order of two to three percent of GNP. Similarly, the popularity of the American security connection has increased markedly —except, of course, on the extreme left; this change of attitude reflects in part a corresponding one in Peking, which for anti-Soviet reasons of its own has strongly supported since the early 1970s a higher Japanese defense budget and a continuing close Japanese-American security tie.

The Japanese perceive a Soviet threat in two entirely separate areas, the northern and the southern approaches to the Japanese islands.

In 1945 Moscow took from the collapsing Japanese Empire the islands of Sakhalin and the Kurils. For complex historical reasons, Japanese irredentism toward these "Northern Territories" confines itself to a demand for the two smaller islands (or groups) of Habomai and Shikotan, which the Japanese have always considered to be attached to Hokkaido rather than the Kurils, plus the larger islands of Etorofu and Kunashiri just to the north. For powerful reasons of its own relating to the naval impor-

13. Derek Davies, "Suzuki Surrenders to Austerity," *Far Eastern Economic Review* 16 January 1981, pp. 24-26.

tance of the Kurils and its nervousness over other (especially Chinese) claims to territory currently controlled by the Soviet Union, Moscow is most unlikely to return any of these islands to Japan; in fact, in 1979, significant Soviet forces were stationed on the disputed islands for the first time, apparently partly in retaliation for the signing of the Sino-Japanese peace treaty with its obnoxious (to Moscow) antihegemony clause. All this casts serious doubt on occasional Soviet hints and statements that the islands might be returned to Japan as part of a peace settlement, no such treaty having yet been signed between the Soviet Union and Japan since World War II. The doubt is powerfully reinforced by the fact that Moscow is concerned over what it regards as the emergence of an entente directed against it and comprised of Japan, the United States, and China.

Japan has only a small petroleum stockpile and imports about 90 percent of its vast requirements from the Middle East, principally the Persian Gulf, hardly an area noted for political stability. Tokyo tries to keep on good terms with the supplying countries, not by the normal expedient of selling them arms (that is forbidden by Japanese law) but through technical assistance, credits, and occasional verbal slaps at Israel. Once pumped and exported, the oil has to get to Japan if it is to be of any help. On its way it must pass first across the Indian Ocean and next through the narrow Malacca Strait (between Malaysia and Sumatra), or, if carried in supertankers, then through some channel to the east of Java, usually the Lombok Strait (between Lombok and Bali). Then the oil wends its way across the South China Sea, which is dotted with the numerous and scattered Spratly Islands (disputed among China, Taiwan, Vietnam, and the Philippines), then usually through the relatively wide Bashi Channel (between Luzon and Taiwan), and finally parallel to the Ryukyus chain on the Pacific side. At countless places along this long route, but above all at the chokepoints, tankers carrying oil to Japan or returning to the Middle East would be vulnerable in time of war to attacks, conceivably rising to the level of a blockade, from Soviet submarines and naval aircraft. Such a scenario, however, although understandably the source of much nervousness in Japan, appears realistic as has already been suggested only in case of something approaching general war, in which event everyone—including the Japanese—would have even more interesting things to think about than the interruption of the Western Pacific sealanes.

THE KOREAN CONFRONTATION[14]

For the past century Korean life has been dominated by a series of brutal events arising out of interaction among the same four powers: China, Japan, Russia, and the United States. Fifty years of harsh Japanese colonial rule were followed by the division of the peninsula into American and Soviet occupation zones in 1945, the emergence of two hostile states separated only by the

14. For background see David Rees, *Korea: The Limited War* (New York: St. Martin's Press, 1964); Young C. Kim and Abraham M. Halpern, eds., *The Future of the Korean Peninsula* (New York: Praeger, 1977); Morton Abramowitz, *Moving the Glacier: The Two Koreas and the Powers*, Adelphi Papers No. 80 (London: International Institute for Strategic Studies, August 1971).

38th parallel, the invasion of American-defended South Korea by Soviet-supported North Korea in 1950, three terrible years of war, and severe tension that survived the fragile armistice of 27 July 1953 and persists to the present day. The Republic of Korea, guaranteed by a security treaty with the United States and the presence of American forces, faces a rigidly totalitarian, implacably hostile, and militarily somewhat stronger (especially in aircraft and armor) northern neighbor.

According to the latest and best available estimates, the North Korean forces confronting South Korea center on some 40 divisions, including two armored ones, an abundance of artillery, and a powerful, although essentially defensively equipped, air force whose most advanced aircraft is the MIG-21. Against these, the Republic of Korea disposes of roughly 20 divisions (each larger than its North Korean counterpart) and armored and air forces that are somewhat smaller than those of the opposition.

Under these conditions no country could develop a liberal democracy or sustain it if it had one, and South Korea is no exception. On the other hand, the rigid personalist dictatorship of President Park Chung Hee has been succeeded, after a stormy transition, by a somewhat more relaxed, although still basically authoritarian, regime under another former military man, President Chun Doo Hwan.

Since the Korean war, Pyongyang has often put forward proposals seemingly aimed at ultimate unification of Korea, but they have usually been made at times when it seemed possible to destabilize the South through such contacts and have often been withdrawn or dropped when the South appeared to be on a steady course. In 1972-73, largely, it appears, as the result of the atmosphere generated by the improvement of Sino-American relations at that time and perhaps some backstage Chinese pressures on Pyongyang as well, North-South talks took place but without significant result. During the period of turbulence following the death of Park, the North claimed to feel an interest in further talks but then backed away as the Chun government began to stabilize. President Chun has made proposals of his own for North-South contacts, including one for an exchange of visits between himself and North Korean President Kim Il Sung, only to be rebuffed.

The U.S.-South Korean alliance of 1954 has been counterposed since 1961 to alliances linking North Korea with the Soviet Union and China. These are all defensive in fact as well as in name; none of the external powers wants its Korean partner to attack its adversary. Indeed, Moscow probably and Peking certainly approve of the American military presence in South Korea as a stabilizing influence, but neither can say so in public for fear of driving Pyongyang into the presumably waiting arms of the other party to the Sino-Soviet confrontation. The Soviet Union's need to conciliate North Korea is less than China's because of the great disparity in their power, and Moscow has given informal indications that it would welcome a "German" solution for Korea ("One nation, two states"), under which the two states would coexist peacefully and refrain from claiming one another's territory. Such an outcome, however desirable from everyone's point of view (except

perhaps Pyongyang's), is not in sight at present.

For the political reasons just indicated, and because of the defensive strength of South Korea and the continuation in force of the American security commitment, the chances of another North Korean invasion à la 1950 appear rather small. However, the South Koreans are the ones under the gun, and they can hardly be blamed for feeling nervous. They do.

AMERICAN SECURITY INTERESTS AND STRATEGY IN EAST ASIA[15]

The Nixon Doctrine, announced in mid-1969 and still going strong, says in effect that the United States will continue to protect its allies and other important friendly states against possible attacks by other major powers, but with air and seapower rather than (with the evident exceptions of Western Europe and South Korea) with ground forces, as occurred in Vietnam. The United States made a powerful contribution to the dramatic improvement in Sino-American relations that began soon after 1969 by modifying its mil-

15. For background see Robert A. Scalapino, *Asia and the Road Ahead: Issues for the Major Powers* (Berkeley: University of California Press, 1975); Ralph M. Clough, *East Asia and U.S. Security* (Washington, DC: Brookings Institution, 1975); Bernard K. Gordon, *Toward Disengagement in Asia: A Strategy for U.S. Policy* (Englewood Cliffs, NJ: Prentice-Hall, 1969); "The Asian-Pacific Region: Implications for U.S. Policy, 1975-1980," *Orbis* 19(3) (Fall 1975); *China and U.S. Far East Policy, 1945-1966* (Washington: Congressional Quarterly, 1967); *United States-Soviet Union-China: The Great Triangle* (Washington, DC: Government Printing Office for House International Relations Committee, 1976); Fred Greene, "The United States and Asia in 1980," *Asian Survey* 21(1): 1-13 (January 1981).

itary posture and strategy from one designed for two and a half wars to one adequate, supposedly at any rate, for one and a half—meaning that China was no longer seriously regarded as a likely adversary or as a significant threat to Asia. As already indicated, the eruption of the armed Sino-Soviet confrontation in 1969 was a major reason for this shift of American strategic perceptions.

The shift went further. Under the Carter administration, the so-called "swing" strategy emerged, under which American forces in the Western Pacific, especially naval forces, were considered available for redeployment if and when necessary to the Indian Ocean and even farther afield. In addition, the Carter administration decided to withdraw the only remaining American Army division, the Second, from South Korea, another (the Seventh) having been pulled out in 1971; this was partly designed as punishment for the Park government's unacceptable record on human rights. These policies, coming not long after the American withdrawal (undefeated, as it happened) from Indochina and the resulting disaster, clearly operated in a manner adverse to the interests and influence of the United States in East Asia and the Western Pacific. No one remembered (but every one should have) that in 1905 Britain transferred the capital ships of its China Squadron to the Home Fleet to face the German High Seas Fleet; the result was that British power was not significantly increased in home waters and British influence was very nearly eliminated from the Western Pacific.

Both the swing strategy and the plan to withdraw the Second Division from South Korea were abandoned in 1978-79 as a result of

sharply increased intelligence estimates of North Korean strength and the rapid growth of Soviet power in the region.[16]

At present American forces in East Asia and the Western Pacific consist largely, in addition to the Second Division in Korea, of two regiments of the Third Marine Division on Okinawa and the 25th Army Division in Hawaii; 10 Air Force fighter squadrons based in Korea, Okinawa, and the Philippines; most of a Marine air wing in Japan, and a squadron of B-52s on Guam; and the famous Seventh Fleet, which homeports at Yokosuka (in Japan) and has another large base at Subic Bay (in the Philippines) and controls two carrier task forces as its cutting edge.

It is clear that, as all American presidents since Nixon have affirmed, the United States intends to remain a Pacific, although not truly a continental Asian, power. It will not repeat the British mistake of 1905. In fact, the United States began even under Carter to strengthen, rather than continuing to reduce, its forces in the Western Pacific. As an essential supplement it has also begun to strengthen its existing strategic relationship with Japan and even to explore the possibilities of a new one with China, essentially for (defensive) anti-Soviet purposes. The United States wants, and occasionally prods, Japan to improve its defensive posture, especially in the critical fields of air and submarine defenses. In spite of the serious complication

16. One of the first signs of the shift was a speech by Secretary of Defense Harold Brown on February 20, 1978, in which he blew taps over the previous "Europe first" approach of the Carter administration by asserting: "We cannot be strong in Europe and weak in Asia."

created by the postnormalization American relationship with Taiwan, and above all by the announced intent of the United States to sell "selected defensive" arms to the Republic of China (on Taiwan) and by Peking's confrontation with Vietnam, the United States has had some limited success in getting strategically closer to a China that does not seem to have decided what it needs from the United States—let alone how to pay for it—and that has not yet gotten its politicoeconomic "act" together. In addition, the United States must adjust its policies to rapidly changing political conditions in South Korea, an advanced case of regime fatigue in the Philippines where there are important American bases, and assorted other problems elsewhere in the region. East Asia has never been an easy region for a power seeking to exercise influence, to say nothing of acquiring predominance.

THE UNITED STATES AND THE SINO-SOVIET CONFRONTATION[17]

The Sino-Soviet territorial-dispute-cum-military-confrontation

17. For background see Robert L. Pfaltzgraff, Jr., "China, Soviet Strategy, and American Policy," *International Security* 5(2): 24-48 (Fall 1980); A. Doak Barnett, "Military-Security Relations Between China and the United States," *Foreign Affairs* 55(3): 584-97 (April 1977); Allen S. Whiting, "China and the Superpowers: Toward the Year 2000," *Daedalus* 109(4): 97-114 (Fall 1980); Edward N. Luttwak, "Military Modernization in the People's Republic of China: Problems and Prospects," *Journal of Strategic Studies* 2(1): 3-16 (May 1979); William V. Garner, "Arms Control and the China Card," *Arms Control Today* 10(7): 1-2, 6-8 (July/August 1980); Harlan W. Jencks, "The Chinese 'Military-Industrial Complex' and Defense Modernization," *Asian Survey* 20(10): 965-89 (October 1980); Harold C. Hinton, "The United States and the Sino-Soviet Confronta-

is, of all the adversary relationships in the world, perhaps the most likely (or least unlikely) to escalate to the level of a war between two major powers, with the serious possibility of general war. If such a Sino-Soviet war should occur, in spite of the powerful disincentives on both sides, it would seriously harm American interests by confronting the United States with the choice of allowing China to be defeated and perhaps crushed, with very destabilizing effects on the international equilibrium of East Asia and possibly the world, or involving itself directly in some fashion with potentially awesome consequences.

President Nixon reportedly declared at National Security Council meetings in 1969 that the United States could not allow China to be "smashed" by the Soviet Union,[18] but it is not clear that his administration did a great deal to prevent such an outcome, beyond the undeniably important creation of a basis for a "normal" relationship with the PRC.

The Carter administration went further in this direction. Not only were full diplomatic relations established with the PRC at the end of 1978, but Sino-American strategic discussions were held, with results that the sensitivity of the subject has rendered obscure, during visits by Zbigniew Brzezinski (May 1978), Secretary of Defense Harold Brown (January 1980), and Under Secretary of Defense William J. Perry (September 1980) to China, and by Vice Premier (now also Defense

tion," *Orbis*, 19(1): 25-46 (Spring 1975); Michael Pillsbury, "U.S.-Chinese Military Ties?" *Foreign Policy* No. 20: 50-64 (Fall 1975).
18. Kissinger, *The White House Years*, p. 182.

Minister) Geng Biao to the United
States in May 1980. Soon after the
Brown visit, theUnited States began
to license for export to the PRC a
wide range of "dual use" (potentially
both civilian and military) but "non-
lethal" technology and equipment,
in spite of the objections felt and
expressed in Moscow, Taiwan, and
elsewhere in Asia to the effect that
this was a "tilt too far."[19]

It is likely that the Reagan administration will continue the process of
developing strategic cooperation
with, and perhaps actual arms sales
to, the PRC, but for important political and military reasons on both
sides this relationship is likely to
stop well short of an alliance, even
an informal one.

It is widely argued, in the United
States and elsewhere, that China
does not really need Western
(including American) arms, mainly
because it cannot hope even with
such help to come anywhere near
eliminating the vast Soviet military
lead, that it could not absorb them
for obvious technological reasons,
that in any case it could not pay for
them, and that, if so armed, China
would arouse dangerous alarm in
Moscow and might even attack one
or more of its Asian neighbors—
Taiwan or Vietnam, for example. It
is clear that, in spite of the backwardness displayed by its armed
forces during the brief 1979 war
with Vietnam, Peking has been in no
hurry to purchase arms abroad.
Nevertheless, it has shown a definite
interest in doing so, especially with
respect to American arms. It can
also be, and has been, argued that
highly selective inputs, including

such things as aircraft engines and
trucks as well as such essentially
defensive weapons as antitank and
antiaircraft missiles, could substantially enhance Peking's military
posture at relatively low cost and
should therefore be carefully considered. The current realities of China's international position, which
Peking has given clear evidence of
understanding, make it very
unlikely that China, with or without
foreign arms, will attack any of its
Asian neighbors, even Taiwan.

There is little doubt that China, in
spite of its serious weaknesses, is a
significant actual and potential
strategic asset for the United States.
It already "ties down" one-quarter of
Moscow's ground forces and a somewhat smaller fraction of its air
power. Any future increase of China's military strength is likely to be
targeted on the Soviet Union and is
more likely to push Moscow into
increasing its own force levels in
the Far East than into actually
attacking China, unless some other
consideration more powerful than
this also began to operate. To the extent that Moscow is "tied down" in
the Far East, it is obviously less able
to move militarily in the Middle
East or Europe, and in view of its
historic and massive anti-two-front
complex it is unlikely to want to do
so. It is therefore a sound strategic
instinct that led the Reagan administration to hint that a Soviet invasion of Poland might push the
United States into transferring
arms to China.

THE UNITED STATES AND CHINA[20]

During the difficult Sino-
American negotiations leading to

19. See I. Aleksandrov (pseud.), "Peking:
A Course Toward Wrecking International
Detente under the Guise of Anti-Sovietism,"
Pravda 14 May 1977.

20. For background see Michel Oksen-
berg, "China Policy for the 1980s," *Foreign
Affairs* 59(2): 304-32 (Winter 1980/81).

"normalization" at the end of 1978, Peking's fundamental position was that the United States must cut all political and military ties with Taiwan. This the Carter administration was willing to do with one important exception, which Peking, under the stress of the Soviet-Vietnamese treaty of friendship (an alliance in everything but name) signed in November 1978 and the rapidly ensuing Vietnamese invasion of Cambodia, decided to ignore for the time being without really accepting: the continuing sale of "selected defensive" arms to Taiwan, with no veto for Peking on the types or amounts of such sales. Substantial arms transfers of this kind were authorized, although not actually made, during the last year of the Carter administration.

The Reagan administration not only gave every evidence of intending to continue arms sales to Taiwan but for a short time went so far as to talk of restoring an "official" character to the American relationship with Taiwan. Strategic considerations predictably prevailed, however, and for obvious reasons: China was still considered much more important to American interests than was Taiwan. The exact way in which the two essentially incompatible relationships were to be optimized was evidently controversial within the Reagan administration and at the time of writing (April 1981) is reportedly under review. On the other hand, President Reagan fairly promptly took some steps to reassure Peking, which had felt seriously concerned over what it took to be Reagan's unfriendly and pro-Taiwan attitude, that no major policy change was intended, among them the sending of former Presi-

dent Gerald Ford to China in March 1981.[21]

The first serious issue bedeviling Sino-American relations under the Reagan administration is likely to involve its response to Taiwan's request to buy the F-16, an advanced fighter bomber and therefore a weapons system with some offensive—and also deterrent—capability against the mainland.[22] Peking has signaled in advance its strong objections to any such transaction by reducing the level of its diplomatic relations with the Netherlands in retaliation for the sale of some Dutch submarines to Taiwan.[23]

Peking's politicolegal position is that the act of diplomatic recognition by the United States takes priority over American domestic legislation, meaning specifically the Taiwan Relations Act passed by Congress in March 1979. The Reagan administration concedes the point but denies any real incompatibility between the two documents. This is a doubtful one, since the Taiwan Relations Act designedly goes rather far in perpetuating an American relationship with Taiwan, even if technically an unofficial one; it affirms, for example, a continuing American interest in the security and prosperity of Taiwan and the determination at least of Congress that the island shall be provided with adequate means for its defense.

Sino-American trade began in the early 1970s and, so far as American exports to China were concerned, grew fairly rapidly at the opposite ends of the spectrum of

21. *Washington Post* 14 March 1981; *New York Times* 22 and 28 March 1981.
22. *Washington Post* 9 March 1981.
23. *Washington Star* 2 March 1981.

technological sophistication: long range aircraft, electronics, other equipment, and grain and fiber. Expansion was especially impressive during 1979, the year following diplomatic normalization. In August of that year Vice President Walter F. Mondale visited China, stated the American interest in seeing it become a "secure and strong and modernizing" country, announced the availability of an Export Import Bank credit of up to $2 billion over five years, and concluded an agreement to assist China's vast hydroelectric development program.

Almost immediately after that, however, America, like other trade with China, began to feel the full effects of a "readjustment" policy decided on in Peking at the end of the previous year and originally scheduled to last through 1981 but likely on present indications to continue until the mid-1980s. Offers of credit were ignored, and contracts were cancelled, postponed, or not signed at all on a wide scale. American firms trading with China drastically cut their staffs in Peking.[24] Although the results of seismic surveys for possible offshore oil conducted in the South China Sea by foreign (including American) companies would not be known publicly until the fall of 1981, it appeared improbable that anything in that line would do much to lift China's foreign trade, and the level of activity of American firms trying to trade with China, out of the doldrums.

THE UNITED STATES AND JAPAN[25]

Until the advent of the Reagan administration, at any rate, there was a widespread belief among Japanese, including the conservative establishment, that the United States was a "has been" power. This attitude contrasted, and yet coexisted, with a profound national inferiority complex; a book by an American scholar with the strikingly overdone title *Japan as Number One* sold much better in Japan than in the United States, even though it was supposedly aimed at American audiences. The validity of the idea that Japan was in many ways "superior" to the United States and therefore a useful model for it in those respects was challenged by, among other things, the fact that in a Kawasaki-owned plant in the United States American workers, under Japanese management, outperformed their Japanese counterparts.

Japanese automobiles, electronics, and steel continue to sell well on the American market, often at prices that appear to reflect skillfully disguised dumping. In November 1980, nevertheless, the U.S. International Trade Commission ruled that no case for Japanese exports damaging the American automobile industry had been proved. Meanwhile, the Japanese government and Japanese industry have been erecting very effective barriers to the sale of American products on the Japanese market. American and other foreign automobiles are subjected to 105 special "safety" tests that are not imposed on automobiles produced in Japan. An American businessman in Japan was recently jailed because he dared to import foreign whiskey and undersell the absurdly overpriced Japanese equivalents.

---

24. *Wall Street Journal* 18 March 1981.
25. For background see Kenneth L. Adelman, "Japan's Security Dilemma: An American View," *Survival* 23(2): 72-79 (March/April 1981).

Considering the size of Japan's gross national product (approximately $600 billion), not only its defense budget (about $10 billion, or slightly under one percent of GNP, by far the smallest percentage of any major industrialized country) but the size of Tokyo's financial contribution to the support of American forces based in Japan largely for its protection (roughly $1 billion per year) seems distinctly modest. The same could be said of Japan's foreign aid program (around $2 billion annually in recent years, tied to Japanese goods and services).

Under these circumstances, the profound American conviction that Japan is not pulling its weight in the "partnership" is understandable, although also debatable. So is the recurrent American urge to prod Japan to do better on all these fronts.

Other problems have also dogged the relationship. The U.S.-Japanese Security Treaty, although somewhat revised (in favor of Japan) in 1960, is still highly asymmetrical; the United States assumes responsibility to help defend Japan (subject to American "constitutional processes"); Japan assumes no obligation whatever to help defend the United States or American interests in the Western Pacific. Largely for domestic reasons, the Japanese Self Defense Forces have been very slow to begin conducting joint maneuvers and otherwise cooperating with the American forces in the region, although this situation has recently started to improve. Because of its almost total lack of natural resources and the skyrocketing price of oil since 1973, Japan has naturally moved rapidly ahead with a nuclear power program; the Carter administration, because of its obsession with the possibility of nuclear weapons proliferation, repeatedly

harassed Tokyo on this issue even though the Japanese government has signed and ratified the Nonproliferation Treaty and clearly has no present intention of developing nuclear weapons.

The Carter administration tried to popularize the Brzezinskian concept (or slogan) of trilateralism, under which it was held that there existed among the United States, Japan, and Western Europe not only economic comparability but economic, political, and even ideological compatibility that ought to find its reflection in close cooperation.[26] Largely in order to humor Carter and Brzezinski, the West Europeans went along to a degree with trilateralism and its institutional expression, the Trilateral Commission, but they had (and continue to have) objections to Japanese behavior that are very similar to those felt in the United States. It appears very unlikely that trilateralism will survive the change of administrations in Washington, except perhaps as a buzz word. Curiously, the Chinese have recently begun to express interest in joining the Trilateral Commission—hardly an example of flawless timing.

THE UNITED STATES AND KOREA[27]

The assassination of President Park Chung Hee in October 1979 ushered in conditions under which the South Korean military rose

26. On the exiguous security aspect of trilateralism see *The Common Security of Japan, the United States, and NATO* (Cambridge: Ballinger, 1981).
27. For background see Ralph N. Clough, *Deterrence and Defense in Korea: The Role of U.S. Forces* (Washington: Brookings Institution, 1976); Han Sungjoo, "South Korea and the United States: The Alliance Survives," *Asian Survey* 20(11): 1075-86 (November 1980).

more than ever to the top of the political system and North Korea appeared to consider that the time for some major initiative might be at hand. The Carter administration objected to both these tendencies; despite its distaste for the first, it warned Pyongyang not to indulge in the second. The Carter administration was profoundly unhappy over the death sentence for sedition pronounced by a South Korean military court on the prominent opposition politician Kim Dae Jung.

The Reagan administration, on the other hand, felt less disposed to take an interventionist stand on the issue of human rights in foreign countries including South Korea and somewhat more inclined to emphasize American military commitments overseas. It knew that any effort to bargain with President Chun Doo Hwan's government over the fate of Kim Dae Jung would be undignified, ineffective, and in fact probably counterproductive, yet it wanted to establish a friendly relationship with Seoul in contrast to the Carter administration's generally unfriendly one. Fortunately, Chun desired the same improvement and realized that the chances of attaining it could be significantly enhanced by statesmanlike moderation on his part. In January 1981 he commuted Kim Dae Jung's sentence to life imprisonment, lifted martial law a few months earlier than had been expected, set in motion the transition to constitutional government in lieu of emergency rule—with himself still as president, to be sure—and proposed an exchange of visits with Kim Il Sung. These steps clearly contributed, although for reasons of face on both sides they could not be an explicit precondition for, an invitation to visit the United States that was formally extended

the day after President Reagan's inauguration. The visit (in early February) was an outstanding success—from the diplomatic point of view, at any rate. Among other things, President Reagan announced firmly that the withdrawal of the Second Division was not contemplated. He also reaffirmed the Carter administration's position that the United States would not negotiate bilaterally with North Korea, as constantly demanded in Pyongyang, without the participation of the Republic of Korea.

Since that time there have been indications that the Reagan administration is giving favorable consideration to a South Korean request for the sale of 36 F-16s.[28]

In recent years the South Korean economy has become badly inflated, largely because of generous wage increases aimed at keeping labor contented, with a marked and adverse effect on the price-competitiveness of South Korea's exports. As the Chun government realizes, the answer to this problem is to be found essentially at home, but it hopes that the United States will help by facilitating in one way or another the sale of Korean products on the American market (color television sets are prominently mentioned in this connection) and the export of American rice, South Korea having experienced unusually cold and wet weather during the summer of 1980.

THE UNITED STATES AND
INDOCHINA

The hard-won Paris Agreement of January 1973 did not gain a "decent interval" for South Vietnam. Massive North Vietnamese

28. *New York Times* 27 March 1981.

violations of the agreement, supported with heavy arms shipments from the Soviet Union and China inasmuch as the United States was no longer involved directly in the war, produced the rapid collapse of the non-Communist governments of the three Indochinese states (Vietnam, Laos, and Cambodia) in 1975 and naturally worsened the already strained relationship between Washington and Hanoi. It was scarcely improved when Vietnam began not only to seek diplomatic recognition but also to demand aid and even reparations from the United States and continued to be less than fully cooperative on the emotive issue of the MIAs (American military personnel reported missing in action in Indochina).

Nevertheless, by 1978 the Carter administration felt an active interest in establishing diplomatic relations with Vietnam, if possible. American-Vietnamese normalization proved not to be so, however. For one thing, by that time Sino-Vietnamese relations were strained to the point where the United States could probably not have normalized its relations with both, and of the two China was by far the more important to American interests. Furthermore, even the usually tolerant Carter administration was outraged by Hanoi's sharp tilt toward Moscow, its ruthless expulsion of thousands of its residents, and its massive invasion of Cambodia. The progress toward recognition, never breathtaking, came to a screeching halt in late 1978 and has not been resumed. Partly by way of retaliation, the United States has supported the continued representation of the pro-Chinese and anti-Vietnamese Pol Pot regime, its penchant for genocide notwithstanding, in the United Nations.

Recently this stand has begun to weaken somewhat in parallel with the apparent trend toward a position on ASEAN's part favorable to an anti-Vietnamese coalition in Cambodia with the participation of Pol Pot's Khmer Rouge but under the leadership of someone else, possibly the indestructible Prince Sihanouk.

THE UNITED STATES AND ASEAN

Like everyone else, the United States greeted the formation of ASEAN in 1967 with its standard attitude reserved for Southeast Asia outside Indochina: benevolent indifference. The interest, what there was of it, lay in the resources of the region, not in its governments and still less in a newborn regional organization. Before ASEAN was 10 years old, however, it began to be taken much more seriously. It had demonstrated some effectiveness at negotiating collectively on trade issues with Japan, the Common Market, and the United States. It has yet to develop a significant collective security role, but that is less surprising and less impressive than the fact that it has survived for more than a decade.

For nearly 30 years Thailand has been viewed by American officialdom both as possessing considerable strategic importance and as being vulnerable to attack and/or subversion by China and/or Vietnam. The Manila Pact of 1954 and its concomitant structure, the Southeast Asia Collective Defense Organization (misnamed SEATO by consciously misleading analogy with NATO), were put together by the United States largely in order to protect Thailand. Although the SEATO mechanism lapsed in 1976, the treaty survives, and the United

States is also committed to come to the defense of Thailand if necessary by a unilateral commitment made in 1962. Even though the Thai expelled the important American strategic air bases and electronic monitoring facilities from their soil in 1975-76 as an act of appeasement of Hanoi, the United States has been selling arms to Thailand at an accelerated pace since 1978, Vietnam being the perceived threat.

Partly because of the improvement in Sino-American relations, but even more because of China's potential as a constraint on Vietnamese expansionism, Thailand established diplomatic relations with Peking in mid-1975, at the same time as the Philippines and a year later than Malaysia. Indonesia and Singapore have yet to do the same. Jakarta claims to regard Peking and its own Chinese population as a serious threat, at least in a long-term sense, and quietly approves of the idea of a strong Vietnam as a buffer and counterweight to China. The Indonesian military elite also seems to consider the fostering of an image (essentially a myth) of Chinese expansionist tendencies in the region helpful to its own long-standing quest for preeminent influence in Southeast Asia.[29] In recent years the United States, which encouraged Indonesian Chinaphobia in the 1950s, has been trying with little success to soothe it. Singapore has been holding off, mainly because it does not want to offend its huge, dangerous southern neighbor by anticipating it in extending recognition to the latter's proclaimed *bete noire*.

To the United States, Indonesia is important primarily for its enor-

mous natural resources, especially Sumatran oil. This is nothing new; the United States risked and got war with Japan in 1941 mainly because it refused to acquiesce in Tokyo's obvious intent to dominate and exploit the resources of what was then known as the Dutch East Indies.

A long-standing political connection and the presence of large American investments and bases continue to render the Philippines one of the most important countries in Asia to the United States. The government of President Ferdinand Marcos has been less than an ideal one from the American—to say nothing of the Philippine—point of view; for a time Marcos appeared to be threatening to squeeze the United States out of its bases, and even to make them available to the Soviet Union, unless suitably appeased with a large dollop of aid. He won, by and large; at the end of 1978, in addition to some largely atmospheric concessions to Philippine sovereignty over the bases, the American tenure of which was guaranteed at least until 1983, Marcos was promised $1 billion in aid.

THE OUTLOOK

Fortunately for American interests, there is little likelihood in the near future of a major war in East Asia, except perhaps in Korea and conceivably between China and Vietnam and/or the Soviet Union. There is little chance of any presently non-Communist country going Communist in the near future.

But even in the absence of extreme contingencies, there is still a need for the United States to maintain a strong and effective military presence in the Western Pacific and South Korea in order to promote international stability and Ameri-

29. See Barnard K. Gordon, "The Potential for Indonesian Expansionism," *Pacific Affairs* 36(4): 378-93 (Winter 1963-64).

can "credibility"; to wipe out, if possible, the psychological and political effects of the American withdrawal from the Vietnam war and the ensuing inevitable debacle; and to counterbalance with deterrent effect the current, fairly rapid Soviet military buildup in the region. The United States need not fail in these missions; if it does, the failure is more likely to be caused by a lack of determination and effectiveness on the American side than by objective difficulties, impressive though these are.

ANNALS, *AAPSS*, 457, September 1981

The Rapid Deployment Force: Problems, Constraints, and Needs

By JEFFREY RECORD

ABSTRACT: The character and capabilities of the Rapid Deployment Force formed by the Carter administration in the wake of the Soviet invasion of Afghanistan do not reflect sufficient appreciation of the two pivotal conditions governing any U.S. attempt to mount a credible military defense of its vital interests in the Persian Gulf region: (1) the lack of secure military access ashore in the region, and (2) an unavoidable reliance on forces already committed to the defense of Europe and other areas outside the Gulf. The problem of access is critical, since the present RDF is composed largely of units whose ability to go ashore is dependent upon uncontested prehostilities entry into ports and airfields, and whose ability to sustain combat, once ashore, is contingent on the availability of a massive, land-based logistical infrastructure. In effect, the utility of the RDF as an instrument of U.S. military power in the Gulf region has been staked on the presumed political goodwill under crisis conditions of unstable potential host regimes whose security interests are not identical to those of the United States. In lieu of secure access ashore, the present RDF should be replaced by a sea-based and sea-supplied intervention force supplemented by enhanced amphibious assault and other forcible-entry capabilities.

Jeffrey Record is a senior fellow at the Institute for Foreign Policy Analysis and the author of a study of the Rapid Deployment Force recently published by the Institute.

DETERRENCE of overt Soviet aggression in the Persian Gulf region and preservation of uninterrupted access to Persian Gulf oil remain the two principal rationales underlying the Rapid Deployment Force (RDF), formed by the Carter administration in the wake of the Soviet invasion of Afghanistan in December 1979.

An assessment, therefore, of the utility of the Rapid Deployment Force as an instrument of U.S. military power—the purpose of this article—must be made in the context of the two pivotal conditions governing any U.S. attempt to mount a credible military defense of its vital economic interests in the Gulf. Those conditions are (1) the lack of secure military access ashore in the region, and (2) unavoidable reliance on forces already committed to the defense of Europe, Northeast Asia, and other areas outside the Gulf region.

Unfortunately, it is not at all apparent that the Department of Defense has fully grasped the profound operational and logistical implications of either condition. An intervention force has been created that is critically dependent for success or failure in combat on the presumed goodwill of unstable potential host regimes in the region, whose interests in the Gulf are far from identical to ours; and no attempt has been made—in the form of expanded force levels—to resolve the dilemma inherent in the Carter Doctrine's imposition of a major, new strategic commitment upon forces already severely taxed by pre-Afghanistan obligations.

AN ILLUSTRATIVE WAR GAME

Evidence of this strategic incomprehension was abundant in a recent war game conducted in summer 1980 by the U.S. Readiness Command, the parent military authority of the RDF. The game, known as *Gallant Knight* and conducted largely on computers, postulated a successful U.S. defense of Iran against a full-scale Soviet invasion.[1]

The prospect of a Soviet invasion of Iran has been publicly raised by the Chairman of the Joint Chiefs of Staff, General David C. Jones, and is drawing the increasing attention of RDF contingency planners. Preparation for a U.S. defense of Iran is becoming more and more evident in the character and planned capabilities of the RDF. Testifying in March 1981 before a Senate Armed Services Subcommittee, Jones stated that the 26 Soviet divisions deployed opposite Iran are being rapidly upgraded and warned of a possible Soviet thrust into that country, already at war with neighboring Iraq.[2] *Gallant Knight* entailed the commitment of some 325,000 U.S. troops to Iran and the Arabian peninsula in an attempt to block a Soviet invasion through the Trans-Caucasus. The war game sought to preserve Iran's oil-rich province of Khuzistan by halting Soviet forces in the rugged terrain of the Zagroz Mountains.

Leaving aside the question of whether the Congress and the nation would be willing to shed American blood on behalf of a rabidly anti-American government whose most significant foreign policy act to date has been the taking and torturing of U.S. diplomatic personnel, it is not at all obvious that Iran is militarily defensible against a Russian attack, at least by the United States.

Strategically, the commitment of substantial U.S. forces to Iran would automatically endanger the defense of Western Europe: Most of the ground combat and tactical air force units that have been earmarked for the rapid deployment mission are also assigned to the no

1. John J. Fialka, "Panel to Probe Pentagon Infighting on Proposed RDF," *Washington Star* 3 March 1981. Additional information on Gallant Knight was provided to the author by sources in the Department of Defense.

2. David Halevy, "U.S. Military Chiefs Warn of Soviet Thrust to the Gulf," *Washington Star* 13 March 1981.

less critical mission of reinforcing NATO.

No military force can be in two places at the same time, and it is difficult to envisage any major shooting war between the United States and the Soviet Union confined—or confinable—to Iran or the Gulf alone. As noted by Senator William Cohen, Chairman of the important Senate Armed Services Subcommittee on Sea Power and Force Projection, "In all probability such a conflict would spill over into at least the European theater, raising the grim prospect of a war on two independent fronts against an adversary possessing superior forces on both, and enjoying the advantage of interior lines of communication."[3]

However, even were the United States liberated from the strategic penalties associated with utilizing forces already committed elsewhere, the U.S. defense of Iran currently postulated by Pentagon force planners seems less the product of real-world considerations than it does that of the "world of Disneyland," as one member of the Joint Chiefs has privately remarked.[4]

Against the 26 Soviet divisions now deployed opposite Iran, the United States can count not a single ground combat unit stationed anywhere ashore in the greater Gulf region. To mount a defense of Iran, RDF ground and tactical air forces, almost all of which are based in the United States, would have to be flown or shipped to the Gulf. Unfortunately, the United States today

does not possess the strategic airlift and sealift capabilities sufficient to move the requisite military forces to the Gulf in time.

It is noteworthy that *Gallant Knight* was played with lift capabilities (including the controversial proposed CX air transport) not scheduled for service until the late 1980s, and that even with these projected additional capabilities it took some six months to deploy to the Gulf those forces war gamers deemed necessary for an effective defense of Iran. One wonders what the Russians will be doing during those 180 days.

A defense of Iran also would require prehostilities access not only to Iran but also to the Arabian peninsula. Pentagon planners concede that no major U.S. fighting force in Iran could be logistically sustained without the creation of a support infrastructure on the peninsula. Access to air bases in Turkey is also considered essential for the purpose of mounting an air interdiction campaign against Soviet forces pouring through northwestern Iran. Finally, it is presumed that the U.S. Navy will be able to keep open the critical Strait of Hormuz against anticipated attacks by Backfire bombers, Soviet attack submarines, and Soviet tactical air forces operating out of Afghanistan.

These are heady—indeed, mind-boggling—assumptions. No country on the Arabian peninsula to date has been willing to permit the United States to station forces in its territory, even in peacetime. In a crisis, would the Turks, the Saudis, and the Omanis be prepared to expose their countries to potential Soviet retaliation for the sake of assisting the United States in defending Iran? Would the government of Iran, even in the face of a Soviet invasion, be pre-

3. Opening Statement of Senator William Cohen before the Hearings on the RDF of the Senate Armed Services Subcommittee on Sea Power and Force Projection, 3 March 1981.

4. In a conversation with the author in January 1981.

pared to invite onto its own soil forces of the "Satanic" United States? Could the U.S. Navy keep open any narrow body of water within easy reach of massive land-based Soviet airpower?

The burgeoning focus of RDF contingency planners on a defense of Iran is a focus not just on something that may be inherently indefensible but on what is perhaps the least likely to materialize of all the threats now confronting the preservation of uninterrupted U.S. access to Persian Gulf oil. One suspects that Soviet military units in the region, many of which are already tied down in Afghanistan, have stayed out of Iran less out of dread of what the United States could do to stop them than for fear of the occupation costs associated with attempting to digest a population of 40 million hostile Islamic religious fanatics.

Far more likely and immediate threats face the United States in the Gulf, including internal instability of the kind that toppled the shah of Iran and regional wars among oil-producing states like that now being played out between Iraq and Iran. To assume (as the Pentagon appears to be doing) that a massive, firepower-oriented, logistically cumbersome, and land-dependent intervention force of the type now being created with an eye to defense of Iran against overt Soviet aggression would possess equal utility in dealing with lesser, more diffuse, and more pressing threats defies both logic and common sense.

THE PROBLEM OF ACCESS

Secure military access ashore in the Persian Gulf is essential, certainly in contingencies entailing a prolonged land campaign. To get ashore, intervention forces must have access to ports, airfields, and other reception facilities. To stay ashore, they require continued access to proximate logistical support bases. Neither is available to the RDF in the Gulf region.

With the exception of the tiny atoll of Diego Garcia, some 2500 miles from the Strait of Hormuz, the United States possesses no military bases in that vast area of the world stretching from Turkey to the Philippines. (In contrast are the large Soviet installations at Cam Ranh, Socotra, and Aden, and long-standing Soviet access to the Iraqi bases at Umm Qasr and Al Basrah.) Nor are prospects favorable for the establishment of a "Subic" naval facility or "Clark" air force base in the region. As confirmed in 1980 by Robert Komer, then Under Secretary of Defense, "the countries [in the area] . . . most emphatically do not want formal security arrangements with us."[5]

The political sensitivity of potential host nations to a permanent U.S. military presence on their own soil is certainly understandable and is manifest in their refusal to permit the peacetime stationing of any operationally significant U.S. forces on their territory. Such a presence "would validate the criticisms of radical Arabs about how the conservative [Gulf] states are toadies of the imperialists" and would thus "increase the chances of the internal turmoil that constitutes the main potential threat."[6] Moreover, many

5. *Department of Defense Authorization for Appropriations for Fiscal Year 1981, Hearings before the Committee on Armed Services,* United States Senate, 96th Congress, Second Session (1980), Part 1, p. 445 (hereinafter cited as *Hearings*).

6. Richard K. Betts, *Surprise and Defense: The Lesson of Sudden Attacks for U.S. Military Planning,* a draft manuscript scheduled for publication by the Brookings Institution, pp. ix-14.

Gulf states continue to regard U.S. support for Israel as a greater threat to the security of the Arab world than the prospect of an "Afghanistan" on the Arabian peninsula. Some even suspect the United States of coveting the peninsula's oil fields, a suspicion reflected in the following statement of Sheik Sabah al Ahmad al Sabah, Kuwait's Foreign Minister:

Defend us against whom? Who's occupying us? We haven't asked anybody to defend us. Yet we find all these ships around asking for facilities. It's all a bit like a film with two directors—Russia and the U.S. How will the film end? Perhaps with both big powers agreeing, "O.K., these oil fields belong to us, and those to you. We'll divide up the region from here to there." Is that how it will end?[7]

To its credit, the Department of Defense appears acutely cognizant of the political barriers to establishing a permanent U.S. military presence ashore in the Gulf region, and accordingly has pursued the alternative of gaining contingent rights of access to selected facilities in time of crisis. Agreements along these lines have been concluded with Kenya, Somalia, and Oman.

Yet simply having the promise of access to facilities on a contingency basis is no substitute for U.S.-controlled and -operated bases whose use is not subject to momentary political calculations of host governments. The same internal political considerations that deny the United States a permanent military presence ashore in the region could well be invoked to deny the United States access to facilities in the event of a crisis, irrespective of the agreements that have been negotiated.

It is worth recalling that during the October War of 1973, the United States was denied overflight rights by NATO allies, countries usually regarded as more reliable than non-treaty U.S. "friends" in the Gulf.

The operational and logistical difficulties posed by lack of secure military access ashore in the Gulf region are compounded by the lack of politically reliable and militarily competent U.S. client states in the region, whose assistance could be vital in a major contingency, particularly a prolonged one. The internal political fragility of potential U.S. friends and allies in the Gulf is exacerbated by the questionable capabilities and competence of their military establishments. The present Iraqi-Iranian war has done little to enhance the dismal military reputation of the Arab world, and national military forces on the Arabian peninsula are negligible in size, questionable in quality, or both.[8] Enormous defense expenditures on the part of many Gulf states appears to have produced little in the way of technically competent, properly integrated, and well-led military forces. Even the large and experienced armies of Iraq, Iran, and Pakistan have been demoralized by defeat, revolution, or internal division along political or ethnic lines. In short, U.S. intervention forces could expect little effective support on the battlefield, even from host nations requesting intervention.

The adverse consequences of local military incompetence should not be underestimated, although U.S. intervention would, of course,

7. "Preserving the Oil Flow," *Time* 22 September 1980, p. 29.

8. See Abdul Kasim Mansur (pseud.) "The Military Balance in the Persian Gulf: Who Will Guard the Gulf States from Their Guardians?," *Armed Forces Journal* (November 1980).

benefit from it in contingencies involving aggression by a regional state. While many commentators pronounced the Guam (Nixon) Doctrine "dead on arrival" in the wake of the collapse of South Vietnam in 1975, the doctrine's fundamental premise remains as valid today as it did when promulgated in Guam in 1969: The sustained application of major U.S. military power in the Third World is not likely to succeed if unsupported by viable and competent local regimes capable of assuming a significant burden of the land battle. This is surely one of the principal geostrategic lessons of U.S. intervention in Indochina. Rushing to the defense of any nation either unwilling or sufficiently incapable of defending itself is to rush into the potential abyss of another Vietnam. As former Secretary of Defense Brown noted in testimony before the Senate Armed Services Committee in 1980, "the United States cannot defend . . . people in the [Gulf] region who are not willing to participate in their own defense. You need a significant political base and . . . effort by the people in the region."[9]

On what grounds, however, can the United States count on "a significant political base" "effort by the people in the region," particularly the kind of effort that would be required in the face of aggression by a Soviet client state or by the Soviet Union itself? The availability of such support is ultimately a function of the political stability of the regime supplying it; its effectiveness is a product of the size and competence of the regime's military forces. In the Persian Gulf, the West for decades enjoyed in the shah of Iran a powerful and seemingly stable local client committed to the

defense of shared interests. Yet, which potential Western client among the littoral states of the Persian Gulf and Indian Ocean today can be regarded as both politically stable and militarily competent? Somalia? Oman? Saudi Arabia? Kuwait? The United Arab Emirates? Pakistan? All of these states are governed by military regimes or semifeudal monarchies whose social and political fragility renders them vulnerable to internal overthrow by Soviet-sponsored leftist groups or the forces of religious fundamentalism now sweeping the House of Islam.

In short, in the Persian Gulf region the United States possesses none of the critical operational and logistical benefits that it enjoys in comparative abundance in Europe and in those other areas of the world (such as Korea) where large U.S. military forces are firmly ensconced ashore and can count on the support of powerful and reliable allies. As emphasized by Lt. General Paul X. Kelley, Commander of the Rapid Deployment Force, the United States will have to "start from scratch" in the Gulf against potential adversaries with large military forces already in place in the region or along its periphery.

There are sizable U.S. forces in-place in Western Europe—with the exception of naval forces in the Indian Ocean, we have none in Southwest Asia.

There are sizable amounts of prepositioned supplies and equipment in Western Europe for reinforcing units—we have none in Southwest Asia.

There is an in-place command and control system in Western Europe—we have none in Southwest Asia.

There is an extensive in-place logistics infrastructure in Western Europe—we have none in Southwest Asia.

9. *Hearings*, Part 1, p. 35.

There are extensive host-nation support agreements between the U.S. and Western European countries—we have none in Southwest Asia.

There is an alliance of military allies in Western Europe—there is no such alliance in Southwest Asia.[10]

THE PROBLEM OF INSUFFICIENT FORCE

Even were military access in the Gulf not a problem, however, the commitment of any sizable U.S. force to combat in the region would automatically weaken the defense of no less critical U.S. interests elsewhere in the world. The decision to form the RDF from *existing* military units, almost all of which are already earmarked for NATO and the Far East, has served to widen what, even before Afghanistan, was a substantial gap between U.S. commitments abroad and capabilities to defend them. The decision makes it virtually impossible to deal effectively with a significant military challenge in more than one area at a time. As noted in 1980 by William Perry, then Under Secretary of Defense for Research and Development, "the really troublesome problem we have is how do we accommodate [a] NATO buildup and the Persian Gulf buildup at the same time? That is the rub."[11] Army Chief of Staff Edward C. Meyer stated flatly that present U.S. force levels are "not sufficient to repel a Soviet assault [in the Persian Gulf] without jeopardizing our NATO commitment."[12] Chief of Naval Operations Thomas B. Hayward testified that the present "1 1/2-ocean

Navy" of the United States cannot meet the "three-ocean commitment" imposed by the Carter Doctrine.[13]

Although U.S. military planning since 1969 has called for capabilities adequate to wage simultaneously a major conflict in Europe and a lesser conflict elsewhere (the so-called "1 1/2-war" strategy), the simple truth is that U.S. force levels, now lower than at any point since the Korean war,[14] are not sufficient to meet the demands of more than one sizable conflict at a time. The "1/2-war" in Vietnam was waged in no small part by U.S. forces earmarked for European contingencies. Similarly, the two U.S. carrier battle groups now deployed in the Arabian Sea were drawn from NATO's Southern Flank and the Western Pacific.

Even the planned increases in the size of the U.S. Fleet from the present 440-odd vessels to 600 is unlikely to be adequate. It is in any event highly doubtful whether the U.S. Navy, under the current All-Volunteer Force, is capable of manning a 600-ship fleet; existing shortfalls in skilled personnel are so severe that comparatively new vessels have been retired from active patrolling.

The strategic risk inherent in reliance on forces committed to both

10. Statement by Lieutenant General P. X. Kelley on Rapid Deployment Force Programs, before the Senate Armed Services Subcommittee on Sea Power and Force Projection, 9 March 1981, p. 5.

11. *Hearings*, Part 6, p. 3,275.

12. Ibid., Part 2, p. 745.

13. Ibid., Part 2, p. 785.

14. A benchmark year widely used for comparison with the present is 1964, the last year preceding the U.S. buildup in Vietnam. For example, in 1964 personnel assigned to the active armed forces totalled 2.685 million compared to 2.059 million in fiscal year 1981; the active U.S. fleet contained 803 vessels compared to the present 418; the U.S. Air Force fielded a total of 439 active squadrons of all types compared 253 today; and strategic sealift vessels numbered 100 compared to the present 48. In 1964 the United States allocated 8.4 percent of its gross national product to defense compared to less than 5 percent in the fiscal years 1977-1980.

Gulf and non-Gulf contingencies would be profound in circumstances involving a U.S.-Soviet confrontation. By virtue of interior lines of communication, larger forces, and greater proximity to both Europe and the Gulf, the Soviet Union could, by feinting in one area, divert rapidly deployable U.S. forces away from the true point of decision.

The U.S. defense establishment currently lacks much latitude to cope with sizable contingencies [in the Persian Gulf]. The Soviet side, whose large forces afford more flexibility, could sponsor several widely-separated hot spots at the same time, with assistance from allies and friends.

Possible application of U.S. military sinew to ensure petroleum imports from the Persian Gulf should be viewed in that perspective.

Our active status strategic reserves are too few to fight even a modest war in the Middle East without accepting calculated risks that uncover crucial interests elsewhere. Even "best case" forces would probably prove insufficient against the Soviets, whose abilities to project offensive power beyond their frontiers have improved impressively in recent years.[15]

This is not to suggest that present U.S. forces could be no better postured than they are today. On the contrary, the readiness, structure, weaponry, and logistical sustainability of many units are not optimized for many conceivable contingencies in the Gulf region. More fundamental is the comparatively small amount of real combat power generated by the present

15. John M. Collins et al., *Petroleum Imports from the Persian Gulf: Use of U.S. Armed Force to Ensure Supplies* (Washington, DC: Library of Congress Congressional Research Service, 1980), p. 16.

structure of U.S. military forces. The product in large part of low "tooth-to-tail" ratios and reliance on individual (versus unit) replacement policies characteristic of a continuing orientation toward protracted conflict, the problem is nowhere more visible than in the U.S. Army. In contrast to the Soviet army, for example, which fields a total of 173 divisions from manpower base of 1.8 million active-duty personnel, the U.S. Army musters but 24 divisions (including eight National Guard divisions) from a base of 775,000 active-duty personnel. Finally, the present acute shortage in strategic lift capabilities—a shortage that cannot be overcome for at least half a decade—constrains U.S. ability to move military forces into the Gulf in a timely fashion.

Thus existing U.S. forces are simply insufficient in size to meet the requirements of defending the Gulf without reducing the capacity of the United States to meet its commitments elsewhere. In the absence either of larger forces or of forces fundamentally restructured to maximize combat power, the price of effective deterrence in the Gulf is a degradation of deterrence in Europe and Northeast Asia. Conceivably, this dilemma could be resolved by the assumption by allies of a greater portion of their own defense, thereby releasing U.S. forces for other missions. Unfortunately, prospects for compensatory Japanese and European defense investment of the necessary magnitude are not encouraging. Japan seems content to remain a military eunuch for the indefinite future; and many of America's NATO allies—including Germany—appear unwilling or unable to meet even pre-Afghanistan pledges for real increases in military spending devoted to the defense of Europe.

THE RDF MISMATCH

It might be assumed that the problems of access and insufficient force would have impelled the Pentagon toward both larger force levels and the creation of an instrument of intervention based primarily on seapower and supplemented by robust amphibious assault and other forcible-entry capabilities. An RDF of this kind would be comparatively free of dependence on the political goodwill of unstable, potential host governments in the Gulf region and able, if necessary, to gain access ashore without invitation.

Such, unfortunately, has not been the case. In terms both of forces earmarked for the rapid deployment mission and of the means chosen to enhance their ability to deploy rapidly to the Gulf, the present RDF's utility is questionable in contingencies not involving prehostilities access ashore, willingly granted.

As shown in Table 1, most of the military units now assigned to the RDF are not only already committed to NATO, but are also dependent for entry ashore and subsequent sustainability on friendly ports, airfields, and logistical facilities. Only the carrier battle groups and the national Marine Amphibious Force[16] are deployed or deployable afloat and logistically supportable from the sea; only the Marines and the Army's 82nd Airborne Division

possess the ability to enter territory controlled by hostile forces. The remaining units earmarked for the RDF, which organizationally consists of little more than a new headquarters charged with identifying, training, and planning the employment of existing forces suitable for Persian Gulf contingencies, are completely land-dependent.

The presumption that the RDF will enjoy uncontested entry ashore in the Gulf is further apparent in the strategic mobility programs associated with the force and in the absence of any proposed increases in amphibious assault capabilities. To speed the deployment of RDF forces from the United States to the Gulf in a crisis, the Pentagon has requested funding authority to develop and produce a new strategic air transport (the CX); a flotilla of fast sea transports; and a total of 12 specialized logistics ships, known as Maritime Prepositioning Ships, aboard which will be stored equipment and 30 days' worth of combat consumables for a complete Marine division.[17] The MPS vessels, which will be maintained on station in the Indian Ocean, represent partial compensation for the inability to preposition equipment and supplies ashore.

None of the proposed ships and aircraft, however, possess any defensive capabilities; all will be unarmed, and the ships will be manned by civilian crews. As such, their utility, like that of the bulk of the forces they will be carrying, is completely dependent on friendly reception ashore.

---

16. Each of the Corps' three Marine Amphibious Forces consist of a division and an associated air wing. None are formally earmarked for the rapid deployment mission. Currently only a battalion landing team is actually deployed in the Indian Ocean.

17. For a detailed description of this and other proposed strategic mobility programs associated with the RDF, see Jeffrey Record, *The Rapid Deployment Force and U.S. Military Intervention in the Persian Gulf* (Cambridge, MA: Institute for Foreign Policy Analysis, 1981).

TABLE 1
TENTATIVE RAPID DEPLOYMENT
JOINT TASK FORCE COMPOSITION, 1981

UNIT	NATO EARMARKED?	LAND-DEPENDENT?*
Ground Forces		
(Army)		
18th Airborne Corps HQ	No	Yes
82nd Airborne Division	Yes	Yes
101st Air Assault Division	Yes	Yes
9th Infantry Division	Yes	Yes
24th Mechanized Division	Yes	Yes
194th Armored Brigade	No	Yes
6th Cavalry (Air Combat) Brigade	Yes	Yes
2 Ranger Infantry Battalions	Yes	Yes
(Marine Corps)		
1 Marine Amphibious Force	?†	No
U.S. Air Force Units		
1 Air Force HQ	?	
12 tactical fighter squadrons	Yes	Yes
2 tactical reconnaissance squadrons	Yes	Yes
2 tactical airlift wings	No	Yes
U.S. Navy Forces		
3 carrier battle groups	Some‡	No
1 surface action group	Some‡	No
5 aerial patrol squadrons	Some‡	Yes

*Dependent for commitment ashore on access to secure ports and/or airfields, or dependent for subsequent operations ashore on a shore-based logistical infrastructure.
†Marine Amphibious Forces are considered available for contingencies worldwide.
‡A significant proportion of U.S. naval vessels currently deployed in the Indian Ocean belong to the U.S. 6th Fleet in the Mediterranean. Maintenance of a naval presence in the Indian Ocean at the expense of NATO-oriented naval forces is likely to continue throughout the decade.

CONCLUSIONS

Given the operational and logistical obstacles confronting the effective application of U.S. military power in the Persian Gulf region, logic and common sense would seem to dictate replacement of the present RDF by a small, agile, tactically capable intervention force that is based and supplied from the sea and is supported by expanded sea power, especially forcible entry capabilities. Such an intervention force would stress quality at the expense of size, immediate responsiveness at the expense of delayed augmentation from the United States; sea-based power projection capabilities at the expense of air-transported

Army forces and land-based tactical air power; and logistical self-sufficiency at the expense of dependence on facilities ashore. The present composition and capabilities of the RDF are the product less of impartial military judgment than they are of the bureaucratic desire of each service for at least a "fair share" of the rapid deployment mission.[18] As such, the present RDF can

18. See Fialka, "Panel to Probe Pentagon Infighting"; Robert C. Toth, "Military's Bureaucracy Curbs Emerging Unit," Los Angeles Times 1 December 1980; Richard Burt, "Army and Marines in Battle over Command of Rapid Deployment Force," New York Times 10 December 1980; and James R. Schlesinger, "Rapid(?) Deployment(?) Force(?)," Washington Post 24 September 1980.

and should be replaced by a new variant of the Navy-Fleet Marine Force "team" utilizing tried and tested organizational structures and operational doctrines associated with the successful projection of power from sea to shore.

Specifically, I propose the following: (1) the transfer of the primary responsibility for the rapid deployment mission to the U.S. Marine Corps and (2) an expansion in forcible-entry capabilities through increases in present levels of amphibious shipping and naval gunfire support.

Given the peculiar obstacles to and requirements for successful U.S. military intervention in the Persian Gulf, a strong case can be made for transferring the mission to the U.S. Marine Corps. Leaving aside the fact that a Marine Corps general already has been appointed to command the Rapid Deployment Joint Task Force, the lack of any real prospect for establishing an operationally significant peacetime U.S. military presence ashore in the Persian Gulf region (to say nothing of the potential unwanted political and military entanglements such a presence would invite) virtually dictates primary reliance on sea power, and especially on the kind of sea-based capabilities to project power ashore long associated with the Marine Corps.

The Marine Corps is the sole repository of U.S. amphibious assault capabilities, an essential component of any credible U.S. intervention force in the Persian Gulf. Moreover, unlike the Army, which must rely on another service for tactical air support, the Corps has its own air arm, not only compatible with carriers and other sea-based air platforms but also highly integrated with both carrier-based naval aviation and

Marine ground forces. In short, in contrast to the Army—the Corps' principal competitor for bureaucratic control of the rapid deployment mission—the Marine Corps is fully compatible with sea power: the necessary foundation of a U.S. military presence in those areas of the world where U.S. forces are not stationed ashore. There is also the Corps, long-standing history of successful expeditionary operations in the Third World and its record as the nation's recognized "force in readiness," of being the "first to fight."

Essential to any credible U.S. intervention force in the Persian Gulf is a robust U.S. forcible-entry capability. The present level of U.S. amphibious shipping is less than one-half that of the planning requirement specified by the Joint Chiefs of Staff; and naval gunfire support capabilities have been permitted to dwindle to patently unacceptable levels. Serious consideration should be given to expanding the level of amphibious shipping from the present 1.15-MAF lift capability[19] to a minimum 2.33-MAF lift capability—the JCS planning requirement. A 2.33-MAF capability would permit the uninterrupted deployment in the Indian Ocean (or other Third World crisis areas) of at least one full amphibious assault brigade (compared with the present occasional visits of a battalion-sized landing force), as well as sufficient redundancy for larger assault operations.

19. A Marine Amphibious Force (MAF) consists of a division, air wing, and associated support units. The present level of amphibious shipping is capable of moving only 1.15 MAFs; even then, however, it would take the Navy some 30-45 days to assemble in one place the shipping necessary for a MAF-sized assault, since the vessels are scattered among naval commands throughout the world.

As for naval gunfire support, the U.S. Navy retains in reserve some four *Iowa*-class battleships (mounting nine 16-inch guns apiece) and two *Salem*-class heavy cruisers (each with nine automatic 8-inch guns).[20] The reactivation and refurbishment of one or more of these vessels would certainly enhance Marine Corps forcible-entry capabilities against lightly or even moderately defended beachheads, if not against heavily defended shores. The presence in the Indian Ocean of such vessels, with their awesome

20. The Reagan administration's proposed Fiscal 1982 Five-Year Defense Plan calls for the return to active service of at least two of the *Iowa*-class battleships.

and easily visible capacity for destruction, would contribute to deterrence.

A sea-based RDF admittedly would have limited utility in contingencies demanding sustained combat inland, beyond the reach of amphibious assault forces and carrier-based air power. Prosecution of sustained inland combat, however, would be contingent upon secure coastal military lodgements, which can be gained only by the ability to project power ashore. Moreover, unlike forces withheld in the United States for rapid deployment to the Gulf region, a sea-based RDF has the advantage of already being there.

ANNALS, *AAPSS*, 457, September 1981

Maritime Doctrines and Capabilities: The United States and the Soviet Union

By ROBERT J. HANKS

ABSTRACT: During the past two decades, the sea power of the Soviet Union has undergone remarkable growth in size as well as capability. At the same time, that of the United States has suffered steady decline. Moscow has moved deliberately to exploit its new-found maritime outreach for political purposes, while ensuring that its sea power will be capable of successfully discharging far more important wartime functions. The maritime lessons that clearly have been assimilated by the leaders in the Kremlin have just as obviously been ignored by Western governments in general and the United States in particular. Unless these present trends are re-versed, the outlook for Western industrialized nations—heavily dependent on use of the seas as they are—is grim. Indications from the Reagan administration suggest that a resuscitation of the American Navy is about to begin. There is a very long way to go, however, and if in the meantime U.S. allies and friends do not make a serious effort to assume their fair share of the burden, they may find themselves left in the lurch if the United States is ultimately forced to take unilateral action to protect its own interests, the needs of its allies notwithstanding.

Rear Admiral Hanks, a 1945 graduate of the U.S. Naval Academy, retired in 1977. His active-duty assignments included command of a destroyer, a destroyer squadron, and the U.S. Middle East Force, along with duty as Director of Strategic Plans and Policy for the Navy Department. Over the past 20 years he has written extensively on political-military affairs, his latest works being The Unnoticed Challenge: Soviet Maritime Strategy and the Global Choke Points *(1980) and* The Cape Route: Imperiled Western Lifeline *(1981). His current activities include a position as Senior Political-Military Analyst for the Institute for Foreign Policy Analysis in its Washington office.*

S INCE 1960, a massive shift has taken place in the American-Soviet naval balance. With formal assumption of leadership of the Soviet Navy by Admiral Sergei G. Gorshkov in June 1956, that country's navy began a spectacular expansion, one which has continued ever since. Rewarded for his early efforts, Gorshkov was promoted to the newly created rank of Admiral of the Fleet of the Soviet Union in 1967—five stars—thus finally achieving equality with the commanders of the Russian ground and strategic rocket forces.

As a result of Gorshkov's successes, it has quite rightly been said that the Russian Bear, heretofore essentially a land animal, has learned to swim. Moreover, it is now abundantly clear that the bear has done so in the salt water that comprises all the world's oceans. In short, the USSR has become a global maritime power of the first order.

Concurrently, the navy of the United States has undergone precipitate decline. Serious erosion of American sea power began during the interminable years of the Vietnam war. From 1965 onward, when massive U.S. intervention in that region steadily escalated, funds appropriated for the U.S. Navy were expended almost exclusively on combat operations. Monies originally budgeted for warship overhauls, combat aircraft replacement, and new ship construction were systematically diverted to support the wartime requirements in Southeast Asia.

These adverse trends in relative naval prowess were accompanied by a demonstrated determination on the part of the Soviet Union to exploit its new-found maritime capabilities for political purposes.

Moscow has subsequently done so in myriad ways, all largely designed to achieve Soviet state objectives while avoiding any direct military confrontation with the United States. At the same time, U.S. foreign policy, under the stewardship of President Jimmy Carter, was increasingly perceived internationally as indecisive and vacillating. Taken together, the foregoing elements produced a marked reduction in American influence around the world, along with a commensurate rise in that of the Soviet Union.

Precisely how the two superpowers will adapt to these changed circumstances, with respect to their national objectives and strategies, remains to be seen. It is nonetheless manifest that the way they do so will profoundly affect the world of the 1980s.

The American electorate's rejection of Jimmy Carter on 4 November 1980 and accession to power by Ronald Reagan may well give rise to important changes on the world scene. Certainly, nations on both sides of the superpower struggle now believe that a fundamental shift in American foreign policy was signaled by the election. Nonetheless, whether the changed perception of the United States will be borne out by subsequent international events is a very large unknown.

Significant imponderables, of course, continue to color the present-day global environment. As suggested, they include the future maritime balance between the United States and the Soviet Union, along with the manner in which the USSR will utilize its new-found naval strength. Pertinent as well is the question of how the United States and its allies will react to Soviet initiatives. To understand these issues, it is necessary to review the recent history of the Soviet Navy and, particularly, the impact made by Admiral of the Fleet of the Soviet Union, Sergei G. Gorshkov.

THE RISE OF SOVIET SEA POWER

In 1955, Premier Nikita S. Khrushchev decided that the course then being navigated by the Soviet Navy was wrong. Accordingly, he sacked its commander-in-chief, Admiral Nikolai G. Kuznetsov, and turned the reins over to the next ranking officer, Admiral Sergei G. Gorshkov. Roughly a year later, Khrushchev elevated Gorshkov from acting commander in chief to full command of the Soviet Navy and handed him a set of explicit orders. In effect, he told Gorshkov to scrap all large surface ships then in the Soviet Navy and devote his efforts solely to building "rocket-firing" submarines. Enthralled by the emerging guided-missile technology and convinced of Gorshkov's political reliability, the Soviet premier expected his new naval commander not only to carry out his instructions but to sell the new Soviet maritime strategy to the latter's seagoing confreres. But Khrushchev reckoned without Gorshkov's strategic acumen and political agility. It is true that the new Soviet naval commander embarked on a huge building program designed to produce a monstrous submarine force—ballistic-missile and attack boats, diesel as well as nuclear-powered—but he also set out to fashion a true blue-water surface fleet.

Confronted with a U.S. Navy considerably larger and far more powerful than that of the USSR, possessing one of his own that was clearly inferior to the U.S. Navy with respect to the cutting edge of

modern sea power—aircraft carriers and marine assault forces—Gorshkov sought a way around these critical deficiencies until such time as he could convince the essentially land-bound mentality of those in the Kremlin that he should build these types of naval power. Like Khrushchev, he settled on the embryonic guided missile and thereby stole a march on the American navy that the latter is still trying to overcome. Eventually outlasting and outmaneuvering his mentor, Gorshkov managed to achieve precisely what he had set out to do. It seems abundantly clear that he exploited Soviet political reverses—Jordan in 1957, Lebanon in 1958, and the Cuban missile crisis in 1962, for example—to make a fundamental point to his superiors: Any nation harboring ambitions of global influence, let alone worldwide dominion, must necessarily become a major sea power.[1]

There are some analysts in the West who argue that the true watershed in Soviet naval history came with the Cuban missile crisis, featuring, as it did, the abject retreat Khrushchev was forced to make in the face of relative Soviet naval impotence and clear American strategic nuclear superiority. If, however, one examines the Soviet fleet of the early 1960s and then factors in the leadtime inherent in modern warship construction, it becomes evident that the origins of the present Soviet surface navy lay further back in time. In fact, *Kynda*-class cruisers and *Kashin*-class destroyers—new-generation ships

1. For a detailed discussion of this point with respect to the two crises in the Eastern Mediterranean, see Jacob C. Hurewitz, "Changing Military Perspectives in the Middle East," in P. Y. Hammond, ed., *Political Dynamics in the Middle East* (New York: Elsevier, 1972).

at sea in 1962—could have been conceived only in the 1950s at roughly the time Gorshkov came to power. As for the Cuban fiasco, one must logically conclude that the shrewd Russian admiral used this and similar Soviet international reverses with telling effect to further hammer his basic thesis home inside the walls of the Kremlin.

In any event, there can be little argument with the contention that Gorshkov has succeeded in remarkable fashion. Today outnumbering the U.S. Navy by a wide margin, the Soviet Navy has now begun to close extant gaps in the final two categories of naval power wherein the United States has always enjoyed a decisive superiority: aircraft carriers and amphibious assault forces.

After years of disparaging the power and utility of the aircraft carrier—when the Soviets had none—Gorshkov embarked on a clearly evolutionary program to add this vital capability to the Russian Navy. He started with the small and relatively unsophisticated helicopter carriers of the *Moskva*-class, following these ships with the more versatile *Kievs*, which carry a combination of helicopters and the new vertical take-off, fixed-wing aircraft known in Western military circles as the Forger. Based on this progression, astute Western observers predicted that Gorshkov's ultimate objective was acquisition of a capability to take meaningful tactical aviation to sea. They did not have long to wait for their suspicions to be confirmed.

In early 1980, reliable reports claimed that the USSR had begun building a nuclear-powered attack aircraft carrier of some 80,000 tons displacement. Along with rumored construction of the lead ship of this new class at Severodvinsk—a prime

nuclear-propulsion shipyard—came additional reports of Soviet experiments with shipborne catapault and arresting gear equipment.

How many of these or similar ships they intend eventually to build will go far toward determining the issue of U.S. versus Soviet naval superiority. The aircraft carrier evolution in the USSR, coupled with ongoing production of four completely new classes of nuclear-powered cruisers—including the huge 22,000-ton *Kirov*-class battlecruiser—together with accompanying procurement of underway replenishment ships of the 36,000-ton *Berezina*-class and 13,000-ton *Ivan Rogov*-class amphibious ships, suggest that Gorshkov's actual goal is a Soviet Navy—on the American model—capable of projecting power to any spot in and along the periphery of the world's oceans, in peacetime or in wartime.

THE DECLINE OF THE U.S. NAVY

As already noted, while Admiral Gorshkov was working diligently to fashion such a maritime capability for the USSR, the navy of the United States was suffering steady reductions. The reasons for the decline are myriad. First, there is the increasing complexity of the modern warship with its proliferation of very expensive weapons systems. Second, the pernicious effects of continuing inflation in the United States have driven the costs of even the most simple men-o'-war to incredibly high levels. In addition, the Navy Department must shoulder a sizable portion of the blame as a result of its less-than-superb management of shipbuilding contracts once they have been awarded. For example, altogether unnecessary design changes permit contractors, who submit irresponsibly low initial bids, to dash to the cash register and get well financially on such alterations subsequently ordered by the Navy. Nor are other segments of the U.S. government free of responsibility. Stubborn adherence to single-year appropriations, as opposed to multi-year financing, and refusal to permit realistic estimates for inflation have further aggravated the basic procurement problems.

Several other factors have also played important roles in the progressive U.S. naval decline. Of foremost significance was the long war in Vietnam. Electing to provide for "guns" as well as "butter," President Lyndon Johnson thereby assured that the developing war in Southeast Asia could be prosecuted only at the expense of future U.S. military prowess. In no instance was this more true than with respect to the U.S. Navy. For the Vietnam conflict not only wore out existing ships and aircraft at an accelerated rate, due to the high tempo of combat operations, but simultaneously caused a devastating hiatus in new ship construction and aircraft procurement, since available budgetary funds were almost wholly absorbed by demands—fuel, ammunition, and repair parts—of the war itself.

Once this unhappy conflict came to an end, aging U.S. ships were eliminated from the fleet at a rapid pace. Either totally obsolescent or far too expensive to modernize and maintain, their retention on active service could no longer be justified. At the same time, rampaging inflation served to reduce the numbers of new warships and combat aircraft that could be procured to replace them.

Over all of these difficulties hovered an internal Navy dispute

concerning how the available budgetary dollars should be spent. The nation's strategic nuclear requirements inevitably took first priority. Before any serious attention could be given to general-purpose forces, the needs of the sea-launched leg of the strategic nuclear triad had to be satisfied. The costs associated with this effort annually ate up a disproportionate share of the U.S. naval budget.

Once those funds were set aside, there arose the historic arguments among what former Chief of Naval Operations Admiral Elmo R. Zumwalt, Jr. characterized as various "unions" within the naval service.[2] That is, parochial pressures were constantly exerted by aviators, submariners, and surface sailors, each seeking to maintain the viability of their own communities. The heart of this seemingly endless debate was the "mix" of ships that should be acquired with the remaining funds. Essentially, the dispute amounted to an intense tug-of-war over large, sophisticated carriers and submarines on one hand and greater numbers of less complex, less expensive surface ships needed for the many other sea power tasks on the other. The disagreements thus spawned have never been satisfactorily resolved.

EFFECTS OF THE
U.S. SEA POWER DECLINE

This vicious circle was compounded by the fact that, as the Soviet naval threat grew, a shrunken American Navy could no longer count on a powerful British Royal Navy to help it meet the developing challenge at sea. Moreover,

2. Elmo R. Zumwalt, Jr., *On Watch* (New York: Quadrangle/New York Times Book Co., 1976), p. 63.

while overall American naval capability continued to shrink, demands for its services inexorably rose. The Carter administration abruptly came face-to-face with the dilemma thus posed, first in the wake of the Iranian Revolution with its accompanying seizure of the U.S. Embassy in Teheran, and then subsequent to the brutal Soviet invasion of Afghanistan.

Confronted with a nearly complete absence of U.S. bases in the Indian Ocean—symptomatic of the inexorable loss of U.S. military access worldwide since the end of World War II[3]—the American president found himself ensnared by an inability to deploy anything but naval power to the region. Yet, he discovered that these crises were occurring at precisely the time when the defense policies of his own administration had still further reduced the number of ships in the U.S. Navy. To expand the minuscule American military presence then in the Indian Ocean, President Carter learned that it would be necessary to "borrow" an attack aircraft carrier battle group from the U.S. Seventh Fleet in the Western Pacific. When, in response to the Soviet invasion of Afghanistan, Washington decided to send a second carrier group to the Indian Ocean, the requisite ships were similarly drawn from the Seventh Fleet, leaving that famed unit without a single aircraft carrier for the first time since its establishment. To maintain continuously such a two-carrier force in the Indian Ocean while not permanently stripping the Seventh Fleet, Carter was ultimately forced to halve the traditional U.S. carrier

strength assigned to the Sixth Fleet in the Mediterranean Sea.

The resultant reduced power of these forward-deployed fleets thus offered eloquent testimony to the condition to which the U.S. Navy had been allowed to descend by the time the 1980s dawned. Like the carrier groups, the Marine contingent and its assault shipping being maintained in the Indian Ocean are also alternately drawn from these alternative sources.

In the Pacific Far East, as well as in NATO Europe, America's friends and allies watched with alarm as these ships departed their traditional stations. As with the ill-conceived Carter plan to pull all U.S. ground forces out of South Korea, these latest American moves were seen as a further reduction in American commitment to the common defense. Particularly in East Asia, Japan, China, and other nations believed their concerns were abundantly justified. In addition to Washington's Korean pullout initiative, they had only recently been witness to a public debate in the United States over the so-called "swing strategy."[4]

Long carefully concealed, this is a plan to shift sizable elements of American military power from the Pacific Ocean area to the Atlantic in the event of a major war in Europe. There can be little doubt that for years Tokyo had been privately, albeit painfully, aware of the swing strategy's existence. Public revelation, however, directly on the heels of Carter's Korean ploy stirred appreciable political waves throughout Japan.

3. See Alvin J. Cottrell and Thomas H. Moorer, *U.S. Overseas Bases: Problems of Projecting American Military Power Abroad* (Beverly Hills, CA: Sage, 1977).

4. For a more complete examination of the "swing strategy" see Robert J. Hanks, Rear Admiral USN (Ret.), "The Swinging Debate," *United States Naval Institute Proceedings* 106: 26-31 (June 1980).

Further, one can reasonably conclude that Peking—having only recently elected to "open to the West" in an attempt to enlist allies in its anti-Soviet campaign—also looked aghast at these developments. Supremely pragmatic as they are, the Chinese leaders must have begun to entertain serious doubts about their new international policies.

Thus, insofar as the United States is concerned, the picture in the early 1980s is one of acute uncertainty. A remarkably expanded Soviet Navy—one capable of projecting meaningful military power into distant seas for the first time in Russian history—confronts a diminished U.S. Navy whose commitments have grown rather than receded.

Finally, yet another difference between American and Soviet approaches to the utilization of maritime power adds to Washington's problems. In the United States, only naval forces are the responsibility of the government. Other aspects of sea power—the merchant marine, fishing fleets, oceanographic survey and research, and so on—are matters for private enterprise. By contrast, every maritime element disposed by the USSR is under the direct control of Moscow. Certainly, Admiral Gorshkov operates on this premise:

It is reasonable to consider that the totality of the means of harnessing the World Ocean and the means of defending the interests of the state when rationally combined constitute the sea power of the state, which determines the capacity of a particular country to use the military-economic possibilities of the ocean for its own purposes.

It is legitimate to consider the sea power of the state as a system characterized ... by the presence of links between its components (military, merchant, fishing, scientific research fleet, etc.).[5]

Thus, Moscow operates not only naval forces but all other segments of sea power in a carefully integrated fashion so as best to promote the USSR's national interests. There is little prospect that either the Soviet or the American approach to the utilization of sea power will change appreciably in the foreseeable future.

Then, of course, it is important that one not overlook the problem of growth within regional navies around the world. Development of "smart" weapons, particularly the guided missile, along with the ability to launch them to great ranges from relatively simple platforms, both airborne and seaborne, has compounded the threats confronting major sea powers. It is altogether possible, for instance, that a tiny country possessing this capability could inflict significant damage on ships belonging to one of the superpowers. In such circumstances, the imperative to retaliate could conceivably lead to uncontrolled escalation between the major nations on each side of the conflict. In light of all the foregoing factors, one must view the future with something akin to alarm.

THE OUTLOOK

As for that future, the USSR can be expected to continue to exploit its newly developed maritime capabilities—naval, merchant marine, and other—in a controlled campaign to advance Soviet state

5. S. G. Gorshkov, *The Sea Power of the State* (Annapolis, MD: Naval Institute Press, 1979), p. ix.

objectives. Moscow's inferred goals include extension and expansion of Soviet influence on a global scale while simultaneously decreasing that of the United States and the West.

One must assume that the foremost aims of Soviet maritime strategy will be to seek to control—directly or indirectly—Western access to the two great raw material "treasure houses" whose resources sustain the modern industrial state: the Middle East with its petroleum reserves and southern Africa with its wealth of nonfuel minerals.

Second, the Kremlin can be expected to forge a series of interlocking overseas bases from which its expanded naval forces will be in a position to influence—in peacetime—international events, as well as to interdict—in wartime—those sealanes carrying the foregoing commodities to the West.

In this context, the words of Gorshkov are instructive:

With the emergence of her navy on the oceanic expanses, the Soviet Union has gained new and wider possibilities for its use in peacetime to ensure her state interests. Finding themselves in foreign ports, Soviet naval seamen—representatives of the various Soviet nations and specialties—feel themselves ambassadors of our country.

Friendly visits by Soviet seamen offer the opportunity to the peoples of the countries visited to see for themselves the creativity of socialist principles in our country, the genuine parity of the peoples of the Soviet Union and their high cultural level. In our ships they see the achievements of Soviet science, technology and industry. Soviet mariners, from rating to admiral, bring to the peoples of other countries the truth about our socialist country, our Soviet ideology and culture and our Soviet way of life. ... Official visits and working calls of our ships to foreign ports make a substantial contribution to the improve-

ment of mutual understanding between states and peoples and to the enhancement of *the international authority* of the Soviet Union [italics added].[6]

Here is the classic naval presence statement, and in this light a recent excursion of the Soviet Navy into the southern Indian Ocean bears mention. On 30 January 1981, South African forces attacked and destroyed three African National Congress headquarters 15 kilometers from the center of Maputo in Mozambique. Pretoria asserted, with considerable justification, that the attack had been directed solely at bases from which terrorists had been operating inside the Republic of South Africa. Shortly thereafter, Soviet warships appeared off Mozambique's two main ports—Maputo and Beira—demonstrating that Moscow was determined to support the Mozambique government under the terms of the Treaty of Friendship and Cooperation the two nations had signed in 1977.[7] This is only the most recent example of the extent to which the political employment of the Soviet Navy has grown in direct proportion to its enlarged size and expanded outreach.

Thus the evolving character of the Red Navy—as well as that of other aspects of the USSR's maritime power—lead inescapably to a fundamental conclusion. It is axiomatic that the evolution of trends in naval and other maritime power, plus changing patterns in the uses to which that strength is put, necessarily provide solid clues to the ultimate strategic aims of a possessing nation. With respect to the USSR, it would be the sheerest of follies to ignore the evidence now at hand.

6. Ibid., pp. 251-52.
7. "Soviet Ships Lying off Mozambique," *Baltimore Sun* 20 February 1981, p. 4.

One therefore comes to this question: What should the response of the United States be? Given the shift in relative naval prowess that has occurred during the past two decades, it is abundantly clear that resuscitation of the U.S. Navy, as well as that of other elements of American maritime power—particularly the merchant marine—must be undertaken as a matter of urgency if this new challenge is to be met. It is also obvious, in view of the long leadtime involved in warship construction and the production of modern combat aircraft, that such a rebuilding effort will not only be long term but exceedingly expensive.

Given such circumstances, it is equally obvious that, for the immediate future, the United States will be compelled to look to its allies for assistance. In view of the facts of natural resource life, there can be little argument that with the far greater dependence of Japan and the nations of Western Europe on raw materials and markets in the Third World, they should be bearing a major portion of the responsibility for Western industrial stability. For political reasons, however, such assistance may very well not materialize, even though the requisite aid can take many forms, not all of which would necessarily require dispatch of allied armed force to distant regions.

Nevertheless, it would be a grave, perhaps fatal, mistake for Japan and Western European nations to conclude that the United States—concerned with its own issues of energy and nonfuel mineral shortages—would undertake, unilaterally, military action that would simultaneously solve their resource problems. After all, American industry is far less hostage to raw materials lying beyond the seas than are its allies. Moreover, those states should understand that while the spirit of isolationism in the United States might be moribund at the moment, it most certainly is not dead. The notion that the American body politic would sanction the shedding of American blood to preserve *Western* access to either or both of the aforementioned "treasure houses" while its allies stood supinely by beggars credibility. This is a lesson that allied leaders and their peoples will ignore at their peril.

Still, the United States may find it necessary to take unilateral military action to protect its own interests. After all, the U.S.—despite its continental scope—is an island nation in an increasingly interdependent world. It is now, and has been throughout most of its history, heavily reliant on the seas for access to raw materials and to markets for its manufactured goods. As energy and nonfuel mineral supplies within the nation's continental boundaries have been progressively depleted, that dependency has grown accordingly.

The USSR, on the other hand, has historically been a "have" nation insofar as such resources are concerned. Although the situation may shift with respect to energy in the not-too-distant future, the relative positions of the two superpowers remain essentially unchanged. Thus, the maritime strategies of the two nations can be expected to be diametrically opposed.

The United States' maritime strategies, should be oriented toward control of discrete portions of the world's sea-lanes when and where they must be used to support the nation's industrial and, therefore, economic as well as political well-being. From Moscow's perspective, its strategy should focus on denying such use to the United States and its allies while concurrently expanding Soviet influence and control along the paths and littorals of those seas. Given developments within the two navies in the past 20 years, it seems clear that the Soviets have learned this lesson and have taken concrete steps to put it to good use, while the United States and its various allies have not.

Whether the Reagan administration will produce the level of American sea power rennaissance required is uncertain. Insofar as naval forces are concerned, the Reagan defense budget is a most favorable indication.[8] But there is a long way to go, and one must conclude that time is very short. Under Gorshkov's tutelage, the Soviet fleet continues to grow in technological sophistication and capability. Allied assistance—provided in their own interests—can ease the present burdens to a considerable extent as the United States moves to redress the international maritime balance. In the long run, however, unless those allies make an effort to shoulder their fair share of the burden, they are likely to find themselves left in the lurch as the United States undertakes whatever measures might be required to ensure its own well-being, the needs of its allies notwithstanding.

8. John J. Fialka, "Budget to Boost Naval Power," *Washington Star* 4 March 1981, p. 1.

Obsolescence, Declining Productivity, and the American Defense Mobilization Infrastructure

By LEON S. REED

ABSTRACT: Numerous problems affect the mobilization capability of U.S. defense industry. These include legal requirements; the recent growth in lead times—perhaps the most meaningful indicator of defense industry responsiveness—and factors which determine this responsiveness, such as the adequacy of raw material supplies, investment in new processes and technologies, machine-tool industry capacity, availability of subcontractors, contractor productivity, and requirements imposed by socioeconomic policies. Mobilization capability is not a static phenomenon: it can either improve or deteriorate. Efforts to improve mobilization capability will also increase the efficiency of defense industry and its ability to meet near-term demands; failure to address these problems over the near term will result in continued deterioration of industry mobilization capability and responsiveness to short-term as well as long-range needs.

Leon S. Reed is employed by The Analytic Sciences Corporation, where he specializes in analyses of defense industry capability and industrial mobilization planning. Previously, he was senior professional staff member with the Joint Committee on Defense Production, U.S. Congress, and a professional staff member of the Senate Committee on Banking, Housing and Urban Affairs. In the mid-1970s he was co-leader of the first comprehensive congressional review since the 1950s of the defense industrial base and emergency preparedness and mobilization plans and capabilities.

This article is based on a paper presented by the author at the Tenth Annual Conference of the International Security Studies Program of the Fletcher School of Law and Diplomacy, Tufts University, held in Cambridge, Massachusetts, May 4-6, 1981.

INDUSTRIAL mobilization capability and the degree of obsolescence and declining productivity of the defense industrial base are closely related. If we were to project current capabilities into an environment of rapidly increasing demand for defense products, it would be likely to mean mobilization of an increasingly inefficient and unproductive defense industrial base. Inattention to the fact that mobilization may be necessary—that preparedness for war is the ultimate purpose of defense production programs—may account, at least in part, for this declining productivity and capability. Although many other factors contribute to defense mobilization capability—in a positive or negative fashion—the levels and relevance of investment in new processes and technology may be the most important single determinant of industrial readiness. An obsolete and unproductive industrial base cannot mobilize or even meet near-term demands effectively.

What follows is an assessment of the current status of defense industrial responsiveness, some of the factors that account for the present situation, and some alternative programs and reforms that could improve the current situation. Although many other factors are vital for mobilization capability—such as military manpower, maintenance and repair depots and operations, and transportation facilities—this article will consider only industrial production capability.

Efforts to understand mobilization capability must begin with an analysis of industry's ability to meet present-day defense requirements, because it is this capability which provides the baseline for expansion of production. If the defense industry cannot meet near-term needs, its prospects for meeting vastly increased mobilization requirements cannot be considered promising. Many reforms that could improve mobilization capability would also, if implemented today, improve the ability of defense industry to meet near-term, continuing needs; conversely, failure to address these problems in the near term would likely result in continued deterioration of defense capability and of mobilization potential.

It is useful at the outset to establish distinctions between two terms: surge and mobilization. Aside from stipulating that surge falls somewhere short of mobilization (in terms of increased rate of production and stress on society), there is little agreement on the distinction between the two terms. When does surge stop and mobilization begin, or, for that matter, when does everyday defense contracting let off and "surging" begin?

However, two useful distinctions can be made. First, while everyday production and surge would be carried on, for the most part by existing contractors, full mobilization would undoubtedly involve massive conversion of commercial producers. Second, while situations short of mobilization would be carried out under existing legal authorities and constraints (at least given current planning), mobilization would undoubtedly involve wholesale suspensions of present legal requirements and augmentation of existing presidential authority to control production and stabilize the economy. These two characteristics have a significant effect in determining the adequacy of industrial response under these two scenarios.

Many factors influence the ability of industry to mobilize or to meet increased demand for defense materiel. Some of the most important factors are

—the raw materials stream, including mining and processing;

—the adequacy and productivity of contractors' and subcontractors' industrial facilities, including especially the ability of the machine tool industry to meet increased demand;

—the availability of skilled labor in adequate quantities and with sufficient skills to operate the available machines;

—the adequacy of the government-industry planning system; and

—the legal structure underlying the system, both in terms of the authority it grants the government to conduct mobilization planning and in terms of any special obstacles which these requirements impose on near-term procurement and/or surge/mobilization planning and requirements satisfaction.

Serious deficiencies have been identified in all of the previously described areas. Many of these problems are closely related. For instance, raw materials supply problems can result in limiting the capacity of processing and refining industries. Efforts to increase stockpile holdings of some critically short materials (such as titanium sponge) could further strain existing supplies and have a serious impact on defense production programs. Similarly, shortages of skilled labor can affect the willingness of industry to expand capacity by installing new equipment.

Moreover, it is not clear that attempted solutions to any single problem can be accomplished without implications for other problems. For instance, investment incentives could have a variety of effects on defense industry. In terms of manpower, some types of investment could greatly increase demand for machinists, computer programmers, engineers, and other skilled workers currently experiencing job shortages. Other types of investment, in robots or computer-aided machinery, for instance, could moderate the demand for some labor skills, such as machinists, while increasing the need for other skills. Efforts to encourage industry to invest in new machinery could also strain the capacity of the machine tool and similar industries, which, because of severely limited capacity and expansion capability, have long been a critical bottleneck to defense expansion efforts. Thus, efforts to improve mobilization potential must attack the problem on a broad front. Uncoordinated efforts could solve one problem at the expense of others.

LEGAL AND ADMINISTRATIVE SYSTEM FOR PREPAREDNESS AND MOBILIZATION

Any effort to understand defense production and mobilization capabilities must consider the system of laws that establishes emergency preparedness planning and guides the defense production and mobilization system. Two acts of Congress, both more than 30 years old, establish the basic structure for industrial preparedness and mobilization planning: the National Security Act of 1947 (50 U.S.C. 401 *et seq.*), and the Defense Production Act of 1950 (50 U.S.C. App. 2061 *et seq.*). Both acts reflect the style of their times. They are very flexible, provide only general policy guidance, and grant authority in a relatively unconstrained fashion.

The National Security Act of 1947 directs the National Security Resources Board (now, as a result of the many executive branch reorganizations, the Federal Emergency Management Agency—FEMA) to undertake and to advise the president on mobilization planning. Specifically, FEMA is directed to develop plans for

—industrial and civilian mobilization to make the maximum use of the nation's manpower in time of war;

—the stabilization and conversion to a wartime footing of the civilian economy;

—unifying the activities of federal departments and agencies engaged in activities important to the war effort or mobilization;

—rationalizing potential supplies of and requirements for manpower, resources, and productive facilities;

—establishing adequate reserves of strategic and critical materials (that is, the National Defense Stockpile);

—the strategic relocation of industries, services, government, and other essential economic activities.

The National Security Act is potentially very powerful legislation. Only two weaknesses have been identified, both of which could probably be corrected by administrative action. First, the act defines and contemplates a relatively small coordinating entity within the Executive Office of the President (EOP).

This function has been reorganized on numerous occasions, but it was not until the 1974 creation of the Office of Preparedness, within the General Services Administration, that the function left the EOP. It is possible that the disharmony between FEMA's legislative charter and its current organizational status accounts for some (though by no means all) of the confusion about FEMA's proper role in emergency planning.

Second, while the act provides a relatively complete definition of the types of actions that should be planned for, these authorities are all oriented toward mobilization. No official basis exists to plan for mobilization-type activities in situations short of mobilization, though the nonmobilization "surge," with greatly increased defense demand but without wholesale conversion of the economy, may be both more likely to occur and more stressful to defense industry. The failure to provide in the law for planning for this situation represents a major void in U.S. preparedness efforts.

By contrast, the Defense Production Act (DPA) of 1950 contains both general authority for industrial preparedness and mobilization planning and specific authority for priority contract performance, allocation of materials, control of hoarding, financial assistance to assist defense contractors or to increase supplies of critical materials, and consultation with industry on industrial preparedness programs. The scope of the authorities contained in the DPA was perhaps best described by Paul Kreuger, Assistant Associate Director of FEMA for Resource Preparedness:

The easiest way to say what we can do and can't do under the DPA is that the entire synfuels program could have been funded, could have been authorized, using the existing authorities in Title III of the DPA. There was no necessity really for all of that legislation. ... We can make direct government loans. We can make loan guarantees. We can guarantee certain levels of production. We can guarantee prices. We can fund research and development. All of this is in the area of materials.

If you look in the back of the Act, the materials are defined in a very broad sense, to not only include what we think of as common materials, but also processes, ideas, concepts, so that the authorities are quite sweeping, quite broad.[1]

These authorities are available every day; they are not keyed to a state of war or declaration of national emergency.

Individual provisions in the DPA either affect or could affect nearly all the problems mentioned earlier. Because of the importance of the DPA, and because its provisions provide a useful structure for discussion of these problems, the following sections will discuss specific problems in the context of relevant provisions of the DPA which represent either problems or potential solutions to the problems.

Lead times

Unlike the problems mentioned elsewhere, increasing lead times should be regarded as a symptom, rather than a cause, of ailments in the defense industrial base. Between 1977 and 1980, according to the Defense Science Board, lead times for many weapons systems, components, and subsystems increased rapidly. For example, in 1976, the lead time for aluminum forgings was 20 weeks; by 1980, this had increased to 120 weeks. The 1976 lead time for traveling wave tubes (35 weeks) had more than doubled (to 95 weeks) by 1980. Titanium lead times increased steadily, from 40 weeks in 1976 to 46 weeks in 1977, 60 weeks in 1978, 70 weeks in 1979, and 104 weeks in 1980. Aircraft landing gear lead times were 52 weeks in 1977 but had increased to 120 weeks in 1980.[2]

Even a "DX" priority rating, supposedly a recognition of utmost urgency and highest national priority, did not guarantee timely delivery or protect against growing lead times. DX-rated aluminum small forgings experienced lead time increases from 55 weeks in 1978 to 125 weeks in 1980. Similarly, lead times for DX-rated titanium large forgings increased from 65 weeks in 1978 to 108 weeks in 1980. Electronic parts showed similar lead time growth: DX-rated microcircuits increased from 25 weeks (1978) to 51 weeks (1980), while DX-rated integrated circuits rose from 25 weeks to 62 weeks (1980).[3]

There were many causes for increased lead times, including insufficient capacity, or imbalanced capacity, at subcontractors and vendors; competition from commercial orders, especially in the booming commercial aircraft industry; labor problems at some key subcontractors and vendors; and failure to apply or enforce defense priorities.

Title I of the DPA provides authority to the president to

1. Statement in *Capability of the U.S. Defense Industrial Base,* Hearings before the Panel on Defense Industrial Base, Committee on Armed Services, U.S. House of Representatives, 1980, pp. 1367-68.

2. *Report of the Defense Science Board Summer Study Panel on Industrial Responsiveness,* Office of the Undersecretary of Defense for Research and Engineering, January 1981, pp. 30-31.

3. Ibid., p. 31.

"require that performance under contracts or orders (other than contracts of employment) which he deems necessary or appropriate to the national defense shall take priority over performance under any other contract or order" (50 U.S.C. App. 2071 (a)). Priority ratings of DO or DX are applied to virtually all defense weapons systems procurements, and regulations of the Office of Industrial Mobilization (Department of Commerce) stipulate that priority ratings attached to prime contracts must flow down through all subcontractors, vendors, and suppliers. However, there is general agreement that the DPS has been used ineffectively.[4]

The parallel Defense Materials System (DMS), concerned with allocation of critical materials, appears to function effectively, but its utility is limited by the fact that its coverage represents 1950s materials utilization patterns and fails to consider changes in supply and utilization patterns since that time. The DMS currently establishes "set-asides" for the following materials: steel, aluminum, copper, and nickel allow.[5] The former administrator of DPS/DMS testified: "The DMS is an outgrowth of experience that was gained during the Second World War and during the Korean conflict when it was found that through control of these particular commodities,

we could basically control U.S. industrial production."[6]

The limited coverage of the DMS, not applying to such vital defense materials as titanium, cobalt, and other critical materials that are in short supply and/or suffer from processing industry capacity limitations, undoubtedly contributes to long lead times and higher program costs. Given the changes in usage and patterns and supply sufficiency since the 1950s, it is not necessarily true that control of the four named materials still permits basic control of production. Even if this were true, such a macroeconomic approach ignores the potential for materials allocation to mitigate specific supply shortfalls for materials such as titanium.

Although no legislative permission would be needed to designate new materials, this has proved difficult. A recent effort to establish a set-aside for titanium was cancelled after the proposal was published in the *Federal Register*, principally due to titanium producer opposition to the proposed government control.

Priorities and allocations are important for other reasons than their potential for controlling lead time growth. In wartime, these systems would assume much greater importance. Bernard Baruch, head of the World War I mobilization effort, referred to priorities as the "synchronizing force" for war production efforts.[7] A critical short-

4. Defense Science Board, pp. xvii and 63-64; also, testimony before House Armed Services Committee, by the Honorable Dale Church (pp. 131, 135), Jerry R. Junkins (pp. 304-8, 318-21), General Alton Slay (pp. 475-77, 661-62), General John R. Guthrie (p. 743) and Wallace Brown (pp. 1010-52).

5. DMS regulations require that producers of these controlled materials "set aside" designated quantities and types of production each month for allocation to defense projects.

6. Testimony of Wallace Brown before House Armed Services Committee, p. 1015; see also testimony of General Alton Slay, p. 509.

7. Bernard M. Baruch, "Priorities: The Synchronizing Force," *Harvard Business Review* Spring 1941, pp. 261-70. For discussions of the application of priorities immediately before and during World War II, see John M. Martin, "Present Status of Priorities," *Harvard Business Review* Spring 1941,

coming of industrial preparedness planning appears to be that the current DPS/DMS is uniquely ill-suited to wartime needs when any or all of the following would be required:

—prioritization between different defense projects, based on relative urgency *and* on the degree to which the program could be completed in a timely fashion;

—broad allocation of many materials;

—priorities and allocations for industrial and essential civilian production; and

—renewed enforcement efforts to deal with a potentially higher degree of violations.

Although DPS/DMS has a potentially important role to play in reducing lead times, it is not a panacea. There is no substitute for capacity. Other industrial improvement and planning measures will be necessary to bring lead times under control. Lead times may be the most accurate gauge of the responsiveness of defense industry and have a direct impact on defense readiness. Increased lead times have a direct

pp. 271-85; Donald M. Nelson, *Arsenal of Democracy, The Story of American War Production* (New York: Harcourt, Brace and Co., 1406), pp. 90, 110-11, 119, and 349-90; and R. Elberton Smith, *The U.S. Army in World War II—the Army and Economic Mobilization* (Office of the Chief of Military History, 1958), pp. 507-49. Application of priorities in the Korean conflict is discussed in *Progress Report No. 10*, Joint Committee on Defense Production (JCDP), U.S. Congress, 26-27 November 1951, and in *Annual Reports* of the JCDP, 1951, and subsequent years. More recent status of the DPS/DMS was discussed in *Defense Priorities System*, Hearings before the Joint Committee on Defense Production, U.S. Congress, 22 and 23 May 1975, and in the *Annual Report* of the JCDP for 1975.

impact on near-term readiness by delaying delivery of programmed systems. Reducing lead times would mean automatic improvements in near-term readiness due to the shortened delivery periods.

Lead times also affect surge and mobilization capabilities, but the relationship is not as direct. Although reduced lead times are a necessary precursor to improving mobilization capabilities, such reductions will not necessarily improve these capabilities. Instead, project-by-project analysis would be needed to determine the impact of reduced lead times in one area on other potential bottlenecks in an environment of increasing production rates.

Expansion of productive capacity and supply for strategic and critical materials

The United States is dangerously dependent on foreign suppliers for many strategic and critical materials, including some of the most important for defense programs. Shortages of critical materials can affect industrial responsiveness in no fewer than five ways: (1) by increasing lead times, if materials are unavailable or in short supply; (2) by limiting domestic processing capacity; (3) by adding to costs, if suppliers increase prices; (4) by forcing use of substitutes; and (5) by making it impossible to meet existing or expanded program needs due to supply interruptions.

Stockpiling of critical raw and processed materials has been the traditional way of protecting against materials vulnerability. However, for many reasons, the present U.S. stockpile is seriously out of balance. Of 61 individual materials and family groups in the stockpile, shortfalls exist for 37. In the case of 23, stockpile holdings equal half or less of approved goals.[8] Although serious questions exist about the realism of the present goals, although many of the deficits are for relatively low-priority items, and although greater attention could probably be given to the potential for increasing imports "on warning," it is nonetheless clear that it will take a very expensive and long-term effort to bring the stockpile up to adequate levels.

It is possible, however, that stockpiling should be regarded only as a last resort. Actual purchase of a material can be expensive and can place an unacceptable strain on already limited supplies (among them titanium sponge). Furthermore, stockpile purchases alone cannot reduce foreign dependence, solve raw materials supply problems in times short of national emergency, or, perhaps most important, correct processing or production industry capacity shortages. Indeed, it may be impossible to buy some of the most critically needed materials, precisely because the short-supply situation which creates the need for stockpiling prevents any action that would tighten supplies further.

An alternative exists in the form of Title III of the DPA, which authorizes virtually unlimited financial assistance for projects to expand domestic capacity and supply of critical materials, including energy resources. However, despite the potential for use of these authorities, no new awards of financial assistance have been made since 1967. FEMA has proposed four Title III

8. Federal Emergency Management Agency, *Stockpile Report to the Congress*, January 1981, p. 3.

projects—for titanium processing, cobalt, guayule rubber cultivation, and refractory bauxite. All four of these projects are significant because they could increase domestic capacity for materials for which substantial stockpile shortfalls presently exist. At relatively small cost, these programs could reduce stockpile goals, thus freeing limited acquisition funds for other purchases.

Title III can also be used more broadly to grant loans or loan guarantees to government contractors for virtually any project that would promote improved defense production efforts. This authority, like the authority for critical materials, has remained unused for nearly 15 years.

Contractor investment

While lead times may be the most basic indicator of industrial responsiveness, investment in new processes and technologies may be the most important determinant of this responsiveness. A great deal of attention has recently been focused on the problem American industry is facing in forming capital for plant modernization. It should come as no surprise to find that defense contractors suffer from these problems that affect American industry generally.

However, defense industry also suffers unique investment disincentives that grow out of DoD depreciation and cost reimbursement policies. Interest has traditionally been an unallowable expense on defense contracts. Depreciation of equipment has traditionally been allowed only at a very slow rate. However, while government cost-reimbursement policies have tended to ignore investment costs, labor has always been recognized as a legitimate, allowable input. In addition, cost projections have been based on historic (allowable) costs, and target profit rates have been based on these cost projections. Thus, as DoD's Profit '76 Task Force acknowledged, contractors have had little incentive to reduce costs, especially if cost-reduction measures would involve reductions in allowable costs (labor), increases in unallowable costs (investment), and overall reductions in incurred costs (and, thus, profits). The Profit '76 Task Force reached very broad conclusions about the contribution of new investments to productivity and the negative impact of DoD cost and profit policies on contractor investment and productivity. However, the reform initiated as a result of this study effort was comparatively modest, and, according to the GAO, was unlikely to provide a significant incentive for new investments.[9]

A second investment disincentive, the unallowability of interest, was partially corrected in 1976 with the issuance of Cost Accounting Standard (CAS) 414, which allowed the imputed rate of interest for facilities capital as a contract charge. Working capital is not covered by CAS 414, however, and the reimbursement rate for facilities capital is limited to the Treasury borrowing rate, which is currently below the rates most contractors must pay for facilities capital.

Perhaps the most significant investment disincentive is posed by DoD depreciation policy, mandated by CAS 409, which was issued by the Cost Accounting Standards Board in 1975 under the authority of Section 719 of the Defense Production Act. Because the cash flows resulting from any expenditure are vitally important, the rate at which a new investment can be depreciated plays an important role in determining a contractor's willingness to make new investments. CAS 409 requires that depreciation for contract costing be based on the historical useful life or the estimated economic useful life of the given piece of equipment, which is perhaps the slowest depreciation rate prescribed by any governmental body in the world. While this procedure undoubtedly minimizes short-term government expenditures by limiting the rate at which contractors will be reimbursed for new investments, it can pose a substantial disincentive for contractors to make new investments. General acceleration of tax depreciation policies to spur corporate investment will have little impact on the defense industry unless CAS 409 is also modified. Due to a unique situation that has existed since 30 September 1980, CAS 409 and other cost accounting standards may be the only government regulations that can, at present, be modified only by an act of Congress.[10]

9. General Accounting Office, *Recent Changes in the Defense Department's Profit Policy—Intended Results Not Achieved* (PSAD-79-38), 8 March 1979. See also *Defense Industrial Base, Part II: Department of Defense Profit '76 Study*, Hearings before the Joint Committee on Defense Production, U.S. Congress, 18 November 1976; and *Department of Defense Contract Profit Policy*, Hearings before the Committee on Banking, Housing and Urban Affairs, U.S. Senate, 21 March 1979.

10. The Cost Accounting Standards Board was denied an appropriation for FY81 and ceased to exist on 30 September 1980. Although the CAS remained in effect, no authority, other than an act of Congress, presently exists to modify, amend, repeal, or grant waivers from CAS requirements. An effort to transfer CASB authorities to the Office of Federal Procurement Policy, sup-

Government-owned machinery

Inadequate as industrial investment has been, it is probably in better shape than is the government-owned tool base. Congress has given the government contradictory directions regarding government-owned tools. While the Defense Industrial Reserve Act specifies that the government should retain an "essential nucleus" of government-owned tools to meet current and emergency needs, it also directs the government to make the maximum use of privately owned industrial facilities. Short-term budget reductions have led to a sentiment to "do it next year," resulting in a rapidly aging machine tool base. While industry has relied heavily on government-owned tools, the government has failed to modernize its own machinery. According to the Defense Science Board, more than 20,000 of 26,000 government-owned metal-cutting and metal-forming tools in contractor plants (including government-owned, contractor-operated plants) are in excess of 20 years old. Little is being done to modernize this base.

Machine tool industry capacity

Efforts to promote increased industry investment in new machinery are likely to be constrained by the limited capacity and responsiveness of the machine tool industry. In past mobilization efforts, this industry has constituted a critical bottleneck. One of the classic studies in the field concluded: "This component of production, relatively small in dollar value, was the main bottleneck of industrial mobil-

ization in World War II and after the outbreak of war in Korea."[11]

The machine tool industry suffers from a variety of problems that serve to limit its capacity and responsiveness. These include decentralized structure, limited investment capital, fluctuations in demand, and skilled manpower shortages.

For all these reasons, the machine tool industry has traditionally been unable, or unwilling, to expand its capacity to meet increased demand. To cope with this problem, the Machine Tool Trigger Order Program (or M-Day Tool Program) existed until 1969, under the authority of the DPA, for the purpose of minimizing machine tool bottlenecks during emergencies. Under this program, standby contracts were signed with various machine tool producers, requiring them, in time of emergency or upon order, immediately to begin producing designated types and quantities of machine tools. In 1971, the DoD requested that the Tool Program be reactivated, and in 1974 an interagency committee made the same recommendation. However, little has happened since that recommendation was made. Several years ago standard contracts were developed and offered to machine tool producers, but these contracts were refused, reportedly because of the machine tool producers' reluctance to accept government requirements and contractual restraints at a time when a machine tool "seller's market" existed. It is ironic that the conditions which create the greatest need for such a program may also

ported by the OMB and GAO, failed in the 96th Congress due to major contractor opposition to elements of the proposed legislation.

11. George A. Lincoln, *The Economics of National Security* (Englewood Cliffs, NJ: Prentice-Hall, 1954), p. 209. See also Nelson, *Arsenal of Democracy*, pp. 127-28, 140, 152.

maximize the resistance of machine tool manufacturers to get involved in such a program.

Other productivity problems

Lack of investment, while important, is not the sole cause of unsatisfactory productivity in defense industry. Inefficient labor utilization practices also play no small role. For example, in the general turmoil surrounding release four years ago of the "DoD/OMB Aircraft Capacity Study," one conclusion that was generally overlooked was that most of the extra costs represented people, not machinery. For instance, the senior DoD procurement official, testifying about this report, stated:

> For the most part, this cost consists of indirect labor, i.e., engineering, marketing and administrative personnel, retained in anticipation of and to enhance obtaining additional government business. Twenty-five percent or less of the extra capacity costs is associated with under-utilized plant and equipment.[12]

Another study, by the Air Force Systems Command, found similar inefficient direct labor utilization:

> Manufacturing costs are about 42 percent of direct costs on a typical production contract. About 50 percent of this cost represents nonproductive labor caused by inefficiencies of one kind or another. If it were possible to achieve only a 20 percent improvement in labor productivity, approximately one billion

dollars could be saved on contracts at 11 of the major Air Force contractors.[13]

Many factors may account for poor labor productivity. The DoD/OMB study recommended absolute limits on contractor indirect labor charges. Hand in hand with enforcement, however, should be increased stability in procurement and increased investment incentives to achieve improvements in labor utilization. In addition, the impact of legal and administrative compliance and reporting requirements on contractor productivity should be considered.

Other legal requirements

Many other laws, most of which appear to have little bearing on defense contracting or mobilization, can also have a serious negative impact on industrial responsiveness, productivity, and mobilization capability. These are the numerous procurement and "socioeconomic" laws, many of which have been approved by Congress within the past 15 years, and most of which have never been reviewed by the committees most concerned with defense production.

It is not unprecedented for the United States to apply socioeconomic policies to defense contracting efforts in time of war. In 1953 alone, the Office of Defense Mobilization issued several manpower policies dealing with some of the same subjects as present-day "affirmative action" policies. These included Defense Manpower Policy No. 7 (DMP-7), providing for more effec-

---

12. Testimony of the Honorable Dale Church, Deputy Director for Acquisition of the Directorate of Defense Research and Engineering in *Defense Industrial Base, Part IV: DOD Procurement Practices*, Hearings before the Joint Committee on Defense Production, 30 September 1977, p. 34.

13. Cited by Senator William Proxmire in *Federal Acquisition Act*, Hearings before the Committee on Armed Services, U.S. Senate, 5 October 1978, p. 44.

tive utilization of older workers in the defense program; DMP-9, calling for emphasis on increasing opportunities for handicapped workers and more effective use of such workers in the mobilization program; and DMP-11, providing for special assistance to returning Korean veterans in obtaining suitable training or employment.[14]

What is new is the breadth of coverage of present-day requirements, the detailed compliance requirements, and the punitive enforcement provisions. Socioeconomic legislation in the fields of environmental protection, employment practices, and subcontractor/prime contractor preference, as well as general procurement law, has become so detailed that the industrial response in World War II and in the Korean war should probably be considered irrelevant to the environment of the 1980s.

These new requirements can have any of the following negative impacts on defense procurement and on mobilization capabilities: diversion of effort, in order to comply with detailed reporting and review requirements; delay in approval of reports or in initiation of contracting efforts; and additional expense, due either to the delays or to additional compliance efforts. Reporting requirements under defense contracts can have a negative impact on contractor productivity, because the work necessary to comply with the requirements would be considered to be indirect, nonproductive labor.

Perhaps most serious in terms of their effect on mobilization potential, though, are those requirements

14. ODM submission to *Third Annual Report*, Joint Committee on Defense Production, U.S. Congress, 1954, p. 71.

which act as barriers to entry for new firms or prevent initiation of production under new government contracts. These requirements include preparation of Cost Accounting Standards disclosure statements, which must be approved before a new contractor or subcontractor can initiate production; a former CASB senior staff member estimated that preparation and approval of a disclosure statement for a new contractor or subcontractor could take as long as six months. They also make necessary the preparation and approval (and litigation, if necessary) of environmental impact statements, needed for any major federal actions significantly affecting the environment (including new plant construction, Title III projects, and weapons projects such as the MX); preparation and approval of an affirmative action employment plan; and preparation, approval, and negotiation into the contract of a detailed small and disadvantaged business subcontractor utilization plan. This requirement is especially burdensome and must be developed anew for each contract.

None of these requirements was present, in anything like their present form, even during the Vietnam conflict. Significantly, none was written or considered by the Armed Services Committees, normally considered to be the committees in the Senate and House of Representatives, respectively, most concerned with defense matters. In most cases enforcement authority, as well as waiver authority, lies with agencies other than DoD, and provisions for suspending the requirements during emergencies are not specified. It is important to remember that bureaucratic bottlenecks can delay mobilization efforts just as much as production-capacity bottlenecks. Defense procurement procedures, only some of which were mandated by Congress—such as qualified bidder's lists, first-article approval requirements, preaward surveys, and complex specifications and quality control procedures—can also delay and add to the costs of defense programs.

In all likelihood, these requirements will not be repealed. They probably should not be repealed, even in wartime. The United States has always placed a high priority on protecting its values, and this may be even more important in wartime than in peacetime. As stated earlier, policies such as those under discussion were applied, to some extent, during World War II and the Korean war. Indeed, some socioeconomic policies—such as the requirement for contracting in labor surplus areas—may become more important in wartime because of the impact of localized labor shortages and surpluses.

Instead, what is needed is a reassessment of the miscellaneous socioeconomic requirements and procurement procedures that can inhibit industry's ability to respond to near-term or mobilization requirements. The probable effect of these requirements on defense production was generally not considered at the time these requirements were enacted, and should be now. In some cases such a review might disclose methods of avoiding impairment of defense production while still ensuring satisfaction of the original purpose of these requirements.

CONCLUSION

Preparation for industrial mobilization has been considered irrele-vant for many years because it has been assumed that future conventional wars will occur with little warning and will be very short. Clearly, the ability of industry to increase production significantly, or to mobilize, over the short term is so questionable (especially with existing legal constraints) that mobilization planning—at least on a broad scale—should be considered irrelevant under such a scenario. The increasing complexity of modern weapons systems, lengthening lead times, and the declining number and capacity of subcontractors contribute to this problem.

However, there is an element of self-fulfilling prophecy in these assumptions. If the United States assumes that it will not begin to mobilize industry "on warning," and if it continues to assume that industrial preparedness is irrelevant, then such preparedness probably will be. If the United States refuses to take advantage of "warning," and if it continues to allow mobilization capabilities to deteriorate, then mobilization plans will be lacking, mobilization capability will not be provided, and future conventional wars, in all probability, will be "short" due to the inability of U.S. industry to sustain its forces.

Since the Korean war, industrial preparedness planning has frequently been forced to take the "back seat"—first to the doctrine of massive retaliation, then to Vietnam war consumption requirements, and then to the requirements for force structure modernization. Declining defense budgets and DoD's self-imposed imperative to perpetuate the major aircraft manufacturers also contributed to the low priority for IPP.[15]

15. For discussions of mid-1970s industrial base planning, see *Defense Industrial*

However, this does not need to be the case. Defense production capacity is not foreordained, nor is it static. This capability can improve or deteriorate. If legislative packages were introduced and approved to provide necessary legal authorities and reform burdensome requirements, if proper investment incentives were furnished, if government and industry initiated effective industrial preparedness planning to include both broad industrial improvements and planning for wartime expedient measures, if the DoD initiated programs to correct deficiencies in the lower tiers and to attack known and prospective bottlenecks, and if effective programs were initiated, under the stockpiling program and the DPA, to correct raw materials and materials processing shortages, the

Base, Part IV: DOD Procurement Practices, Hearings before the Joint Committee on Defense Production, 29 and 30 September 1977; Civil Preparedness Review, Part 1: Emergency Preparedness and Industrial Mobilization, Report of the Joint Committee on Defense Production, February 1977, pp. 55-96; Colonel Harry F. Ennis, Peacetime Industrial Preparedness for Wartime Ammunition Production (National Defense University, 1980); and Jacques S. Gansler, The Defense Industry (Cambridge: MIT Press, 1980).

result could be a robust defense industrial base which could support more realistic and useful military planning.

These improvements in defense industrial capability should be of concern to everyone, regardless of ideological perspective. Conservatives should favor programs to improve defense industrial capabilities, because their efforts over the near term to expand defense capabilities are likely to be frustrated if inadequacies in the defense industrial base are not corrected. Liberals and arms control advocates, likewise, should favor these initiatives because they will ensure that defense dollars are not spent profligately and because a sound, economic, and expandable defense industry capable of responding to increasing needs provides the assurance necessary to back up arms control agreements.

Efforts to improve industrial mobilization capabilities should begin with the strengthening of the ability of the industrial base to meet near-term defense needs. Failure to address these problems in the near term will result in continued erosion of defense capabilities and a continued decline in mobilization capabilities.

ANNALS, *AAPSS*, 457, September 1981

Arms Control in the 1980s

By WILLIAM HADLEY KINCADE

ABSTRACT: Despite the reversal of détente, and perhaps even because of it, negotiated arms control agreements will continue in the 1980s to offer solutions to security and related problems that cannot be adequately managed in the absence of mutual restraint. To the existing motives for arms limitation—coping with the existential dilemma of nuclear weapons in a conflictual world and avoiding the worst costs of an unbridled strategic competition—will be added the requirement for greater predictability and calculability in the strategic environment than emerging weapons and surveillance technologies will provide. At the same time, the difficulties of conceiving, achieving, and sustaining support for arms limitation agreements will be greater than in the past, owing both to technological and political developments. Those who endorse arms control as an approach to security problems must find solutions to the many vexing problems this enterprise faces. There are, first, the technical challenges: innovation, verification, and the prevention of costly and provocative deployments. In addition, there are institutional and political challenges. Answers to some of these problems can be found by examining the record of negotiated security in the nuclear age and by making the lessons of this record available both to the policy makers and the public.

William H. Kincade is a senior associate of the Carnegie Endowment for International Peace and executive director of the Arms Control Association. A graduate of Princeton, he earned his Ph.D. in international relations at the American University. From 1963 to 1970, he served as an intelligence officer in the U.S. Navy, attaining the rank of lieutenant commander. Before taking his present posts, he was staff director of the Joint Committee on Defense Production of the U.S. Congress. He is the co-editor of three books on arms control and the author of numerous articles on arms control and other security issues.

TWENTY-FIVE years have passed since arms control was born out of the dual recognition that human safety and national security require the regulation of nuclear and thermonuclear weapons and that international disarmament discussions, as they existed, were not going to provide a mechanism for limitation.[1] During most of that period, the United States has enjoyed a significant lead over all other nuclear weapon states in both the qualitative and quantitative dimensions of nuclear arsenals. Moreover, these weapons, measured by cost per unit of destructive power, were comparatively inexpensive and were often considered more or less straightforward substitutes for other types of military force. As a consequence, American presidents and their defense advisers could afford to view arms control as a potentially useful but not essential component of security policy. For national leaders, more often than not, what tipped the scales in favor of particular limitation proposals was less the urgency of the problem of a nuclear war than the hope of avoiding additional defense costs, the need to demonstrate a commitment to peace, and the desire to prevent the spread of nuclear weapons to new countries or new areas, such as Antarctica, outer space, and the seabed.

The conditions that allowed arms control to be treated as optional and not essential have ended. As was anticipated by many early advocates of negotiated limitation, the Soviet Union has drawn abreast of

1. For a longer discussion of the U.S. arms control experience, see William Hadley Kincade, *American Interests in Strategic Arms Control: Past Present, and Future*, Occasional Paper, Chicago Council on Foreign Relations, 1980.

the United States in at least the crude measures of nuclear strength. There is little in recent history to warrant the view that the Soviet Union will fail to maintain its hard-won position of equivalence. The belief that the Soviet leadership will relinquish its new status and concede self-evident nuclear superiority to the United States has a weak foundation, even (or especially) in view of Soviet economic and political problems.

Of equal importance, staying on the strategic high wire and avoiding a plunge into the nuclear caldron below has become progressively more difficult for the superpowers as technological innovation has produced weapons that greatly increase the incentives for striking first in a crisis—or, more precisely, that, in principle, increase the penalties for *failing* to stike first, if there appears to be a reasonable chance the other side is contemplating a nuclear attack. Paradoxically, the growth and improvement of nuclear weapons have reduced to an even more discouraging level the penalties for initiating nuclear war for profit, but the same developments have made more possible and more desirable a preemptive or damage-limiting attack. The likelihood of a so-called catalytic nuclear war that neither superpower wants is now higher than a nuclear exchange instigated by either side for perceived gain ever was.

Moreover, owing partly to the condition of parity, partly to the ravages of inflation in the United States, and partly to the fact that most of the "easy" innovations in strategic weaponry have been achieved, each additional increment of nuclear firepower—Trident, MX, and new bomber—will be purchased at a cost far higher than that of baseline forces, such as Polaris/ Poseidon, Minuteman, and the B-52. Cruise missiles may prove an exception. The $100 billion MX missile system will give us 200 missiles and 2000 reentry vehicles at a price greatly in excess of the less than $20 billion life-cycle cost (in 1981 dollars) of the 1000 missiles and 2000 reentry vehicles in the Minuteman system it augments.

Any hypothetical advantage this could confer on the United States, furthermore, may be undercut even before MX deployment is completed by Soviet exploitation of its existing capacity to increase the number of its reentry vehicles or by a Soviet decision to field its own mobile missile, perhaps without the surveillance safeguards contemplated for MX. Indeed, the United States could suffer a net security loss by stimulating the rivalry in ICBMs, the only type of weapon in which the Soviet Union has some advantages.

As the various costs of the strategic competition grow while producing, at best, more and more marginal gains, arms control becomes not an option in U.S. defense policy but an imperative. Negotiated agreements are the only sensible means now available for confining Soviet strategic potential, bringing predictability to the strategic environment, and avoiding the economic and domestic political penalties of an unregulated rivalry. This is not to say that the imperative character of negotiated security will necessarily be widely appreciated or accepted in the United States. History is littered with the carcasses of men and governments who could not read the handwriting on the wall.

Although in 1981 the American administration did seem to endorse the notion that there is a simple correlation between nuclear hard-ware and national security, this may well change as the long-term implications of an aggravated strategic competition for its economic revitalization policies sink in. The Reagan team, at least ostensibly, has left open the arms control option. Its interest in this prudent course may quicken when the American public and the economy begin to feel the full impact of President Reagan's five-year defense plan.

As projected, defense spending would grow from $162 billion in fiscal year 1981 to over $343 billion in fiscal 1986, an expansion three times as great as that of the Vietnam war. With federal spending of this magnitude and with substantial reductions in personal and business taxes, achievement of a balanced budget will rest on roseate assumptions about inflation rates and the impact on the economy of hopeful public expectations. These assumptions raised eyebrows among economists and defense analysts, as well as, more importantly, on Wall Street. Something in the defense program thus probably will have to give; the areas where restraint can most easily be achieved are the big-ticket strategic systems.[2]

Security interests—including economic interests—then, increasingly require strategic arms limitation for their fulfillment in an

2. Arms control undertaken primarily for cost-avoidance reasons, however, may not produce the best results. Some of the weapons most prejudicial to durable, verifiable agreements—such as MIRVs or cruise missiles—may not be the most expensive, while more "controllable" weapons, such as manned bombers, could have very high price-tags. For an analysis of the possible impact of the Reagan program, see Lester Thurow, "How to Wreck the Economy," *New York Review of Books* 14 May 1981. See also R. James Woolsey, "A Strategy of Fudging Numbers," *The Washington Post* 28 April 1981.

altered world. Nuclear superiority is yesterday's answer, not today's. As long as SALT is observed, there is a basis for believing the leadership of the United States will come to appreciate this situation, by an indirect route if not a direct one. Should it not, subsequent administrations will be under even greater pressure to do so.

Nevertheless, arms control in the 1980s will face serious problems and severe tests, which may make even the difficulties of the 1960s and 1970s seem simple by comparison. Thoughtful observers agree that arms control is now in political, conceptual, and institutional disarray, if not in a crisis.[3] Aggravating these problems is a generational change. Many of the midwives of the idea of arms control have retired from the field, or they bespeak approaches that are less and less relevant to today's circumstances. A successor generation of thinkers (as opposed to practitioners) is not clearly in evidence. And there is much to discourage promising talent from entering the field.

Yet clearly the problems that confront arms control will not be solved by detractors and skeptics on either the left or the right. Solutions must be found by individuals committed to the principle that negotiated arms agreements can enhance American and world security. No one else will assay the task.

3. See, for example, Leslie S. Gelb, "The Future of Arms Control: A Glass Half Full," *Foreign Policy* 36 (Fall 1979); Barry M. Blechman, "Do Negotiated Arms Limitations Have a Future?" *Foreign Affairs* (Fall 1980); Joseph J. Kruzel, "Arms Control and American Defense Policy: New Alternatives and Old Realities," *Daedalus* (Winter 1981); and Duncan L. Clarke, "The Future of Arms Control and A.C.D.A.," testimony before the Committee on Foreign Affairs, House of Representatives, U.S. Congress, 8 April 1981.

The purpose of this survey, however, is not primarily to provide solutions. Nor is its method to canvass possible futures for different negotiating initiatives already undertaken. Rather, the objective is to establish an agenda and stimulate thinking by exploring current and foreseeable problems that arms control must solve if it is to make a contribution to U.S. security during the 1980s. The focus is on nuclear arms limits, since, without progress in this area, other initiatives are likely to prove barren.

PRELIMINARY STEPS

The original intellectual capital of arms control needs to be reevaluated and replenished in light of the lessons of 20 years of negotiating experience. Equally urgent is the task of explaining in comprehensible terms the principles and promise of arms control to audiences beyond the community of specialists. Even the small but consistent constituency for arms control often labors in ignorance of basic military, technical, and diplomatic factors. Too few understand arms control in a comprehensive way— how to conceive it, how to achieve it, and how to build and sustain support for it. Arms limitation has been for some time an insider's game.

With some notable exceptions, there has been too little intimately informed, systematic analysis that is relevant to both policy and public concern.[4] Insufficient attention has been paid to separating that which

4. Some notable exceptions are Gerard Smith, *Doubletalk* (New York: Doubleday, 1980); Raymond L. Garthoff, "Negotiating with the Russians: Some Lessons from SALT," *International Security* (Spring 1977),

works in arms control from that which does not, to describing the conditions associated with success or failure, to generating new conceptions, and to making these understandings available to the public.

The perpetuation of these conditions will contribute still further to the ready acceptance of simplistic notions of arms control—either negative or positive—to false expectations, to unnecessary incoherence in policy, and, at times, to a conceptual rigidity among supporters of arms control. Negotiated security is a long-haul enterprise that already faces many permanent obstacles: resolute opposition, periodic changes in policy and personnel owing to domestic politics, and ups and downs in international relations. It would be easy to ascribe its slow progress to these conditions alone.

What is needed instead is a willingness to rethink arms control broadly in light of past and future challenges—both political and technical. Arms limitation is not a solution for a major human problem; it is a technique for managing this problem, for preventing its worst excesses. As such, arms control must evolve as conditions change. If it becomes too rigid and pretends too much, if its trials are blamed solely on demonic forces, or if its partisans regard it as a final truth rather than an important instrument, then arms control will suffer the fate its detractors wish for it—an idea that failed.

and "Mutual Deterrence and Strategic Arms Limitation in Soviet Policy," *International Security* (Summer 1978); Robin Ranger, *Arms and Politics, 1958-1978: Arms Control in a Changing Political Context* (Toronto: Macmillan, 1979); and Thomas W. Wolfe, *The SALT Experience: Its Impact on U.S. and Soviet Strategic Policy and Decisionmaking* (Santa Monica, CA: Rand Corporation, 1975).

TECHNICAL CHALLENGES

Judging from recent negotiating experience and projections of future technology, the three principal technical problems requiring solution in the 1980s are:

—the advent of a presumptive counterforce capability in both Soviet and American arsenals, a capability that appears to undercut arms control agreements based on the mutual vulnerability of urban-industrial centers;

—a widening gap between the rate of improvement in surveillance technology and the increasing capacity of new weapons (mobile ICBMs, modern cruise missiles, etc.) to evade high confidence surveillance; and

—a similar gap between the arms control negotiating process and the weapons development process that results either in interminable talks or agreements susceptible to rapid obsolescence due to the deployment of new technologies.

Innovation

To many, the only or best foundation for arms limitation is a technological condition in which the population and industrial centers of both superpowers become necessarily—if not by choice—the primary targets of survivable, retaliatory forces. This circumstance prevailed from the time of Hiroshima and Nagasaki until about the mid-1970s, because available weapons, although often aimed at traditional military targets, could not dependably hit them or do so without causing considerable collateral damage to the surrounding area. A nuclear capacity constrained by technology to large-scale urban-industrial damage is considered conducive to arms control, since the threat to devastate major cities by itself provides an effective deterrent and the vulnerability and comparatively small and unchanging number of important cities keeps weapons requirements to a relatively low level. In such a situation, the objective of arms control in the United States was to help stabilize this condition at the lowest level of forces consistent with the requirement for an adequate and survivable second-strike threat. This would both prevent the economic burden and diminish the risks attendant on a nuclear competition in which neither side could hope to evade the basic condition of vulnerability anyway.

Yet when nuclear arsenals improved in numbers and capability in the 1970s, it became possible to contemplate striking, with higher confidence of success, more discrete counterforce targets such as an adversary's strategic or conventional forces, command and control systems, administrative and political centers, industrial infrastructure and recovery capacity, and so on. As a consequence, target lists and the requirements for offensive weapons expanded. So did the apparent incentives for striking first, in order to evade a possible first strike by the other side—a first strike that seemed to undercut retaliatory capability substantially or to render it meaningless.

Under these emerging circumstances, the incentives and conditions for achieving durable arms limitation agreements would appear to diminish drastically, if not to vanish altogether. Hence a good deal of energy has been devoted to freezing the nuclear balance in a state that is regarded as more favor-able to enduring agreements and to the comparatively low levels of forces deemed necessary for retaliatory attacks on major cities. Nevertheless, improvements in weapons yield-to-weight ratios, in guidance systems, and in multiple warhead technology have not been forestalled. While the benefits and penalties of initiating a nuclear exchange continue to tilt toward the deficit side of the ledger, the technological fact is that counterforce capability has advanced considerably, at least on paper. Although it may be preferable to negotiate agreements under technological circumstances that favor countercity assumptions, the dominant strategic perception of the 1980s will be that counterforce targets come first and countercity exchanges will be reserved for the ultimate blow, if necessary.

An important task for arms control, then, is to work out the implications of this shift from countercity technology to an era of presumptive counterforce technology. It will be a highly uncongenial enterprise for some. Yet the value of arms limitation will not vanish in this new, counterforce setting. In fact, the need for the order and predictability that arms limitation can bring to the strategic environment will probably increase in coming years, as new and hybrid systems create a far wider range of plausible threats to challenge contingency planners and budget officials. Both supporters and opponents of arms control have largely ignored the fact that much of the comparative orderliness in the strategic balance of the 1960s and 1970s was a product of the technological limitations inherent in the first generations of strategic weapons. As these "natural" limitations are eroded, the requirement to preserve order and calculability through careful and mutual management of forces grows greater.

Reinforcing the military interest in a more, rather than less, predictable threat milieu is the political interest in avoiding misunderstandings that could precipitate a nuclear exchange desired by neither side but made more possible in a fragile, "use-them-or-lose-them" balance of counterforces. Further buttressing the need for negotiated security in a counterforce world is the continuing economic interest in cost-avoidance, for the variety of new threats suggested by emerging offensive and defensive weapons implies strategic program growth of staggering proportions in the 1980s.

This further implies the maintenance, unchanged, of the current Anti-Ballistic Missile (ABM) Treaty of 1972 and its 1974 protocol. It remains not only the best guarantee of the ultimate deterrent threat against cities but also a brake on the further refinement of counterforce weaponry. Despite beguiling assertions that ballistic missile defenses could produce a more benign strategic competition, the inevitable result of expanded ABM systems would be a race to improve counterforce weapons through such expedients as maneuvering and precision-guided reentry vehicles and similar innovations designed to penetrate defenses that would, in any case, remain "leaky."[5]

The low-altitude ballistic missile defense or interception system now under consideration in the United States does not represent a technological breakthrough; it cannot, for example, provide stationary missile silos effective protection against an attacker determined to overwhelm

or destroy the interception system itself. To be effective in shielding fixed silos, low-altitude defenses must be supplemented by a high-altitude interception system, of which there is no near-term prospect.

To be effective in guarding ICBMs based in a semimobile, deceptive mode—such as one the Carter administration proposed for MX missiles—a low-altitude interception system must itself be based in such a way as to avoid revealing its own location and that of the MX missile it is defending. No operationally satisfactory means of meeting this requirement has been found.[6]

Perhaps the strongest argument against U.S. adoption of ballistic missile defenses (BMD), however, is that if the Soviets in turn deploy BMD technology of even uncertain effectiveness, it would necessarily raise doubts about the penetrativeness of American warheads and especially of the far less numerous British, French, and Chinese warheads. This would amount to undercutting a strong, combined deterrent threat to the Soviet Union for the sake of a highly dubious defensive gain for the United States alone.

How arms control can best function in a counterforce epoch will be influenced in part by the program choices of the superpowers in the next few years and in part by the rate of development of new systems. While security negotiations cannot turn back the technological clock to the era of predominantly counter-city weaponry, it should continue to have as one of its goals the curbing of

5. On this point see Albert Carnesale, "Reviving the ABM Debate," *Arms Control Today* (April 1981).

6. I am indebted to Prof. Jack Ruina of MIT for illuminating these points.

developments that increase incentives in a crisis for a damage-limiting, preemptive first strike. Simple, numerical limits, for example, can help to constrain counterforce capability and thus help avoid crisis situations wherein initiating a first strike may seem the lesser of two evils. A ban on the deployment of antisatellite or other space-oriented weaponry, or an agreement not to target command and control facilities, would further reduce the chance of catalytic war. Restrictions on submarine forces and on certain antisubmarine warfare advances or techniques would aid in the preservation of both the high survivability of missile submarines and the overall predictability of the strategic environment.

Verification

A task that is, if anything, still more challenging is the design of the surveillance technologies and techniques that are the sine qua non of effective arms control. Weapons now emerging will be less susceptible to monitoring with adequate confidence than the large systems and associated facilities that have been dominant for the last 20 years.[7] The newer systems can be more readily obscured and concealed than older ones, if there is a desire to do so. In the emphasis on advances in surveillance technology over the last two decades, it has been largely forgotten that the most important items to be monitored—launch platforms—have been comparatively visible and that surveillance measures, to some

7. The widening gap between surveillance technology and the concealment potential of new weapons is discussed in William Hadley Kincade, "Over the Technological Horizon," *Daedalus* (Winter 1981).

degree, have been tailored to these systems. Even the ballistic missile submarine must return periodically to special bases. Newer weapons, especially cruise missiles, will in themselves be harder to detect and analyze as to performance, while the new multiplicity of launch platforms can escape high confidence surveillance.[8]

The obvious supplement to a surveillance technology being undercut by new weapons technologies is agreements tht contain measures to assist verification. Although sometimes overly specific in their language, which prevents a residual vagueness useful for challenging Soviet behavior, the SALT II agreements were distinguished by the way they aided U.S. surveillance of Soviet systems.[9]

Given characteristic Soviet resistance to divulging information, the concessions gained by U.S. negotiators in this area were considerable. A short list of the verification aids in SALT II would include (1) extension of the SALT I provisions regarding "national technical means" of verificaiton (for example, by forbidding encryption of relevant missile test data); (2) detailed definition of treaty systems and terms; (3) counting rules that classify deployed or test systems on a "worst-case" basis; (4) requirements for functionally related design differences or externally observable design

8. The verification problems of cruise missiles are analyzed in William Hadley Kincade, "Cruise Missiles as an Arms Control Problem," in Richard K. Betts, ed., *Technology, Strategy, and Politics: Cruise Missile Development and U.S. Policy* (Washington: Brookings Institution, forthcoming).

9. This point is treated at length in the author's "Verification and SALT II," in William Hadley Kincade et al., *SALT II and American Security* (Cambridge, MA: Institute for Foreign Policy Analysis, 1980).

characteristics on certain weapons; (5) exchange of data that must be independently confirmed to be accepted; (6) advance notification of weapons tests; (7) prescribed procedures for dismantling and destroying excess weapons so as to make this process more visible; and (8) restrictions on missile reload capacity.

Yet even more aids to surveillance will have to be written into future agreements to cover the kinds of weapons likely to dominate the strategic environment in the next 10 years or so. A variety of limitations or specifications applying to a single class of weapons will increase the probability that a violation or potential violation is detected, if not at one stage or by one surveillance technique then at another stage or by another technique. Providing additional "checkpoints"—limiting both the overall number and the deployment areas of, for example, ground-launched cruise missiles—would make it more likely that clandestine activity would be observed. Limits on numbers, performance, deployment areas, tests, types of launcher, and the like will have to be combined in an overlapping way to provide adequate assurance that any significant violation would be discovered immediately and, of equal importance, that even a potential violation has a reasonable chance of being "seen."

Arranging a series of verification measures relevant to new weapons technologies will be formidable task for arms control in the 1980s and negotiating them will be even more arduous. However, when one considers the alternatives to a world without arms control—the deployment of Soviet cruise missiles, mobile ballistic missiles, or other less monitorable systems in the absence of agreed

aids to verification—the challenge seems worth accepting. More important, without such measures, the United States will return to the condition of information insecurity of the 1950s, when intelligence gaps were inevitably translated into bomber and missile gaps.

Prevention

As the arms competition continues to shift from a quantitative to a qualitative character, the interests of the superpowers in avoiding a technological duel that adds more to costs and perils than it adds to security presumably will also grow. These incentives may be reinforced by increasing volatility in the Third World, especially in states adjoining the superpowers or considering the development of their own nuclear forces. The unsettled conditions in the Third World not only create temptations for involvement and escalation, more and more they force the superpowers into a reactive mode; neither possesses the control it once had over developing countries.

If bilateral and international conditions increase the value of arms control agreements, then an imperative for arms limitation in the future will be better synchronization of weapons development and weapons diplomacy. This, fundamentally, is what is implied by the calls for better integration of arms control considerations in overall security policy.

While, on its face, the idea of negotiating on systems in the research and development (R&D) phase is met with skepticism, halting steps have already been taken in this direction. In the ABM Treaty and subsequent protocol, the United States and the USSR limited the deployment of ballistic missile defenses to trivial levels but permitted research on ABMs, with some restrictions. In the unratified SALT II treaty and protocol, there are provisions limiting undeployed systems (air-launched cruise missiles, MIRVed cruise missiles, and the like, and pledging negotiations on other, as yet undeployed weapons. The arrested Anti-Satellite (ASAT) negotiations looked toward some kind of ban or restriction on weapons before or at an early stage of deployment.

This form of preventive or preclusive arms control is similar to that found in the Antarctic, outer space, and seabed treaties, except that it deals with the hardware instead of geographical areas. The great advantage of preclusive arms limitation, in principle, is that it makes the negotiating process more synchronous with the weapons research, development, and acquisition process; it gives negotiators more time to accomplish their objectives and facilitates verification.

Negotiations aimed at preclusive agreements in the future may help to close the gap that frequently opens between the tortoise of diplomacy and the hare of technology.[10] What is now needed is a systematic effort to work out ways of conducting negotiations of this type without compromising other interests, such as the requirements for secrecy, a viable R&D program, and a robust, efficient defense industrial base.

10. Technological innovation in specific sectors tends to be rather slow and cumulative; it is the fact that it is occurring across so broad a front that lends military-technological innovation its hare-like qualities. On the phenomenon of "technology creep," see Deborah Shapley, "Technology Creep and the Arms Race," a three-part series appearing in *Science* 22 and 29 September and 20 October 1978.

Maintaining sound R&D programs and an adequate industrial infrastructure would be essential to the conduct of parallel weapons negotiations, since they provide (1) the incentive for the other party to remain at the bargaining table, (2) the information needed to understand the nature and potential of emerging technologies, and (3) the necessary insurance against the failure to reach an agreement or a termination of an agreement already reached. Indeed, circumstances can be foreseen under which expanding the breadth and depth of military R&D would, in principle, serve the cause of improving security through arms control.

The costs of a more aggressive R&D effort or of a sturdy but underutilized industrial base might be offset by eventual savings in procurement or operations and maintenance costs achieved by limitation agreements. Yet they may not; one of the unpalatable realities that arms control advocates may have to face in the 1980s is that defense budget reductions and weapons limitations may be independent variables that cannot be maximized simultaneously. For a variety of reasons, the price of effective arms controls may be the expansion of certain sectors of defense spending—the costs of surveillance, R&D, smaller defense orders, and so on—at least initially.

Thus negotiations on emerging weapons would not visualize limiting military R&D itself. What is envisioned is treating an arms control agreement as a security product of the R&D process at least equal in value to a deployed weapon system. Hence, the objective would be to examine the feasibility of negotiations during all major phases of weapons acquisition with a view to agreements that would, for weapons mutually seen as provocative or otherwise undesirable, preclude (1) large-scale deployments, (2) any deployment at all, or (3) prototyping and advanced system testing, depending on where agreement can be reached.

Preclusive negotiations would permit the playing of so-called "bargaining chips"—weapons in development but as yet not in the field—without necessarily converting them to deployed systems. In fact, such a negotiating regime would depend in some measure on the leverage implicit in developmental systems advancing toward a production decision. Yet the bargaining chip approach to arms negotiations was to a large degree discredited during the Ford administration because the weapons gathered institutional momentum and deployment seemed inevitable. It was further discredited in the Carter administration, which was accused of negotiating only with "paper"—that is, future—systems.

No serious student of arms limitation has argued, however, that developmental systems can be ignored in arranging arms control regimes or that concern for future adversary deployments is a negligible factor in sustaining interest in negotiations. What is needed is a more orderly, thoughtful, and constructive way of harnessing this mutual fear of the other side's emerging weapons in the negotiating process. It may be facetious, but still instructive, to observe that, in principle, strategic arms control might have progressed further by now if it had initially concentrated only on new offensive technologies— for example, a ban on MIRVs, flight test limits to constrain guidance improvements, and restrictions on cruise missiles—and proceeded to numerical limits on existing systems after the main lines of the provocative innovation had been curbed. The United States would not now be contemplating MX or air-launched cruise missiles, in order to stay ahead of Soviet MIRV potential.

One of the keys to any successful negotiation between antagonists is to formulate a match between the greatest fears of the two hostile powers. This generally involves matching their current or projected strengths, irrespective of whether they are in the same area. A notable feature of the SALT II agreements, for instance, is the single subceiling limiting both air-launched cruise missile (ALCM) aircraft, which the United States wants and the Soviet Union fears, and MIRVed ICBMs, which the Soviet Union wants and the United States fears. By linking in this fashion the strengths and fears on both sides, a counting rule that treats dissimilar systems alike permits some flexibility to each side while forcing limits and trade-offs on both.

Efforts to initiate negotiations during research and development could be established on this principle. If, hypothetically, the Soviet Union is most worried about future advances in American strategic antisubmarine warfare, while the equivalent U.S. concern is for Soviet improvements in prototype antisatellite weapons, then talks on these issues could be initiated, most likely in parallel rather than in combination. To facilitate the arrangement of such packages, some kind of joint agenda-setting mechanism is required, as well as, perhaps, a technological foresight capability.

Though it has never been exercised to its full extent, the broad mandate of the Standing Consultative Commission (SCC) appears to have ample latitude for incorporating the agenda-setting function. By increasing the frequency of SCC meetings beyond two per year, the Soviet and American commissioners could explore possible combinations of issues that would make promising negotiating packages. Talks on two or more such packages could proceed but with staggered meetings, so that those working on one set of issues would have the opportunity to assess the implications for their own work of discussions on other packages.

Although the SCC commissioners might play some role in it, the technological foresight function is primarily a national one. Foresight for this purpose doubtless would involve intense internal debate over what emerging adversary systems to accord highest precedence and where to be willing to compromise in one's own R&D programs in pursuit of restrictions. However, such debates will take place in any case. Institutionalization of the controversy at an earlier stage of developmental technology would only concentrate attention more productively, by assuring that the debate went on when it was most relevant to crucial military and diplomatic decisions.

The approach described would satisfy the need (1) to address military-technological innovation at an early enough stage to allow meaningful agreements and (2) to sustain a comprehensive approach to problems that are deeply intertwined while "incrementalizing" the negotiating process so that it does not collapse from issue-overload and a surfeit of false hopes and promises. The suggestions made here are far from comprising the only strategy that can be conceived for relating diplomacy to technology. Yet all such approaches probably face similar obstacles and objections, including (1) avoidance of disclosure of R&D plans and information; (2) national differentials in technological innovation and verification capability; (3) the difficulties of coping with incremental improvements—technology "drift" or "creep"—and agreeing on what constitutes necessary or harmful modernization; and (4) the impact of such negotiations on the development and acquisition process.[11]

If we accept for arms control in the 1980s the modest but worthwhile goals of achieving predictability in the strategic environment, avoiding the worst costs of unregulated competition, and preserving the option of more significant limitations, then its character will probably be that of regulating, not terminating, modernization programs, keeping deployments to lower levels than might otherwise occur. Even without negotiations, economic pressures in the United States and the Soviet Union could well impose de facto limits on deployments in any case. Thus the choice is not between some arms control and no arms control, but between haphazard, ad hoc, unilateral arms limits and mutual, codified constraints. The advantage of the latter course is that it would avoid the uncertainties and consequent spasms of fear that arise from (1) unsystematic, self-imposed limitations, and (2) the loss of the surveillance benefits that are conferred by agreed verification provisions.

11. The pros and cons of negotiating weapon systems during R&D are weighed in the author's "Arms Control at the Source: Weapons Acquisition and Negotiation," paper delivered at the Biennial Meeting of the Section on Military Studies of the International Studies Association, Pittsburgh, Pennsylvania, 4 October 1979.

Under these circumstances, the foreseeable problems may prove more manageable than they seem at first glance. For example, the difficulty of containing the institutional momentum that grows up behind a developmental system will be less where the objective of concurrent negotiations is (1) to fix deployment at certain levels rather than forestall it entirely or (2) to constrain an emerging Soviet weapon that provides the justification for an American R&D program.

It may be objected that the proposed talks would falter on the U.S. fear of divulging too much information or on Soviet unwillingness to admit to or divulge information on its own programs. If so, nothing would be lost in trying this tack. But the SALT process and the SCC meetings have already produced lessons on how to negotiate without revealing sensitive information. Moreover, the state of scientific and technical intelligence, and projections based on it, is such that we can anticipate with confidence adequate for this purpose the direction and rate of Soviet technological innovation. If the Soviet Union refuses to respond to negotiating initiatives involving its R&D programs, then it will have to reckon with the implications of such a stance for parallel or offsetting U.S. programs.

INSTITUTIONAL CHALLENGES

Masked by the oft-reopened discussions of how to organize the Arms Control and Disarmament Agency (retain its semiautonomous status, effect a merger with the Department of State or with the Defense Department) is the more fundamental question of how to integrate arms control considerations earlier and more productively into the overall development of American security policy. Diplomats, specialists in security issues, thoughtful defense officials, and members of the armed services agree that this is a priority objective for arms limitation and that the lack of an integrated approach has been a major contributor to the rocky road arms control has traveled to date.[12]

The innovation of Arms Control Impact Statements represented in part an early effort by Congress to raise arms limitation issues during the planning and development process. While they have no doubt helped in this regard, they have also stimulated a variety of discontents not necessarily helpful to the image of arms control or to the Arms Control and Disarmament Agency (ACDA). More recently, it has been proposed that ACDA have a seat on the Defense Systems Acquisition Review Council (DSARC), a panel within the Office of the Secretary of Defense that selects, monitors, and approves development and production programs.

While such organizational, informational, and decision-making innovations can play a role in improving security policy formulation, such approaches are likely to be bereft of any real meaning without a basic change in attitude among relevant actors, perhaps especially the uniformed services. There are some real signs that this evolution in attitudes is taking place. This

12. Another contributor has been the increasing specialization and lack of coordination within the agency itself. In carrying out the recommendations of the Odeen Report on national security policy-making in the Carter administration (see Philip Odeen, "Organizing for National Security," *International Security*, Summer 1980); however, ACDA did establish a policy planning and coordination element to assure better intra-agency policy integration.

results partly from the pressure of anticipated resource constraints and an appreciation for the heavy burdens implicit in an unregulated superpower rivalry. It also owes much to the experience of some of the services' most competent officers, who have served on SALT and other delegations, in ACDA, or on the SCC and whose pragmatic attitude toward arms control is now trickling down to others. Although the uniformed opponents of arms limitation continue to have the most impact politically, its uniformed practitioners are having a significant effect operationally. If developments along these lines could be encouraged and broadened, then it would probably make little difference what visible or formal arrangements were made institutionally, unless they tended to frustrate early, consistent, and meaningful policy coordination on an interagency basis.

As to the status of ACDA, the arguments seem to be fairly well balanced regarding semiindependence or merger with one of the larger bureaucracies. However, all such cases are highly speculative and depend on arguable assumptions about how the American national security bureaucracy operates. Recognizing that, as Duncan Clarke points out, the effectiveness of ACDA is primarily a product of a president's personal interest or support, one might conclude that it made little difference how the U.S. arms control effort was institutionalized.[13] It must also be recognized that, even with presidential support, arms control faces

numerous bureaucratic competitors. John Foster Dulles's dismantling of an embryonic arms control bureaucracy in the Eisenhower administration and the hamstringing of negotiators in the Carter administration are cases in point. In view of these circumstances, there is reason, on balance, to retain ACDA in its present form.

But it should not be imagined that this will necessarily provide a strong prop for arms control. The larger task is to create in other agencies and in the Congress an appreciation for arms control that will facilitate ACDA's work. If arms limitation considerations are to be effectively integrated in security policy formulation, they must be taken into account in the weapons acquisition and strategic planning processes earlier and more consistently, not in the sense of constraining them, but as options for reducing potential threats.[14] The institutional arrangements for carrying this out matter less than encouraging the recognition of the arms control option as a contributor to U.S. security.

13. Duncan L. Clarke, *Politics of Arms Control: The Role and Effectiveness of the U.S. Arms Control and Disarmament Agency* (New York: Free Press, 1979), passim.

14. Of the legends surrounding arms control, perhaps the most fallacious is the myth that arms limitation considerations have been pervasive in the development of American defense policy, especially strategic planning and weapons acquisition. The limits attributed to arms control have far more often been a product of efforts by national leaders to hold down defense costs, probably in response to the generally widespread public opposition to increases in defense spending that existed from about 1953 to 1978 or 1979. Presidents and defense secretaries may have hoped that arms control would provide a mechanism and justification for spending limitation, but the cases of significant arms control impact on American strategic planning and weapons acquisition decisions are hard to find. Easier to document is arms control's lack of influence; see Clarke, *Politics of Arms Control.*

POLITICAL CHALLENGES

An obvious lesson of the past and challenge for the future is that arms limitation or reduction agreements do not sell themselves. Thirty years of opinion polls, not surprisingly, register frequent majority support for some kind of negotiated restriction of the nuclear menace, just as—with somewhat less consistency—they reflect interest in civil defense. Through negotiations or defenses, or both, the public wants relief from the threat of nuclear war.

In both cases, however, the judgment is passive and nonspecific. When negotiators produce an agreement, when civil defense officials produce a plan, and when pollsters get down to specifics, the public often proves to be skeptical and unwilling to take the nominal risks or make the sacrifices implied by either the arms control or civil defense initiatives presented to them.[15] The exceptions to these generalizations are the Limited Test Ban Treaty (LTBT) of 1963 and the SALT I agreements of 1972. Both President Kennedy and President Nixon—capitalizing respectively on the enormous foreign policy prestige of the Cuban missile crisis and the opening to China—skillfully exploited the advantages of their office to provide arms control with its two high-water marks.

In sharp contrast, President Carter failed to mount the "bully pulpit" that comes with the presidency,

15. These observations are based on the author's analysis of 30 years of Gallup poll data on public opinion regarding security issues. In 1961, Samuel Huntington linked arms control and civil defense as the "country cousins of American strategy" in *The Common Defense: Strategic Programs in National Politics* (New York: Columbia University Press, 1961), pp. 353ff. Both have had checkered careers in the 20 years since then.

appeared incompetent regarding security issues generally, gave equivocal signals to the public in his Soviet policy, and consistently missed opportunities to preempt an often misleading strategic debate and to capture an increasingly apprehensive political center. As a result, he could not secure approval for a treaty that would have done far more for American security than either the LTBT or SALT I. It is fair to speculate that, had the Soviet brigade in Cuba incident never occurred or been mishandled, SALT II would still have failed to be ratified, so fragile and easily upset was its support in the Senate and the country.

Several lessons can be drawn from this capsule history. Early or "breakthrough" agreements are easier to negotiate and ratify. A strong president and a strong, unambiguous presidential voice are essential to convince elites and the general public that a particular treaty merits their approval. The public must repose confidence in its military forces and in the competence of the president on security matters before it will accord support for agreements with the Soviet Union, of which there are powerful, irreducible fears and suspicions. It is to this understandable public fear and distrust that the opponents of SALT II played so successfully, often with the unwitting assistance of President Carter.

For exponents of arms limitation, these lessons have corollaries that may seem distasteful because the impulse to endorse arms control is often just that—a well-meaning impulse rather than a politically and militarily reasoned approach to American security interests and to the existential dilemma of nuclear weapons.

The first corollary is that arms limitation agreements should not be overrated. As in the past, their impact on strategic competition will not be highly visible, although it will be important from a security standpoint in ways that are not (or have not been) readily communicated to mass publics (for example, the numerous verification provisions of SALT II that make it easier for the United States to monitor Soviet developments, a benefit ignored during and since the SALT debate).

Presidents, more than professionals, have been guilty of overselling arms control as the centerpiece of East-West relations or as a prelude to peace and disarmament. But it is up to the professionals to resist this political temptation, so as to avoid creating expectations that must be deflated when a specific contract is unveiled. In retrospect, linking SALT with détente was an error, perhaps unavoidable, but one which created the impression that arms limitation and détente were synonymous, when in fact the value of arms control—if not its negotiability—rises in periods of hostility.

Nevertheless, arms limitation should not be underrated. Its capacity for bringing order to an increasingly volatile strategic environment, for providing predictability to defense planners and budgeteers, and for regulating a competition that always bears a worrisome risk of escaping control are benefits that need to be promoted. What this suggests is that arms control must be straightforwardly justified to the public as it has always been justified within the government: a tough, sensible response to the problem of providing adequate deterrence and defense in a troubled world of finite resources, not a harbinger of East-West accord or world peace.

To make this case to the American people, proponents of arms control will be well advised to separate arms limitation from disarmament —of which there is a deep-seated and probably unchangeable public skepticism—as well as from what has come to be perceived as the liberal foreign policy agenda—that is, opposition to the draft, increasing foreign development assistance, cutting defense budgets and reforming defense contracting, unilateral withdrawal of U.S. troops from overseas, and so on. While cases might be made for some of these objectives, practical politics indicates that they must be made separately. The public is notoriously unenthusiastic about package deals in security policy. People sense, if not see, that enormous difficulties and risks are involved in remaking foreign and defense policy all at once; the magnitude of such a change discourages rather than attracts support.

By linking several issues together, skepticism of one component can spread to the entire ensemble. Arms limitation has its own rationale quite apart from the justification for other initiatives. There is little to be gained and much to be lost by creating the impression that support for arms control requires an attitudinal change across the entire range of foreign and defense policy issues. Just to influence current attitudes about the contribution of arms control to national security is a large enough task in itself.

This leads to a related corollary. The job is not, as some hold, to create a mass movement, such as brought about policy changes in civil rights, abortion issues, environmental pollution, or the Vietnam war. Arms control is too complex and continuous an enterprise—and one that addresses problems most often viewed as too remote from daily life—to support the kind of major or grass-roots movement other issues have generated. Highlighting the dangers and consequences of nuclear war is useful, especially in the face of a tendency to make it seem endurable; but after a point this stimulus produces numbness and apathy, not the energy or appetite for action. And mere fear of nuclear war can provide an argument for a more aggressive competition and for larger nuclear arsenals.

What is needed instead is a broadening and deepening of efforts to explain arms control in ways that increase appreciation of its fundamental common sense and that meet the legitimate concerns of Americans for their safety. When negotiated security is portrayed—as it should be—as a pragmatic answer to these concerns, rather than misidentified as a "liberal cause," support will be more durable. The roller-coaster ride that SALT II took in the polls of the late 1970s reflected three things: the basic desire of the American people to limit the nuclear threat, their lack of a firm understanding of how arms control could achieve this, and the weaknesses and vulnerabilities of efforts to demonstrate the advantages of negotiated security. What should be created, then, is not a constituency, which will not work, but a deeper appreciation and a broader awareness from which a consensus can be forged when specific agreements are produced, as Kennedy and Nixon did.[16]

16. For an interesting interpretation of the Eisenhower and Kennedy approaches to public opinion and arms control, see Eugene J. Rosi, "Public Opinion and National Security Policy: The Nuclear Testing Debate," in *American Defense and Detente:*

To do this, supporters of arms limitation will have to adopt new tactics and become better informed. In too many cases during the lengthy SALT II debate that began in 1977, the nongovernmental advocates simply did not know the issues as well as the opponents of the treaty, especially those questions related to Soviet policy and military activities. Persuasive arguments were available, but either they were not made at all or they were not made in terms the public could readily grasp. SALT defenders too often started with the emerging treaty, where critics lodged their case, instead of with the first principles on which the treaty depended and which the public could comprehend —indeed already believed, if opinion polls are any guide.

Moreover, SALT advocates for too long played an inside game, watching developments among elites, senators, and executive officials, instead of building general support among the public, as both Kennedy and Nixon had done even before treaties were signed. Ultimately, of course, the approval that counts must come from the Senate and, indirectly, from the elites to whom senators harken. But gaining this approval is facilitated by widespread public support that requires prior cultivation and cannot be taken for granted.

Yet the public is unlikely to accept arms control when it harbors doubts about the adequacy of American military forces. Accepting both the real and perceived risks of depending on treaties for security requires self-confidence. Although the Uni-

Readings in National Security Policy (New York: Dodd, Mead, 1973). For Kennedy's effort to gain public support for the limited test ban treaty, see Theodore H. Sorensen, *Kennedy* (New York: Harper & Row, 1965).

ted States maintains demonstrable leads in the relevant dimensions of strategic forces—warheads, survivable airborne and seaborne forces, advanced technology base, and system quality—some supporters of arms limitation have, in other contexts, caricatured our civilian and military leadership as capable only of making wrong-headed decisions. SALT opponents took up this theme in their own way, arguing that U.S. forces were in drastic decline and that the cause was civilian leaders under the thrall of arms control for as long as 10 to 20 years. The public responded by withdrawing support for SALT, reversing over a decade of opposition to military spending increases, and insisting on bigger defense budgets and new leadership.

Clearly, Soviet actions finally prompted much of this change in the climate of opinion, but the polls reflected the onset of a shift on defense spending well before the SALT II Treaty was concluded. And the extent of the fluctuation could have been cushioned had Americans not been told for so long by left and right alike that something was amiss with American strategy, leadership, and defense forces. Thus, paradoxically it will seem to some, domestic acceptance of arms control depends heavily on the public perception that U.S. strategy, plans, leaders, and forces are adequate to their tasks. This perception, in turn, must rest on reality and also, since it will never be fully self-evident, on the efforts of arms control proponents to demonstrate the basic adequacy of our strategy and forces while recognizing mistakes where they have been made.

Creating political support also requires correcting the misapprehensions and distortions fostered by

the strategic debate of the last five years or so and by the low level of public knowledge about American strategic planning. A short list of common misconceptions would include the following notions: (1) American strategic planning has been limited solely to targeting Soviet urban-industrial areas and not to military forces. (2) Arms control is infeasible if targeting doctrine is not thus restricted. (3) Soviet and American nuclear war plans are fundamentally opposed and mutually exclusive, instead of differing in emphasis. (4) Successful negotiations are incompatible with different strategies, doctrines, or plans. (5) The Soviet Union has somehow discovered a way of turning the old expedients of running, digging, and hiding into a civil defense program that will be highly effective against today's larger and more capable nuclear forces.[17] A misconception of a different kind is that the United States is in a better bargaining position if it insists on linking arms agreements to Soviet behavior elsewhere *before* their negotiation or approval. This implies that it would be difficult to give up what one does not have. The shrewder approach would be to acquire leverage on other behavior through the explicit or tacit threat to annul an agreement from which the Soviet Union is already drawing benefits.

These and similar misunderstandings undercut support for negotiated agreements no matter what their provisions. They gain currency because they contain partial truths and because the public

17. Arms control specialists themselves often adopt these interpretations; see, for example, the treatment of American strategy in the Kruzel, "Arms Control and American Defense Policy."

has little or no appreciation of what is involved and what is at stake in military planning and strategy. The surface validity of simple-minded concepts is accepted as truth. Themselves often unaware of the history of defense decision-making, the strategic milieu, or military science, well-intentioned advocates of arms limitation have too frequently been unable to resolve these alleged problems and have thus lost credibility with the public.

Finally, arms control exponents will have to make some very hard choices in the coming years as regards priorities, choosing, for example, between (1) more costly and more verifiable systems—a follow-on bomber—and (2) cheaper but largely unverifiable systems—sea-launched cruise missiles—or (3) systems that can only be verified through the aid of treaty provisions that are probably nonnegotiable in the climate of East-West relations we can now foresee—ground-launched cruise missiles. Making a fetish out of cutting the defense budget has already inclined many congressmen supportive of arms

limits to prefer systems that negotiations probably cannot control. This presents arms control with insoluble dilemmas for the future and will rob it of its potential, over the longer term, for having a systematic influence on defense budgets.

For arms limitation to succeed in the 1980s, many conditions will have to be met, not all of them subject to the influence of those bespeaking arms control. But the fundamental requirement of political support will require of advocates an approach that is far more astute, informed, politically judicious, and relevant to the security concerns of Americans than were the efforts of the late 1970s. Up to now, too many people have called for arms control agreements and too few have helped to figure out how, in the real world, they can be achieved, supported, and sustained. These efforts cannot be independent of one another. If the advocacy for arms limits outpaces imaginative yet pragmatic solutions to the many obstacles that lie in their path, then arms control cannot succeed politically or technically.

ANNALS, *AAPSS*, 457, September 1981

Personnel Recruitment and Retention: Problems and Prospects for the United States

By WILLIAM SCHNEIDER, Jr.

ABSTRACT: In the development of an adequate defense capability, the United States faces no more formidable problems than those associated with personnel recruitment and retention. The replacement of the draft by the All-Volunteer Force has resulted in substantially higher financial costs, which have been met by reducing force readiness and modernization. Because of its aging population structure, the United States is likely to face higher personnel costs in the next decade in competition with the civilian economy. The AVF has resulted in problems of productivity and quality of personnel needed to perform complex tasks and to operate complicated weapons systems. Although a return to conscription would provide the armed services with a broader cross-section of U.S. society and spread more equitably the burden of military service, the high turnover associated with conscription would increase training and operating costs. The author suggests that the United States, except in the event of a national emergency requiring rapid expansion of forces, will continue to rely on volunteerism. He addresses options such as lengthening the initial tour of duty and reforms is compensation structure as means toward the resolution of military personnel recruitment and retention problems.

The author is Associate Director for National Security and International Affairs of the Office of Management and Budget, Executive Office of the President, Washington, D.C.

THE military manpower question has become the central problem in our national ability to acquire and maintain the military strength we need to cope with the reality of Soviet military power. Despite its inferior resource base, the Soviet Union, with a population only slightly larger than that of the United States (260 versus 220 million), has managed to deploy more than twice as many personnel in its armed forces (4.5-4.8 versus 2.1 million) and over 10 times the number of active-duty Army divisions (173 versus 16) as the United States. In part these disparities reflect the higher national priority afforded defense in Soviet resource allocation (12-15 percent of GNP compared to less than 6 percent in the U.S.), as well as unique tactical and operational concepts used by the Soviets which require higher manning levels.[1]

Nevertheless, the broad national consensus surrounding the need for a more effective national defense posture has made it necessary to review all dimensions of our defense posture, including policies for recruiting and retaining military personnel. The anomaly of a protracted peacetime draft was suspended in 1973 in favor of an all-volunteer system to recruit military personnel. Between 1964 and the mid-1970s, military personnel costs rose from 48 to 60 percent of the defense budget, largely driven by the post-1973 costs of adjusting to the all-volunteer force.[2] These increases in cost were met partly by reducing the rate of growth of investment in operations and maintenance accounts and partly by lowering the share of defense expenditure accounted for by procurement and military research and development. In short, the full costs of the all-volunteer force were not met by internalizing these costs in the form of higher real growth in defense expenditure; they were met by the expedient of diminishing force readiness and modernization.[3]

In addition, military manpower has been reduced. Since 1964 (the last pre-Vietnam fiscal year) active-duty forces have been reduced by 600,000, with half of that reduction accomplished since the end of the conscription in 1973. Within the scope of reduced manpower requirements, the all-volunteer force has generally met its accession requirements. Had military manpower not been reduced, it is likely that both readiness and modernization would have been far more substantially curtailed during the 1970s than was actually the case.

As the issue of conscription versus voluntarism has become highly politicized, it is often overlooked that whether the new accessions are induced by a draft or volunteer system is simply an input to the armed forces; it does not directly influencs the efficiency of the military system

---

1. For example, the Soviet Union employs a unit rather than individual replacement in combat. Although this system permits a smaller division "tail" in the form of combat maintenance and support, it requires a far larger divisional force structure to provide for the replacement of an entire TO&E unit in combat. U.S. practice equips a division with an organic logistics support infrastructure to sustain combat indefinitely with casualty replacements supplied on an individual rather than unit basis. The Soviet system is similar to the one employed by the German *Wehrmacht* in World War II. See J Erickson, *Soviet Military Power* (London: Royal United Services Institute for Defense Studies, 1971); and W. V. Madej, "Effectiveness and Cohesion of the German Ground Forces in World War II," *Journal of Political and Military Sociology* Vol. 6 (1978).

2. *Annual Defense Report, FY 1975*, (Washington, DC: Department of Defense); and *Staff Papers on Defense Manpower Costs*, (Washington, DC: Office of Program Analysis, U.S. Genveral Accounting Office, December 1975).

3. See a discussion of this problem in S. L. Canby and R. A. Butler, "The Military Manpower Question," in *Arms, Men, and Military Budgets: Issues for FY 1977* (New York: Crane, Russak, 1976), p. 183.

or its performance in combat. The efficiency of the military system is influenced by a host of variables relating to the organization and management of the armed forces. The performance of the armed forces turns on operational and tactical considerations. Neither issue is uniquely dependent on the manner in which accessions are induced. Indeed, historical examples of successful volunteer and conscription systems abound.[4]

This article seeks to address only the component of our overall national problem of military power that relates directly to the issue of recruitment and retention of military personnel. Other specialists have addressed these issues, but they remain the most significant and difficult to resolve of any of public policy problems surrounding U.S. defense policy.[5] Their complex-

---

4. Perhaps the most successful large-scale example of voluntarism was the 1914-16 experience of the British Army, which was entirely composed of volunteers until the initial enthusiasm with the conflict (World War I) wore off. U.S. experience with voluntarism is limited to special units in time of war; although during World War II the German armed forces were composed largely of conscripts in the *Wehrmacht*, a large element of the armed forces were volunteer—the *Waffen-SS*. Effective military performance from both volunteer and conscripted units was obtained. A well-documented study of the U.S. and German armed forces during World War II is contained in M. van Creveld, *Fighting Power: German Military Performance, 1914-15* (Potomac, MD: C&L Associates, December 1980).

5. For a discussion of the linkage between the personnel problem and other issues of defense policy, see S. L. Canby et al., "An Alternative Analysis of the State of U.S. General Purpose Forces: The Need to Restructure for Combat Effectiveness," (The Heritage Foundation, 1980). See also M. Binkin, "Military Manpower in the 1980s: Issues and Choices," *International Security Review* (Fall 1980).

ity precludes extended consideration here.

VOLUNTARISM OR CONSCRIPTION?

U.S. defense policy requires a substantial active-duty military force to support the objectives of U.S. foreign policy. By historical standards, the present level of U.S. forces is high. The U.S. has nearly 10 times as many men under arms today as it had before World War II, reflecting the demands of contemporary strategy for strategic forces deployed at a high order of readiness, and extensive forward-deployed general-purpose forces to cope with regional contingencies with very limited warning.[6]

The needs of U.S. strategic forces emphasize personnel with a high order of technical competence and continuity of assignment among military personnel. The personnel demands of the general-purpose forces (although they, too, have a significant technology-driven component) are designed for close combat and as a mobilization base for wartime expansion. The former requires a long-term volunteer force; the latter requires a (relatively) short-term force owing to the latter's need for a physically vigorous force to meet the dangerous and demanding environment of close combat.

---

6. The U.S. armed forces expanded from less than 250,000 troops in 1939 to more than eight million by the end of the war. The U.S. Army was composed of 89 divisions (compared with only 16 today). Readiness requirements demand forces capable of operating at high orders of effectiveness in a matter of minutes (such as ICBM and strategic bomber crews) to 48 hours (forward-deployed forces in NATO). Meeting such demanding readiness requirements requires high manning levels compared to our historical experience, when "warning" could be measured in weeks.

The vexing property of this structure of military personnel requirements is that no single system is a perfect match in both peace and war. Voluntarism in peacetime will provide ample accessions to meet the needs of the technology-driven component of U.S. forces provided incentives are properly structured. However, voluntarism is less effective as a means of meeting the quantitative and qualitative demands of the general-purpose forces in times of war. The use of conscription to fill high-turnover segments of the general-purpose forces will generally induce highly capable individuals to volunteer for service in the skilled segment of the armed forces (currently more than half of the enlisted strength of the armed forces compared with only 15 percent in the combat arms). The effect of these observations is that experience suggests that voluntarism is not suited to the manpower demands of large conflicts, but conscription is ill-suited to the needs of U.S. peacetime forces. From the perspective of U.S. peacetime requirements conscription would solve some of the problems that have emerged from U.S. post-1973 experience with voluntarism: Assuring the technology-driven components of the Navy and Air Force of high-quality, draft-induced volunteers (to this one might add the Reserve and Guard forces as well if no significant changes were made in their current operating practices), it would provide the armed services with a cross-section of U.S. society, and conscription would more equitably spread the burden of military service.

Left unaddressed by conscription are a considerable number of problems. The high turnover associated with conscription would increase training and operating costs due to the demands of the training base. The retention and experience problem central to productivity in the armed forces would be exacerbated by the rapid turnover of noncareer conscription-induced volunteers in technology-driven specialties. Thus, unless conscripted troops were obliged to serve protracted active-duty tours, the costs of maintaining the military personnel system could increase while its technical performance could decline.

Continued reliance on voluntarism appears to be the most likely course for gaining the new accessions needed by the armed forces over the course of the next decade, providing these demands are not increased substantially by either management action (for example, reduction in the average first-term length of tour) or international circumstances (such as a conflict requiring expansion of the current peacetime force structure). The current implementation of the all-volunteer force concept tends to increase the costs of its operation and to produce inefficiency in the operation of the armed forces contrasted to what could be the case if reforms were introduced.

PROBLEMS IN THE ALL-VOLUNTEER FORCE

The all-volunteer force (AVF) has become thoroughly embedded in the operating practice of the Department of Defense, but there have emerged a number of difficult problems in its implementation that affect the performance of the entire defense establishment.

Cost

As noted elsewhere, the increased budgetary cost of the AVF over its predecessor (conscription) has imposed a substantial reallocation of defense resources away from R&D, procurement, and operating accounts to military personnel. Indeed, many of the characteristics of the draft-based force prior to 1973 continue in the current force; only its overt budgetary costs have undergone major changes. To be sure, the economic costs of the military personnel system have not changed. In fact, while the explicit budget cost of the AVF may be greater than that of the system it replaced, its real economic costs (the real burdens of the labor and capital resources of society) may be lower because lower opportunity cost volunteers replace higher opportunity cost conscripts.[7] The AVF is superior from the perspective of efficiently using real resources, but is expensive in budgetary terms because of the high costs of inducing voluntary accessions and retaining scarce skills.

The high budgetary cost of the AVF nevertheless forces difficult intragovernmental resource allocation choices. Internalizing the full budget cost of the AVF requires either reducing overall military power (post-1973 practice) or shifting resources from the civil sector of government to the military sector.

Training base

Related to the direct cost of the AVF are the direct and indirect costs induced in the armed forces through the operation of the complex of institutions and facilities

7. The real economic costs are virtually impossible to calculate, since they vary with individual circumstances. With the AVF in place, the market mechanism provides the most effective means of sorting out those with higher opportunity costs.

required to train new accessions. The relatively short turnover of new accessions (three to four years) produces a requirement for 250-300,000 new trainees per year. This requirement imposes a substantial burden on the active forces by necessitating a diversion of resources, both human and material, to maintain authorized strength. As the training establishment employs operational equipment in the course of its activities, a high annual rate of accessions increases the burden on operations and maintenance accounts and accelerates the rate of wear on equipment that could otherwise be deployed with operational forces. Thus, the thin margin of equipment acquisition beyond that needed to fill unit TO&E (Table of Organization and Equipment) is diminished by the need to meet training demands.

Productivity

A substantial portion of the technology-driven sector of the U.S. defense establishment resembles the modern corporation in many ways more than does the classic model of a military organization. The need for long-service personnel with skills in advanced technology contrasts sharply with the needs of an infantry division where the demands are dominated by the need for a youthful and vigorous (and thus relatively high-turnover) force. It is unlikely that a modern business corporation could build a productive work force in the face of the kind of first-term accessions burden the armed forces must cope with, nor could it effectively operate with the high rates of turnover of trained personnel that has afflicted the armed forces since 1973. However, the productivity problem in the armed forces is largely a first-term accession problem. If first-term accessions could be stabilized for a time period twice as long (that is, six to eight years) as currently exists, the loss of productivity arising from the brief period available to a new accession to employ his training could be reversed.

Quality

One of the most controversial criticisms of the AVF is the concern about the quality of volunteers in AVF. Anxieties about the issue intensified recently when it was discovered that an error in test evaluation resulted in understating the number of Category IV (the lowest mental category from which recruits are normally accepted for military service) by a factor of six (the number of Category IV recruits was revised upwards from 8 to 48 percent).

This issue begs the question about whether or not performance on the Armed Forces Qualification Test (AFQT) is useful for predicting performance in the armed forces. Evidence appears to suggest that Category IV recruits meet current proficiency standards nearly as well as those in higher mental categories, even though more investment in training is required to allow those in Category IV to attain minimum proficiency.[8]

The question of the quality of the armed forces under the AVF is not likely to be resolved entirely on the basis of standardized testing results. Broader individual and unit performance measures that capture the effects of greater training, longer initial terms of service, and operational and tactical concepts which most effectively employ military personnel will be more persuasive in resolving this controversy to the satisfaction of the various antagonists than any plausible test battery developed by a psychologist.

Flexibility

The United States' experience with mobilization (either general or limited) in this century has tended to exacerbate concerns about the usefulness of the AVF concept to meet military contingencies. U.S. mobilization has always required a reliance on conscription, not only for active duty manpower but for the maintenance of adequate reserves as well. The argument made by critics of the AVF focuses on the inability of the AVF to meet accession requirements associated with a serious military contingency, or to provide for the retention of needed specialists during a protracted crisis.

Conscription is well suited by its coercive properties to the demands of a mobilization contingency and to sudden and unanticipated manpower demands. However, one cannot overlook the costs imposed on a peacetime military establishment by retaining the practices associated with conscription. These costs may serve to compromise readiness and modernization objectives, thereby reducing the responsiveness of the armed forces to a serious military contingency.[9] The problem is a

8. See various hearings before the Committee on Armed Services of both the U.S. Senate and the House of Representatives in connection with the FY 81 Department of Defense authorization bill for further discussion of this complex issue.

9. The practices associated with a conscription-based manpower system tend to drive resources away from R&D, modernization, and readiness when they are applied in an AVF context.

difficult one, in that conscription appears to be the most effective instrument for general mobilization (à la World War II), while voluntarism is the most effective system for peacetime recruitment. A satisfactory mechanism for the transition from limited mobilization (peacetime active units plus reserves) to general mobilization is lacking in current concepts.

The criticisms that have been directed at the implementation of the AVF reflect real concerns. The increasing visibility being given to military performance has focused greater attention on the level of confidence reposed in the recruitment and retention concepts embodied in the AVF. The post-1973 period has permitted the transition from conscription to voluntarism, but without many of the cost and performance benefits its advocates had expected. Given the range of criticisms to which the AVF has become subject, the operational issue is the extent to which its implementation can be reformed to capture the benefits inherent in the concept.

REFORM OF THE AVF

The transition from conscription to the AVF reflected a policy of seeking to reproduce the structure of the recruitment and retention system (absent, of course, the element of coercion) that existed in the pre-AVF. The consequences of this policy, de facto or by design, have diminished the ability of the military personnel system to supply the personnel needed at reasonable budget costs. These defects of design are particularly important in the realm of military compensation and current recruitment and retention concepts.

Military compensation

The military compensation system has three properties that constitute a relic of traditional military compensation policy that is often at odds with an effective policy for the AVF:

—deferred compensation rather than higher entry-level pay;

—an emphasis on in-kind benefits rather than cash; and

—standardized compensation rather than adjustments for skills, burdens, and risks.

The unique military retirement system and the pattern of career compensation reflected the pre-AVF policy of seeking to distribute total compensation in a manner heavily favoring deferred compensation. The discounted present value of deferred compensation—often attractive to career cadres—provided little in the way of an incentive to first-term enlistees whose economic preferences heavily discount future income. During the period when conscription was the predominant means of first-term accessions (either directly or conscription-induced), the effects of this phenomenon were perverse. Highly capable and educated conscripts with a low propensity for a military career displaced less educated volunteers in competition for skilled occupational specialties. This exacerbated the problems associated with a high rate of turnover in skilled billets. Efforts to increase incentives through additional increments of deferred compensation had little leverage over inducements to enlist but substantially increased costs during the implementation of the AVF.

This dimension of the problem has another component associated with the military establishment's preference for in-kind benefits. Emphasis on such benefits increases the total cost of military compensation but has little visibility in the size of the total compensation package to military personnel. Pay perceptions tend to be driven by basic cash compensation, yet more than half of total military compensation (compared with less than 25 percent in the private sector) is provided in the form of deferred compensation.

The third dimension of the traditional military compensation package—compensation for skill differentials—has received considerable attention through a complex set of enlistment and reenlistment bonuses. This has served to adjust the traditional preference for standardized compensation for all personnel of a given time in grade but has not entirely displaced the practice. A radical construction of this problem extends to standardized compensation among the services. In the AVF, service in the Army is relatively less attractive than service in either the Navy or the Air Force. Yet the practice of standardized compensation makes it necessary to compensate a given rank in the Army at the same level as the Navy or Air Force. As a result, the Navy and the Air Force frequently enjoy the benefits of a large queue of high-quality recruits while the Army faces great difficulty in recruiting such individuals within the current interservice pay structure.

As a result of the characteristics of the military compensation structure, the AVF goes to greater expense to recruit and retain personnel than would be the case if conventional economic analysis guided the formulation of compensation policy. However, achieving substantial reforms has to be treated as an evolutionary enterprise. With decades of experience and the careers of hundreds of thousands of active-duty and reserve personnel associated with the current system, one cannot expect to alter the system either swiftly or easily. Such incremental changes will contribute to a reduction in the cost of the AVF without reducing its potential contribution to national security.

Recruitment and retention policy

The training of military personnel represents one of the highest cost elements of the military manpower system (currently in the $12-$15 billion range, and possibly higher when all costs are included).[10] Training costs are affected by the level of annual accessions needed to maintain the desired service and strength. The number of annual accessions required is in turn determined by the length of the initial term of service.

The conscription-based manpower demands were substantial—upwards of 400,000 or more individuals annually. This figure has been reduced by one-third as a result of a modest increase in the length of the initial tour of duty and reductions in desired service strength. From the perspective of training requirements, the AVF retains many of the properties of the conscription-based accession system and thereby serves to increase the cost of the military personnel system.

If the initial term of service were lengthened from the current average of three to four years to six to

10. See *Staff Papers on Defense Manpower Costs*, ibid.

ten, the number of accessions could be cut by 50 percent or more annually, with similar reductions in the direct (for example, operations and maintenance expenditure) and indirect (such as wear and tear on operational equipment and the diversion of skilled manpower to the training base) costs of the training establishment. Some of the savings generated by reductions in the cost of the training base could be used to pay the higher initial costs of inducing longer first-term enlistments. This could be effective if the compensation takes the form of cash payments rather than deferred income.

Further, military productivity would be increased if changes in personnel rotation policy were made to permit fuller exploitation of the higher levels of effectiveness implied by longer tours of duty within a given military occupational specialty (MOS). Such productivity could feed back in the form of lower accession requirements as well, although it is unlikely this will happen in force structure-dominated circumstances such as ground combat units or tactical air squadrons.[11]

Closely associated with recruitment policy is retention policy. One of the current problems that has emerged from the (appropriate) attention given to the retention of middle-level skilled personnel in the armed forces is a career-heavy force

moving inexorably toward retirement in the military system.[12] Just as a first-term force, which requires a large number of annual accessions, can pose serious budget and performance problems, so too can a career-dominated force impose serious difficulties. What is required is an AVF with a pattern of long first-term enlistments coupled with a retention policy that constrains reenlistments to 10-20 percent of accessions. This selective retention policy would minimize the number of personnel eligible for retirement and reduce pressures for costly non-cash-deferred benefits for the career force.

THE MILITARY PERSONNEL
OUTLOOK FOR THE
UNITED STATES

It appears likely that at least modest changes will be made in the U.S. military personnel system— even in the absence of significant pressures for force structure change. The need to cope with the magnitude of Soviet military power makes it necessary that the United States develop an effective and responsive military force with appropriate hedges to accommodate a potential mobilization contingency. The cost of maintaining the current system is unnecessarily high. Incipient trends toward the use of short first-term enlistments and GI Bill legislation to induce volunteers promise to raise training costs in the first instance and discourage retention in the latter case unless their use is carefully controlled. Costly incentive programs

11. The experience of the United States with civilian technicians performing maintenance is instructive in Air National Guard units A civilian technician is about three times as productive as his active Air Force counterpart, who must perform all the productivity-reducing tasks imposed by current operating practices. A similar technician-oriented system in the Swedish air force has a plane-to-man ratio nearly four times that of the U.S. Air Force. See Canby et al., "An Alternative Analysis," p. 8.

12. For example, due to the effect of new incentives for middle-level career personnel, the U.S. Army is now facing the highest fraction of career miltary personnel in its active-duty force in history.

aimed at middle-level retention create similar risks of increasing costs unless their use is carefully monitored.

The decline in the military-eligible age cohort during the 1980s poses the risk of higher budget costs for the recruitment and retention of military personnel when there is competition with the civilian economy. This is a problem widely shared in the industrialized nations of the West and will increase the need for more imaginative solutions, especially with respect to the need to structure reserve forces capable of responding to meet a future military contingency.

It is unlikely that conscription will be reintroduced in the United States without a major stimulus in the form of a significant deterioration in the international environment or a refusal on the part of Congress to meet the budget cost of AVF. The short-run costs of reintroducing conscription do not appear to be worth the benefits it would provide to meet peacetime military personnel requirements.

ANNALS, *AAPSS*, 457, September 1981

A National Arms Control Policy for the 1980s

By JAMES E. DOUGHERTY

ABSTRACT: The SALT decade saw two balances—strategic and European—tilt against the West. Arms control policy requires better integration with U.S./Allied defense planning needs. It must address differences in superpower deterrence doctrines and negotiating requirements and NATO dependence on non-NATO areas. Policy in each arms control forum should be judged according to criteria of Western security interests and international strategic stability.

James E. Dougherty is professor of politics, St. Joseph's University, Philadelphia, and senior staff member, Institute for Foreign Policy Analysis, Cambridge, Massachusetts. For 20 years he has had a particular interest in arms control and negotiations.

THE arms control policy of the United States cannot be developed in isolation from defense policy; much less can it be formulated in a manner antithetical to defense. The specious argument has been propagated that the more we spend on the military, the less national security we really have, and the even more bizarre corollary argument that by reducing our defense budget and rejecting new weapons systems we somehow further the cause of arms control. Those who act on such advice further the cause of unilateral disarmament, but they do not advance toward the goal of genuine arms control, which is to make the world safer against the danger of war by enhancing international strategic stability.

In an era of dynamic, rapid technological change—a subject which opponents of defense prefer not to discuss because it exposes the shallowness of their assertion that "we have enough"—American national security must be based on continuing programs of military weapons modernization in the nuclear, conventional, and unconventional sectors—all carefully conceived in light of a comprehensive and coherent national strategic concept. Arms control policy is supposed to strengthen deterrence, not weaken it. It should be compatible with the essentially defensive ethos of the United States. It should also be consistent with, and promotive of, the basic security interests of those allies to whose defense we are committed.

SALT I AND SALT II

In recent years, the United States has found itself increasingly unable to achieve a viable strategic arms limitation agreement with the Soviet Union because of a growing perception at home and abroad that its own strategic military position relative to that of the Soviet Union had been deteriorating for the last decade, ever since the signing of SALT I. During the SALT I negotiations, each of the superpowers had a serious concern about the other side's deployment plans. The Soviet leaders feared that the United States was ahead in ABM technology and that if the Safeguard system was put in place around as many as four ICBM sites it might later be upgraded into a fairly effective nationwide antimissile defense force. American military planners were worried about the possibility that the new Soviet heavy missiles, once MIRVed, would render U.S. land-based ICBMs vulnerable to a Soviet first strike. The ABM Treaty of 1972 and a subsequent protocol concluded in 1974 led to the abandonment of ABM deployment by the United States. But the Soviet Union refused to alter its position on heavy missiles, and the United States had to be content to defer the possibility of attaining essential equivalence based on equal aggregate strategic forces until SALT II. It gradually became clear that the negotiation for the SALT II Treaty had failed to produce any substantial modification in the rate at which Soviet strategic capabilities were being deployed during the 1970s.

The Nixon-Ford administration had proceeded with SALT II negotiations on the assumption that certain planned improvements in existing weapons systems and certain projected new weapons systems would be realized on schedule. Even if those expectations had been fulfilled, there probably would have been a vigorous debate in the Senate over the SALT II agreement that was finally signed in Vienna in June 1979 by President Carter and Soviet President Brezhnev. What seems likely is that Ford and Kissinger might have been able to negotiate a somewhat more favorable (though not drastically different) agreement and to convince the Senate that, in view of strategic modernization programs that were under way, ratification was in the U.S. national interest.

PRESIDENT CARTER'S MILITARY CUTS

During its first two years in office, the Carter administration cancelled the B-1 bomber, slowed down both the Trident I submarine and the Trident II missile program, as well as R&D for cruise missiles, decided against deployment of the enhanced radiation weapon after badly mishandling it politically in the European alliance context, and cut the naval shipbuilding program. In fact, the Carter administration, while irritating the Soviet leadership by stressing human rights as a foreign policy issue, seemed to bend over backwards to demonstrate a willingness to reduce reliance upon military force in the conduct of international affairs and even to move toward operationalizing a concept close to President Carter's heart—finite deterrence as the route to substantial disarmament—without inducing the Soviet Union to make reciprocal concessions.

Far from reciprocating the Carter administration's gestures with any acts of self-abnegation on its own part, the Soviet Union continued its steady military buildup—nuclear and conventional, at the strategic level and in the European theater—without any signs of abatement. Unlike American defense spending curves, which showed periodic sharp rises and falls as a result of the Korean and Vietnam wars, a graph of Soviet military expenditures manifests no peaks and valleys, only unrelenting effort. It should be borne in mind that in the Soviet state-controlled economy, the military budget in the last decade has not undergone erosion by inflation—for example, in manpower costs. Instead it has been increased in support of a military program unprecedented in scope and magnitude for a state during peacetime.

THE TILTING BALANCE

There have been endless arguments since the mid-1970s over the degree to which the global strategic nuclear balance and the European theater-nuclear balance have tilted to the disadvantage of the West. It is not my intention to delve into the dismal statistics of various strategic indicators such as throw-weight, megatonnage, numbers of missiles and warheads, accuracy, hardening, hard-target kill capability, and related factors. Regardless of what the current objective military balance may be—and perhaps no one knows exactly—two facts are incontrovertible. First, the statistical trends have been running against the United States and NATO for the last 10 years. Testifying as Secretary of Defense before the Senate

Foreign Relations Committee in July 1979, Harold Brown said that he expected those trends to continue to be adverse through 1985, even if the SALT II agreements were ratified.[1] In other words, what once was considered an advantageous U.S. strategic position has been, and still is, undergoing long-term erosion. Thus, whereas U.S. strategic nuclear superiority could once compensate for the West's deficiencies in conventional forces, this is no longer the case. In our strategic-military literature, discussion of the impending "window of vulnerability" has become commonplace.

Second, a long-range adverse tilt in the military balance has been widely perceived in the United States and abroad. This perception is a political-strategic phenomenon, and it has produced political-strategic effects. For several years after the Vietnam war, the United States had been seen to be moving into a more passive—some have called it neoisolationist—phase of foreign policy history while the Soviet Union had been perceived as becoming an increasingly dynamic and assertive actor in the international system in Asia, the Middle East, Africa, and Latin America. Meanwhile, Western Europe appears to have been drifting toward what some in Western Europe fear to be a condition of "Finlandization." Within such an uncongenial environment, it was not surprising that the SALT II Treaty stood little chance of Senate ratification even before the Soviet invasion of Afghanistan in December 1979.

1. Charles W. Corddry, "Vance, Brown Start SALT Debate with Hawkish Attitude," *Baltimore Sun* 10 July 1979; see also *New York Times* 10 July 1979.

SALT AND U.S. DEFENSE PLANNING

American policy makers and strategic analysts in growing numbers had become wary of the effects the SALT process had exerted upon U.S. strategic planning over the course of a decade. Although they could find no persuasive evidence that SALT had done much to restrain the Soviet Union from doing what it was technologically and economically capable of doing, they were convinced that the SALT process was retarding U.S. defense efforts. Soviet planners tailored their SALT negotiating positions to the force goals they wanted to achieve during the lifetime of the treaty. In contrast, the United States often allowed the hope that an arms limitation agreement was close at hand to determine its strategic force planning and to provide specious justification for delays of several years in needed modernization programs. Virtually every proposal for a new U.S. strategic weapons system, even when fully compatible with the provisions of SALT I and the expected terms of SALT II, was likely to face opposition on the grounds that it was unnecessary and represented a wasteful expenditure in light of an "imminent agreement," and that to proceed with it would violate the "spirit of arms control" if not actually jeopardize the agreement being negotiated. The net result of such an approach was to create a backlog of modernization needs and a mounting demand for crash programs to catch up, because SALT was allowed to become a tool of defense budgeteering in Washington rather than a negotiating process for stabilizing the strategic balance.

Not until the latter part of 1978, when the Carter administration began to realize that SALT II was in trouble, did it attempt to convert the Senate critics by adopting a tough-sounding tone on defense—calling for a doubling of civil defense preparations, MX development and deployment, and a five percent increase in real terms in defense spending. But the change did not come in time, nor was it sufficiently substantial to reverse the anti-SALT tide. The President himself had not been a model of political prudence in his dealings with the Senate, especially when he made an unveiled threat to bypass the power to advise and consent by casting SALT II in the form of an executive agreement rather than a treaty. The administration's problems were compounded by the discovery of, and the focusing of public discussion on, a Soviet combat brigade in Cuba and subsequently the seizure of hostages in the American Embassy in Tehran. The latter event ushered in a long period of American frustration and apparent impotence. Weeks before the Soviet invasion of Afghanistan, SALT looked as if it would be unratifiable in the prevailing political environment in the United States and in light of deteriorating trends in the U.S.-Soviet relationship.

THE DEMISE OF SALT II

The demise of SALT II was inevitable once a substantial number of senators reached the conclusion, in the words of the Armed Services Committee report, that the agreements were "not in the national security interest" of the United States. The American people have been told for many years that arms control is supposed to contribute to a more stable and peaceful world without placing either superpower at an unfair military disadvantage.

They were willing to support an equitable SALT II agreement which would fit that description of purpose. But a set of accords that made so many policy makers and analysts apprehensive had to be fundamentally flawed. In order to be viable, an arms limitation treaty must command the confidence of an overwhelmingly majority of the Congress and public alike. Any accord that "squeaks by" in a narrow vote after an acrimonious debate that leaves the country deeply divided (does it foster or undermine national security?) is not a sound diplomatic instrument. It does nothing for the cause of arms control. Unless both sides can live comfortably with a treaty that impinges vitally upon their national security, that treaty is bound to come under strains which may prove unbearable, leading to its eventual collapse by abrogation or withdrawal under circumstances likely to heighten rather than attenuate international tensions.

President Carter committed a significant error of political judgment in presenting such a flawed treaty to the Senate. It is regrettable that the United States placed itself in the awkward position of negotiating a treaty that in the end could not be ratified. Some advocates of ratification pointed out that senatorial rejection would duplicate the fatal mistake of 1920, when the United States disinherited the brainchild of President Wilson—the League of Nations. They said the United States would be made to look inconsistent and unsure of itself, incapable of charting a steady course in the conduct of foreign policy. In a sense they were right. Unfortunately, there were some unfavorable consequences. Worldwide there were probably many who thought that the United States seemed to be erratic in its policy behavior. Our European allies, having been urged by Washington to endorse the SALT II agreements despite some misgivings over provisions of the protocol relating to range limitations on cruise missiles and exclusion of the Soviet SS-20 launchers targeted against Western Europe, were at least for a while perplexed (even though some may have felt relieved) at the U.S. reversal. Furthermore, some Western Europeans opposed to the deployment of a new NATO theater-nuclear force (Pershing IIs and cruise missiles) have contended erroneously that Europe's acquiescence in the Brussels TNF modernization decision of December 1979 was contingent upon the ratification of SALT II. But it is the total pattern of U.S. behavior in recent years that must be faulted for its unpredictability. The fault lay more in the negotiation of SALT II than in its rejection. It was traceable to the fact that U.S. arms control policy had been allowed for too many years to proceed along a track that diverged from the essential requirements of U.S. planning for its own defense and the defense of its allies.

SOVIET AND U.S. DOCTRINES

It will be necessary for the United States to integrate arms control and national defense planning much more effectively than in the recent past. Account also will have to be taken of a monumentally important fact that became abundantly clear to Western strategic analysts during the years of negotiating SALT II: the fundamental difference between the American and the Soviet approach to deterrence and arms control. The difference is one of strategic doctrine and of force posture planning. For a decade and a half, the official U.S. philosophy informing both posture planning and arms negotiations had been the McNamara Doctrine of mutual assured destruction (MAD). Many in the Arms Control and Disarmament Agency, under Democratic and Republican presidents, remained confident for a long time that the United States must and could "educate" Soviet planners and bring them around to an American view concerning deterrence, strategic stability, force level requirements, and arms control itself. By the late 1970s, however, it had become apparent that the Soviet Union was not prepared to be so "educated" by the United States. Soviet military literature pointedly repudiated the concepts on which the MAD doctrine rested. That literature emphasized instead the crucial importance of the preemptive nuclear strike if nuclear war should appear inevitable and imminent and of preparations for waging, winning, surviving, and recovering from such a war. Whereas the United States, in its traditional approach to deterrence and arms control, had called for restraint in the deployment of first-strike counterforce capabilities, Soviet strategic doctrine and weapons acquisition policies were derived from a sharply contrasting philosophy that exacerbated Western concern over the global nuclear balance and the growing vulnerability of U.S. land-based ICBMs.

This analysis is not meant to suggest that the Soviet Union is any less interested in deterring nuclear war than is the United States. In my opinion, even though Soviet communist ideology rejects the notion that peace can be achieved so long as capitalism has access to formidable nuclear military power, nevertheless the wartime destruction of the Soviet Union—which has no counterpart in American experience— reinforces a preference for an operational strategy that will enable Moscow to achieve its foreign policy objectives without nuclear war, unless the Soviet heartland itself is threatened. Soviet leaders have long been convinced that the most effective way to deter an unwanted nuclear war (one initiated by capitalist states) is to be prepared to fight, win, survive, and recover from such a war. Many of those Western analysts who for decades treated reports of Soviet active and passive defense eforts with ridicule are still inclined to believe that Soviet military theoreticians are engaged in "whistling past the nuclear graveyard." Nevertheless, we have seen mounting evidence of Soviet R&D programs in strategic defense designed to overtake the United States, together with a commitment by Moscow to civil defense programs designed to ensure the survival at least of elite cadres needed for the formidable task of postattack recovery in the event of a nuclear war.

REVISION OF DOCTRINES?

Within the last year or two, a few arms control Sovietologists have perceived signs that Moscow may be shifting toward the U.S. concept of deterrence through mutual assured destruction. But thus far the evidence that can be marshalled in support of this position has not been convincing. Subtle semantic modifications in the publicly professed doctrine of the Soviet leadership, far from reflecting a profound strategic "metanoia," may be little more than a tactical maneuver designed to dissuade the United States from the necessity of embarking on new defense modernization programs. Such a development in Soviet political rhetoric is an interesting one and will bear careful watching in order to determine whether it eventually has any significant effect upon Soviet strategic deployments, future arms acquisition policies, and willingness to negotiate arms limitation agreements that take into fuller consideration American and Western European security apprehensions.

One might argue that the Soviet strategic philosophy of nuclear deterrence and arms control has produced a more noticeable impact upon the policy of the United States than vice versa. American strategic thinkers have become steadily more disenchanted with the doctrine of mutual assured destruction on moral, military, and political grounds. The new strategic doctrine known as Countervailing Strategy, which was embodied in Presidential Directive (PD) 59 in August 1980, represented a logical culmination of a line of thinking that can be traced back to Defense Secretary James Schlesinger's 1974 call for selective targeting and limited nuclear options. Indeed, one can find adumbrations of it in the Kennedy administration's strategy of "flexible repsonse" in the early 1960s. The Joint Chiefs of Staff were never enthusiastic about the MAD doctrine, which was never the exclusive basis for American operational planning. That doctrine, however, did exert a powerful controlling effect upon the strategic force procurement policies of the United States for two decades. After the new Countervailing Strategy was announced in 1980, the head of Strategic Air Command, General

Richard Ellis, and other top-ranking U.S. commanders noted that even with a significant program of modernization (including ALCM, Trident, and MX), the United States would be in no position to make the Countervailing Strategy militarily credible until 1986.[2] In short, the declared doctrine would not be backed up by an appropriate force posture.

One of the main dilemmas long faced by American strategic planners has been the moral-political one. Some critics of MAD condemned it as ethically monstrous, politically absurd, and without any coherent military meaning because of its conceptual emphasis on holding hostage the civilian population of the Soviet Union instead of concentrating principally on the destruction of military targets. Others questioned the deadly logic of deterrence which, it was said, involved a senseless, spasmic revenge from the grave. But the only alternative deterrent is one which envisages the capability of carrying out a limited or selective strike that would make the cost of aggression excessively high in terms of military forces and other strategic resources. Soviet strategic deployments during the last decade were so extensive that some ardent proponents of SALT II, anxious to calm American misgivings over the growing vulnerability of fixed, land-based missiles, began to suggest that the United States could easily circumvent its difficulty by going to a policy of "launch on warning" or "launch under attack/assessment." That type of reasoning sent shivers down the spines of the more experienced advocates of strategic stability.

2. "New U.S. War Plan Called Unworkable," *International Herald Tribune* 22 August 1980.

Indeed, for the Carter administration to assert that, as a result of the deteriorating U.S.-Soviet strategic balance, the United States might be compelled to consider such a destabilizing option constituted in itself a serious indictment of the SALT process. Clearly, during a decade of SALT the most accurate component of the U.S. triad of strategic forces, the land-based ICBM, had become vulnerable to a Soviet attack.

One of the most important contributions the Reagan administration can make toward U.S. national security and the security of its allies will be to develop a coherent strategic concept synthesizing the basic requirements of deterrence, defense, and arms control. Pending the emergence of such a concept— one which can generate a broad consensus—it will be necessary to postpone nearly all arms negotiations with the Soviet Union.

THE INDIAN OCEAN

For all practical purposes, the illconsidered effort (undertaken largely as a result of pressure from certain senators) to seek an agreement limiting naval armaments in the Indian Ocean at a time when the Soviet Union was building up its military presence in the Horn of Africa is now dead. During the last few years the Western allies have become steadily more concerned, in the face of growing political turbulence along the Cape Route, to shore up the sea lines of communication on which they depend for the flow of oil and other critical raw materials. The principal maritime allies have been strengthening their naval presence in that volatile region, and the United States is now acquiring and improving airfield, seaport, and prepositioning facilities for its

Rapid Deployment Force in Oman, Kenya, and Somalia. Barring a genuine subsidence of the threat to Western interests in the vicinity of the Persian Gulf, the prospect for negotiations that would serve the interests of the United States and its allies is bleak.

Three other sets of negotiations the United States should reassess unilaterally are those pertaining to chemical weapons, antisatellite (ASAT) weapons, and a comprehensive nuclear test ban. It is probable that both superpowers perceive some problems in subscribing to any set of arms limitations, but in these areas the problems are more serious for the United States than for the Soviet Union—in light of present military asymmetries.

Chemical warfare

The Soviet Union now leads the United States in chemical warfare capabilities (especially in the NATO/Warsaw Pact equation). But there can be little doubt that Soviet leaders have a great deal of respect for the U.S. chemical industry and that they would like to freeze their present advantage by entering a chemical wapons convention that would obstruct U.S. efforts to catch up without requiring any reduction in chemical warfare capabilities already produced and deployed. In an age of binary weapons, both sides need to worry about the problems of control and verification. But Moscow can always count on a variety of internal monitoring mechanisms within the United States to police an agreement—the opposition party, the press and electronic media, and opponents of U.S. defense programs. The United States must rely on a more limited range of information emanating from the USSR—

such as the sources that brought to light in 1979 the Sverdlovsk incident, apparently in flagrant violation of the Biological Weapons Convention, indicating that the Soviet Union may have been engaged in the manufacture of biological weapons.

Antisatellite weapons

Both superpowers rely on satellites for a variety of purposes: military (warning, reconnaissance, communications, and navigation), civilian (meteorology, civil communications, and scientific investigation) and also to verify compliance with arms control agreements. The Soviet Union carried out ASAT tests before the United States began to develop an ASAT capability of its own. When the United States proposed a ban on further testing, the Soviet Union sought to link such a ban to a discontinuation of the U.S. space shuttle, which Moscow suspects of possessing an antisatellite capability. Perhaps what the United States really needs is an "antisatellite-killer-killer" to prevent the Soviet Union from destroying American satellites either at low altitudes (where it now possesses a limited operational capability) or at higher geosynchronous altitudes (where most U.S. satellites orbit the earth and where the Soviet Union has not yet developed an ASAT capability). Regardless of the strategic doctrine a superpower espouses, its military leaders will deem it crucially important to have a secure reconnaissance and warning system both before and after the initiation of hostilities. This will enhance deterrence, defense, and arms control. Any use of satellite killers or satellite blinders on a large scale must be regarded as part of a strategic attack and would be bound to

make for uncontrolled escalation following the breakdown of deterrence. It is in the interest of strategic stability, therefore, to obtain a verifiable ASAT agreement.

Comprehensive test ban (CTB)

Although both superpowers have undoubtedly learned a great deal about warhead design from underground testing during the 18 years since the signing of the Limited Nuclear Test Ban Treaty, the requirements of modernization and of occasional stockpile-proof-testing make both sides wary of entering into a comprehensive nuclear test ban of more than limited duration— for example, three or five years. The Soviet Union appears sufficiently confident of its vast nuclear weapons lead over China to have overcome its earlier reluctance to sign a treaty to which the PRC did not adhere. Despite the gains made by the United States in developing national technical means of detecting nuclear tests, American policy makers are still not certain that a CTB would be verifiable over a long period of time, and they would prefer it to contain provision for a small number of low-yield tests. But Soviet negotiators have never agreed to that, nor to the exact duration of a CTB. Because of differences in the two systems, it is presumed that a complete ban on nuclear testing would have a more adverse effect on U.S. than on Soviet capabilities for preserving scientific/technological laboratories and staffs in a state of competent readiness. But the most important reason for the United States to examine carefully all future Soviet proposals relating to CTB is that, for the next five years, the testing and development of a new strategic and theater-nuclear force will represent a much greater security imperative for the United States than for the USSR. After a decade of vigorous testing and development of several missile systems by the Soviet Union, the United States must now try to catch up.

NONPROLIFERATION

The one arms control area in which nuclear weapons powers share a continuing interest in cooperation is nonproliferation. American policy makers have probably been correct to assume that a world of 10 or 15 or 20 nuclear weapons states would be more dangerous than a world of a half-dozen. Doubling or trebling the number of nuclear weapons states is bound to render problems of international arms control more intractable than they are already and would—statistically at least—increase the probability of nuclear war. Within recent years, nations regarded as possible leading candidates for entry into the nuclear club have included Argentina, Brazil, South Africa, India, and those interested in an "Islamic bomb"—especially Pakistan, Iraq, and Libya. Prime potential suppliers of nuclear technology include France, the Federal Republic of Germany, Canada, Japan, Italy, Switzerland, the Netherlands, and Belgium. It is obvious that the United States, the original sponsor of the nonproliferation regime, cannot sustain it without the cooperation of other countries capable of exporting nuclear materials. Growing dissatisfaction with the adequacy of IAEA controls on the export of technology from supplier states provided one of the justifications for the Israeli attack in June 1981 on Iraq's Osirak reactor, which set an ominous prece-dent for one of the most highly dangerous approaches imaginable for dealing with the problems of proliferation and nuclear blackmail.

It will become increasingly difficult to discourage states from acquiring nuclear weapons, but uncontrolled proliferation may not be inevitable. Having paid a political price for pressing some of its closest allies in the 1960s to promote the Nonproliferation Treaty, the United States should not now abandon as either worthless or hopeless the effort to retard or stretch out the process of nuclear weapons diffusion in Asia, Africa, and Latin America. It may be possible to provide incentives for candidate countries to continue to practice restraint and to be satisfied with a "demonstration of ability" standoff in regional rivalries such as that between India and Pakistan.

But the United States will not be able to succeed if it pursues a Canute-like policy of ordering the waves to recede. It cannot prevent forever the construction of reprocessing and separation plants throughout the Third World. Moreover, while continuing to remind the world that unbridled proliferation will be destabilizing, the United States should avoid offending those allies that have a significant economic stake in civilian nuclear energy by lecturing them publicly on the dangers of the plutonium economy and of nuclear sales without safeguards against diversion. The allies are aware of the need for controls. In the past, they have often suspected the United States of adopting a "holier-than-thou" attitude while seeking to reserve a large portion of the international nuclear materials market for itself. For the future, the United States will require an evenhanded policy, one which recognizes the economic interests of allies and Third World countries in civilian nuclear power, as well as the implications of conventional arms transfer policies for proliferation pressures abroad. Finally, in order to improve mutual understanding among supplier and consumer countries, it should follow up the initiatives embodied in the now completed International Nuclear Fuel Cycle Evaluation (INFCE). While working for agreements with the principal suppliers on terms and procedures for the international transfer of nuclear materials and equipment, the United States will do well to demonstrate to the less developed countries a sensitivity to their concern over an assured flow of supplies for their nuclear power industries for the use of nuclear power as a source of energy.

NATO THEATER-NUCLEAR MODERNIZATION

In December 1979, more than two years after Chancellor Schmidt first urged the creation of a NATO long-range missile force to redress the East-West nuclear imbalance in the European Theater, the Alliance Defense Ministers decided to deploy in Western Europe 108 Pershing IIs and 464 ground-launched cruise missiles capable of reaching targets in the Soviet Union. This decision was necessary because, throughout the decade of SALT negotiations, Western Europeans had witnessed the steady deterioration of their regional security posture as the United States first lost strategic superiority and then, in the eyes of many, could no longer be sure even of strategic parity. Meanwhile, the Soviet buildup of intermediate-range missiles capable of striking targets in

Western Europe proceeded unabated. Most of the tactical nuclear weapons the United States had deployed in Europe in the 1960s were of very short range. At the present time NATO has no land-based missiles capable of reaching the Soviet Union. Western Europeans have been understandably fearful that if the Soviet Union ever attacked and if the war should become nuclear all of the Soviet Union's 5000 Eurostrategic weapons—including the new SS-20s and Backfire Bombers—could strike targets in Western Europe, whereas about 5000 of NATO's 7000 nuclear warheads could not be delivered to targets in the Soviet Union. (The other 2000 would have to be delivered by NATO aircraft against formidable Soviet air defenses or by SLBMs that lack the accuracy and counterforce capability of the SS-20.) Given the Warsaw Pact's three-to-one edge in tanks and two-to-one margin in artillery, tactical aircraft, and armored fighting vehicles for infantry, as well as its superior capabilities for waging chemical warfare and rapidly mobilizing and reinforcing with trained reserves, NATO allies have experienced apprehension about the trends and have become increasingly uncertain about the credibility of the U.S. security commitment.

Western European governments have insisted with varying degrees of intensity that the decision to deploy new-generation theater-nuclear weapons in Europe should be related to East-West negotiations over such forces. The United States has agreed to proceed with negotiations but without postponing the NATO TNF deployment scheduled to begin in 1983. During the last few years, antinuclear sentiment has been on the rise throughout Western Europe. The United States cannot be insensitive to the delicate political situations confronting Western European governments, but it must continue to insist that the Alliance not concede to Moscow a monopoly right to modernize theater-nuclear forces, thereby increasing the vulnerability of Western Europe—if not to the danger of overt military attack, certainly to the possibility that at least some of the allies living in the westward shadow of projected Soviet power will be gradually transformed into neutralized states with their political compasses oriented increasingly toward Moscow. If the subtle process of Finlandization is to be reversed, a greater degree of Eurostrategic symmetry must be achieved through a combination of deployment and negotiation.

At the Rome meeting of NATO Ministers in May 1981, Secretary of State Haig assured the European allies that the United States would be ready to enter East-West negotiations over theater-nuclear forces by the end of this year.

CONCLUSION

It remains in the national interest of the United States to pursue modes of arms control which are equitable to all parties, which are verifiable and which will enhance the stability of the international strategic, political, and military environment. SALT II collapsed because, in the eyes of many, it codified a superpower relationship that failed to advance the basic objective of stra-

tegic stability. The United States should not seek an arms control treaty merely for the sake of obtaining agreement or for vaguely defined goals in superpower relations. Yet in the last decade administrations of both political parties at times oversold the SALT process as the centerpiece of a foreign policy in which the ephemeral atmospherics of détente were assigned a higher priority than the substance of strategic stability.

At the present time the conditions for meaningful strategic arms negotiations with the Soviet Union do not exist. Before it can negotiate with confidence, the United States must first put its own house in order and develop a more coherent strategic concept upon which adequate force modernization programs can be based and from which criteria for arms control negotiations and agreements can be derived. There is no need to strive for superiority in strategic forces, or in theater-nuclear forces, or across the conventional spectrum. But it is essential that the United States acquire the capabilities to deprive the Soviet Union of any "window of opportunity" that might tempt its leaders to take imprudent risks in a future crisis. It is not necessary for the United States to procure every new weapons system available. But a steady and efficiently planned effort to increase our deterrent capabilities and our overall defense readiness is in order. Once we have taken such action, it will be possible to work out with the political realists in Moscow an arms control agreement that will serve the security needs of the United States and its allies.

ANNALS, *AAPSS*, **457**, September 1981

The Superpower Relationship and U.S. National Security Policy in the 1980s

By ROBERT L. PFALTZGRAFF, Jr.

ABSTRACT: In retrospect, the United States has experienced repeated failure in the efforts of successive administrations over the last decade to bring about an improved relationship with the Soviet Union because of fundamentally different Soviet and American security interests and objectives and conceptions of the role of force in international politics. The debate in the United States about the SALT II Treaty provided the basis for a broader discussion of the adequacy of American defense capabilities in light of the growth of Soviet capabilities and the manifest propensity to extend Soviet influence by direct means, as in Afghanistan, or by the use of surrogates, as in Africa. In the years ahead, the United States faces the need both to rebuild its military forces and to fashion a global political strategy that deters the Soviet Union from exploiting whatever advantages may be perceived to accrue from vast military capabilities during this period of vulnerability in which interests vital to the United States and its allies will be at stake.

Robert L. Pfaltzgraff, Jr., is Professor of International Politics at the Fletcher School of Law and Diplomacy, Tufts University, and President of the Institute for Foreign Policy Analysis, Inc., Cambridge, Massachusetts, and Washington, D.C. His recent publications include Contending Theories of International Relations *(Second Edition);* The Atlantic Community in Crisis: A Redefinition of the Transatlantic Relationship; Arms Transfers to the Third World: The Military Buildup in Less Industrial Countries; Soviet Theater Strategy: Implications for NATO; SALT II and U.S.-Soviet Strategic Forces; The Soviet Union and Ballistic Missile Defense; Energy Issues and Alliance Relationships: The United States, Western Europe and Japan; Intelligence Policy and National Security; *and* Power Projection and the Long-Range Combat Aircraft: Missions, Capabilities, and Alternative Designs.

IN the United States in recent years there has been a dramatic transformation in outlook toward the Soviet Union. This is based on several factors which will affect pro- foundly the American conception of the Soviet Union in the years ahead and the policy options available to the United States in coping with what has been described as "the present danger." To understand the evolution of this changed outlook toward the Soviet Union, it is essential to assess, first and foremost, the apparent differences that emerged between the United States and the Soviet Union in their respective conceptions of détente in the early to mid-1970s. Furthermore, it is necessary to examine the principal features of Soviet foreign policy during the last decade. Last but not least, crucial to an understanding of the nature of the foreign policy problems confronting the United States in its relationship with the Soviet Union in the years just ahead is an assessment of the changed superpower strategic military balance that has emerged in the last decade.

DÉTENTE:
CONTRASTING APPROACHES

The apparent differences between the United States and the Soviet Union in their respective conceptions of détente result from the idea, in retrospect, that détente was oversold to the American public and was based on illusion, even within much of our official policy community, in the early to mid-1970s. Although the failure of détente diplomacy is now deeply rooted in the American outlook toward the Soviet Union, three successive presidents tried variants of détente diplomacy with the Soviet Union—Nixon, Ford, and Carter. Even though their conceptions of Soviet-American relations differed substantially, the results of each seem to have been at least less than satisfactory and at most potentially disastrous to the security interests of the United States. The Nixon-Ford-Kissinger approach sought a conception of linkage between Soviet behavior in one category and of foreign policy in another. An attempt was made in the principles of coexistence, to which each side agreed in May 1972, to establish a kind of code of conduct for superpowers based on the exercise of unilateral restraint and the avoidance of efforts by either side to gain advantage in regional issues at the expense of the other. The Nixon-Ford-Kissinger approach sought to balance the Soviet Union in an East-West context by the conclusion of SALT accords codifying parity and by normalizing American relations with China and at the same time encouraging, to the extent feasible, the growth of surrogate powers in various regions of the world. Moreover, Soviet behavior in one category, especially trade, would be linked to Soviet behavior elsewhere. It was hoped that the Soviet Union would come to have a vested interest in détente because of its existing and potential benefits.

The Carter administration's approach to U.S.-Soviet relations was fraught with paradox, reflecting the apparent split within his own administration on U.S.-Soviet relations. It will be recalled that Carter came to office as a critic of the Nixon-Ford-Kissinger approaches to relations with Moscow. He sought at the same time to subordinate U.S.-Soviet relations to other, allegedly more important, global issues—those of the Third World. He attempted to align American policy, in the United Nations for example, with Third World aspirations. This idea reached its zenith in President Carter's 1977 Notre Dame Speech: "Being confident of our own future, we are now free of that inordinate fear of communism which once led us to embrace any dictator who joined us in that fear. I am glad that's being changed." At the same time, Carter sought to make human rights a central element in U.S.-Soviet relations, together with the achievement of arms limitation agreements—the SALT. He held to a belief that unilateral restraint on the part of the United States would produce reciprocal action on the part of the Soviet Union. Perhaps even more than the Nixon-Ford-Kissinger policy, Carter's efforts were a failure and were perceived as such by a growing number of his countrymen and eventually by most of those who voted in the election of 1980. Toward the end of his administration, and particularly after the Soviet invasion of Afghanistan in December 1979, there were important manifestations of a changing outlook on his part—in particular, the withdrawal of the SALT II Treaty from Senate consideration, although Carter had promised in the presidential campaign to resubmit the treaty to the Senate if he was reelected. Here it is doubtful that the SALT II Treaty would have achieved Senate ratification even before the Soviet invasion of Afghanistan unless accompanied by vast increases in American defense capabilities to cope with the growing challenge posed by the Soviet Union as a result of its substantial military buildup in the 1970s.

These successive failures in American efforts to bring about an improved relationship with the Soviet Union set the stage for a debate that erupted in the United States in the late 1970s, both about the nature of America's role in the context of U.S. national interests and the implications of the growth of Soviet strategic-military power for the security of the United States and its allies. Of major importance in this debate was the repeated evidence of a fundamental difference between American and Soviet approaches to regional security issues. It may be argued that Kissinger had understood the nature of the Soviet Union as what he termed an imperial power—a state in the imperial phase of its history and behaving much as such states could be expected to behave in their international relationships. Although (or because) the American willingness to devote adequate resources to national security and to foreign policy had apparently declined in the post-Vietnam period, it was essential for the United States to call on whatever restraints existed to contain Soviet power. This was the context in which the United States made repeated efforts to call into being—as if it were possible to do so—a global system of several power centers and to evolve with the Soviet Union and a détente relationship. Perhaps we were engaged in a kind of holding action until a new consensus could be forged in support of American foreign policy.

AMERICAN EXPECTATIONS AND SOVIET STRATEGY

Whatever may have been the intention, the effects of U.S. policies of the early 1970s was to produce unwarranted expectations of immediate success—a generation of peace" or a "new structure for global peace," as the terms were widely used— although by the end of the 1970s the United States had begun to enter a new phase in its foreign policy. It was the widening gap between American expectations and Soviet policy —in Angola, Yemen, Somalia, Ethiopia, Southeast Asia, and finally Afghanistan—that produced the coup de grace for the Soviet-American relationship envisaged in the

1970s in the United States and many of the assumptions on which it was based. The evidence mounted that Moscow held to a conception of détente, acknowledged by the Soviet leadership itself, in which periodic improvements in relations with the United States in no way diminished the need for continued struggle against "Western imperialism." Whereas we had perceived detente often as an end in itself—that is, as a condition of peace and global stability—the realization grew in the United States that, for the Soviet Union, détente was a process or means toward an end; that struggle, not stability, was postulated by the Soviet leadership to be inherent in international political relationships. Thus by the end of the 1970s the United States had come full circle, from a conception of containment in a generation after World War II that rested on broad bipartisan consensus until the Vietnam war but which was shattered until the mid- to late 1970s and which has begun to be restored in the form of a new nationalism (some would say neoconservatism) massively demonstrated in the 1980 election.

Of perhaps equal importance to the changed approach to U.S.-Soviet relations was the realization in the American strategic-military affairs community that fundamental differences existed between the superpowers in their respective conceptions of strategic stability and military doctrine. Translations of Soviet literature and the study of Soviet military concepts yielded abundant evidence that the Soviet Union placed emphasis on concepts of surprise and preemption, as well as the integration into a doctrinal framework of strategic offense and strategic defense. Strategic-military deterrence had different force level requirements for the Soviet Union in contrast to the United States. It was pointed out that if nuclear war was unthinkable in the United States, in the Soviet Union emphasis was placed on the means to survive a nuclear exchange. The recognition of such asymmetries led to a belief that American conceptions of strategic doctrine, grounded in mutual assured destruction with its emphasis on the targeting of the populations and urban centers of the adversary, were inadequate in a strategic relationship in which one's adversary held to a fundamentally different conception of deterrence with doctrine and forces configured principally to destroy the strategic forces of the United States. While Americans concluded that military power was irrelevant in light of the global issues of the late twentieth century, the Soviet Union continued to amass huge military capabilities, apparently in support of political objectives.

With a growing appreciation of differences between the doctrines espoused by the Soviet leadership and those of the United States, it was only logical to relate such statements to strategic nuclear force levels and to the trends that were manifest in the Soviet strategic force program. If Soviet doctrine stressed preemption and surprise, together with the survivability of the Soviet Union in the event of nuclear war—eminently sound military concepts and objectives—there was mounting evidence of Soviet strategic programs in keeping with such concepts. The Soviet air defense and civil defense programs, about which there was controversy in the United States related more to their extent and effectiveness than to their existence, were cited in support of Soviet doctrine. In contrast, the United States, perhaps in keeping with the concept of mutual assured destruction, had in effect abandoned air defense after about 1970. Similarly, Moscow's deployment of several fourth-generation ICBM launchers, the hardening of launch sites and facilities for elites, and the deployment of ICBMs with throw-weight and accuracy potentially capable of destroying all or a major portion of the U.S. Minuteman force gave evidence of a perceived relationship between Soviet strategic doctrine and the force levels that were being developed and deployed in its support.

Such was the context within which the SALT II Treaty debate took place in the United States. The American approach to SALT had been premised upon the MAD Doctrine of the United States. Those who rejected this doctrine usually had serious reservations about a SALT II Treaty that appeared principally to codify a strategic military balance that was tilting ominously away from the United States. The split in the American strategic-military affairs community between proponents of MAD and those who emphasized a much stronger defense posture based on counterforce was in part a division between proponents and opponents of the SALT II Treaty. A third approach may be noted: It was argued that the treaty did not reduce substantially the strategic forces of either side and therefore could not be said to constitute genuine arms control. It was such a

dissensus that ultimately helped defeat the SALT II Treaty.

The debate over the SALT II Treaty was really a debate about U.S.-Soviet relations—past, present, and prospective. Critics of the treaty argued that in the decade of SALT the Soviet Union had achieved not only parity with the United States but also an increasing measure of superiority in most categories of strategic forces. In the decade of SALT, the Minuteman vulnerability problems had grown. The Interim Agreement on Offensive Systems signed in May 1972 had conceded the Soviet Union a quantitative edge in ICBM launchers, while the SALT process since 1972 had done little, if anything, to restrain a qualitative Soviet improvement. In short, the SALT process as practiced for a decade had been perceived increasingly to be a kind of strategic cul-de-sac for the United States. Clearly, with or without SALT, we would face the need for major new strategic programs in the 1980s if we were to counter the Soviet buildup. Opponents rested their case on the fact that the treaty codified a superpower strategic military relationship grossly disadvantageous to the United States. Proponents were often able only to argue that, without the treaty, the United States would be even worse off because the balance would tilt even more away from the United States. The recourse, both sides came to agree in principle, lay in American defense modernization programs designed to rectify perceived deficiencies in the U.S. military force posture.

In retrospect, it may be argued that just as the United States expected too much from a détente relationship with the Soviet Union, it placed excessive hopes in SALT and in arms control more generally. By the early-1980s, the dominant view has come to be that arms control policy would be no substitute for an adequate strategic doctrine or for effective defense modernization programs in the United States. Thus the election of 1980 symbolized, in foreign policy, the rejection of a large number of prevailing assumptions of the 1970s about U.S.-Soviet relations, including the previously fashionable view that military power, relative to other instruments of statecraft in foreign policy, was of little importance to the United States.

PROSPECTS FOR THE NEXT DECADE

What, then, are the prospects for U.S.-Soviet relations in the 1980s? Much American analysis in recent years has focused on the phenomenon of "window of vulnerability" for the United States, which is said to translate into a "window of opportunity" for the Soviet Union. The extent to which the Soviet Union presses whatever advantages may be said to accrue to it in the years just ahead will determine to a substantial degree the nature and extent of stability or instability in the Soviet-American relationship. Will the Soviet Union seek to exploit U.S. vulnerabilities during a period in which the United States is rebuilding its military capabilities? Will the Soviet Union engage the United States in crisis diplomacy in which Moscow's advantages will be substantial at progressively higher rungs in a hypothesized escalatory ladder—in a Cuban missile crisis in reverse scenario? In that crisis the United States held both a local and regional conventional advantage and strategic-nuclear superiority. While the Soviet Union enjoyed a

military edge in certain other crises, as in the successive tests of Western will in Berlin, the United States had been superior in strategic-nuclear forces. As a result of trends in the last decade, we face the prospect of inferiority at both levels until and unless basic changes are made in our overall defense posture.

Although many in the United States initially viewed without alarm the growth of Soviet military capabilities as contributing to stability, since Moscow presumably would be more inclined to negotiate arms ceilings once it had attained parity with the United States, the question now arises whether the Soviet Union can be expected to acquiesce in a similar fashion in American efforts to narrow or eliminate a military gap favoring the Soviet Union. The ability to answer that question would enhance our understanding of the prospects for the U.S.-Soviet relationship in the years ahead. Unless the Soviet Union had come to embrace American conceptions of deterrence, strategic stability, arms control, and the presumed disutility of military power in the late twentieth century, there would be little reason to expect Moscow to behave toward the United States as the United States did toward the Soviet Union while Moscow was narrowing the gap.

Perhaps evidence of resolve and of strengthened national will on the part of the United States, seen in sharp contrast to the vacillation in American policy of recent years, will provide the deus ex machina which will be sufficient to deter the Soviet Union from exploiting whatever advantage may be perceived to accrue from the vast military capabilities accumulated during the last decade. It is conceivable that the United States will thus transform weakness into strength even in the

absence of sufficient military capa-
bilties. But it is equally plausible to
assume that the Soviet Union will
assess the correlation of forces as
being maximally in its favor just
before or precisely at the time the
United States begins to narrow the
gap in military capabilities. In this
event, the point of maximum danger
in international crisis to the United
States would seem to lie in the years
just ahead. The approximate time of
such a period of maximum danger
depends on whether the military
advantage favoring the Soviet
Union widens before its narrows, or
when or whether it is transformed
from the edge enjoyed by the Soviet
Union to a "margin of safety" for the
United States.

To be sure, the Soviet Union faces
numerous vulnerabilities, both during its period of maximum opportunity and subsequently. It is
conceivable that its formidable
problems in Poland will deepen and
spread and that repression by Moscow will be met with resistance. The
prospect exists that the vulnerabilities of today will be magnified for
the Soviet Union in the next decade
or generation. These include declining productivity and an aging population as a result of present and
prospective demographic trends;
nationalities problems; repeated
failures in agriculture and in the
nonmilitary-industrial sector; and
problems of reliability often noted in
the forces of the Warsaw Pact and
underscored by events in Poland. If
such problems can be expected to
create growing vulnerabilities for
the Soviet Union in the next decade,
does this not reinforce the notion
that the maximum opportunities
available to Moscow will fall within
the next several years?

ALTERNATIVES FOR THE UNITED STATES

What, then, are the policy options
available to the United States in
fashioning a global strategy in the
years ahead? It is possible that the
communication of national resolve
by the United States to its principal
adversary will elicit deference even
in the absence of requisite strength,
and that such signals will deter the
Soviet Union from miscalculation in
its relationship with the United
States. But it can be argued that
without the substance of power the
United States risks a humiliating
situation in which its bluff is called
by Moscow. Would it not be preferable for the United States to
acquiesce in Soviet probes until
American power is reconstituted? If
the United States faces the specter
of a Cuban missile crisis in reverse
scenario, would it not be less damaging to American interests and prestige to avoid by whatever means
possible a confrontation with the
Soviet Union in the next several
years? To answer such questions in
the affirmative is to embrace a policy of appeasement based on weakness and to acknowledge the
implications of the failure of past
American détente policies toward
the Soviet Union.

To adopt such an approach is to
assume, furthermore, that the United States necessarily has the luxury
of choosing between defending its
interests with whatever means may
be available or accommodating—if
only temporarily and tactically—to
the superior power and designs of
the Soviet Union. Although in the
abstract sense such choices are theo-
retically available, in the real world
they confront vital interests for

which such compromise based upon expediency may be impossible because of the nature of the interests at stake. The most obvious example can be found in a destabilization of Saudi Arabia in which the Soviet Union becomes, or threatens to become, the dominant influence, with attendant consequences for Western Europe and Japan and for the United States itself.

In keeping with the notion of a world in which economic power has been diffused, the United States can make an effort to achieve a more equitable sharing of the burdens of international security with its allies, notably with Western Europe and Japan. Although there remain substantial differences between the United States and its allies stemming from their respective interests in relations with the Soviet Union (for example, West German trade with the Soviet Union and the tangible benefits flowing from intra-German normalization), the United States will seek from its allies a fair share of defense both within their immediate regions and perhaps—although to a lesser extent—outside. Central to its strategy in the late twentieth century is the preservation of alliance relationships. Although the power and the threat of the Soviet Union have grown, the United States faces—especially in Western Europe—allies whose policies are conditioned by domestic constituencies and constraints which lead governments toward policies divergent from what the United States, in this new phase of American policy, is likely to consider an adequate response to perceived dangers. In the years ahead, moreover, the Soviet Union can be expected to maintain its efforts to reinforce such tendencies as a means of encouraging what has been termed the Findlandization, or

perhaps the "Hollandization," of Western Europe. Soviet policy will be designed to strengthen those forces, as in the Netherlands, opposed to NATO modernization, including the deployment of new-generation long-range theater-nuclear systems, even while the Soviet Union continues to deploy counterforce-capable SS-20 systems targeted against Western Europe, China, and Japan at the rate of an additional unit every five days.

Groups opposed to NATO modernization have achieved momentum in Western Europe. In some respects, however, their perspectives have not been at odds with many of the policies and attitudes prevalent in the United States until recently. For more than a decade, successive American administrations urged upon our allies policies of détente and support for strategic arms control. SALT was initially an American, not a European, idea, although its most fervent supporters in the official policy community are now to be found not in the United States but in Western Europe. Just as present European perspectives are the product of forces that have been shaped over many years, policies of consistency and strength manifested by the United States will help to strengthen those within and among our allies who hold a common appreciation of security interests and needs. But such a change will not necessarily come overnight. Thus if there is a lack of policy synchronization between the United States and its allies, the causes lie not only in a quest among allied governments for greater independence but also in American policies of the past decade now discarded in the official American policy community but which remain deeply rooted as part of the prevailing orthodoxy within certain elites abroad.

EQUILIBRIUM IN EAST ASIA

Of equal importance to the United States is the preservation and—to the extent necessary—the strengthening of relations with allies and friendly states in East Asia. In that region we have seen the evolution of a security framework over the last decade that contains as principal actors the Soviet Union, Japan, and China, in addition to the United States. This regional system has been described as quadrilateral in its key actor membership, although it affects, and is affected by, relationships between and among lesser states—notably the two Koreas. It is asymmetrical in nature as a result of the vast differences in the major categories of military and economic strength of its members. Only the United States possesses relatively balanced capabilities encompassing both the military and economic sinews of power. Over the last decade whatever incentive existed among at least some of the major actors to follow a policy of equilibrium with respect to the other members of the system—notably with China and the Soviet Union—has been replaced by a policy, especially in the case of the United States, of de facto alignment with China against the Soviet Union and, in the case of Japan, a quest for rapidly expanding trade with China. (The future of Japan's economic relationships with China now seems less certain as a result of the apparent setbacks in the four modernizations in China.)

The security framework that has evolved in East Asia over the last decade has been set within the broader global strategic framework outlined earlier. That is, the manifest growth of Soviet military power, the outward thrust of Soviet policy into the littorals of the Indian Ocean, and the marked deterioration in relations between Moscow and Washington have deeply influenced alignment patterns in East Asia and can be expected to continue to do so in the years just ahead. Hence, elements of a classical balance of power model serve as useful reference points for analyzing regional security at the macrocosmic level.

In this respect the United States and China have evolved a series of parallel interests, together with a common assessment of the threats posed by the Soviet Union. As the momentum of Soviet efforts in military modernization has grown, together with the propensity of the Soviet Union to make direct or indirect use of such power for political purposes, the American relationship with China has been transformed from a framework based on equilibrium, or equidistance, to one providing for alignment—but not formal alliance—with China against the Soviet Union. In 1981 the ultimate extent of an American alignment with the PRC against the Soviet Union remains undecided; however, the scope of the relationship would be determined in the future, as historically it has been in the case of other states in the international system, by perceived dangers emanating from the Soviet Union. In the United States the assertion of a new nationalism, or a neoconservatism, in foreign policy based on the conclusion that the principal strategic threat stems from the Soviet Union coincided by and large with the strategic assessment emanating from Beijing. This included the assertion by China that the Soviet Union was, and is, pursuing a two-pronged strategy in which pressure was applied to the West against NATO and to the East against China and Japan. China contributes to the contemporary regional and global security system by holding down on its frontier with the Soviet Union approximately one-quarter of Soviet military strength. To the East and to the West the Soviet Union has been effectively contained by China and by NATO, respectively. Therefore, the Chinese assessment continues, the Soviet Union has pushed southward into regions adjacent to the strategically vital Persian Gulf and into the oceans in an effort to outflank Western Europe and to encircle China. This so-called two-pronged Soviet strategy, to which Chinese spokesmen have frequently referred in recent years, is worth outlining here because it represents —from the standpoint of a growing consensus of American analysts—an accurate assessment of Soviet strategy. Thus we may speak of parallel Sino-American interests in Soviet containment based on a common strategic appreciation which, nevertheless, does not necessarily translate into identical policies.

Although the differences between China and Japan with respect to security perspectives in and beyond East Asia are substantial, there has been a considerable change in the Japanese outlook on regional and international security issues in recent years. This results from four principal factors: the Soviet invasion of Afghanistan; the strengthening by the Soviet Union of its military forces in the northern territories seized from Japan at the end of World War II; the sustained maritime buildup by the Soviet Union in the seas adjacent to Japan at a time when the United States had drawn down its forces because of security interests in the Indian Ocean-Persian Gulf; and the threats posed to energy in the Persian Gulf region upon which Japan is so vitally dependent. As a result, Japan and

the United States seem to be evolving a consensus on the international security environment to an extent hardly imaginable even a few years ago, although Japan's domestic consensus is not yet sufficiently strong to support what the United States, and even some in Japan, would like to see Japan bear as a fair share of the security burden in the Western Pacific. Once again, as in the case of the European-American relationship, there is a lack of synchronization between Japanese and American policies based to some extent on differing domestic constituencies in each country.

What will be needed in the Japanese-American relationship in the years ahead will be a conception of security in which Japan can play a somewhat greater maritime defense role in the Western Pacific and an increased economic role outside the region. As in the case of alliance relations elsewhere, this will call for a sophisticated combination of American leadership and consultation and a joint assessment of the global and regional security environment on a continuing basis, leading to an appropriate division of labor based on more adequate force levels on the parts of both Japan and the United States.

But the principal conflict arena, it is widely assumed, lies not in Western Europe or in East Asia but in the Southern Hemisphere, in politically unstable Third World countries, some of which are important producers of minerals on which the United States and its allies are vitally dependent. Although much attention has been focused on the Persian Gulf, the potential for instability and conflict elsewhere is abundant. The causes of such conflict can be found in local social, economic, and political circumstances, in the upheavals that have followed the end of Western empires in such regions, in the arming of revolutionary groups by outside powers, especially by the Soviet Union, and in Moscow's use of surrogate forces from Cuba. A decade ago the United States sought unsuccessfully to reach agreement with the Soviet Union that neither superpower would exploit such instability for unilateral advantage. In the 1980s the United States faces the immediate need to halt Soviet-Cuban arms transfers to such groups and to take other steps designed to prevent forces compatible with American interests from being overwhelmed by Soviet-Cuban-supported groups. In large part, this is the meaning of American policy in El Salvador set in broader strategic context.

COALITION-BUILDING AND DEFENSE MODERNIZATION

Thus the alternative to a discredited conception of détente is the pursuit by the United States of policies designed, first and foremost, to maintain and build coalitions of strength in support of vital interests while undertaking necessary defense modernization programs. In defense this means steps to strengthen each of the legs of the triad of strategic forces and to increase their survivability in light of present or emerging asymmetries favoring the Soviet Union. Defense modernization necessarily encompasses general purpose forces as well as strategic nuclear capabilities. It includes the modernization of maritime forces, as well as the development of a rapid deployment capability and the refurbishing of reserve forces. It means consideration both of the nature of future conflict and the creation of adequate doctrines and strategies, together with correction of deficiencies in the American defense mobilization base both in its industrial infrastructure and in manpower-personnel dimensions.

Last but not least, the policy of the United States toward the Soviet Union must be set within a framework which has military as well as political-economic dimensions. Burden-sharing with allies should encompass the concept of fair share for each ally in defense, but it should also contain the notion that alliance partners contribute to the sharing of nonmilitary burdens as well—what in Japan has been termed "comprehensive security." The alternative to détente, moreover, to the extent possible, must seek to exploit existing and emerging Soviet vulnerabilities —to turn the Soviet Union inward to cope with its own formidable problems and thus to relieve outward pressures by Moscow on the United States and its allies. To set forth such basic guidelines for American policy toward the Soviet Union is to acknowledge the existence of risks, especially in a period of maximum Soviet military power. However, to fail to take such steps would pose even greater potential risks for the United States and other peoples whose security will depend ultimately on the strength and clarity of purpose of the United States in the years ahead.

Book Department

INTERNATIONAL RELATIONS AND POLITICS

LOUIS RENÉ BERES. *Apocalypse: Nuclear Catastrophe in World Politics.* Pp. xvi, 315. Chicago: University of Chicago Press, 1980. $20.00.

The purpose of this book, according to Beres, is to signal the enormous danger of nuclear catastrophe in world politics and to suggest a strategy for world-order reform so that this danger can be avoided. The danger arises from the possibility of the United States and the Soviet Union using weapons from their immense nuclear arsenals, from the possibility of other states using nuclear weapons as a consequence of the proliferation of nuclear capabilities, and from the possibility of terrorists causing nuclear explosions. The first two parts of the book explore these possibilities and their consequences. The third part of the book, which accounts for somewhat less than 30 percent of the total pages, advances proposals to minimize these possibilities.

The book is effective in sounding the alarm. Dangers outlined in general terms are illustrated by scenarios that are both chilling and plausible. Because the danger of nuclear catastrophe is appalling, it may seem to be a cavil to raise the issue; nevertheless, at times Beres is unduly pessimistic. It is most unlikely that there will be 100 countries with nuclear weapon capabilities by 1995; and even though the People's Republic of China may have rhetorically supported proliferation, its behavior has been as cautious as that of the nuclear superpowers. The danger is real enough even with more realistic and conservative assumptions.

The more important criticism of the book is that the proposed strategy for world-order reform is not very promising. It is mainly a compilation of proposals that are by now long familiar. The superpowers should adopt strategies of minimum deterrence, accept a comprehensive test ban, renounce the first use of nuclear weapons, and support effective arrangements for nuclear-free zones. Successful nonproliferation appears to depend on the simultaneous acceptance by the superpowers of a dispersion of power and tightened bipolarity. Targets of terrorists must be protected, ways must be found of thwarting the realization of terrorists' objectives, and governments must be willing to bargain with terrorists.

That elements of this strategy appear to be—and are—contradictory is not the most serious problem. The most serious problem is that this strategy was available and pursued, at least to some extent, during the 1970s, yet the danger of nuclear catastrophe may be even greater in the early 1980s than it was in the late 1960s. Creative new suggestions firmly based on an analysis of why this strategy produced such limited results are urgently needed.

Beres achieved one of his purposes—signaling the danger—and he succinctly summarizes the conventional wisdom about how to avoid the danger. Even though specialists will find little new in the book, it should be widely read. Perhaps more was not achieved in the 1970s because the public had become complacent. Reading this book would surely jar one's complacency.

HAROLD K. JACOBSON
University of Michigan
Ann Arbor

GEOFFREY BEST. *Humanity in Warfare.* Pp. xi, 400. New York: Columbia University Press, 1980. $25.00.

Even "in the most unpromising circumstances of war, humanity can often quite surprisingly break through," claims Geoffrey Best, author of *Humanity in Warfare* and professor of history in the School of European Study, University of Sussex. Defining humanity as the observance of "prohibitions and restraints on how" human beings fight wars, and asserting that historical attempts to preserve and exercise that humanity have generally been clothed in "codes of custom and even law," Best assigned himself the task of tracing such restraints from the middle of the eighteenth century to the present.

In the pursuit of his objective, Best rejects the "just war" approach since, among other things, wars are "just" or "unjust" according to who defines them. He also makes clear that, for all human beings, it is a moral and practical victory to limit the nastiness of war, even when we are frustrated by our failure to abolish it and regardless of whether a given war is adjudged just or unjust.

The author begins his study in the middle of the eighteenth century because there existed what he calls an "enlightenment consensus" on the law of war and limited warfare, despite the legal, philosophical, and political differences within that consensus. He then shows how the latter was disrupted, where not destroyed, by the revolutions in the latter half of the century and by the Napoleonic wars. However, the human need to limit the cruelties of warfare expressed itself in the reemergence of ideas and movements in the half-century preceding World War I which gave birth to the Red Cross, the first Geneva Conventions, and the regulations and conventions which resulted from the Hague Conferences of 1899 and 1907. In the rest of the work, Best shows how the two world wars wreaked havoc on those efforts and presents the post-World War II attempts to create legal frameworks to control warfare.

The book, thoroughly researched and supported by elaborate notes and a rich bibliography plus a chronological guide, is a significant contribution to our understanding of the sociopolitical forces within which attempts at controlling the conduct of war have taken place. It lacks balance in some areas—for example, it is Eurocentric and does not sufficiently consider what F. Brown, in *Chemical Warfare: A Study in Restraint*, shows to be technologically conditioned restraint. But such is minor. Best, like Louis Henkin in *How Nations Behave*, demonstrates that law can be a bearer of human ideals, notwithstanding our falling short of its commands; and that it can help us to understand, if we are willing to emphasize it through a focus on human rights, that "men and women are not citizens of their nations alone."

The work was written for all who have an interest in understanding the struggle to limit warfare. With Sydney Bailey's *Prohibitions and Restraints in War* and F. Bonkovsky's *International Norms and National Policy*, one has the basis for the conduct of a lively seminar on restraints in warfare.

WINSTON E. LANGLEY
Boston State College

HARRY HOLLOWAY and JOHN GEORGE. *Public Opinion: Coalitions, Elites, and Masses.* Pp. xii, 286. New York: St. Martin's Press, 1980. $14.95. Paperbound, $8.95.

It is not clear exactly who the ideal audience for this book might be. In a time in which "public opinion" is widely reported to have defeated one president and to have elected another, this book will tell the general reader almost nothing about why Carter lost and Reagan won.

As an introduction to the field of public opinion for undergraduates and beginning graduate students, the book is flawed by Holloway and George's limited (but mixed) aspirations. Although they do not report any original research of their own, they make no claim to offer a comprehensive survey of the current literature on public opinion either. Instead, they devote a large portion of their text to a summary of superficial truisms about the influential role of family, education, religion, ethnic differences, and social class in shaping popular values. (Their contention is that these factors are influential; they offer little specific material about *how* these shape specific values.) Moreover, the studies included seem to have been chosen less for their representativeness of the state of current research than for the fact that they tend to support (or do not contradict) Holloway and George's contention that "ordinary people's opinions really do matter"—or because the studies need refutation in order to clear the way for their preferred interpretation.

On the other hand, as a sophisticated argument addressed to professional colleagues, the book is flawed by Holloway and George's cavalier refusal to define key terms. "Public opinion," after all, is initially a metaphor, not a scientific constant. Until it is operationalized—by specifying what is being counted, and how—the term can do little more than suggest a vague poetic image of transcendent collective sentiment. Although they acknowledge that "perplexed students . . . want to know what 'public opinion' means," they confess feeling "a twinge of annoyance" at the inquiry, and the best they can offer is a vague allusion to public opinion "in the sense of a governing majority that shapes public policy." The key terms in the subtitle are likewise glossed over as if their meanings were universal and self-evident: "by coalitions we mean basic political groupings that have shaped the American polity"; "elite theory, the idea that a relatively small and homogeneous group dominated the system with little constraint from the masses"; "what we mean by 'the masses' is much like what the politician means when he refers to 'the public.' They are not the leaders, usually, but they are not dimwits either."

Some of the most provocative elements of Holloway and George's argument apparently vanished somewhere during the editing process. In the preview of the structure of the book in Chapter 1, readers are told that "Chapter 14 sums up the themes of our opening chapter on coalitions, elites, and masses. Here we try to spell out the relationships between elites and masses and, in addition, the theory of the dominant coalition, which we consider the most persuasive interpretation." Chapter 14 turns out to be an assessment of "The Democratic Potential Unfulfilled," and there is no mention—much less a "theory"—of dominant coalitions.

The book concludes with a four-page appendix entitled "What Pollsters Do and How They Do It." A more thorough treatment of the material covered there would seem to belong squarely in the middle of Chapter 1.

JAMES TODD HAYES
Gustavus Adolphus College
St. Peter
Minnesota

JOHN G. KELIHER. *The Negotiations on Mutual and Balanced Force Reductions: The Search for Arms Control in Central Europe.* Pp. x, 204. Elmsford, NY: Pergamon Press, 1980. $25.00.

The negotiations on Mutual and Balanced Force Reductions—MBFR in the jargon of international diplomacy—have gone virtually unnoticed in the United States in comparison with SALT and other more highly publicized arms limitation negotiations. John Keliher, whose service on the U.S. MBFR delegation in Vienna has provided him with many insights into the negotiating process, has written an informative analysis of both the evolution of the negotiations and of the positions taken by the major participants. Keliher begins with a discussion of the major importance of the German question in East-West discussions on arms control during the first two decades after World War II. Until the late 1960s all Soviet proposals for arms limitations in Europe had as a central focus the acceptance of measures that would effectively neutralize West Germany.

He then traces the developments during the period 1968-73 that led to the negotiations. The central portions of the book concern the preparatory consultations of early 1973, the initial stages of the negotiations, and an analysis of the major proposals presented by the two sides. For the reader interested in the content of the proposals presented by the negotiating teams from both the East and the West, Keliher has provided adequate detail without permitting his narrative to become enmeshed in minutiae. Moreover, his judicious use of source material and documentation makes eassier the reader's search for materials relevant for further research.

After discussing the issues that have been of primary importance in creating the impasse in the negotiations—the data base that determines the size of the Warsaw Pact force reductions and the limitations that will apply to forces outside the Central European region—Keliher presents an interesting set of recommendations designed to permit the negotiations to break out of the impasse. During what has now become an eight-year period of negotiations no real progress has been made on these central issues, and Keliher suggests that a new approach might be considered which focuses on the realignment of forces in Europe rather than on mere force reduction. This would call for the establishment of zones on both sides of the East-West "boundary" in which only defensive military equipment would be permitted. This, he maintains, would result in greater ease in monitoring, although he is aware of some of the potential risks involved in such an approach.

The Negotiations on Mutual and Balanced Force Reductions is well written and makes an important contribution to the growing literature on East-West security relations and arms control negotiations.

ROGER E. KANET
University of Illinois
Urbana-Champaign

W. SCOTT THOMPSON. *National Security in the 80s: From Weakness to Strength.* Pp. 524. San Francisco: Institute for Contemporary Studies, 1980. Paperbound, $8.95.

MICHAEL BRECHER. *Decisions in Crisis: Israel, 1967 and 1973.* Pp. 479. Berkeley: University of California Press, 1980. $24.95.

The Vietnam syndrome paralyzed actions in our basic interests and only now, as America's international predicament is increasingly obvious, are there belated stirrings. Both Democrats and Republicans have been to blame, say the 17 contributors to *National Security in the 1980s: From Weakness to Strength.* Many of them were security advisers to presidential candidate Reagan, and this allegedly could color their defense perspectives. Yet all were authorities in their fields: former public servants Paul Nitze and Fred Ikle, defense experts Democratic Senator Sam Nunn and Richard Burt of the *New*

York Times, and informed scholars. This makes the book a remarkable aggregate of information and argument whose theme is the need for a crash effort to counter a dangerous threat.

The volume looks at what can be done in the short and long term to overcome our weakness. With a section on "Quick Fixes" is a general discussion among the volume's authors and invited participants, such as a Reagan political campaign representative and a White House Brzezinski staff member. The strategic rebuilding section and conclusion also have discussions. There are tabular summaries of what might be done and where we stand with the Soviet Union. One lists some immediate fixes to the U.S. strategic nuclear capability. Another shows the relative technological balance. Relevant graphs and tables are interspersed.

Following the Cuban missile crisis the Soviets, by annual increments of at least five percent in the true military budget increase, now have the advantage of America through a spectrum of weaponry. While some significant categories remain in which the United States has an edge, the Soviet trend is expected to continue at least through the mid-1980s. To opponents of responsive increased U.S. defense spending the authors have a rejoinder. In percentage of all spending, we are at the lowest for defense since FY 1940 and at the lowest percentage of GNP since 1947-48. During the Korean conflict it was, relative to GNP, three times higher than today. President Carter, in a speech on the matter, described the post-Afghan situation as the greatest crisis for the United States since World War II.

With the U.S. force posture decline, a projected three to five percent real growth in such spending can do little more than sustain the present force status, according to the authors. Also, everyone knows from press stories of the inadequacies of our service arms. For global action the Navy has suffered deterioration, being spread thin in coping with three-ocean commitments. One proposed early fix would install cruise missiles on submarines and surface ships. Also, the shipbuilding budget should be increased by at least 30 percent. As for aircraft, their procurement should rise 100 percent. There should be a rapid program of multiple vertical shelters for each Minuteman, thus heavily adding to such missile survivability. Higher manpower levels for increased forces would be essential and inevitably would call for a form of national draft. We should avoid gadgetry and costly questionable weapons. We need quantities of field-maintainable, durable weapons systems.

America has no national security strategy, the contributors agree. The war colleges are needled for much study of management techniques (civilian-useful) but nothing about the art of war. Cost-high technology weaponry derives in part from this lack of strategy, since theoretic simulations of firepower impact dictate heavy logistics components for combat units. Meanwhile we have failed "to produce an acceptable infantry combat carrier or scout car." The few days of oil the U.S. has in its so-called "strategic petroleum reserve" have no relevance to a prolonged conflict or possible interdiction of supply lines for raw materials. The current purported "1½-wars" strategy is assertedly bankrupt, with three feasible war theatres: Western Europe, the Persian Gulf, the Western Pacific—and conceivably a half-war in the Caribbean and Central America. A superior armed Soviet Union could threaten or act to immobilize us, so there would be no time for a massive production buildup.

There are some arresting conclusions: Political aims have risen as military means declined. Defeat for Nato could come in other areas. Despite foreseeable Western efforts, we cannot live the 1980s without a grave Persian Gulf crisis. To play the China card could fruitlessly raise tensions and bring a possible war with the USSR. A shock like the Chinese over the Yalu in the Korean conflict is needed to get sudden major increases in the defense budget and a national draft. "Prudence of the most compelling sort is [essential] until our military capability is substantially rebuilt." Engage in a political-propaganda contest worldwide with the Soviet Union and resist its thrusts wherever made. Avoid a showdown—always have an "escape hatch," for full Soviet military power could oblige us to back down.

Clearly, if such a sobering projection should be the prospect for Americans, hard times are coming.

International crisis behavior studies in depth are the objective of a major project covering a sample of 25 varied cases, each from the perspective of a single state. Each study is to apply kindred methods of quality and quantity analysis while refining certain conditions typifying a crisis. Representative of the project is the fine volume authored by its director, Michael Brecher, with the cooperation of Benjamin Geist. Using the agreed techniques, they dissect how Israel's decision makers handled sequential issues surrounding the 1967 and 1973 wars.

Symptomatic of the realistic approach, an early chart on crisis behavior uses the designation "coping" instead of "management," of which other writers are fond. However, there is divided opinion among the project scholars as to whether threat perception creates stress or whether stress is a combination from threat, time, and war likelihood. Could it not also be that stress as a crisis factor changes as threat perception shifts with time and likelihood of war?

In format the three stages of the two wars are termed "pre-crisis," "crisis," and "post-crisis." Each studies the identified decisions, how and by whom made, the backgrounds, personalities, and motivations of the decision makers, together with the psychological environment and decision flow. There follows a comparison of the two wars at that stage.

A significant Israeli decision, according to some writers, is not accessible for the study's record. This they consider to be the deliberate attack of 8 June 1967 on the U.S. communications ship *Liberty*. The volume's sole citation is from President Johnson's account reinforcing the Israeli public announcement of

error. Dissenters claim that the tragic episode was the result of Israel's decision to prevent U.S. electronic intelligence of its preparations to seize the Golan Heights on 9 June, which Washington feared could spark Soviet intervention. Subsequent acts do give credence to an American-Israeli coverup.

In the book stress and decision choice are given final evaluation in dimensions such as core inputs, costs, importance, complexity, and novelty. During the two great crises facing Israel's governors stress brought more receptivity to new information. With its decline, receptivity became more biased. Similarly with more stress there was more scope and frequency of consultation. Options seemed to increase with stress, and alternatives were less carefully evaluated. Costs also were assessed as becoming high; decisions were deemed increasingly important. Issue complexity also rises, but even with a stress decline the issue areas involved in decisions reach a maximum. In addition, added stress brings more unprecedented choices, while even in a decline such choices stay at their peak.

There is a fascination about the study stemming from its satisfying yet complex combination of scope and detail, use of environmental narrative and personality vignettes, and tables and numbers. Indeed it materially adds to an understanding of how crisis decisions eventuate, and that is its whole purpose.

ROY M. MELBOURNE
Chapel Hill
North Carolina

AFRICA, ASIA, AND LATIN AMERICA

ISEBILL V. GRUHN. *Regionalism Reconsidered: The Economic Commission for Africa.* Pp. xiv, 154. Boulder, CO: Westview Press, 1979. $20.00.

Isebill Gruhn, a political scientist on the faculty at the University of California at Santa Cruz, has done previous research in the field of African technical and economic cooperation for the promotion of national and continental goals. In 1967, she received her doctorate at the University of California at Berkeley and has published articles on African topics in *The Journal of Modern African Studies* (October 1971) and subsequently in *International Organization* (Spring 1976). Moreover, she has undertaken fieldwork in Africa in 1965-66 in connection with her dissertation and a decade later in preparation for this book. Her observations and experience with the personnel and environment of the commission headquarters in Addis Ababa, Ethiopia add enormously to the quality and texture of her thought and writing.

This book, which is deceptively diminutive, reflects comparative political science at its best, especially in Gruhn's illuminating juxtaposition of this United Nations economic arm in Africa with its parallel organization for Latin America once headed by the renowned Raul Prebisch. Although the Economic Commission for Africa (ECA) is neither as old nor as distinguished as the Economic Commission for Latin America. Gruhn's comparison cannot be said to be invidious to the African organization; her candor reflects her concern over what she perceives as an organizational schizophrenia for the ECA. Utilizing the title of a classic study on indirect rule by Lord Lugard, Gruhn builds her analysis on the "dual mandate" (Lugard's term) of ECA, that is, it must serve its parent organization in New York (the General Assembly and Economic and Social Council of the United Nations) and its constituents, which are the different African member states.

Those who are new to African studies will appreciate her brief, but accurate, survey of the visionaries, such as Senghor and Nkrumah, who added a sense of conviction and pride to the cultural and political imperatives of African unification to regain the lost paradise of precolonial Africa. Still others will find most useful her synopsis of the major points in the literature on regional cooperation and integration. She is well aware of the difficulties scholars and African statesmen have had in trying to adjust theories to fit

declining expectations concerning the ability and inclination of these states to advance the common regional good, often by making painful political sacrifices and also trying to blend these theories and greater practical awareness into the higher plan of what is now termed the "New International Economic Order."

Her analyses of the activities, work programs, budget, staff, and organizational structure of ECA constitute the central portion of the book (Chapters three and four). Her study focuses not only on the organizational deficiencies of ECA but also on the legacies still facing some of its client national states and their inadequate economic resources and staffs. She explains why ECA has had little success in projecting an image of an organization staffed by Africans (rather than by expatriates), devoted exclusively to African concerns, and a source of theory that is peculiarly suitable to economic conditions in Africa. At the rhetorical level, ECA finds itself competing with the Organization of African Unity, and at the technical working level it becomes ensnared in the web of other United Nations agencies which have resident representatives in various locations in Africa. It is Gruhn's contention that

for Africa, a key obstacle to development during the past decades has been an inadequate institutional and manpower capacity with which to translate capital into meaningful development. Equally important has been Africa's lack of institutional and manpower capacity with which to generate and then maximize new resources for development.

She concludes that the commission's

inability to clarify its mission, its attempts to come up with development strategies and then carry out projects and programs based on those strategies, and its inability to develop bureaucratic efficiency and a high-quality staff, have all combined to give the ECA a mixed reputation among its clients— and have led to bureaucratic malaise at the ECA itself.

This book is indeed a welcome addition to any upperclass or graduate course syllabus in the fields of public administration, international organization, the politics of developing areas, development administration, international political economy, and African politics and international relations. Unquestionably, it is also a sorely needed and scholarly addition to the literature. Nevertheless, the book could be improved in subsequent editions with the inclusion of a map, a chronology, a more thorough index, a fuller and more fastidiously organized bibliography, and were the publisher to eliminate the irksome typographical flaws. Such minor changes, were they incorporated in a paperback edition, would not only put the book within the financial reach of students in American and African universities but also would make it more attractive as a basic reference work for university libraries.

RICHARD DALE
Southern Illinois University
Carbondale

GORAN HYDEN. *Beyond Ujamaa in Tanzania: Underdevelopment and an Uncaptured Peasantry.* Pp. xii, 270. Berkeley: University of California Press, 1980. $18.50. Paperbound, $7.95.

For those concerned with African social change and economic development, this is the next book you should read. Hyden has skillfully pursued his objective or producing the intellectual equivalent of the African *chapati* (fried unleavened bread): a non-Western-centric model of development theory and practice derived from and appropriate to a structurally anomalous African setting. Hyden argues that modern society has everywhere been achieved at the expense of the peasantry, and that only in Africa have peasants eluded "capture" by the state and the harness of modernization. The work manifests an inevitable and profound ambivalence between admiration and respect for the logic and resilience of the peasant mode of production, and resignation that development in either capitalist or

socialist terms must involve increased agricultural productivity through transformation of this peasant "economy of affection."

As described by Hyden, the peasant mode of production involves an orientation toward small-scale production by self-sufficient domestic units, primarily for their own subsistence, and is grounded in affective ties of common descent, residence, mutual assistance, and local autonomy. The study represents a history of the elusiveness of the "small" faced with intervention by the "big" in Tanzania: Faced with colonial and postcolonial state action, the peasantry has resisted or used the "exit option." Hyden criticizes two prevailing development theories through his proposition that the "small is powerful": Dependency theory has overemphasized the role of international economic relations, for the root causes of "underdevelopment" lie in the narrow productive base of peasant production; and modernization theory has overemphasized the role of technology and the benefits of change and has ignored the systematic logic of the peasant mode of production.

The *"Ujamaa"* program of socialist development in Tanzania aimed, in Hyden's terms, to apply the principles of the "economy of affection" as a nationwide strategy of development, the central pivot of which became the "villagization" of the rural areas. The assumption that if government efforts were directed at assisting the peasant economy, the peasants would become open to government influence proved wrong, for it ignored the fact that all regimes are in an antagonistic relation to the peasantry, since, given the fact that the peasantry does not need other classes, it must be exploitative. He concludes that *Ujamaa* has not had a significant impact on peasant production.

Beyond Ujamaa develops the argument that "small is beautiful" in Africa, that the peasant mode of production works according to its own logic and has prevailed. But finally Hyden questions whether indeed "small is really beautiful" given its inflexibility faced

with pressures for national development; and he suggests that the development task "will imply the use of force."
After his stimulating analysis of the
commonality of the predicament of
colonial and nationalist governments,
and capitalist and socialist development, it is disappointing that in the end
he is not able to develop the potential of
the "small" for a strategy of African
development, rather than retreating to
unfortunate Western inevitabilities,
which leaves a trace of leaven in the
otherwise admirable African chapati.

JOHN G. GALATY
McGill University
Montreal
Canada

KENNETH LITTLE. *The Sociology of
Urban Women's Image in African
Literature.* Pp. x, 174. Totowa, NJ:
Rowman & Littlefield, 1980. $27.50.

Kenneth Little invites the reader to
survey a deeply complex, painful, and
significant matter: the roles women
play, and who they become, in a process
of urbanizing an ancient and village-
centered Africa. In at least two important recent works—Carolyn Merchant's
The Death of Nature and Susan Griffin's
historical study of women and nature—
images of women have been intimately
tied to decisive concepts of nature,
science, technology, and modernization
in the postindustrial world we now
inhabit. Merchant has shown, for
example, that modern science has transformed a concept of the nurturing, holis-
tic, living cosmos into fragmented, inert,
dead matter to be exploited, depleted,
and raped (like a wanton woman) with
impunity.

Little's exploration of African literature produces conclusions that are
similarly enlightening, with respect
to the life conditions of contemporary
urban women. The table of contents
suggests the following characterizations
of women: girl-friends, good-time girls,
wives, "free" women, mothers, courte-
sans, prostitutes, "political" women, and
workers. Many of these characters, as
African women today, have the tragic

experience of *not* being integrated as
whole, free, loved, productive human
beings in their own new urban settings.
In addition, men often do not form sustaining, productive, and loving relationships with the women who have become
central in their lives.

In fact, the African urban scene
emerges from Little's survey of the
literature in a much more familiar,
Durkheimian cast. Instead of representing a better, more humane stage in
the relationships between men and
women, urban life often introduces a
loss of human identity and belonging in
comparison to the former tribal existence. One illustration of this anomie is
Nuruddin Farah's *From a Crooked Rib*,
in which Ebla, "an illiterate and completely unsophisticated girl," finds her
way via caravan to the nearest town and,
after seductions and abandonment, mar-
ries for money and contemplates suicide.
Ebla is quoted in this self-reflection:

For sure this world is a man's—it is his
dimension. It is his and is going to be his, as
long as women are sought and bought like
camels. As long as this remains the system
of life. Nature is against women.

The web of urban relationships constructed by men to which women must
adapt themselves is perceived by Ebla
as awesome and equivalent to nature
itself, hostile to the plight of women.
Little has this insightful comment on
Ebla's experiences: she has fled the
rural areas to gain freedom in the city
but has not found either freedom or
peace of mind;

... what she discovered is that urban society
provides no kind of niche for women who
want to be independent. Things might be
different if she were rich or had the means
of becoming so. Instead, she finds that the
only marketable thing she has to offer is her
sex. And sex, in this world dominated by
men, is a low-priced commodity.

A more encouraging side to this body
of African literature does exist, however, in its depiction of women as political critics or fighting for political
rights, especially in the context of wage-

labor. A vivid example of political critique is found in Okot p'Bitek's *Song of Lawino*, in which a traditional woman charges her society with corruption:

I do not understand
Why all the bitterness
And the cruelty
And the cowardice,
The fear
The deadly fear
Eats the hearts
of the political leaders!
Is it the money?
Is it the competition for position?

Little quotes G.-C.M. Mutiso, who stated in his *Socio-Political Thought in African Literature* (1974): "To put these words into the mouth of a woman who is supposedly a traditionalist is to stress the point that women have a serious social responsibility to criticize and participate in the social order."

The most impressive African work in this study is one that treats women's leadership in the political protest movement associated with the Senegalese railwaymen's strike from October 1947 to March 1948. In Ousmane's *God's Bits of Wood*, we learn that African women without any prior political experience took the initiative in this fierce labor struggle, both strategically and physically, defeating the French colonial regime. The remarkable historical drama focuses on women organizing a long, strenuous march on Dakar in the face of armed colonial troops. The troops open fire on the women, killing two leaders, but the rest succeed and then carry a banner in commemoration that reads, like Brechtian dialogue: "Even bullets could not stop us . . . we demand family allowances."

Little's survey concludes that images of women in African literature do, for the most part, reflect social reality, with the exceptions of women in the professions and civil service who are not well represented. These exceptions are serious, though, and Little ends his book with a special challenge for female African authors:

. . . why is it so difficult to find as a central character a female doctor, lawyer, high-ranking civil servant, director of a public

service, and so on? In real life such persons do exist. Surely it is time for this fact to be signalized in the literature of the novelist in particular? Until it is done the charge of male chauvinism may be difficult effectively to rebut.

My one reservation, amidst praise for Little's treatment here, is that his book is rather short on analysis. Only nine pages of thoroughgoing analysis follow the greater part of his study which attempts, briefly, to weave conclusions in and out of character-portraits drawn from the literature. Little's conclusions are so important they merit elaboration. But if quantity has been slighted, one may still appreciate this study's undiminished quality.

KAREN HERMASSI
University of California
Berkeley

JOSEPH L. LOVE. *São Paulo in the Brazilian Federation 1889-1937*. Pp. xx, 398. Stanford, California: Stanford University Press, 1980. $25.00.

The book before us is "one of three independent and coordinated studies on the regional dynamism of Brazilian federalism"; that is, John Wirth's on Minas Gerais, Robert Levine's on Pernambuco, and Love's on São Paulo. They are different in themselves, hardly "separate but equal," paying no more than lip-service to their common goals, methodologically put together along social science lines. The only thing that reminds us of the larger context is the introduction to Love's book, initialled by all three authors, and Love's conclusion where he reverts (somewhat lamely) to the idea of the Grand Project that was meant to show different facets of the same phenomenon in the Federative Republic of Brazil.

Love's monograph deals with social, economic, and political elites (a loaded word that carries with it quaint Marxist connotations of exploitation) in eight chapters: man and the land, the economy, society and culture, state politics, the political elite, state and nation, toward integration, and fiscal federalism. The conclusion addresses itself to the validity of the regional approach to the problems of politics and economics in Brazil, a theme that it touches upon quickly and as quickly puts aside. We are left to wonder whether or not the ambitious collaborative scheme of the three well-known and well-intentioned academics, sharing the belief that understanding must come through social science, was worth it after all.

We are in the presence of an exhaustively, overwhelmingly researched book—full of data, lists, figures, tables, appendices—that analyzes the structures that made possible the rise of São Paulo from the backward province that it was when the monarchy came to an end (an exercise in scholarship that will not help to dislodge São Paulo from the invidious position that it enjoys as the most ignored of the major urban complexes of the Atlantic basin). Did Love dull his sensitivies as his massive effort progressed, discard his intuitions, disregard other more luminous paths along which his historical imagination may have wanted to take him?

These strictures to the contrary notwithstanding, the book is still a splendid achievement of its kind. One reads it with surpassing interest; admires the scholarship that went into it, the abundance of sources that supports its assumptions. If I have concluded that a book with this orientation and these concerns was not to my liking, it is because I would have preferred something that would have made São Paulo come alive (as Richard Morse, on a wider canvas, made it come alive). Even its social science *mise-en-scène* would not have disturbed me had I discovered in it the intellectual dimension that is so apparent in the *Annales* school of French historical investigation.

Love has given us a series of very professional position papers that must surely be of use to people in and out of government intrigued by the challenges of underdevelopment, modernization, and dependency. I am not convinced that Third World paradigms have much to teach us about the uniquely Luso-tropical reality that is Brazil.

MANOEL CARDOZO
Catholic University of America
Washington, D.C.

STEPHEN R. MacKINNON. *Power and Politics in Late Imperial China: Yuan Shih-kai in Beijing and Tianjin, 1901-1908.* Pp. xii, 260. Berkeley: University of California Press, 1980. $18.50.

Stephen MacKinnon's study of Yuan Shih-kai is one of the latest additions to a long list of fine historical works on the politics and society in China in the early twentieth century. Through a study of Yuan's career before 1911, MacKinnon seeks to reveal the influence of imperialist powers, particularly England, in domestic Chinese politics and the relationship between central/provincial authority and local elites. More specifically, MacKinnon challenges a popular thesis among students of Chinese history that Yuan's rise to power before 1911 is an indication of the decline of the power of the Manchu court in Beijing (Peking).

Toward these ends, MacKinnon marshaled a large amount of primary and secondary sources, much of them in Chinese, to demonstrate the resilience of the Manchu authority in Beijing in spite of the multitude of internal and external woes. His study shows that (1) the Manchu court in Beijing exercised decisive power over appointment of civil and military officials at the national and provincial level; (2) the court in Beijing received most of the taxes collected in the provinces; (3) the loyalty of most commanders of the Beiyang Army was either toward the court in Beijing or independent of Yuan; (4) a major cause of Yuan's political influence and status in the Manchu regime was support of Yuan by the imperialist powers—England in particular—whom the Empress Dowager Ci-xi (T'zu-hsi) feared; and (5) the success of Yuan's reform programs in the province of Chili (Hebei today) hinged on the support by local elites.

Overall, MacKinnon's book makes two noteworthy contributions to scholarly studies on modern China. First, it presents an all-around and perceptive analysis of the background to Yuan Shih-kai's rise to and maintenance of political eminence in the Manchu regime. Second, delving into the complex background of Yuan's political career, MacKinnon throws into sharp relief the major constituents and their interrelation of the political system of Manchu China.

As to MacKinnon's attempt to challenge the thesis that Yuan's rise to power meant a decline in the effective power of the Manchu court, I do not think he has accomplished his objective. That the Manchu authority in Beijing exercised effective control over the politics and economy of Chili province where the court resided or Shandong (Shantung), the southern defense perimeter of Chili, cannot be regarded as an indication of the "vigor" of the central authority in Beijing vis-à-vis regional powers. To prove the latter point one needs to measure the extent of the Manchu's effective power over the whole empire before and after the occurrence of imperialist attacks and peasant rebellions in the nineteenth century. MacKinnon admits this defect of his study in a parenthetical remark on page 10 in which he acknowledges the need to explore North-South differences. But his later generalizations and conclusion do not heed that qualification. Consequently the book concludes, on one hand, that the Manchu authority was vigorously and violently resisted by provincial authorities in 1911 over the question of constructing railways but, on the other hand, contends that neither regional concentration of power nor peasant uprisings seriously threatened the Manchu regime. What, then, one might ask, had brought the Manchu regime down so abruptly after the revolt on October 10, 1911?

ALAN P. L. LIU
University of California
Santa Barbara

JANICE PERLMAN. *The Myth of Marginality: Urban Poverty and Politics in Rio de Janeiro.* Pp. xxi, 341. Berkeley: University of California Press, 1979. Paperbound, $6.95.

MARIE-GHISLAINE STOFFELS. *Os Mendigos na Cidade de São Paulo: Ensaio de Interpretucao Sociologica.* Pp. 295. Rio de Janeiro, Brazil: Paz e Terra, 1977. No price.

Janice Perlman's *The Myth of Marginality* was much praised, and deservedly so, when it appeared in 1976, and the paperback version under review will serve to circulate more widely the book's much-needed contributions. Perlman's work relies on well-designed survey research in the slums or *favelas* of Rio de Janeiro and uses the results of this research to explode various myths of marginality that have flourished virtually since the establishment of social science as an academic way of life during the nineteenth century. Marginality theory at its unvarnished worst holds that the poor in developing, industrializing societies are an apathetic, incompetent, disorganized, and probably dangerous mass of people who could be suffered to disappear with no loss to society's productive output or culture. The theory was and is intensely elitist and class-biased, and Perlman argues that its raison d'être was to justify middle-class and elitist exploitation and repression and to construct a blame-the-victim ideology that made poor or marginalized people scapegoats for observed social ills. In relying on empirical research in the famous, colorful Rio de Janeiro *favelas*, Perlman demonstrates that the *favelados* are none of the above. In fact, they believe in the efficacy of hard work, seek to create a life around durable material possessions, budget rationally and save money, value formal education, pursue upward social mobility, believe in community organization to defend their rights, eschew radical politics, and work through and usually in support of the established political system even when it can be demonstrated that they are repressed, mistreated, and largely excluded from it. However much the Brazilian middle class may scorn and fear the *favelado*, these hard-working and hard-pressed slum dwellers have responded by accepting middle-class aspirations.

The work of discovering aspirations has been occurring for some time in Brazil. The famous sociologist Guerreiro Ramos explained in 1950 that blacks who formed the lively black theater movement were demonstrating serious professional and artistic aspirations, a fact seldom noted in Brazil's elitist, racist society which tended to interpret black achievements as entertaining or folkloric. In the early 1960s, historian Jose Honorio Rodrigues asserted that a populist Brazil had national aspirations: to be economically independent, to undertake certain social and political reforms, and to develop an independent foreign policy that reached out to new and even revolutionary nations. Perlman has now discovered that the *favelado* is a relatively conservative, easily coopted aspirant after petit bourgeois success. The *favelado* is a socially integrated producer and consumer, though as such he is exploited and cheated.

Perlman's empiricism convincingly exposes the biases and errors of marginality theory. Yet, despite all the evidence drawn from sampling real-life experience, the book creates a kind of abstraction or ideal type—the *favelado*—and may profitably be contrasted with Marie-Ghislaine Stoffels, *Os Mendigos na Cidade de São Paulo*, which was published at roughly the same time (1977) but has been little noted in professional journals. Nobody, certainly not Stoffels, seems to know how many tens of thousands of *mendigos* or beggars inhabit the streets of São Paulo. They are officially scorned in elitist ideology as deviants because they seem to reject the work ethic. They are constantly subjected to overt police harassment. Marginality theory has virtually no place for them. They are submarginal. The life of the beggar is almost unknown and his history remains secret.

Though a doctoral dissertation, Stoffels's book is conceptually impressive in the way it places its subjects in a landscape that includes time (history), space (the streets of São Paulo), economic superstructure (begging as badly paid labor), and ideology (the doctrine of the beggar as a deviant to be corrected by police repression mitigated by occasional state social assistance). Stoffels concludes that begging in São Paulo is a logical—and sometimes even a desirable—form of labor under Brazilian capitalism, and shows how it requires skills, training, in-group cooperation, and existential self-definition. The results are earned income for tens and perhaps hundreds of thousands of hard-working individuals and a life that generally rises above unrelieved material and emotional desperation.

It is unfortunate that Stoffels's thoughtful and unusual book is not available in English translation and must therefore be limited to specialists who can read Portuguese.

PHILIP EVANSON
Temple University
Philadelphia
Pennsylvania

NICOLA SWAINSON. *The Development of Corporate Capitalism in Kenya, 1918-1977.* Pp. xiv, 306. Berkeley: University of California Press, 1980. $20.00. Paperbound, $8.50.

This is a pioneering study in corporate capitalism in a Third World situation; indeed, it is the first monograph-length treatment of the subject in an African context. Swainson, a visiting lecturer at UCLA, draws on impressive research to examine corporate development in Kenya during three distinct historical periods: the interwar years, from 1945 to 1963, and the era of independence down to 1977. The study is in large measure based on four years of research conducted while the author taught in Nairobi and Dar es Salaam, and its findings are as impressive as they are certain to be controversial.

Closely argued and replete with numerous tables, this work "is concerned to examine the underlying mechanisms of capitalist development in Kenya" with its primary focus being "on patterns or corporate accumulation in the economy." However, the actual parameters within which Swainson works include not only economic considerations but the political conditions underlying development as well. While a rather turgid prose style and the complexity of the subject make for difficult reading, there is no question that this book will further fuel the fires of debate centering on the bogeyman of European "underdevelopment." While by no means the final word on the subject, this book does provide real insight into the whole question of Europe's economic relations—both before and after independence—with Africa. Basically, capitalist development is presented as being a matter of interaction between domestic capital and foreign investment, and as such will pose problems for those who adhere to theories that center on the pervasiveness of neocolonialism.

The debate on development in the postimperialist era (if indeed the present merits that description) is certain to continue, but this is a work, carefully documented and scrupulously fair in its conclusions, which none but the most myopic in the currently fashionable "dependency" school of thought can ignore. It sets the tone and pattern for similar studies of other African countries as well as Third World settings on other continents, and as such is a work which will certainly influence and inspire enterprising researchers for some time to come. It deserves to be read by economists, political scientists, and historians interested in any aspect of non-Western development.

JAMES A. CASADA
Winthrop College
Rock Hill
South Carolina

PETER WOODWARD. *Condominium and Sudanese Nationalism.* Pp. xiv, 221. Totowa, NJ: Barnes & Noble Books, 1980. $22.50.

Although the largest country in Africa, the Sudan, which became independent on 1 January 1956, has not received commensurate attention in the West. This study, which focuses on the era of the Anglo-Egyptian condominium 1899-1956, will sit on library shelves as a minor work for specialists. It is written in pedestrian fashion, sorely needing to portray the forest. While chronologically it covers the twentieth century, the greater stress is on the period since World War II. Unfortunately, the reader will seek more on the era since independence, which is sketchily covered in a concluding chapter.

Nominally under joint British-Egyptian control, the condominium was "a clever sleight of hand by the British." "There was a deliberate attempt to isolate the southern provinces from the north, and to promote an alternative form of development." The movement toward Sudanese independence was influenced by pressures from Egypt, Great Britain, the United States, northern Sudanese "Arabism," and southern Sudanese "Africanism." Woodward shows how the declining imperial giant skillfully fended off Egyptian designs on the Sudan. An Anglo-Egyptian treaty of 1936 asserted that the goal of the condominium was the welfare of the Sudanese. Two years later a Graduates Congress sought that goal. World War II accelerated the drive toward self-government. Egypt during this time harbored the aim of the unity of the Nile. Supporting this objective was the Ashiqqa party; opposing it, the Umma party. Meanwhile, Governor-General Sir James Robertson feared that "without protection the Southerners would not be able to develop along indigenous lines and would be overwhelmed and swamped by the North."

In November 1953 a national election brought victory to the National Unionist Party favoring union with Egypt. By 1955, however, for reasons Woodward does not make cogently clear, sentiment shifted toward independence. Perhaps southern Sudanese memories of nineteenth-century slavery by the Arabs had not died.

In the all-too-brief concluding chapter, Woodward describes the 17-year civil war ending in 1972. It resulted in southern regional autonomy. (Students of nationalism will see here another example of how nationalism, among other factors, may be shaped by *political* union. The country has remained nominally as one.)

For some years there was much talk of the Sudan becoming a granary for the Arab world. Although a recent development, and although faced with its own regionalism, Sudanese nationalism apparently will not countenance domination by anyone.

WALLACE SOKOLSKY
Bronx Community College,
CUNY
New York

EUROPE

DEREK BIRRELL and ALAN MURIE. *Policy and Government in Northern Ireland: Lessons of Devolution.* Pp. vi, 353. Totowa, NJ: Barnes & Noble Books, 1980. $32.50.

The authors have the twin objectives of describing and evaluating Northern Ireland's institutions of government and policy processes from partition to present day and of utilizing this analysis to examine the pros and cons of devolution in general. The first of these objectives has been achieved with admirable clarity, and for those with an interest in political processes generally or for those who wish to come to grips with the administrative reality of government in Northern Ireland, this book provides excellent source material.

The analysis is scrupulously objective and fair and gives short shrift to several actively promulgated misconceptions of Northern Ireland. Thus, for example, the notion of a British colonial interest in the province is dismissed and the windowdressing nature of the claims to sovereignty by governments of the Republic of Ireland is noted. Above all, perhaps, the notion that Unionist politics was a cause rather than a symbol of ideological intransigence is called into question, although one would have thought that such an important issue merited further perusal than Birrell and Murie allowed.

Scrupulous objectivity, however, cannot conceal the deficiencies of Unionist rule in Northern Ireland. From this careful and restrained analysis emerges a picture of a part-time government, sitting two or three afternoons a week, all Chiefs and no Indians, presiding over a province whose all-too-evident problems were either beyond their modest, amateur capacity to solve or were resolutely ignored for ideological or sectarian purposes. Housing and local government are particularly well-documented examples in this book.

Meanwhile, Westminister simply let things go ahead, ignoring the growing stockpile of political time bombs until, when intervention was unavoidable, it found its own political arsenal empty, save for the nuclear deterrent of abolition. The only part of the entire Stormont machine to emerge largely unblemished is the Northern Ireland Civil Service, remarkably efficient and adaptable even under the many difficulties presented by the change to and awkwardness of direct rule.

As for the lessons to be learned from devolution generally, Birrell and Murie seem unable to make up their own minds. They do argue that it produced legislation geared to local circumstances, but they also present clear evidence of local need being ignored in several areas. They are at pains to point out the limitations on the power of any government, especially in the face of international economic forces, and they do ultimately acknowledge the predominance of political intransigence over institutional apparatus in Northern Ireland. Perhaps the lesson is that devolution is no panacea for local difficulties.

KEN HESKIN

Trinity College
Dublin
Ireland

RICHARD E. CAVES and LAWRENCE B. KRAUSE. *Britain's Economic Performance.* Pp. xiv, 388. Washington, DC: The Brookings Institution, 1980. $18.95. Paperbound, $7.95.

This timely book raises and answers such important questions as these: Why does British productivity lag behind that of almost all other industrial countries? Can Britain's financial structure or tax system or trade unions be blamed for the slow rate of growth of its economy? Will income from the sale of North Sea oil and gas really improve Britain's economic situation in the future?

The book represents a summary of seven papers presented at a May 1979 conference in Ditchley, England. This meeting was sponsored jointly by the Brookings Institution and the National Institute for Economic and Social Research (an English body). The 32 persons represented prominent American, British, and Canadian economists.

The volume under review was edited by Richard E. Caves, a professor of economics at Harvard University, and Lawrence R. Krause, a senior fellow in the Brookings Economic Studies Program. It has extensive footnotes and an excellent index, as well as charts and graphs covering vital points raised by the various economists in attendance.

The volume emphasizes that there are four questions arising from poor performance in any country: Is there an output gap? Is the fight against inflation handicapped by inflationary disturbances from overseas? Have there been crippling mistakes made in national policy? Does Britain (and other countries discussed) lack capacity for adjusting to external shocks?

One theory outlined is that the British economy makes poorer adjustments to external shocks than do other countries "because it has less capacity for internal adjustment." This weakness arises from the microeconomic structure of the British economy.

An economic analyst must look for deficiencies "in the British labor market, industrial organization, the capital market, the educational system, and other aspects of society." The above deficiencies might have been caused by the rapid growth of nonmarket expenditures that diverted resources from the productive sectors of the economy by successively high marginal tax rates that discouraged productive and creative activity, or by some combination of these and other factors. All participants at the meeting, however, did not support this premise; in fact, there were important pros and cons on all issues discussed.

In the last decade, the most important stimulation to the British economy arose from discovery of oil and gas in the North Sea. This discovery should increase Britain's gross domestic product by three percent in 1982, with royalties and petroleum revenue taxes amounting to seven to eight percent of the current receipts of the central government.

Changes are traced by the participating economists from Prime Minister Margaret Thatcher's first budget of June 1979, which was based on long-range consequences of the Conservative program. Modifications of this program have been made from time to time, as British budgetary policies still fail to solve the nation's deep-seated economic dilemmas.

All of the studies in this volume indicate that Britain's economic problems arise largely from its productivity level, the origins of which lie deep in the social system. One approach would be to strike directly at the productivity level itself— by improving industrial relations "by increasing individual incentives through improvement of the allocation of capital (for instance, in small firms) and similar changes."

Methods by which satisfactory economic aims may be achieved are found in the papers in the volume. The review volume concludes: "It is bad enough to endure relative improvement; it must not be made worse by inflation."

This is a challenging book and one that makes a definite contribution to an understanding of the complex problems facing the British economy in the current decade and in the future.

MARY E. MURPHY
California State University
Los Angeles
California

BENJAMIN B. FERENCZ. *Less Than Slaves: Jewish Forced Labor and the Quest for Compensation.* Pp. xxvi, 249. Cambridge, MA: Harvard University Press, 1979. $15.00.

In writing the Foreword to *Less Than Slaves,* Telford Taylor makes the following statement: "Someday soon an enterprising graduate student in history or sociology should write a doctoral thesis entitled, 'What Happened to the Participants in the Nuremberg Trials after the Proceedings Were Finished?'" Benjamin B. Ferencz, author of the work, has most surely begun the process.

The study of the Holocaust and works dealing with the implications fo that event have proliferated in all directions —theology, psychology, and sociology, as well as in "values clarification for the professions of law, medicine, education and business and technology." Indeed, scholars are now aware of the extent to which the Holocaust involved and affected not only all spheres of learning and creativity but all their institutions as well.

Ferencz, an American, was a prosecuting lawyer at the Nuremburg Trials as well as Director of the Jewish Restitution Successor Organization. His study is an account of the attempts made to get the German government to provide proper indemnity for the labor of the concentration camp inmates. Ferencz points out that while reparation programs were enacted to "pay back" what could "never be made good again," the German government "refused to make any payment for the work performed for private German companies, or for the pain and suffering connected with such labor. No special recognition was accorded the fact that large numbers of human beings had been subjected to conditions of slavery."

Ferencz, with fascinating clarity, supported by German documents, describes the exploitation and murder of human beings for German industrial profit. I. G. Farben, Krupp, Siemens, Telefunken, all flourishing business cartels were not only involved in partnership with the Nazi SS, but in most cases financed and owned the concentration camps. Yet none of these companies, nor the industrialists involved with them, acknowledged their responsibility in the "crime against humanity." In fact, just the opposite was true. Otto Kranzbuhler, defense attorney for Alfred Krupp, was successful in establishing that "German industry's participation in the forced labor program was neither criminal nor blame-worthy." Ferencz uses the case of Friedrich Flick to underline his point. Flick, personally escorted through Auschwitz by Himmler himself, believed that "nobody of the large circle of persons who know my fellow defendants and myself will be willing to believe that we committed crimes against humanity, and nothing will convince us that we are war criminals." Flick, convicted as a major war criminal along with other German industrialists, was released by John J. McCloy, United States High Commissioner for Germany, on 31 January 1951 as part of a "sweeping act of clemency." After release from prison, Flick acquired control of the Mercedes Benz corporation and was referred to at his death as "the richest man in Germany."

Less Than Slaves is a major contribution to Holocaust history.

JOSEPHINE Z. KNOPP
Temple University
Philadelphia
Pennsylvania

A. JAMES GREGOR. *Italian Fascism and Developmental Dictatorship.* Pp. xv, 427. Princeton, NJ: Princeton University Press, 1979. $27.50. Paperbound, $9.75.

Gregor's main thesis is that fascism can best be understood as a mass-mobilizing, developmental dictatorship. Challenging the antimodernist interpretation, which suggests that fascism expressed the resentments and fears of a lower bourgeoisie threatened simultaneously by Bolshevism and high finance, Gregor argues that fascism was dominated by progressive forces attempting to solve the problem of Italy's backwardness. The chief architects of this version of fascism were syndicalists Sergio Panunzio, Roberto Michels, and Paolo Orano.

Gregor explains that, to generate a consensus behind modernization, Mussolini employed patriotic slogans such as the *vittoria mutilata* and "proletarian" Italy, popular themes in a country which emerged from the war feeling cheated and humiliated by ungrateful allies. Hence Gregor's belief that fascism was the intellectual outgrowth of a revolutionary syndicalism married to integral nationalism, a combination that offered a coherent vision of national regeneration and development. Gregor also insists that fascist practice faithfully reflected fascist ideas. In this he has indeed challenged the conventional wisdom.

Gregor certainly is right to point out the productivist strain in fascism, but there are a great many other features of this creed that he either glosses over or ignores. No doubt that fascism liked to be considered as a revolutionary alternative to liberalism rather than merely a postwar nihilist outburst. But nihilist elements there were in the fascist squads that were more responsible in elevating Mussolini to power than the syndicalist intellectuals whom Gregor describes. Fascism also benefited from the Bolshevik peril, which enabled Mussolini to pose as the protector of private property in spite of his hatred of liberalism. Fascism therefore contained both

revolutionary and reactionary elements which, cutting across class boundaries, blurred distinctions between right and left. A complex and puzzling potpourri of conflicting tendencies, fascism resists such easy definition as Gregor's streamlined productivist model.

Gregor's view that Mussolini was guided by his syndicalist mentors is decidedly open to question. Overshadowing any loyalty to philosophical theory was the Duce's scorn for principles and his belief that action itself was the highest virtue. During the depression, it is true, Mussolini did employ New Deal-style strategies whose effect on productivity, however, is difficult to assess. What is known is that these measures did not lead to the creation of a technocratic leadership. In any event the Duce's aim was not to alleviate unemployment and misery. Similar to the mercantilist kings of old, Mussolini intervened in the economy for the purpose of preparing the country for war, and it was that overarching aim that ruined any productivist notion of upgrading Italy's quality of life. Instead of calling Mussolini a Marxist heretic, as Gregor urges, perhaps we should regard him as a socialist apostate.

H. JAMES BURGWYN
Westchester College
Pennsylvania

J. RUSSELL MAJOR. *Representative Government in Early Modern France.* Pp. xiv, 731. New Haven, CT: Yale University Press, 1980. $45.00.

This volume is the culmination of three and a half decades of research and reflective thought. The achievement is impressive on multiple counts. The author's mastery of vast amounts of material is constantly evident, as is his knowledge of and—equally important—"feel" for the operational nature of French governmental institutions. Major's bibliographic and archival research is thorough and of impressive depth; his presentation clear, organized, and well documented.

Major describes the Renaissance monarchies as "popular, consultative, and inherently weak," with more administrative decentralization than is sometimes acknowledged. A central theme is the role of the provincial estates and growth of the people's ability through the fifteenth century to use those estates to resist heavy taxation and for self-government. Yet "the growth of self-government paralleled the growth of monarchical government." Cooperation between people and sovereign soon faded as memory of the disorder of the middle ages weakened, religious divisions developed, and the wars and economic crises of the seventeenth century provoked a constitutional crisis as well. Under these new conditions Henry VI and Sully, especially through the practice of appointing royal tax collectors, "launched a limited but nevertheless clearly conceived attack on the estates." Henry's death brought a short reprieve for the estates and a return to the earlier pattern of relations.

Under Louis XIII it was Michel de Marillac far more than Cardinal Richelieu who worked to dismantle the provincial estates. Indeed, following the former's dismissal, in order to gain domestic peace the cardinal set about "to reverse the governmental revolution he [Marillac] had come so close to achieving by the time of his disgrace." Major concludes by demonstrating that Louis XIV and Colbert worked not so much to destroy municipal and provincial government as to control it through more extensive and effective use of bribes than ever before attempted. The Sun King transformed France into an absolute monarchy "not by reducing the various social classes . . . and destroying the estates . . . but by accepting, indeed strengthening, the society of orders and controlling the remnants of the once vibrant, popular institutions. Louis's system was a personal one which ended the Renaissance balance and cooperation between estates and sovereign without providing the institutional forms of absolutism envisioned by Sully or Marillac; thus it was doomed to failure upon the succession of a weak monarch.

For each phase of this progression, Major examines the relations of the monarch with the estates in various sectors of the realm. He goes into more detail for the confusing period after the Wars of Religion and provides useful information on how the estates of that period functioned. The account is long, and nonspecialists may prefer the projected abridged version which will present Major's interpretation more succinctly. Yet the documentation here offered contains much of interest for the student of the Renaissance and will stimulate further monographs. A review of this fine contribution should not close without a final word of praise for the clean printing and presentation provided by the Yale University Press.

JONATHAN E. HELMREICH
Allegheny College
Meadville
Pennsylvania

TONY SMITH. *The French Stake in Algeria, 1945-1962.* Pp. 199. Ithaca, NY: Cornell University Press, 1978. $15.00.

In sharp contrast with the French experience in Africa South of the Sahara in the last years of the Fourth Republic, the decolonization of Algeria can hardly be described as a model of peaceful political change. Most scholars have explained the failure of the republic to come to grips with the Algerian problem in terms of the regime's structural and institutional weaknesses. For Tony Smith, these explanations are unsatisfactory insofar as they assume the absence of "a common mind on colonial matters" on the part of French governing elites in their handling of Algerian nationalism. In his view, it was not the "système" which was at fault but rather the existence and pervasive influence of a deeply rooted colonial consensus among French decision makers, "the logic of which fixed the Republic on a self-destructive course" in Algeria. This elite consensus had much in common with what D. Bruce Marshall earlier called the "French colonial myth." It rested, in particular, on a

shared anguish . . . at the passing of national greatness, a shared humiliation at a century of defeat, a shared belief that France should retain her independence in a hostile world, a shared fear that her ability to regain national rank would be the consequence of her own internal decadence.

Accordingly, and in ways reminiscent of what had happened during the first Indochinese crisis, the outcome of the Algerian conflict came to be seen by French elites as a test of France's great power status and her image and identity as a nation. From a policy-making perspective, the terms of the French colonial consensus thus did leave some room for minor concessions to local nationalist leaders in Algeria. Its key assumptions, however, excluded political independence and, by the same token, paved the way to the ensuing bitter and bloody confrontation which eventually led to the collapse of the Fourth Republic.

After reviewing the origins of the colonial consensus under the Third Republic and the formative years of the Fourth Republic, Smith develops this thesis through a detailed analysis of the making and implementation of the 1947 Statute and the policies of the various governments in power until 1958. In a closing chapter he shows how De Gaulle redefined the colonial consensus between 1958 and 1962 and made possible French disengagement from Algeria.

One must be grateful to Smith for having written a lucid and compelling book forcing us to reassess some of our conventional views on the Fourth Republic. The regime did have a coherent, if not ill-conceived, Algerian policy, and it was never as enfeebled and indecisive as is still widely believed. I am somewhat uneasy, nevertheless, about Smith's concept of a "colonial consensus" which he presents as the determining causal variable accounting for the republic's failure in Algeria. After all, French decision makers did manage in 1957 to elaborate a "Loi Cadre" that provided for the framework of an orderly decolonization of Africa South of the Sahara. How then does the Deferre Law relate to or fit into the French colonial consensus? On this point the author remains silent despite a brief allusion to France's policy in the Ivory Coast. Also,

it should be noted that colonial expansion, the Empire, the Union Francaise, and France's policy in Algeria after World War II always had their critics. These, however, are either summarily dismissed or altogether overlooked by Smith. Finally, information appearing in two recently published works by C. R. Ageron (*Histoire de l'Algérie Contemporaine*, 1979, and *L'Algérie Algérienne de Napoléon III à De Gaulle*, 1980) cast doubts on the cohesiveness and intensity of the colonial consensus highlighted by Smith. During the war years, De Gaulle himself had acknowledged that Algerian independence was inevitable. If Ageron is correct, then one may wonder why Smith's thesis is superior to other explanations of the Fourth Republic Algerian fiasco focused, for example, on the paralyzing impact of veto groups such as the army, the settlers, and the local bureaucracy which more than once thwarted all reforming efforts from Paris. In other words, Smith is persuasive enough in arguing that French policy makers were influenced by a "backlog of emotional concerns and certain value preferences on how future history should look." His assertion that all other political causal variables (including the regime's weaknesses as well as perhaps De Gaulle's own style) were "secondary" is simply not demonstrated.

Matters of interpretation set aside, these observations should not distract from the overall quality of a book which has unquestionable heuristic value. *The French Stake in Algeria* reveals an impressive degree of careful research and scholarship, and, above all, it is no minor contribution to a more realistic and balanced appraisal of a widely discussed but poorly understood era in French politics.

JACQUES FOMERAND
United Nations

JIRI ZUZANEK. *Work and Leisure in the Soviet Union: A Time-Budget Analysis.* Pp. x, 430. New York: Praeger Publishers, 1980. $26.95.

Stripping it to essentials, this study contains (1) at least 150 tables on working and nonworking time involving different categories of the Soviet population in different geographical areas over a period—with many lacunae in time—of roughly half a century, from the mid-1920s; and (2) accompanying textual discussion of the history of Soviet time-budget research, patterns of everyday life in the USSR, social stratification of Soviet society, and more. As is obvious, the stress is on quantitative data. An all-too-brief discussion of "problems of validity" of the data is offered "instead of a conclusion."

The tables, which occupy between one-third and one-half of the book, are said to derive from materials already published in the Soviet Union, however obscure the source. There is also a rather long bibliography, somewhat sloppily assembled.

It is asserted that this kind of research was "apparently initiated" by American sociologist Franklin H. Giddings, long associated with Columbia University. However, it seems to me that work-leisure surveys for the study of day-to-day human behavior made in a free economic and politically liberal society are quite different from those emerging from a society of planned economy and proletarian dictatorship. Furthermore, what is considered "leisure" in one code may be taken as "work" in another adult study, for example.

Out of this somewhat bewildering array of tables and text one certainly discerns how ambiguous the figures are and how difficult and confusing it is to unravel how long (and intense?) the Soviet work day and work week have been and really are. In any case, the author shows that they are certainly longer than either seven hours a day or five days a week—and often without compensation for extra time worked—in the name of Marxism! And this does not include the large historical category of forced labor.

Of course, Poland is not Russia, but maybe all this gives some insight into current large-scale labor and student unrest in Poland, with demands for a nonworking Saturday and freedom from prescribed courses in Marxism.

This book will have some value to the specialist, if only for the raw materials it presents. But on the negative side, the deplorable truth is that, quite apart from repetitiveness, there is an ill-digested quality to this work. The text, especially, has been poorly prepared for the American reader in terms of spelling, English word usage, and even translations from the Russian.

DAVID HECHT

Pace University
New York

UNITED STATES

THOMAS A. BAILEY. *The Pugnacious Presidents: White House Warriors on Parade.* Pp. ix, 504. New York: Free Press, 1980. $17.95.

As every schoolboy knows, Thomas A. Bailey is the author of some 20 books, including eminently readable and highly successful college texts in American history and diplomacy. In the present work there is a wealth of information but little that is new. Bailey's goal here is to put well-known events in presidential sequence in order to ascertain how each president has handled issues bearing on war and peace. "Our primary concern," declares Bailey, "is with presidential pugnacity that led to war or near war."

The author performs his task in a thoroughly workmanlife, if rather stylized, manner. Each president is treated in a separate chapter as Bailey moves systematically from "George Washington: The Reluctant Warrior" through all that great warrior's successors, including "James Madison: The Scholarly Warrior," Chester Alan Arthur: The Dude President," "Calvin Coolidge: The Sphinx of the Potomac," "Lyndon B. Johnson: The Tormented Texan," and "Jimmy Carter: The Born Again President." The author recounts a few of the most relevant biographical details for each subject but without lapsing into that psychological jargonese now so much in vogue. The bulk of each chapter is a discussion of the way the president dealt with crises that had a potential for conflict. Each president is thus measured on Bailey's "pugnacity scale" and found to be "a warrior," "a man of peace," or something in between.

The result is a work unique in scope if not original in detail. There is no other place to which one can so conveniently turn for a brief accounting of the peace-loving proclivities or the war-making potential of each chief executive. But while in a class by itself, the book is not without problems. Presidential pugnacity may not be as viable a concept as Bailey imagines; and since not all the presidents were pugnacious, both the book's title and subtitle are misleading. Moreover, this is throughout a work far more descriptive than analytical; and, taking the presidents as a whole, it offers surprisingly few conclusions. Finally, and perhaps most significantly, Bailey emasculates some of his warriors by overemphasizing the extent to which they were caught up in forces over which they had little, if any, ultimate control.

Still, this is vintage Bailey, a colorful and interesting work even with its thoroughly familiar facts. Along the way, the song "Adams and Liberty" gets "bawled by thousands of throats," a cold and austere John Quincy Adams proves to be "a veritable chip off the old family glacier," that self-made man Andrew Johnson is, "like many of his kind, inclined to be inordinately proud of his maker," and a determined Cleveland sets "his jaw like flint against the clamor of the crowd." In short, Bailey's presidents, if pugnacious, are dramatically so; and Bailey himself, though technically "retired" for some dozen years now, is as feisty and entertaining as ever.

ROBERT P. HAY

Marquette University
Milwaukee
Wisconsin

PAUL B. BEERS. *Pennsylvania Politics, Today and Yesterday.* Pp. xii, 475. University Park: Pennsylvania State University Press, 1980. $16.75.

Pennsylvania Politics, Today and Yesterday, will probably have only marginal interest for *Annals* readers. The book is a collection of descriptive politi-

cal portraits starting with "John Wanamaker (1838-1922)" and terminating with "Epilogue: Thornburg Election" (the current Republican governor). Its author, a prominent Pennsylvania journalist, ignores 30 years of scholarly struggle with the concept of state political cultures. American researchers have long been told that they are fortunate to have "50 laboratories" in which to observe comparative state politics but have found it difficult, nonetheless, to differentiate between national effects and state particularities. Beers does not acknowledge the problem; he asserts his state's uniqueness simply by pointing to something called "Pennsylvania character." The best advice to the reader would be to skip the introduction and sample the accounts of individuals.

The chronologically arranged sketches—Pinchot, Scott, Scanton, and 42 others are included—give us a great deal of political information. A Harrisburg insider of the 1930s, whose opinion was sought, assured me that the section on Governor George Earle ("The Earle Scandals, Democrats came in on FDR's coattails staged a 'little New Deal' and messed up gloriously") conveyed the amosphere of that time and place very well. Although untheoretical and episodic, the book offers convincing true-to-life accounts of Pennsylvania political events.

More proficient editing might have helped Beers use better his massive amounts of data. Descriptions of a single happening appear on consecutive pages in an unconnected manner and words are used repetitiously: for example, "commissar" to suggest what Pennsylvanians do not want in politicians. (Has anyone discerned a sizable following for commissars among Americans in other states?)

All of this is not to say that Pennsylvania politics cannot funish illuminating events. In the 1976 Senate race, victor John Heinz spent $2.93 million, a record of some kind. One turns with interest to Beers's account of this extraordinary election. Will we finally have an answer to the question, "Can a candidate be sold like soap?" Has the electronic projection of a personable politician obliterated all else? But while we are told that "as the ketchup flowed, the wealthy Heinz was probably the richest U.S. Senator from Pennsylvania ever" and that his wife, "a Portuguese beauty . . . was the daughter of a prosperous doctor," not much more guidance is offered. Too bad.

JANET HANNIGAN

Hunterdon County
New Jersey

JAMES BORCHERT. *Alley Life in Washington: Family, Community, Religion, and Folklife in the City, 1850-1970.* Pp. xiv, 326. Urbana: University of Illinois Press, 1980. $18.95.

James Borchert's study of alley life and culture in Washington, D.C., is an important and welcome addition to the literature of these subjects. It not only pulls together and substantially increases what is known about them but is also a pioneering work methodologically and a major rereading of the evidence interpretively. Its imaginative use of data gleaned from photographs, census manuscripts, and case records has much to teach historical researchers, and its challenge to established views concerning the impact of urbanization on folk migrants is something future writers on the subject cannot ignore.

Borchert's organization follows, in general, the community studies model. He begins by tracing the rise and decline of alley housing in Washington, thus establishing context and setting. He then focuses in turn on alley families, neighborhoods, children, jobs, churches, and folklore, examining each for evidence of the disorganization and pathology thought to characterize alley life, and finding instead a remarkable degree of order, stability, and inventiveness. The older perceptions, he concludes, came from reformers who equated disorder with any departure from middle-class norms. In reality the alley dwellers were remarkably successful in adapting their primary groups and folkways to urban needs, retaining them as ordering mechanisms and using them to prevent dehumanization and anomie.

In his conclusion, Borchert also examines alley life elsewhere and suggests that the Washington experience was probably characteristic of alley dwellers in most American and British cities. At least the evidence available points to striking similarities. In America, he goes on to argue, the alley experience was by no means a peripheral phenomenon. It was a common response to the pressures and constraints of nineteenth-century cities and, for many blacks, a transitional stage in the journey from plantation to ghetto.

If Borchert's work has flaws, they lie in his occasional lapses into folkish romanticism and evidence-stretching. In places his determination to find order becomes a kind of mirror image of the biases noted in reformist accounts. And while he recognizes that alley life was anything but idyllic, some of his depictions come close to making it so. What must have been miserable places to live become warm and vibrant communities sheltering neighborly, humane, and resilient people and allowing them to live meaningful and satisfying lives.

Still, this is an important, useful, and innovative work, made even more valuable by appended essays discussing previous alley studies and the analysis of photographic evidence.

ELLIS W. HAWLEY

University of Iowa
Iowa City

GREG LAWLESS. *The Harvard Crimson Anthology: 100 Years at Harvard.* Boston: Houghton Mifflin, 1980. $12.95.

This excellent anthology from the Harvard student newspaper depicts the life, society, and culture of the university campus from the 1870s to the 1970s. Although Lawless gives prominence to essays that have won the Dana Reed prize for undergraduate writing, he selects articles primarily for their value as sources of social history. Anthony Lewis, in the foreword, suggests that the "microscopic world of Harvard, as The Crimson described and criticized it over the years," reveals much about "the nature of American society then, its economics, its class assumptions, its moral attitudes."

The *Anthology* throws light on many aspects of the history of American student life. The outstanding contributions about academic affairs are a manual (1950) on how to beat the exam system and a haunting study (1972) of the tenure gauntlet. Other items trace the development of student political activity, dormitory life, dating, intercollegiate athletics, and the personalities and policies of successive Harvard presidents. A centennial history of *The Crimson* itself surveys the entire century, and other articles recount the history of campus architecture and the campus novel. The selections are consistently enjoyable, but often thought-provoking as well.

Lawless's anthology regards Harvard more as a unique elite institution than as an example of American academia. Readers will learn much about Radcliffe, Yale, and even Princeton but little directly about the general run of American universities. Many selections betray a trace of Harvard provincialism. The athletic news consists disproportionately of stories about upset victories by Harvard, and the humorous selections feature Cambridge "inside" jokes. An article (1919) on Harvard alumni who served in World War I gives the impression that Yale, not Germany, had been the enemy.

Although campus life (past and present) is a perennially popular subject, there have been few theoretical conceptions to give unified interpretation to its diverse phenomena. Fortunately, there are many such theories to interpret Harvard University. One *Crimson* selection (1975) lists 30 of the theories. Ronald Story's new study, *The Forging of an Aristocracy: Harvard and the Boston Upper Class, 1800-1870*, argues impressively for what the selection calls the "Ruling Class or Training Ground of the Elite Theory." The *Crimson Anthology*, which takes up where Story leaves off, contains much to corroborate his theory. Its capture of the "feel" of campus life, however, should dispel illusions

that the ruling class spends most of its time in deliberately ruling.

JACK P. MADDEX, Jr.
University of Oregon
Eugene

RICHARD LINGEMAN. *Small Town America: A Narrative History, 1620-The Present.* Pp. 547. New York: Putnam, 1980. $15.95.

The dominant impression of Richard Lingeman's excellent study, *Small Town America*, is that life in America's small towns has not changed drastically in the last three centuries. With some exceptions, Americans have founded their towns largely for economic reasons. Also, though opportunities have existed, an informal but often rigid class system has prevailed, forcing the more aggressive to go to the urban centers to seek their fortunes.

Lingeman cites the many traditions that have existed through the years:

the conformity, the suspicion of strangers and new ideas, the informal, personal politics, the avoidance or divisive issues, the reliance on accommodation, the 'neighborliness' accompanied by a proclivity to pry into the private lives of those neighbors, and the sporadic outbursts of populist opposition to centralized authority, whether governmental or economic.

Lingeman, executive editor of *The Nation* magazine, begins his study with an account of the early towns of New England and Virginia. Scholars will find little that is new, but Lingeman does an admirable job of organizing complex material and presenting it in an engaging style. He then moves to the towns of the emerging frontier, sprinkling his tale with anecdotes of Bat Masterson and Wyatt Earp.

The final chapters deal with such themes as small town literary figures and the modern movement back to rural areas. "This movement started as a trickle in the late 1950s," Lingeman writes, "increased in the 1960s, and became a pronounced trend by the mid-1970s." There were several reasons for the trend, among them improved transportation, the decrease in salary disparities between cities and small towns, and the perception that small towns offered a better quality of life.

The book has a useful index, chapter notes, and bibliography.

FRED ROTONDARO
The National Italian
American Foundation

JOHN McCLYMER. *War and Welfare: Social Engineering in America, 1890-1925.* Pp. xvi, 248. Westport, CT: Greenwood Press, 1980. $22.95.

The theme of this series of case studies is that "social engineers" or "experts" did not have a great deal or political power during the Progressive Era, World War I, or immediately thereafter. McClymer's conclusion is that supposed expertise did not ipso facto lead to influence in shaping social policy and programs. Topics covered in the book include the development of settlements and the characteristics of settlement workers, the Pittsburg Survey (1907-9), the early years of the Russell Sage Foundation, the role of experts in assimilation and Americanization of immigrants, experts' response to the war, and the response of experts to the Red Scare in New York State following the war. The case studies are well selected, and, in general, this diverse material is woven together successfully around the central thesis. McClymer has done his homework; evidence is abundant and is very often convincing.

Other strengths of the book include an engaging writing style and an unencumbered view which allows the author to see new relationships. For example, a lasting contribution of the book may be the author's identification of an Americanism Period (1915-24) that spans the war and post-war American politics and society. His suggestion that these years represent a coherent "period" is a fresh and useful perspective.

Overall, the book makes its major point effectively—that is, experts did not have a great deal of political influence between 1890 and 1925. To some extent, however, a straw man has been propped up and knocked down. The straw man is stuffed with statements by Robert Wiebe, Talcott Parsons, and Daniel Bell which relate expertise and political influence. These observations notwithstanding, scholars familiar with the history of settlements and social work, which McClymer see as the fountainhead of social engineering, generally have not suggested that these "experts" wielded a great deal of political power. Uncertainty, limited influence in many situations, and financial precariousness have been well documented. McClymer's case studies do not represent as original an interpretation as he would have us believe.

Some additional shortcomings of the book include an overabundance of citations (for every four pages of text there is one page of notes); a tendency to skip lightly over contradictory evidence; and more than a few overgeneralizations from the case material. These excesses result from his enthusiasm for making his point, but, while somewhat distracting, they do not seriously damage the book.

In general, the strengths outweigh the weaknesses. The case studies are enlightened both as individual accounts and as a series of interrelated events. *War and Welfare* is a well-researched, informative, and readable book.

MICHAEL SHERRADEN
Washington University
St. Louis
Missouri

LEONARD SILK and MARK SILK. *The American Establishment.* Pp. xi, 351. New York: Basic Books, 1980. $13.95.

Shortly before his death, Joseph Schumpeter warned in his essay, "Capitalism in the Postwar World," that the American business establishment was meekly surrendering its power to maintain, as he described it, "capitalism in an oxygen tent." Today, 30 years after Schumpeter's jeremiad, the United States presents a curious spectacle of a capitalist society whose establishment, with self-effacing honesty, has experienced a "failure of nerve." This sense of insecurity pervades *The American Establishment*. The Silks portray the post-Vietnam Establishment as deeply insecure, somewhat bewildered, and not sure of the future.

The Silks pursue their subject through its institutions: Harvard University. *The New York Times*, the Ford Foundation, the Brookings Institution, and the Council of Foreign Relations. Concluding chapters discuss big business and the Establishment and the Establishment in politics. Nevertheless, the authors warn that "the Establishment is more than a collection of worthy and visible institutions; it is a spirit, a ghost, a force." This description of the Establishment is rather vague and leaves the reader wondering what links the Brookings Institution to *The New York Times*, or the Business Roundtable to the Trilateral Commission, other than that these organizations exert some kind of ill-defined power.

Thus the Silks ignore such problems as linkage and definition of power. They show no interest in developing a theory concerning the American Establishment, what it is and how it exerts power, as have New Leftists William Domhoff and Lawrence Shoup. Instead their evident purpose was to write a Fodor-like guide for the interested layman interested in a quick tour of power in America. Their study becomes in the process a compendium of information about important institutions in America. Much of the information, especially historical portions, has been garnered from secondary accounts. And secondary accounts can be misleading. For instance, the authors accept the tale that the Brookings Institution, after a decade of opposition to the New Deal, made its peace with Roosevelt during World War II. Actually the Brookings Institution stood by its criticism of the New Deal/Fair Deal program, specifically on the issues of deficit spending, national health insurance, the extension of social security, and government labor relations. Similarly, the Council of Foreign Relations did not dictate post-war planning policy to the State Department during the war, as the Silks suggest.

Still this book has merits. Leonard Silk's chapter on "Big Business and the Establishment" is astute. He shows that the business community is not a monolith, but is deeply divided over social and economic policy. Furthermore, he argues that clear divisions exist between what he describes as the "intellectual and business wings of the Establishment. Readers will also find the chapter on "The Establishment in the Political Arena" informative in its discussion of modern Republicanism, trilateralism, and Carter's centrist policies.

In summary, this book, written for a popular audience, has value but presents problems for scholars. Clearly it points to the serious need for scholars to address themselves to the role elite groups play in public policy in our society. This issue is far too important to leave to popularizers, even those as good as the Silks.

DONALD T. CRITCHLOW
North Central College
Naperville
Illinois

LORETTA J. WILLIAMS. *Black Freemasonry and Middle-Class Realities*. Pp. 165. Columbia: University of Missouri Press, 1980. $15.00.

Loretta J. Williams claims in her introduction that by examining black, or Prince Hall, Freemasonry "from the colonial period to the present, one can more fully understand the struggles of the black middle-class men." The study "also presents a sociohisotrical perspective on black communities and matters of racial segregation" and "highlight[s] the extreme diversity within the black community." At the same time, Williams hopes to explore "the exclusionary practices, past and present, of mainstream Freemasonry" and "the theoretical implications of this paradoxical phenomenon of racial separation within an ideological brotherhood based upon the values of equality, fraternity, and humanism." Finally, Williams seeks "to develop the concept of pillarization"—the organization of parallel sets of institutions by different groups within a single society—as a mechanism by which to measure a minority group's adaptation to or emancipation from the dominant society.

Any one of these agenda would provide sufficient material for the slim case study presented here, while their interconnections present a tantalizingly rich set of questions for a thick, well-documented monograph. In this book, unfortunately, brevity and complexity coincide to render the history superficial and the sociological analysis confusing. For example, the discussion of pillarization—the supposedly key analytical concept—is contained almost exclusively in the introduction and conclusion, while reference group and relative deprivation theories, concepts of marginality and status incongruity, and notions of strategic elites and status-power dynamics are introduced elsewhere in the text. Moreover, this sociological patchwork is almost wholly unintegrated with the historical narrative in which bits of data are selected from three centuries and all geographic areas. The histories of Freemasonry, Prince Hall Freemasonry, and free blacks are juxtaposed to each other and to sociological theorizing rather than intertwined with them. Simultaneously, references to Mormon and Jewish Freemasonry and to abolitionist Frederick Douglass's critique of black Freemasonry are interspersed in other chapters. Reliance on admittedly sparse data and an unsystematic sampling of personal memoirs and oral histories leaves the reader suspicious of those generalizations drawn by the author.

Williams does point to significant gaps in the analysis of black experiences —in particular, the absence of studies that differentiate the experiences of upper- and middle-class blacks from each other and from those of poor blacks. She claims that "while a subordinate group ... will attempt to offset negative definitions of itself by accentuating unique cultural and behavioral achievements, the greater the group's dependence upon the superordinate group for survival and success, the more it will

pattern itself after the latter in an attempt to gain access to societal rights and privileges." Yet Williams fails to prove, or even seriously speak to, this contention. Because she insists on both the differentiation of the experience of middle-class blacks from their more oppressed brethren and middle-class blacks' identification with and service to those brethren, she cannot adequately come to grips with the class and racial tensions produced by black Freemasons' identification with "the superordinate group." It is, perhaps, Williams's very success in achieving historical empathy with her subjects—black, middle-class Freemasons—that causes her to reproduce rather than analyze those tensions. In this sense, the failure of Williams's study points to the importance of examining the tensions she suggests and reveals in both their historical and contemporary aspects.

NANCY HEWITT
University of Pennsylvania
Philadelphia

SOCIOLOGY

KARL E. BAUMAN. *Predicting Adolescent Drug Use. Utility Structure and Marijuana.* Pp. x, 181. New York: Praeger Publishers, 1980. $21.95.

There are two good reasons why Bauman's recent book should be read. First, this book is an outstanding case study of the application of social science experimental research. Second, Bauman raises important policy questions for treating young drug abusers. Fortunately, the book also is well written. The language is understandable to professional persons who might not be familiar with research complexities, and the materials are arranged in a style that leads the reader easily through the whole research process.

Bauman hypothesizes that utility theory explains marijuana use: Youths will use marijuana when pleasures from use are greater than its displeasures. Bauman tests the extent to which a "utility structure," five interrelated components of a utility theory, contributes to marijuana use among young adolescents. Here one might quibble with Bauman. His explanation of utility theory is much too abbreviated, and little justification is given for his choice of operational definitions of what constitutes a utility structure in a person's life. Ten of the book's 11 chapters describe the research undertaken to test this hypothesis. Bauman studies a panel of seventh graders from a local junior high school who are retested the following year in their eighth grade. Bauman rationalizes the construction of a questionnaire, a pretest of the questionnaire, the protocols for administering the questionnaire, the collection and analysis of data, and the summary of his findings. He even shows how the formal research design required modification to objections, raised by the university which sponsored the research, that legal complications could develop as subjects reported potentially illegal behavior. Bauman forthrightly resolved this and other protocol problems, setting before the public a well-designed and well-executed study.

Even Bauman's final conclusions about his hypothesis fare better than similar social science research: "The analyses consistently revealed statistically significant relationships between the various measures of utility and subsequent behavior with marijuana." Some caveats, however, are in order. There was a high amount of attrition in the sample, so that comparable data were available on fewer than half the subjects originally identified for the study. Furthermore, while Bauman's utility structure was strongly related to marijuana use, most of the variance in marijuana use was not explained by the utility structure. Even with these cautionary notes, Bauman's study is impressive. Most drug treatment programs emphasize efforts to alleviate stress, rebelliousness, or boredom among young people, but these variables were seldom significant to marijuana use in Bauman's study. On the other hand, variables in the utility structure, such as marijuana's attractiveness or availability, were more highly related to marijuana use. Bauman, in a brief and final conclusion to this study, suggests that treatment programs might be improved by providing adolescents with all available information about marijuana and letting them make informed choices regarding their behavior. If Bauman is correct, his suggestion could have important implications for present social programs.

Although not the intent of Bauman's book, this study also contributes to a growing professional concern about healthy young adolescents who become forgotten among problem children in this age group. Bauman's view of marijuana use, confirmed somewhat by his findings, suggests that interest in marijuana is not a sign of a problem child. Instead, marijuana use might be one set of behaviors consistent with the particular utility structure in that child's life. To this extent drug education programs would be valuable for all young adolescents, rather than concentrated on troublesome kids. Bauman's book is a good one which professionals would do well to read, but the high price will probably discourage many potential purchasers.

ANDREW W. DOBELSTEIN
University of North Carolina
Chapel Hill

CHARLES R. FIGLEY and SEYMOUR LEVENTMAN. *Strangers at Home: Vietnam Veterans Since the War.* Pp. xxxi, 383. New York: Praeger Publishers, 1980. $6.95.

Strangers at Home, edited by Charles R. Figley and Seymour Leventman, is a very useful but flawed book: useful for the breadth of treatment it gives the Vietnam veteran; flawed because its authors attempt too much with too little evidence. Simply, *Strangers at Home* attempts to answer a myriad of questions about Vietnam veterans with sketchy and poorly displayed data.

The book has three sections. Section I seeks to inform us on how the Vietnam veteran feels and what makes him feel this way. Section II addresses the degree to which returning veterans have rejoined American society. Finally, Section III investigates the responsiveness of the federal bureaucracy to the Vietnam veteran. Sections I and III are superior to the third.

In Section I case studies are expertly used to explore the circumstances, moods, and attitudes of returning combat veterans, especially veterans who seem not to understand fully what happened to them. The authors attempt to explain selected attitudes and behaviors through the application of sociological and psychological theory. In this context the discussions of "the Gook Syndrome," "Good" and "Bad" wars, "identity vs. confusion," "intimacy vs. isolation," and "primary group" interpretations of combat performance are plausible and interesting to read, although not strongly supported with evidence. Future research will undoubtedly challenge many of the hypotheses found here, but this section will continue to provide direction for analyses during the next several years.

Section III focuses on the political health of the VA system as well as bureaucratic responsiveness to veterans of an unpopular war. With the exception of Chapter 13, this section contains less controversial material than the other two sections and serves as a worthwhile reference on veterans' benefits and legal rights. Moreover, Chapters 14-16 force closer scrutiny of the mental health and drug issues so intimately associated with the Vietnam experience. The chapters dealing with the treatment of veterans' mental problems lead the curious to wonder whether it is the differences of the Vietnam war from other wars or changes in the practices of psychiatry and psychology over time that caused the modern veterans to be handled so differently. This issue is not addressed but should have been, given the other explanations provided.

Section II is where most of the future activity involving this book will focus. Chapters 7-11 report on how the veteran is adjusting now that he is back. In addition to being a good deal more complex than those in either Section I or Section III, the chapters in Section II purport to rely on data. Unfortunately, the data for the material in Chapter 7 are analyzed somewhere else, and the analysis for Chapter 8 is admitted by its authors to be incomplete. The discussion of sample characteristics in Chapter 9 gives us no clue about response rates or data quality. In short, we are left to take much of what the authors report in Section II on faith. This is not good in a book that is loaded with hypotheses that have obvious alternatives.

Taken together, the three sections of *Strangers at Home* provide many insights into the situation faced by the returning Vietnam veteran, but because of the flawed handling of the supporting evidence, this book is likely to be viewed as a preliminary effort rather than a definitive work.

BRIAN CLARRIDGE
University of Wisconsin
Madison

JAMES R. FLYNN. *Race, IQ and Jensen.* Pp. vi, 313. Boston: Routledge & Kegan Paul, 1980. $27.50.

This book is an evaluation of the social, psychological, methodological, and ethical implications of the work of Arthur R. Jensen, psychologist and educator, whose findings on race and intelligence have raised considerable controversy since their initial publication about a decade ago. Jensen's contention that inferior performance by blacks on IQ tests resulted from genetic limitations met with strong opposition in a period when the view of unlimited individual and group environmentally determined potential had been the orthodoxy. For some, Jensen's work seemed to represent a "blacklash" to this "liberal" stance signaling opposition to such policies as busing and affirmative action. James R. Flynn, an American, is currently professor of political studies at the University of Otago, New Zealand. Educated at the University of Chicago, the dustjacket also discloses (presumably as an added qualification) that he was arrested in 1961 while serving as head of the Congress of Racial Equality in Richmond, Kentucky.

While avowing his disagreement with Jensen, Flynn presents the latter's view in a detailed and objective manner. He points out that much disagreement with Jensen stems from ideological opposition and attempts to shift the argument to substantive and methodological levels. He also pinpoints ethical issues involved in raising questions concerning the relationship between scientific research and the value implications of alternative findings. Whether or not Jensen is a racist, for example, cannot necessarily be derived from his factual findings concerning IQ differences between blacks and whites. That such data might be used to justify antibusing efforts cannot be blamed on Jensen. For social scientists, however, the deeper question lies in the sociology of scientific knowledge as to why the revival of such research coincides in time with such policy efforts and their opposition.

To resolve the empirical and theoretical issues, Flynn suggests a more careful environmental approach that seeks to identify external factors accounting for IQ performance differences between the races. In this effort he has been successful, though I feel the main issue still lies in the ethnic and ideological implications of scientific research on behavioral questions of a socially defined "controversial" nature. The book is excellent, thoughtful, deeply felt, lively, and interesting in style. It is highly recommended to all social scientists, especially those working in areas with deep policy implications. The message here is also one of consciousness-raising for those so involved. As such it is a much-needed reminder.

SEYMOUR LEVENTMAN
Boston College
Chestnut Hill
Massachusetts

ERNEST GELLNER. *Soviet and Western Anthropology.* Pp. xxv, 285. New York: Columbia University Press, 1980. $37.50.

Over the past decade increasing contacts with anthropologists from the Soviet Union have made it clear that Soviet anthropology has much in common with anthropology in other countries. One of the most productive meetings between Soviet and European anthropologists took place in 1976 at a conference held at Burg Wartenstein. At this conference a number of Soviet, British, and French anthropologists came together to share ideas, and the papers presented by the participants have now been published. The title of the book, *Soviet and Western Anthropology,* is misleading—or at least the second half of it is. The papers by the Soviet anthropologists do indeed present broad surveys of recent work in the Soviet Union and discuss the theories and methods used by Soviet scholars. However, the papers by most of the "Western" anthropologists deal with limited problems and in no sense provide a broad picture of Western anthropology.

Assuming that the Soviet scholars who attended the conference are representative, Soviet anthropology (which they call *ethnografia*) deals with some of the same subject matter as Western anthropology, but the Marxist orientation sharply defines what is considered significant. There is the expected stress on history, on the development of economic and political systems, and on causal explanations based on the assumption of the priority of the economic infrastructure. It is worth noting, however, that several Soviet authors are not only aware of objections to this assumption but insist that a correct interpretation of Marx requires an analysis of the interplay of "infrastructure" and "superstructure."

One of the major interests of Soviet anthropologists seems to be the study of ethnicity and ethnic groups. This follows from the conception that the role of anthropology is basically pragmatic, to contribute to the establishment of mutual understanding among peoples. Much of the recent work reported in this book involves defining the major ethnic groups in the Soviet Union and providing a basically descriptive account of the customs and institutions that set them apart from mainline Soviet culture.

As was noted earlier, the articles by the British and French contributors to the conference deal with a variety of topics and cannot easily be summarized.

Most valuable as a comprehensive survey of modern Soviet anthropology, this book is also of interest because it provides a number of insights into the status of the social sciences in the Soviet Union. A few of the articles, especially one by Semenov, make significant contributions to Marxist theory.

SETH LEACOCK
University of Connecticut
Storrs

WILLIAM GRAEBNER. *A History of Retirement: The Meaning and Function of an American Institution, 1885-1978.* Pp. x, 293. New Haven, CT: Yale University Press, 1980. $22.50.

A man is useless after 40 and is a candidate for chloroform after 60. That, in effect, was the pronouncement of William Osler in 1905 in his farewell to Johns Hopkins to become Regius Professor of Medicine at Oxford. Most took it as a *jeu d'esprit* in the manner of his Baltimore fellow townsman Mencken, but others countered seriously, citing ancients who never ceased to achieve.

This episode led to proposals to clear the way for the youthfully creative (ages 25-40), among others Carnegie's Foundation for the Advancement of Teaching, which would retire elderly academics. Admiral Dewey warned that we would lose in a naval war unless senior officers were ushered from quarterdecks. The economic pinch of 1907 plus the gospel of scientific management produced discharge slips for some long-time employees in federal service.

With this reminiscence Graebner opens his diligent, illuminating history of older people in the last century who "have been used to service the needs of; larger and more powerful elements of the population." In intimate command of the evidence, fully documented, little escapes his exploration in all quarters. Nor does he omit to give spirited interpretation of the materials, offering informed judgments that persuade assent.

The subject of "senior citizens" demands attention to a host of variables in American society. The three generations under scrutiny have brought multifarious change, mainly gradual but abrupt in later depression and wartime. Improved health and the aging of the population are overall conditions. Technological advance, the shorter workday, tightened competition, corporate business, state capitalism, welfare legislation, growth of labor organization, mass unemployment, social security displacing the poorhouse, the minimum wage, more women in the labor market, and youthful crime all figure in the complex.

Some enterprises are prefacing the retirement ceremony—if such there be—with efforts at preparation for unaccustomed leisure, or perhaps options in incidental gainful employment. The results will depend largely on what communities afford in facilities and solicitude for those suddenly out of harness. The problem reaches back, however, to the endurance of the Protestant work ethic. Too often the work was mentally and emotionally sterile, but fatiguing all the same, and left little time or energy for development of cultural resources in the jobholder. The "golden years" in the next future are likely to be gilt.

Not that well-disposed persons, public and private, lack plans to cherish "the sacredness of the individual" who is defined as superannuated. This good intent, though, comes up against a dilemma which the author emphasizes: "Retirement is being reconsidered because, as an institution, it too has become too costly to maintain and because, as a mechanism of efficiency, it has become counterproductive." Many pension plans of companies, unions, and fraternal orders were without benefit of actuarial structure—if indeed such is applicable in the social system itself—as witness the expectation of higher social security taxes and the paring of services.

Graebner's study will be a handbook of policy makers in the field of retirement.

BROADUS MITCHELL
Hofstra University
Hempstead
New York

ALVIN RABUSHKA and BRUCE JACOBS. *Old Folks at Home.* Pp. vi, 202. New York: Free Press, 1980. $10.95.

WILBUR H. WATSON. *Stress and Old Age: A Case Study of Black Aging and Transplantation Shock.* Pp. xvi. 127. New Brunswick, NJ: Transaction Books, 1980. $12.95.

Twenty years ago the first White House Conference on Aging took place. What has happened since? The major recommendation of that meeting had been to establish a system of Medicare; that has since been done. As the second such White House conference takes place this year, what will be its agenda? Two decades of consciousness-raising and the designation of "aging" as a social problem have led to the accumulation of a great many facts and fallacies, aspects of which the monographs reviewed here assess.

Old Folks at Home, by a fellow at the Hoover Institute at Stanford and a political scientist at the University of Rochester, reports solid research based on a sample of 1575 60-plus-year-old respondents drawn from urban and rural areas across the country. The focus is primarily on housing. Rabushka and Jacobs found a "needs-preference" mismatch between views of the "experts" and what the elderly themselves would like to have government do in their behalf. Great differences exist between the few aged truly in need and the great majority who are not. Most aged were found to be largely self-sufficient and independent. Among elderly homeowners (80 percent of older people own homes fully paid for) the biggest problem was reported to be security in home and neighborhood from the increasing incidence of crime.

Whereas *Old Folks at Home* challenges our preconceptions about Amercia's aged, Wilbur H. Watson, research director at the National Center on Black Aged, focuses on signs of postrelocation mortality, psychosocial distress, and coping behavior among inner-city elderly black people. This research traces the effects of forced migration of elderly, poor, infirm members of minor-ity groups. Observers may come away with a negative image concerning what goes on among populations in "old age homes." However, in tracing the residential relocation of black elderly from inner-city housing in Philadelphia to one of a variety of other kinds of homes, including predominantly white ones, Watson gives us a more hopeful picture. He assumed that patterns of post-relocation responses to stress would build on behaviors learned and reinforced through prelocation coping. The effects of a number of intervening variables on coping behavior were tested. High religiosity, high self-perceived economic status, high physical self-maintenance ability, high mental status, positive disposition to social interaction, and sustained solidary relations with family and friends were found to be significant determinants of positive adjustment to forced residential relocation.

Both of these books present convincing evidence regarding the human resilience displayed by the elderly. Rabushka and Jacobs might have given a clearer picture of the intervals comprising their elderly cohort. Are the same 20 percent of the old folks at home in need to be found among the 60- to 70-year-olds, 70 to 80, or 80-plus years. Or, again, Watson might have given us a better idea of the number of old people's institutions, the black and white populations therein, and the volume of relocation that takes place. What we get are good reviews of the literature, good research, and strong challenges for future action. Both books end with carefully considered policy recommendations. *Old Folks at Home* urges the following measures called for by senior citizens: removal of earning limits in social security payments; repealing minimum wage laws for the elderly; elimination of mandatory retirement; community security services; providing neighborhood security; and reduction of capital gains tax on sale of elderly owned homes. *Stress and Old Age* recommends that future relocation projects take into account the following: elderly preferences for social distance from ethnically divergent others; special efforts to build teams from existing social service and/or nursing departments of the target homes; and, ideally, the agents of intervention should be the offspring, other family members, aged peers, or friendly visitors—deeply sensitive to and familiar with the life situations of the elderly.

PERRY H. HOWARD
Louisiana State University
Baton Rouge

KENNETH E. STUDER and DARYL E. CHUBIN. *The Cancer Mission: Social Contexts of Biomedical Research.* Pp. 319. Beverly Hills, CA: Sage Publications, 1980. $18.00. Paperbound, $8.95.

Kenneth Studer and Daryl Chubin have documented well their thesis that scientific ideas play a vital role in the explanation and predictions of scientific development. They further state and show "that only when contact is maintained with the cognitive domain of science does the sociology of science become relevant to science policy research." This rationale apparently has eluded social scientists until recently, although it is self-evident to scientists and historians of science, tecnology, and medicine. It appears preposterous to think that a special effort must be made to prove the value of scientific ideas to any type of assessment of the scientific endeavor, but one should not take these authors to task, for they fully understand the complex relationships among scientific ideas, ideology, sociology, politics, and economics. The necessity to understand and relate the scientific basis of biomedical projects is only one of the many valuable achievements of this book. Wrapped within a dense forest of facts obtained from published and taped interview references, Studer and Chubin have also shown that "major advances within biomedicine occur when techniques and theories . . . from other fields of science converge to form a biological problem domain [or] cognitive region around which scientists gather

and through which they eventually pass." Other terms for problem domain include "transient network," "research area," "problem area," and "research network."

The problem domain chosen here is the biological phenomenon of cell transformation, which has medical implications when cells develop to produce cancer. Three strands of research domains related to the study of viruses, bacteria, and molecular biology were traced through historical and review articles to discover their contributions toward unravelling the mystery of cell formation in both its normal and abnormal forms. Beginning with a discussion of cell transformation and narrowing the focus to viral transformations, and, finally, extending to reverse transcriptase (RT, discovered in 1970), the multiple dimensions of the twentieth-century research process are revealed and incorporated into the political, economic, and technological factors which helped bring them about. Reverse transcriptase was found to be part of normal cell function (DNA-RNA-DNA) which allows for evolutions or shifting in the genetic map of a cell that provides a basis for theorizing about the origin of viruses and carcinogens.

Passage of the National Cancer Act in 1971 had the greatest extrascientific impact on cell transformation research and especially on the study of viruses as potential carcinogens. With an additional $100 million in federal funds "to launch an extensive campaign to find a cure for cancer" the National Cancer Institute, established in 1937, was bypassed in favor of a mission-oriented, large-scale assault on a complex disease problem. Missions of such magnitude had previously been carried out in the physical sciences under the name of Big Physics. Now Big Biology was to be given its chance to prove how well it could solve a problem of wide concern to all citizens when given massive amounts of money. By 1975 75 percent of all biomedical research was funded by the National Institutes of Health, testifying to the potential impact federal money had on biomedical research.

In their chapter on the politics of cancer Studer and Chubin show how government funding policies in the 1970s facilitated, deterred, and altered the production and recognition of scientific knowledge. Studies of viruses and their role in the causation of cancer were emphasized over all other conceptions of its cause after 1971, when the Laboratory of Viral Oncology was established within the National Cancer Institute. Those researchers who investigated viruses and their relation to cancer were supported after having been discouraged since 1938, when the NCI first began to administer cancer research. In addition to shifting the emphasis on the type of research supported, the method of awarding research support was changed from being primarily through research grants to a large number of research contracts. Between 1971 and 1972 contracts were increased by 47 percent, while research grants increased only 19 percent. Thus the war on cancer increased the shift toward contract research more rapidly than might have occurred. Contracts were awarded to profit-making organizations; and, according to Lawrence D. Longo, "Contract research, which is largely for product delivery or procurement purposes, has the potential of undermining a scientist's commitment to patient, systematic and often frustrating discovery-oriented basic research." Therefore the increasing contracts could and did alter—in some instances, at least—the types of questions and answers posed by cancer researchers. In this one issue of research grant versus contract lies a major aspect of the government's impact on biomedical research—an effect usually discussed in more hypothetical and intuitional terms with undocumented implications. In their research Studer and Chubin have pinpointed a significant way in which government research money does change research by preselecting the types of problems for which it is allocated and the mechanisms under which it is provided.

The reader is instructed by Robert S. Morison in his foreword that the book may be read "as a narrative account of a recent Nobel worthy discovery, an exercise in the sociology of small group behavior, a critique of current theories of scientific creativity, an evaluation of the technique of citation analysis or as an introduction to policy making in an era of Big Science." All these objectives are amply met and are the reason why so much is gained by studying each chapter with care—for this is essential if full value is to be obtained from the six chapters and five appendices. All scientists and social scientists would undoubtedly want to own this book and refer to it periodically. I hope that a distillation of its theses will be prepared for readers who have less interest in the scientific and sociological details but who would like to follow the highlights of "the unfolding of a research journey." The topic is of interest for its bearing on the political, economic, and social factors related to an ongoing scientific quest—the cause and cure of cancer—of major importance to all of us.

AUDREY B. DAVIS
Smithsonian Institution
Washington, D.C.

ECONOMICS

MANUEL CASTELLS. *The Economic Crisis and American Society.* Pp. xiv, 285. Princeton, NJ: Princeton University Press, 1980. $20.00. Paperbound, $7.50.

Castells, professor of city and regional planning at Berkeley, promises to explain the energy crisis, high rates of inflation and unemployment, Watergate, and other social, economic, and political problems of the 1970s as aspects of an underlying structural crisis in an advanced capitalist state. The promise of a new and integrated explanation of our troubled recent past may induce the reader to stay with Castells through the long introductory essay, which sets forth a modified Marxist theory of crises. However, most readers, if they are not already initiated into recent Marxist literature, are likely to find this chapter difficult and tedious. The analysis that follows does not make the effort involved in reading it worthwhile. The analytical chapters are marred by careless use of "facts," unsupported assertions (some quite curious), and a peculiarly bland set of conclusions.

For example, in support of the view that capitalist crises result from insufficient demand resulting from a badly skewed income distribution, Castells tells us that private consumption amounted to 76.9 percent of GNP in 1929 but fell to 62.9 percent during the period from 1961 to 1969. This trend, he says, "is important because it has continued in spite of a systematic selling effort directed against the progressive shrinking of consumer demand." There is no mention of the relative constancy of consumer demand as a percentage of disposable income. We are also told by Castells that total government spending was about 30 percent of GNP in 1960. It was not. Government expenditures *plus* transfer payments amounted to almost 30 percent of GNP, but government expenditures alone were slightly less than 20 percent. We are further told that the Taft-Hartley Act "reversed most of the gains obtained (by labor) during the 1930s. And we are offered as part of an explanation of increased public support for mass transit the curious observation that "a significant portion of the suburban population cannot drive."

What are Castells's conclusions? Among them are: (1) The energy crisis is not a crisis of supply. It is a question of the price of energy. (2) During the 1960s major structural reforms in the economy were pushed by part of the Democratic Party, but this reform went too far and the political ruling class required a Nixon to reverse the process (so as to increase the rate of exploitation). But Nixon went too far: He used the repressive techniques usually used on blacks and the poor on Democrats and so he had to be disciplined. (3) A too-rapid expansion of the money supply is the cause of inflation. (4) American capitalism will not shortly collapse, but

major structural changes will take place.

ANNE MAYHEW
University of Tennessee
Knoxville

WILLIAM R. CATTON, Jr. *Overshoot: The Ecological Basis of Revolutionary Change.* Pp. xviii, 298. Urbana: University of Illinois Press, 1980. $16.50.

A reviewer should be a scholar who has some knowledge of the subject matter of a book he or she is reviewing and of other literature which bears on the matter. But he or she should not be emotionally involved. In this case, however, I have to admit that my sensibilities were affected by the book, for I agree with the point of view Catton put forward and with his conclusions. Indeed, I am at this time working on a study, part of which will echo Catton's views.

The author, a sociologist at Washington State University, believes that mankind has already exceeded what he calls the "carrying capacity" of the earth. He believes that consumption of minerals and energy must slow down or cease and that the increase in population may have already exceeded desirable limits.

The book sees the history of the last 400 years as set out in the two paragraphs that follow.

Four hundred years ago Europeans discovered an unknown continent across the Atlantic Ocean and some other unknown lands. Europe's surplus population could go there. During those years, America and the other new parts of the world provided an escape for too-great population growth. But now America is full. Indeed, the world is full.

About 150 years ago came the Industrial Revolution. Peoples throughout the world, and especially Americans, greatly increased their use of the world's nonrenewable supplies of minerals—in particular, oil and coal. That, in turn, led into what the book called the "Age of Exuberance," by which is meant both vast increases in both population and in industrial growth and the use of industrial products. Industry and advertising (which the author views critically) stimulated use of the new products, while Americans and other peoples of the world carelessly looked forward to continued growth and steadily increasing use of the earth's nonrenewable materials. The book discusses the political impossibility of steps to cease looking for growth, and says that the people of the world looked forward to finding new sources of minerals, especially coal and oil.

Throughout the work uses such words and phrases as "exuberance," "carrying capacity," "drawdown" (meaning theft from the earth of the resources that might be used by future generations), "cargoism" (meaning the belief that new technology will find ways to provide new goods and to meet new problems), and many others which it has to define for the understanding of readers.

It is more a polemic than it is a scholarly presentation of facts. Indeed, it states that Catton's purpose in writing it was to try to lead readers to view his own state of alarm.

It condemns those who forecast that growth will continue and that technology will continue to find solutions to problems that arise, in spite of an increase in numbers of human beings and increases in the use of the earth's minerals. It supports moves to reduce the use of goods, especially oil and coal. It sees as almost inevitable a decline in the growth of population and possible disaster, in the form of increased fighting among men, as demands on food supplies and other products make competition among humans sharper.

Catton finds examples from the animal kingdom and some other cases (Easter Island, for instance) where overpopulation has destroyed resources to such a degree that suffering, fighting, and reduced population follow. That,

he says, is what the world faces in the not-very-distant future.

F. B. MARBUT
Sarasota
Florida

ROBERT J. DWORAK. *Taxpayers, Taxes, and Government Spending: Perspectives on the Taxpayer Revolt.* Pp. xi, 259. New York: Praeger, 1980. $16.95. Paperbound, $6.95.

This timely book analyzes the present trend toward fiscal conservatism in the United States from several perspectives. The author, a professor of public administration, first develops a so-called "Promise Model" to explain, in nonquantitative fashion, the endogenous forces that lead to relative public sector expansion in the mixed American economy. In particular, as the model is applied throughout the book, emphasis is placed on this process as it occurs in the local government sector. After introducing the Promise Model, Part I provides statistical evidence of government growth in the United States in separate chapters within the federal, state, and local government components of the public sector. These chapters could have been strengthened by the inclusion of an inflation-adjustment column in the numerous tables used to demonstrate such growth. Also, tax-shifting assumptions at times appear to be too definitively stated, given the present state of economic literature on tax incidence. Moreover, the statement that tobacco and alcoholic excises are "not regressive" conflicts with the empirical observations of economists.

Perhaps the most valuable contribution of the book is its excellent analysis in Part II of California's famous Proposition 13 (June 1978), which is generally recognized as the spark that set off the national taxpayer revolt, thus igniting the trend toward fiscal conservatism. The remainder of this section of the book considers subsequent fiscal restraint efforts in other states and at the federal level of government. Part III consists of a respectable attempt to educate the taxpayer regarding the local government budgetary process inclusive of ways to interact with this process. The objective of such interaction is to rationalize fiscal decisions by reversing the endogenous forces which otherwise lead automatically to public sector growth. Then, in Part IV various alternatives to higher taxes are considered, including "practical" ways to increase government efficiency, such as cost-benefit analysis and contracting for services, as well as a rather "impractical" voluntary personal service alternative. The latter would give each local government taxpayer the option to substitute labor input for taxes owed to the local government. The final chapter discusses what taxpayers should expect to receive in responsiveness, communications, and the like from local government. In all, it would seem that Dworak's primary purpose of the book—to make taxpayers better informed so that they can more effectively impose their collective will on government—is attained.

BERNARD P. HERBER
University of Arizona
Tucson

F. A. Von HAYEK. *The Counter-Revolution of Science: Studies on the Abuse of Reason.* Pp. 416. Indianapolis: Liberty Press, 1979. $9.00. Paperback, $4.00.

These essays on the origins of totalitarianism, first published in book form in 1952, constitute the link between Von Hayek's criticism of totalitarian thought in *Road to Serfdom* (1944) and his praise of classical laissez-faire thinkers in *Individualism and the Economic Order* (1948). His later works in the history of ideas, such as *The Constitution and Liberty* (1960), merely extend these wartime and immediate postwar essays, most of which appeared in *Economica* before he left the London School of Economics for the University of Chicago in 1950. Like his Chicago colleague and fellow Nobel laureate Milton Friedman, Von Hayek sees his work on the history of ideas as part of the economic theory for which he won the Nobel Prize in 1974.

Von Hayek's historical argument is that the true science and social science of the seventeenth and eighteenth centuries was replaced by the scientism (or positivism) of the École Polytechnique, the Saint Simonians, and the Comtians. The errors of the nineteenth and twentieth centuries, including socialism, thus arise, not in Hegelianism but in the Cartesian reductionism of the engineers of the École Polytechnique. Examples include the influence of École professor Lazare Carnot and his sons on Saint Simon, of Saint Simon and his heirs Comte and Enfantin on Hegel and J. S. Mill, and, hence, by this chain of intellectual inheritance, of the École on both utilitarianism and socialism. The result is the substitution of a "religion of the engineers" for true religion, of the "historicism" of Marx and Buckle for the true history of Ranke, of "scientism" for true science, of the "abuse of reason" for true reason.

Von Hayek argues that the atempt to generalize the solution of engineering problems through "conscious" control and "deliberate" direction is both unreasonable and harmful. He not only reiterates Kant's arguments against the false generalization from science to society, but also employs Whitehead's notion of "misplaced concreteness" to show how the modern belief that planning can improve institutions or cure monopoly rests on the illusion of an "institution" or "monopoly" being a thing rather than a mental construct. Von Hayek believes that knowing where to find a given item for the cheapest price is more "reasonable" than pretending to manage an economy according to preconceived "laws." To know how to respond to the hidden social forces beyond conscious control is the higher reason, as the Classical School of economists contended.

The reissuance of this work prompts at least two questions. First, are we dealing here with politics or science?

Most, if not all, empirical social scientists would certainly deny any connection between Von Hayek's study of economic cycles and his philosophical and historical assertions. And if empiricists accuse Von Hayek of mysticism, the truly religious, like Solzhenitsyn, will undoubtedly accuse him of rationalist materialism. If anything, the technological society seems to have reinforced Bentham's claims of regularity and Carlyle's claims of inhumanity at the expense of the Burkean brand of rationality which Von Hayek sees. Second, if Von Hayek's outlook is not scientifically valid, is it at least politically valid because it suits the Zeitgeist? Statism and bureaucratism, whether or not they be caused in any real sense by positivism or Hegelianism, may have produced a revulsion against utopian planning and a renewed respect for individuality among social scientists such as Berger, Dahrendorf, and Piaget. Yet utopian idealism is no doubt smoldering in the ashes of today's discontent.

For Von Hayek has not solved the problem of individuality versus collectivity by undermining the arrogance of the positivists. What, for example, is his response to Lasch's recent charge that American individualism rests on narcissism or to Von Niebuhr's earlier observation that either individuality or community can be demonic? And if Brave New World might work but shouldn't, some descendants of Rousseau, such as the environmentalists, may have as good a claim on leadership of a decentralized future society as Von Hayek's libertarians. The central problem appears to be one of moral authority, not of scientific accuracy.

THOMAS J. KNIGHT
Pennsylvania State University
University Park

ERRATUM

In the May 1981, volume 455, issue of THE ANNALS, we published reviews of two books in a joint review format: Robert Boettcher, with Gordon L. Freedman, *Gifts of Deceit: Sun Myung Moon, Tongsun Park, and the Korean Scandal;* and Robert T. Oliver, *Syngman Rhee and American Involvement in Korea, 1942-1960: A Personal Narrative.* The reviewer, George Fox Mott, has asked us to indicate that these were two separate reviews, written at different times, and with different review purposes. The Oliver book is a scholar's primary source book, whereas the Boettcher and Freedman appraisal is of another side of the Korean-American relationship coin.

INDEX

CHICAGO Fall '81 Titles

Political Science for All Seasons

NEWS FROM THE WHITE HOUSE

The Presidential-Press Relationship in the Progressive Era
George Juergens
Cloth $25.00   344 pages   November

ORGANIZING
THE EXECUTIVE BRANCH

The Johnson Presidency
Emmette S. Redford and Marlan Blissett
Cloth $21.00   272 pages   Available

THE PRUDENT PEACE

Law as Foreign Policy
John A. Perkins
Cloth $28.00   268 pages   Available

SPEECH
AND LAW IN A FREE SOCIETY

Franklyn S. Haiman
Cloth $22.50   480 pages   November

THE IRONY OF LIBERAL REASON

Thomas A. Spragens, Jr.
Cloth   TBA   December

IMPRISONMENT IN AMERICA

Choosing the Future
Michael Sherman and **Gordon Hawkins**
Studies in Crime and Justice series
Cloth $15.00   144 pages   December

LibertyPress
LibertyClassics

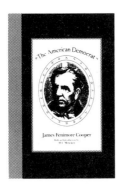

The American Democrat

By James Fenimore Cooper

Introduction by H. L. Mencken

An easily readable study of political democracy as attempted in the United States. Cooper, an aristocrat in mind and manners, defends democracy provided it remains representative rather than direct.

He cites the dangers inherent in direct democracy and describes the elements of character and principle that he feels must be preserved in both people and politics if the republic is to survive.

The Introduction by H. L. Mencken illuminates Cooper's all-but-forgotten place in the history of American political discourse. Hardcover $9.00, Paperback $4.00.

Prepayment is required on all orders not for resale. We pay postage on prepaid orders. Please allow 4 to 6 weeks for delivery. *All* orders from outside the United States *must* be prepaid. To order, or for a copy of our catalogue, write:
LibertyPress/LibertyClassics
7440 North Shadeland, Dept. 232
Indianapolis, IN 46250